CONTEMPORARY CHINA INSTITUTE PUBLICATIONS

The Contemporary China Institute
School of Oriental and African Studies, University of London,
sponsors research on Twentieth-Century China and
seeks to promote such studies in the U.K.

Democracy & organisation in the Chinese industrial enterprise (1948-1953)

Publications in the series are:

Party Leadership and Revolutionary Power in China (1970) *edited by John Wilson Lewis*

Employment and Economic Growth in Urban China, 1949–1957 (1971) *by Christopher Howe*

Authority, Participation and Cultural Change in China (1973) *edited by Stuart A. Schram*

A Bibliography of Chinese Newspapers and Periodicals in European Libraries (1975) *by the Contemporary China Institute*

Democracy & organisation in the Chinese industrial enterprise (1948–1953)

WILLIAM BRUGGER

Discipline of Political Theory and Institutions
Flinders University of South Australia

Cambridge University Press

CAMBRIDGE
LONDON · NEW YORK · MELBOURNE

CAMBRIDGE UNIVERSITY PRESS
Cambridge, New York, Melbourne, Madrid, Cape Town, Singapore,
São Paulo, Delhi, Dubai, Tokyo

Cambridge University Press
The Edinburgh Building, Cambridge CB2 8RU, UK

Published in the United States of America by Cambridge University Press, New York

www.cambridge.org
Information on this title: www.cambridge.org/9780521134293

First published 1976
This digitally printed version 2010

A catalogue record for this publication is available from the British Library

Library of Congress Catalogue Card Number: 75–9284

ISBN 978-0-521-20790-4 Hardback
ISBN 978-0-521-13429-3 Paperback

Contents

Acknowledgements

To Stuart Schram for supervising that part of this work which was once a thesis. To Franz Schurmann and Gregory Grossman for examining it and offering me advice on its revision. To Franz Schurmann also for making available to me his unpublished manuscript on industrial management and to Christopher Howe for letting me consult his rare set of *Tung Pei Kung-yeh*. To Dorothy Wedderburn for her advice on general problems of industrial sociology and to Seymour Broadbridge for advice on Japanese secondary sources. To John Gittings, Michelle Grieve, John Hall, Christopher Howe, David Wilson and Graham Young for advice on content, style and organisation, and to the secretarial staff of the Contemporary China Institute, London and the School of Social Sciences, Flinders University for typing the manuscript in its various forms.

Flinders University of South Australia
February 1974

W. Brugger

Abbreviations

ACFL	All China Federation of Labour (*Chung-hua Ch'üan-kuo Tsung-kung-hui*)
ACFTU	All China Federation of Trade Unions (*Chung-hua Ch'üan-kuo Tsung-kung-hui*) (after 1953)
CC	Central Committee (*Chung-yang Wei-yüan-hui*)
CSMAC	Central South Military and Administrative Committee
CCP	Chinese Communist Party (*Chung-kuo Kung-ch'an-tang*)
CQ	*China Quarterly*
CB	*Current Background*
ECMAC	East China Military and Administrative Committee
ECMM	*Extracts from China Mainland Magazines*
FGM	Factory General Manager (*Ch'ang-chang*)
GAC	Government Affairs Council (or Government Administration Council) (*Cheng-wu-yüan*)
JMJP	*Jen-min Jih-pao* (*Peoples Daily*)
JPRS	Joint Publications Research Service
KMT	*Kuo-min-tang*
NCNA	New China News Agency (*Hsin-hua-she*)
NE	North East (*Tung Pei*)
NEPG	North East Peoples Government (*Tung Pei Jen-min Cheng-fu*)
NWMAC	North West Military and Administrative Committee
PFLP	Peking Foreign Languages Press
PLA	Peoples Liberation Army (*Chung-kuo Jen-min Chieh-fang-chün*)
SW	*Selected Works* (*Hsüan-chi*)
SCMP	*Survey of the China Mainland Press*
SCMM	*Selections from China Mainland Magazines*
SWB	*BBC Summary of World Broadcasts Pt. III*
URS	*Union Research Service*

Introduction

This work started life as a monograph with a very restricted scope. As a student of politics, I attempted to answer the question: how did the new government of China that took over factories in 1948–9 establish control and institute patterns of worker participation in management? My major concern was with authority relationships since the study of politics is in large measure the study of authority – the legitimate use of influence and power. Entering with trepidation a field traditionally occupied by the disciplines of industrial sociology and economic history, I nevertheless felt that only a trans-disciplinary approach is appropriate for an exploratory study in a relatively uncharted field.

In its early form the work could be criticised for lacking relevance to either contemporary problems or general problems of history. I had to satisfy, therefore, a nomothetic imperative which demands that singular generalisations located in a single place at a particular time be related to a much wider perspective. Having already thrown caution to the winds in deciding to enter disciplines with which I was none too familiar, it was but a short step to the presumption of offering, in chapter 1, a historical comparison of the evolution of industrial enterprises in Russia, pre-war Japan and pre-1949 China. Since the work focusses on the adoption by China of a model of organisation and commitment which derived from the Soviet Union, I was led to examine the origins of that model within the context of Tsarist Russian and Soviet industrialisation. In comparing and contrasting certain features of the pattern of industrialisation in Russia and China, I then felt obliged to introduce a comparison with Japan because of the apparent similarities in cultures and nineteenth century industrialising élites. It was another short step from this to involvement in that debate known as the 'logic of industrialism'.

The logic of industrialism debate

The 'logic of industrialism' argument as expressed in its starkest form by Clark Kerr and his associates[1] clearly bears the stamp of the late 1950s and early 1960s and is remarkably similar to that parallel concept in political science – 'political development'. The 'logicians' maintain that the process of industrialisation is not unilinear (a position they mistakenly attribute to Marx) but multilinear; and the particular route a country takes depends upon the character of the industrialising élite, the conflict of cultures in industrialisation, the nature of economic constraints, the historical timing of the industrialisation process and the way in which the labour force is developed. Despite the diverse routes taken however, there is a tendency towards a process of convergence dictated in large part by modern technology. The end process of industrialisation is seen as a situation where ideology fades away once industrial man is no longer faced with real ideological alternatives, where a new and essentially conservative 'realism' takes over, where interest group struggle replaces class struggle and where class war gives way to 'bureaucratic gamesmanship'. In this state of 'industrialism' there will no longer be workers and managers – merely the 'semi managers' and the 'semi managed'. The state-private dichotomy will be blurred as the omnipresent state realises its potential as the largest single employer. More important, as technology restricts freedom at work, increased leisure will give greater scope for creativity; organisation men will be perhaps at the same time the 'new Bohemians' acting out different roles in different contexts in a world of 'pluralist industrialism'.

In the post-1968 world when social scientists have discovered that the 'end of ideology' school was in fact in itself an ideology, when a serious assault was launched against the wider 'ideology of pluralism' and when a new generation of Marxist scholars pointed out the relevance of sophisticated class analysis, such a view as described above seems very quaint. This is particularly so in a situation where large portions of the world seem just not able to industrialise at all. In the past few years, the field of political science has been glutted by the recantations of many of the 'non ideological' gurus of the 1950s and early 1960s though I am not sure to what extent this process has been paralleled in other disciplines. As a consequence of what would almost amount to one of Thomas Kuhn's 'paradigm shifts', scholars have turned increasingly to examining alternative models of development of which the Chinese is perhaps one of the most outstanding. Whilst continuing to explore development processes, they have looked also at the effect upon developing countries of the mechanical adoption of alien systems. Such is my purpose here – to examine the adoption by China of such an alien model of organisation and commitment prior to the development of her own indigenous pattern which was to be based in part upon the earlier experiences of the Communist Party in the wartime liberated areas.

The historical perspective

In Russia, Japan and China, the primary initiative in promoting industrialisation was taken by the state and, in all three countries, the decline of state initiative was followed by the ruthless pursuit of short term profits by individual entrepreneurs. Conscious that the term has been variously defined, I shall refer to this second period as 'primitive capitalism'. In Japan, the industrial entrepreneurs began to develop a collective ethos which according to G.D.H. Cole's formulation qualified them as a 'bourgeoisie', whereas in Tsarist Russia and Kuomintang China, they probably never achieved the degree of collective consciousness that would have qualified them for a more precise definition than merely 'middle class'.[2] It is my belief that an examination of class structure is probably more fruitful in explaining patterns of industrialisation than the concentration on élite-mass relationships that tends to characterise the 'logic of industrialism' school. Such a focus also permits one to relate findings to the impact of imperialism and to explain the appearance in Japan of a 'bourgeoisie' as opposed to the dependent 'comprador class' (*mai-pan chieh-chi*) that appeared in China.

Although in all three countries state control weakened during the period I have referred to as 'primitive capitalism', certain relationships between government and industry persisted. The Japanese bourgeoisie in the pre-war period was never completely free from the mechanisms of government, nor indeed were the Chinese industrialists, who were described by their critics as 'bureaucratic capitalists' (*kuan-liao tzu-pen-chia*).[3] Chapter 1 will briefly discuss the origins in China of such bureaucratic capitalism and the importance of a steadily growing state sector which was to be taken-over relatively easily in 1948–9.

Chapter 1 will also consider the role of managerial ideology. Here, following Bendix, I shall use the words managerial ideology in the broadest sense meaning 'all ideas which are espoused by or for those who exercise authority in economic enterprises, and which seek to explain and justify that authority'.[4] Regardless of the degree of governmental control, industrial organisations in both Japan and China drew even more heavily upon traditional ideology than did their English counterparts a century before.[5] Early English managerial ideology drew upon traditional master-servant patterns of dependence, whereas in Japan and China managerial ideologies drew upon the ethos of a traditional Confucian bureaucracy. Such a situation was to cause great problems when foreign management systems were imported into these two countries be those systems socialist or capitalist.

Although Japan shared with China an organisational ideology based on traditional bureaucracy, she was able to develop from the period of predominantly state initiative through primitive capitalism to a relatively 'advanced' form of capitalism. Elements of traditional bureaucratic ideology were made to serve that transition,[6] which was taken as a model for China in the early period of her own industrialisation. The model was, however, not very effective where a semicolonial atmosphere was heavily weighted against what the Chinese Communist Party referred to as 'national capitalism' (*min-tsu tzu-pen-chu-i*).

Both Russia and China embarked upon revolution before industry had progressed to any more 'advanced' form of capitalism and the experiences of the former which predated the final victory of the Chinese Communist Party by some three decades inevitably provided a basic point of reference for the latter. The insistence of the Kerr school that the historical point of time at which a country embarks upon an industrialisation drive affects the route chosen is obviously correct. A late-comer has its options restricted but it can learn from others' mistakes. This work will argue that China learnt about the mistakes of the Soviet Union only by making some of the same mistakes herself. During the three decades since the Bolshevik Revolution, the Soviet Union had experimented with a number of systems of industrial organisation and it was not always clear exactly which Soviet model would be applied to China nor indeed which elements of the indigenous experiences of the Chinese Communist Party would be retained. Thus not only did prescribed Soviet patterns of organisation and commitment conflict with traditional bureaucratic patterns, not only did they conflict with patterns worked out by the Chinese Communist Party during the war, they also conflicted with each other. The Soviet model itself was ambiguous. Subsequent chapters will attempt to spell out these many contradictions.

The historical introduction will be concerned mainly with macro-political and macro-sociological issues in preparation for the micro-political and micro-sociological discussion which follows. It will attempt also to sketch some features of the macro-economic background which imposed limitations upon the choices open to industrial management in the post 1949 years. This work will note time and again that patterns of organisation and commitment were prescribed for which human, technical and other resources were currently inadequate. Hence another dimension is added to our set of problems. To what extent were prescribed patterns not implemented because they conflicted with tradition, because they conflicted with socialist patterns deriving from the wartime experience of the Party, because they conflicted with each other or because there was a contradiction between policy and resources? There can be no definitive answer in an exploratory study of this kind. The avenues of enquiry can, however, be opened and perhaps eventually the debate might grow in much the same way as that debate (to which we shall return) between the culturalists and economic determinists on the origins and development of paternalist management in Japan.[7]

The historical introduction will end with a brief discussion of three micro-sociological questions: what was the structure of the decision making process that had evolved within large industrial concerns in China by 1949; what was the relationship between staff and line and what was the nature of material and non material incentive. Since the focus of my research has been on the post 1949 period, this discussion and that which precedes it will draw heavily on secondary sources which deal with the Kuomintang period very inadequately. My only excuse for including an impressionistic account that may well be invalidated by future research is that to omit it would be to consign the major part of this work to irrelevance.

The macro-political perspective

Marxian theory stipulated that following the Socialist Revolution, the workers were to be 'masters of society'. The Chinese Civil War of 1946–9 was not, however, seen as constituting a socialist revolution, the preferred term being 'liberation' (*chieh-fang*), and the period which followed was seen not as one of socialism but of New Democracy (*Hsin-min-chu-chu-i*). The workers, however, were still referred to as 'masters' (*chu-jen-weng*)[8] of society. New Democracy was to be a transitional stage between the Democratic Revolution (*Min-chu ko-ming*) and the building of socialism (*she-hui chu-i chien-she*). During this early period, industry designated as 'bureaucratic capitalist' and industry owned by foreign interests was to be taken over by the state[9] but a sizeable private sector was allowed to remain in existence. The state-owned sector of the economy was to 'exercise leadership' over the private sector and to assist in its socialist transformation. The concern of this work, however, will be only with the state sector and more particularly with large concerns in that sector.[10]

The publication during the Cultural Revolution of attacks on Liu Shao-ch'i's 'Tientsin Talks' of April–May 1949 has revealed that there was considerable polemic over the duration of the New Democratic transitional period.[11] It is probably impossible at this remove to assess the extent to which the charges made against Liu were Cultural Revolution rationalisations. What we can say, however, is that, as the Civil War drew to a close, both the policy of the Chinese Communist Party towards the take over (*chieh-kuan*) and reorganisation of industry and the actions of its cadres became less and less radical. The decline in radicalism affected the way in which traditional bureaucratic practices were changed and residues of the old society such as the 'gang boss' system eliminated.

In chapters 2 and 3 the changing political environment will be examined. Chapter 2 will deal with an essentially moderate (even conservative) period following the take over of industry which was remarkably similar to that period in revolutionary Russia following the Bolshevik Revolution but prior to the advent of 'War Communism'. Chapter 3 will deal with the more radical period which followed. The beginning of this period coincided with the outbreak of war in Korea but one should not make too much of the Russian parallel here since, as will be demonstrated, the domestic reasons for radicalisation in China were probably much stronger than reasons associated with the war. The approach followed in these two chapters will be chronological and the following questions will be posed. What were the main institutions involved in the take over of industry and what new institutions were set up following liberation? To what extent did the pattern of take over differ in various parts of the country and to what extent was this due to physical or policy determinants? To what extent did the initial moderate policy encourage the continuance of old forms of organisation and how was this problem dealt with? To what extent did worker organisations become routinised and bureaucratised and to what extent did China offer a parallel to the great debate on the role of the labour unions under socialism that took place in the Soviet Union in 1920?

In these chapters considerable attention will be paid to the relationship between horizontal (local) and vertical (ministerial) linkages in administration for this relationship was to affect vitally the role of the enterprise Party organisation. The years 1949–53 saw the launching of a whole series of political movements throughout industry and an attempt will be made to separate those movements into two types – those that involved widespread mass mobilisation and those that did not – those in which the primary initiative came from above and those in which the initiative came from both above and below. Such an exercise is relevant to the wider context of Chinese politics in which, since 1942, two distinct political styles may be identified – the 'work team' approach which was associated in the Cultural Revolution with Liu Shao-ch'i and the Party bureaucrats and the 'mass association' approach associated with Mao Tse-tung. I shall not argue that such an identification can be established in the New Democratic period but feel that such an exercise may be useful in any future study of comparative political style.

The context of administrative rationality

Although it was not always clear which Soviet model was to be emulated, the presence of Soviet-run industry on Chinese soil in the occupied area of Lushun and Talien close to the heavy industrial base of North East China provided an important point of reference. Most of the major movements launched in Chinese industry immediately after liberation originated in Lushun and Talien, spread first to the rest of North East China and only much later to the rest of the country. In Chapters 4, 5 and 6, a description will be given of the model of administration that derived from Lushun and Talien and how this model was changed as it was applied to other areas. The Movement to Create New Records (*Ch'uang-tsao Hsin Chi-lu Yün-tung*) of 1959–60 which originated here was designed to lay the basis for a process known as 'enterprisation' (*ch'i-yeh-hua*). The term 'enterprisation' was used in a context much wider than industry. It signified a process where units defined territorially (in the industrial sphere these would be factories [*kung-ch'ang*]) or commercially (in the industrial sphere these would frequently be companies [*kung-ssu*]) were redefined according to an external network of economic administration.[12] The model of economic administration was borrowed from the Soviet Union and 'rationality' (*ho-li*) tended to be measured against a hierarchy of goals explicit or implicit in that model. The term 'enterprise' (*ch'i-yeh*) was first and foremost an administrative one and, in the state sector of industry, indicated the lowest level of an administrative network that enjoyed a certain degree of autonomy in the use of funds allocated by the state or borrowed from the state banking system. From the standpoint of political administration, the enterprise was that unit of administration at which 'basic level' Party and mass organisation (labour union etc.) were established. Chapters 4, 5 and 6 will examine to what extent the prescriptions concerning enterprisation were successfully implemented and to what extent they contradicted existing patterns of industrial organisation.

The term 'enterprisation', as used in industry during the Movement to Create New Records contained the following elements. First, records were broken to form the basis for (1) norm determination and the establishment of a planning and accounting system. (2) Rationalisation proposals were put forward to assist in the formulation of norms, incentive systems worked out on the basis of those norms, model workers designated as a further incentive to raise the norms and internal labour agreements worked out tying together norms, wage systems, plans and labour regulations. Finally (3) a responsibility system was worked out to stop the whole process getting out of hand and as a basis for a new discrete command structure.

Chapter 4 will consider item 1 above – norm determination and the establishment of a planning and accounting system. The discussion will be brief since my aim here is not to describe the economic behaviour of management as has been done by Joseph Berliner in his study of the Soviet Union.[13] The purpose here is to pose a number of political and sociological questions. To what extent was there meaningful worker participation in planning and norm determination? To what extent did that participation slow down the planning process? To what extent was participation in planning seen as an educative process and to what extent did that process conform to 'The mass line' – that set of policies formulated by the Communist Party during the war which were designed to reconcile central direction and mass demands?[14] What were the effects upon the political attitude of management of a system of material balance planning that gave priority to output targets? To what extent did the imposition of controls lead to the growth of illegality and finally to what extent were the detailed provisions of the economic accounting system unworkable in a situation where the literacy and technical skills of lower level cadres were quite low? In short, to what extent did the new system of economic administration reveal a contradiction between policy and resources?

Chapter 5 will consider item (2) above – rationalisation proposals, production competitions, incentive policies and labour agreements. As in Chapter 4, the aim here is not to examine the economic determinants and implications of wages policy. This has already been undertaken by people more competent than myself.[15] The purpose here is to examine the relationship between group and individual, the remunerative dimensions of staff-line conflict, the factors taken into consideration in evaluating workers, technicians and cadres and the social consequences of that evaluation, the degree to which workers participated in wage-reform activities and wage formulation, the extent to which the form of wage payment facilitated or hindered worker participation in management and finally the extent to which traditional segmental forms of organisation resulted in deviations from prescribed wage policy. An examination of production competitions and the movements to put forward model workers will tell us something about divisions among workers and indeed their political consciousness, and an examination of labour agreements will tell us something about the degree and nature of routinisation. This latter might also suggest an avenue of enquiry into the question of conciliation and arbitration about which I was able to find little information. In addition, an examination of the role of the labour unions in negotiating such agreements might tell us something about the rapidly changing function of those organisations. Considerable attention will be given to labour agreements in Chapter 5 because, unlike wages policy about which several people have written, no-one to my knowledge has made a study of labour agreements. In the light of the polemic about the various contradictory 'constitutions' which were put forward by different sides in the Cultural Revolution, such a study is long overdue.

Chapter 6 will examine item (3) above – the establishment of systems of responsibility and a new discrete command structure. What was to result from this was a radically new system of organisation based on the Stalinist system of imposed change from without rather than the approach to organisation that had characterised the wartime experience of the Chinese Communist Party – change from *within* existing organisational structures. Before discussing this however, we must establish a framework within which to discuss the questions of organisation and control.

The organisational perspective

In discussing organisation, at the broadest conceptual level, the Durkheimian framework established by Franz Schurmann will be used. Schurmann distinguishes between networks of technological solidarity (between roles and structures) and human solidarity (between total human units) within ideologies committed to the furtherance of change or the preservation of the status quo. In terms of organisational leadership the following matrix emerges:[16]

	Technological solidarity	*Human solidarity*
Commitment to the status quo	Modern Bureaucracy	Traditional bureaucracy
Commitment to change	Modern (Western and Soviet) Management	Chinese revolutionary organisation characterised by 'cadre' leadership

Organisations held together by human solidarity (a term which avoids the religious implications of Durkheim's term 'mechanical' solidarity) tend to be characterised by diffuseness of responsibility. Such was the characteristic of both traditional Chinese and traditional Japanese bureaucracy and also of the forms of organisation developed by the Chinese Communist Party during its period of guerilla warfare behind the Japanese lines (1937–45).

In examining the latter and their reinterpretation in the middle 1950s, Schurmann has shown that organisation characterised by human solidarity need not preclude rapid social and political change. The main reasons why traditional Chinese bureaucratic forms of organisation ossified seem to have been ideological and cultural and due to the fact that there was no strong non-radical middle class grouping capable of infusing life into them. This will be discussed in chapter 1.

Traditional bureaucratic forms of organisation which were applied to industrial undertakings in both nineteenth-century China and Japan make no clear line of distinction between authority and function but do establish excessively rigid criteria concerning *status*. An excessive concern for status and hierarchy tends to produce a reluctance to delegate authority. Secondly, the ethos that dominates traditional bureaucracy is formally collective. In such a situation a convention develops whereby all key decisions must appear to be the product of consensus and be promulgated at the apex of an organisational hierarchy. Potential decisions, therefore, which originate at lower levels must take the form of proposals and may be modified as they pass up the hierarchy prior to promulgation. Information qualifying such proposals must pass through the same bureaucratic filters as the proposals themselves, which frequently results in the higher levels having information inadequate to form any conclusion other than the one previously arrived at. Consequently the authorisation or rejection of such proposals will frequently be on grounds other than the quality of the arguments put forward on their behalf.[17] In addition, a concern for status and a collectivity orientation makes it extremely difficult to determine exactly what the power of any person occupying a leading position is. What might appear to be absolute power might well be constrained by informal groups or groups with outside allegiances who seek to foster their own interests within the formal organisation.

Modern Western or Soviet management, on the other hand, demands that responsibilities be specific and, whether organisation is centralised (with the bulk of key decisions made at the apex of an organisation) or decentralised (with a large proportion of decision-making power delegated to lower levels), each level or organisation should be responsible for certain specified types of policy or operational decisions. Traditionally the simplest way of classifying factory structure is threefold – single line organisation, staff-line organisation and functional organisation (see Fig. 1).

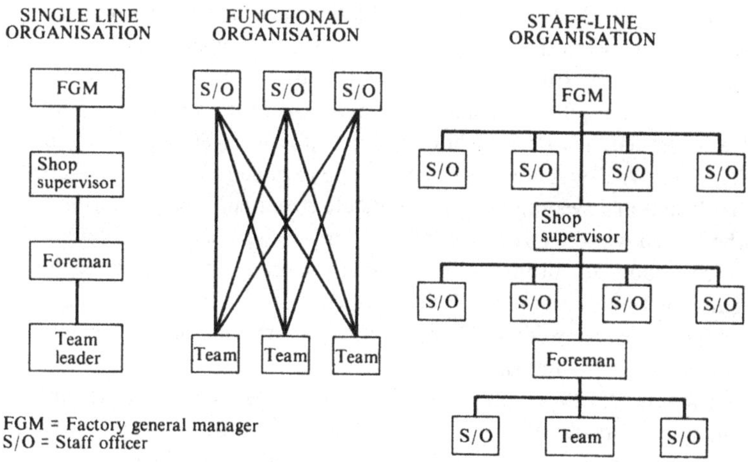

Figure 1

In single line organisation, specialised staff functions (personnel management, engineering, accountancy etc) are performed by line management who issue instructions directly to the shop floor. This principle is suitable only for the small concern since it is based upon the assumption that line management has sufficient expertise and time to perform the functions which would normally be assigned to specialists.

In staff-line organisation, specialised staff have an exclusively advisory role. Their function is to assist line management in making decisions but they themselves may not issue instructions directly to the shop floor. This system assumes that line managers are sufficiently competent to integrate the advice of staff members and process such advice into operational instructions. Specialised staff for their part are required to present as many sides of a particular case as possible, thus producing a very different kind of information flow from the traditional bureaucratic pattern outlined above. Although the staff-line pattern of organisation might eliminate the confusion of the traditional bureaucratic pattern, it might also kill initiative amongst those who feel constrained to act in a situation for which they are not immediately responsible. Secondly, a staff-line system does not readily accomodate patterns of collective decision making and thirdly, there is always the possibility that people at middle and lower levels of the organisation might become atomised and alienated.

In functional organisation, specialised personnel are required to issue instructions directly to the shop floor within limits very clearly defined by their expertise. Ideally, division of labour is worked out with such a degree of precision that there is no need for any line manager to perform an integrative function. When the idea of 'functional supervision' was first put forward at the beginning of the twentieth century, it was associated with the school of 'scientific management' of which Frederick W. Taylor was the most notable exponent.[18] Taylor believed that functional systems would be possible to actualise in a situation where each worker was turned into an unthinking cog in a machine which responded automatically to the specialised commands of each of eight functional foremen.[19] He concluded that workers were by nature lazy and given to 'soldiering' and so all efforts should be directed at cancelling out the human factor.

There is, however, no necessary connection between the functional principle of organisation and a technological conception of solidarity as the Taylor system presupposed. Taylor demanded that the integration on the shop floor of potentially conflicting instructions emanating from a number of functional foremen be achieved by precise written regulations.[20] In other words, integration was held to be inherent in a specified division of labour. I shall refer later to this model of Taylor's as a *technologically integrated functional model*. It is possible, however, to construct a functional model where such integration would be achieved on the one hand by lower level leadership of the 'cadre' type within a network of human solidarity, and on the other by a policy conscious work force. In such a system many of the control processes will of necessity be mechanical and automatic, lest the work force spend most of its time attending meetings. I shall call this model an *ideologically integrated functional model*.

Organisations characterised by staff-line and functional principles differ in their pattern of stratification. In a staff-line system, the number of organisational levels and the number of staff personnel located on them is determined not only by the nature of the work done but also by prescribed norms about the structure of communication and command, independent of the nature of the work. In a functional system, on the other hand, it is ideally only the nature of the work that determines the responsibilities of those who have to supervise it. Consequently where the staff-line principle is employed, there is a greater likelihood that chains of command might elongate, the number of levels of organisation increase and the personnel engaged exclusively in communication proliferate. Since the prescribed Soviet model that was imported into China in the early 1950s was in fact based on this staff-line principle, a consideration of the above problem will be one of the major concerns in chapter 6.

Where the functional principle is employed, however, the need for an additional level of organisation occurs only when a group of functional agents become physically incapable of supervising an increasing number of workers. Despite their attractiveness, functional systems have always been extremely rare in industrial organisation because of the high demands they place upon both management and workers.[21] In a situation where workers are insufficiently skilled and where mechanisms are inadequate to ensure effective integration of conflicting instructions, the adoption of a functional system can result in chaos since an individual worker will be exposed to a whole series of instructions from different sources that he cannot cope with. On the other hand, no organisation can exist in which all technical decisions have to originate from a particular level of line management, for such a system would be incapable of dealing with any emergency situation where technical expertise must be brought to bear upon an immediate problem. It is axiomatic therefore that in any system of staff-line organisation, a pattern of functional relationships will *overlay* the formal structure.[22] Such functional relationships may be formalised, but since it is extremely difficult to forsee all the possible technical and other problems that may occur, a significant portion of the network of functional contacts is usually informal. Chapter 6 will consider what functional overlay patterns persisted in Chinese factories in the early 1950s in violation of the Soviet model and Chapter 7 will give some attention to a particular pattern of functional overlay that could never be dispensed with – that of the Communist Party organisation.

The problem of control

The discussion above assumes a hierarchial form of organisation. In recent years however, a school of industrial sociologists has developed who believe that the concept of pyramidal organisation is inadequate to explain modern industrial organisation. They assert that control processes are not necessarily part of the structure of authority.[23] Control is defined as 'referring solely to the task of ensuring that activities are producing the desired results': it 'is limited to monitoring the outcome of activities, reviewing feedback information about this outcome and if necessary taking corrective action'.[24] Those who reject the pyramid formula divide control into *administrative control* (programmes for production planning, measurement mechanisms, cost-control systems etc.) and *mechanical control* (the automatic control of machine tools, automatic mechanisms for ensuring the continuous flow of production etc.). They maintain that, as the size of an industrial organisation grows, administrative and to an even greater extent mechanical controls become impersonal and automatic and as technology becomes more sophisticated, 'line managers and supervisors increasingly cease to concern themselves with the day-to-day problems of production operations and function primarily as adjustors and supplementers of control processes'.[25] Rather than conceive organisation in a pyramidal sense, these theorists, who seem to envisage the withering away of management, prefer to see organisation in terms of two overlapping spheres, one comprising the design system and the other the execution system. Where the control and authority systems are identical, there is complete identity between the spheres. At the other extreme where processes are completely mechanical, there is complete separation between the spheres.

Clearly any comprehensive study of Chinese management would be required to examine technological determinants and evaluate the relationship between administrative and mechanical control. This exploratory study does not aim at such comprehensiveness and, in any case, the material at my disposal has been insufficient to make any comparison between different technological levels. Secondly, the utility of the above approach increases with technological sophistication and the technological levels dealt with here are not particularly high. Thirdly, since the focus here is on authority, I must perforce concentrate on what has been referred to as *administrative* control. I must, however, anticipate the criticism that this study is weak in its discussion of technological determinants.

Before proceeding any further some mention must be made also of the extraordinary plethora of terms that exist in Chinese which can all be loosely translated by the English term 'control'. The definition of control given above is usually translated by the Chinese word *k'ung-chih*. It is the term that appears in the word 'control figures' (*k'ung-chih shu-mu*) which provided the basis for planning. Control in the sense of *k'ung-chih* may be broken down into two components both frequently translated by the English word 'control'. The first of these, *chien-ch'a* (监察), is taken by Schurmann (from Chou Fang) to mean checking up after the event, in distinction to *chien-tu* (监督), which he translates 'supervision' and which signifies the checking up on actions whilst they are still going on.[26] It is as well to bear in mind however that a number of other terms exist all with slightly different nuances all of which may be loosely translated by the English word 'control'.[27]

Checks on managerial bureaucratism and authoritarianism

Chapter 6 will examine the effects of trying to implement a rigid staff-line system of command which derived from the Soviet Union and will see to what extent this resulted in staff-line tension. It will examine to what extent the implementation of the Soviet system gave rise to 'bureaucratism'. 'Bureaucratism' may be defined here as a process whereby leading personnel in an organisation become cut off from working personnel at lower levels, where they devote an increasing amount of time to just keeping the organisation going without much regard for wider social issues and where intra-organisational communication becomes hidden from outside observers by a process of routinised secrecy. Chapter 6 will enquire to what extent the adoption of rigid staff-line systems gave line management a considerable amount of power and to what extent institutions existed within industrial enterprises that might serve as a check on managerial 'bureaucratism' and authoritarianism.

Chapter 7 will deal with three institutions that were designed, amongst other things, to serve as a check on management – the factory management committee, the enterprise Party branch and the enterprise union branch. The process whereby checks were imposed upon management was part of a general process known as 'democratisation' (*min-chu-hua*) which went together with 'enterprisation' (*ch'i-yeh-hua*) to form the core of policy with regard to industrial enterprises in the period following liberation.

Provision for the establishment of factory management committees upon which worker delegates sat demonstrates clearly what has been referred to as a confusion as to which Soviet model was being adopted, for the prescribed management committees that were set up following liberation were nearer to the Soviet model of 1917 than to the Stalinist model of 1949. The Chinese leadership in 1949 conceived the contradiction between 'democratisation' and 'enterprisation' as similar to the contradiction between democracy and centralism in the theory of democratic centralism (*min-chu chi-chung-chih*). It was felt at that time that one had only to juxtapose the two concepts 'democratisation' and 'enterprisation' for a synthesis to work itself out. It failed to do so, and, in the conflict which followed, the principle of 'democratisation' lost out. It was not until 1957 that Mao Tse-tung felt constrained to spell out the possible antagonistic nature of the twin concepts 'democracy' and 'centralism'[28] at a time when excessive centralism was being criticised and new ideas about democracy put forward. Referring to this early period in 1962, Mao noted that although the measures taken had been necessary, the creativity of the Chinese people had been dampened.[29]

In an unpublished manuscript, Franz Schurmann has suggested that when the Chinese Communist Party uses the word democracy, it can mean one of two things.[30] Firstly, it uses 'democracy' in the classic Soviet sense, contrasting it with 'centralism' and defining it as a situation where decision making is extended further down an organisational hierarchy. Such was the way democracy was used during the decentralisation movement of 1957 when a large amount of decision making power in the industrial sector was handed down to provincial or municipal administration. Secondly, the Communist Party uses the word democracy to mean relatively broad participation in the making and execution of decisions. Such was the way the word democracy was used in the description of mass involvement in industrial management during the Great Leap Forward (1958–9) in the work of Steve Andors. One may further break down this second definition into components familiar to Western political scientists. On the one hand 'democracy' is seen in a participatory sense with a stress on direct mass participation in the making and execution of decisions at the basic level; such a definition immediately raises questions as to the scope of such decision-making, the vertical distribution of power and consequently the relationship between policy formulation and policy execution and between politics, policy and operations. This is the focus of Andors' research mentioned above.[31] On the other hand 'democracy' may be seen in a representative sense and this definition raises the hoary old problem that has concerned students of politics since the time of Rousseau – to what extent does the delegation of sovereignty involve its surrender.

During the Management Democratisation Movement (*Kung-ch'ang Kuan-li Min-chu-hua Yün-tung*) of 1948–51, when factory management committees were set up, it was the representative definition of democracy that held sway in much the same way as during the period when the State Constitution was put forward in 1954. This representative definition of democracy was replaced gradually by a participatory one during the Democratic Reform Movement (*Min-chu Kai-ko Yün-tung*) of 1950–1. Finally, this work will ask whether any of the above definitions of democracy were at all meaningful in the period after 1952 when those institutions designed to act as checks on managerial authority began to atrophy.

The Party and labour union organisations within industrial enterprises are important, not only because they were formally dedicated to the proposition that the working class were 'masters', but also because they were the mechanisms whereby enterprises were linked to local government and the wider political system. Chapter 7 will note that the power of the Party organisation within industrial enterprises varied in direct proportion to the strength of horizontal linkages and where horizontal linkages were weak the Party organisation might be reduced to being just another functional system overlaying the formal managerial structure.

Little attention here will be paid to the role of the labour unions beyond a brief discussion of the Party–union crisis of 1950–1 in Chapters 2 and 3, since unions never really acted as an effective check on management and where they did show some independence, it was in the direction of 'economism' (the search for immediate material benefits at the expense of wider goals). This has been the subject of a study by Paul Harper.[32] A few pages will be devoted in chapter 7, however, to demonstrating the subordinate role of labour unions in the period following the union crisis.

Chapter 8 will attempt to relate the pattern of enterprise 'democratisation' and 'enterprisation' to subsequent events. For a long time scholars have looked upon the events of 1958–9 and 1966–9 as deviations from norms deriving from the Soviet Union and established in the early 1950s. If in fact it can be demonstrated that one of the principal obstacles to the implementation of Soviet models of organisation in the early 1950s was the tradition of the Chinese Communist Party, then perhaps it was the Soviet model that constituted a deviation from the Chinese road to socialism. Such is the inference that I draw from Mark Selden's recent work *The Yenan Way in Revolutionary China*. This study is offered as another contribution to the testing of that hypothesis.

Finally in chapter 8 this work will return to the 'logic of industrialism' debate in discussing how some of the main problems raised in the main part of the study were subsequently dealt with. In dismantling the model imported from the Soviet Union and in attempting to chart their own pattern of industrialisation, it is clear that the Chinese are aiming at something very different from the 'pluralist industrialism' predicted by Kerr and his associates. Other scholars are currently at work documenting exactly what this Chinese road is, and much research needs to be done before we can assess the success of their efforts. All I can do here is to point out some of the avenues of enquiry and some of the persistent problems.

Part I

Historical background

1. The Chinese pattern of industrialisation in comparative perspective

In this chapter, a comparison will be made between the Russian, Japanese and Chinese approaches to industrialisation in the period prior to the Second World War. The aim is two-fold; to locate the process of enterprise formation in the Peoples Republic of China within the historical debate concerning the 'logic of industrialism' and then, to examine three questions of relevance to the subsequent discussion. Firstly, what was the structure of the decision making process that had evolved in large Chinese industrial organisations by 1949 and to what extent was it similar to or different from that of Japan and the Soviet Union which at various times had provided China with models. Secondly, what was the pattern of stratification and segmentation that existed in these organisations and what was the relationship between staff and line. Thirdly, what was the nature of material and non-material incentive that developed in industry in each of these three countries. Additionally, some attention will be given to the evolution of the Chinese labour movement in order to provide background for the discussion of the role of worker organisations in the take-over of factories in the next chapter.

The Russian experience

The 'westernising policy' of Peter the Great (1689–1725) sought to establish the military viability of the Russian state through a number of measures including the state promotion of industry. During Peter's reign, foreign managerial personnel were recruited to establish industrial concerns and attempts were made to train an indigenous managerial cadre. Not long after their establishment, however, many of the new industrial concerns were found to be unprofitable and were turned over to private entrepreneurs the bulk of whom were not aristocrats but were drawn from a traditional merchant class of comparatively low social status. The new entrepreneurial class was especially favoured by the state with regard to government loans and, as a result of the acute shortage of 'free' labour in a serf-owing society, they received in 1721 the right to purchase whole villages of serfs. A situation in which the relationship between the economically privileged middle-class manufacturer and workers under his control approached that of lord and serf resulted in considerable aristocratic resentment.[1]

Aristocratic hostility against the rising middle class led to an erosion of middle-class privileges in the years following Peter's death and a number of edicts were published restricting the right of non-aristocrats to possess serfs. These conservative edicts, however, were only able to hamstring the middle class for a time and with the reign of Catherine the Great (1762–96), a new period of state economic initiative began. Now the discrimination against non-aristocratic manufacturers became less acute as the central government played off aristocracy against middle class in an attempt to strengthen its own autocratic power.

Partly as a result of the non-payment of compensation for runaway serfs, the proportion of 'free' workers in concerns managed by middle class or aristocratic entrepreneurs increased from 39% of all industrial workers in 1797 to 54% in 1825.[2] At the same time there was a corresponding decline in the proportion of so-called 'possessional workers' owned by the state or nobility who worked in either private industry or state industry managed by government officials or leased to private entrepreneurs. A third category, however, 'estate peasants' (serfs) engaged in 'mountain' or other works located on the estates of the nobility increased in number partly as a result of the *obrok* (tithing) system which commuted service obligations into cash payments and which required an increase in the money income of serfs.

Over each of the above types of labour, the form of power exercised by management was largely coercive and a very important form of (negative) non-material incentive was fear. In state-run concerns, wages were higher and conditions of employment better than elsewhere due to the more direct regulation by a state concerned with efficiency and informed by a belief that an excessively coerced work-force was an inefficient one. In enterprises run by middle-class entrepreneurs, there existed a series of regulations governing wages and working conditions which, although rarely enforced, reflected the desire of government to prevent the sacrifice of long-term production goals for the sake of short-term profit for the middle-class entrepreneurs. It is unlikely that factory regulations were imposed for any benevolent motive, for if humanitarian considerations were at all important they surely would have applied to 'estate peasants' who continued to enjoy very low wages, appalling working conditions and the absence of any restrictions on management whatsoever.

The government was quite prepared to restrict a relatively weak middle class but it was not prepared to suffer the economic and political consequences of provoking a nobility which still dominated the central government. It was unwilling therefore to take action against estate works run by the nobility unless such concerns ran into debt. Nevertheless, although committed to a policy of transferring state-run industry to private hands, the government was unwilling to make transfers to the nobility in a situation where transfer resulted in an almost immediate decline in not only wages and working conditions but also profits. This reluctance is reflected in the fact that from 1762–96, the number of serfs in 'mountain works' under the Treasury increased two and a half times whilst those in private hands increased by just over 50%.[3] By the nineteenth century, however, the significance of 'mountain works' in the national economy declined as did the significance of the government as an economic agent. The government had been prepared to intervene directly in 'possessional factories' and indirectly in privately run 'mountain works' when it depended upon such concerns for supplies. By the 1840s, however, other sources of supply were available and attempts to regulate factories ceased.[4]

Perhaps the key reason for abandoning factory regulations was that official control of industrial entrepreneurs might encourage industrial unrest by raising the workers' 'horizons of expectations' which might be an important element in a revolutionary prodrome.[5] On the other hand, the Russian Ministry of the Interior argued that the non-regulation of factories was one of the surest ways to worsen working conditions and thus provoke labour agitation;[6] they were clearly informed by a more classical revolutionary prodrome.[7] In the agitation for the reintroduction of factory regulation, an odd alliance developed between the Ministry of the Interior and large middle-class industrial entrepreneurs in the high-wage modern sector who felt that such regulation would eliminate the marginal producer. By the 1880s, the Ministry of the Interior had already extended its control down to the factories by obliging factory employers to issue passports to workers and by sending police and factory inspectors down to inhibit the growth of labour agitation. It was but a short step from this to the promulgation of a new set of factory regulations limiting the arbitrary actions of management.

The 1840s–80s, therefore, was a period of reduced state intervention in the economy, when middle-class entrepreneurs were unfettered in their pursuit of short-term profits in an atmosphere of cut-throat competition. It was a period which saw cuts in wages, worsening working conditions and high labour mobility. With the emancipation of serfs in 1861, there was a great influx of peasants into the towns but not as permanent labour since former serfs were required to return to their villages periodically for purposes of tax payment and, as a result, the industrial workforce maintained its semi-rural character right into the twentieth century. As far as the Russian bureaucracy was concerned, this was not necessarily a bad thing for it was noted that the existence of a workforce with rural ties would militate against the development of a politically conscious urban proletariat; unemployed workers could be expected to return to the countryside and not 'congregate in a dangerous way'.[8] The existence of a pre-proletarian workforce in an atmosphere of unfettered pursuit of short term profit will be referred to hereafter as 'primitive capitalism'.

In some societies the process of alienation and atomisation characteristic of 'primitive capitalism' and so graphically described by Marx and Engels was diverted by the formation of mutual-aid groups, friendly societies and simulated-kinship structures. During the period of Russia's early industrialisation, however, there was a relative absence of spontaneously organised mutual-aid groups except amongst the Jewish population and in the non-Russian areas of the extreme West and, by the time friendly societies began to show significant growth in the second half of the nineteenth century, such groups became increasingly subject to state control and were often used to limit labour mobility.[9] There was, however, in Russian society a tradition of *sobornost* which stressed moral solidarity within social groups reinterpreted as family units and which might have led to the formation of simulated-kinship structures providing a sense of solidarity and identity for urban workers newly torn from rural families. A precedent might be found in the *arteli* which were ideally self-governing fraternities of artisans but, by the second half of the nineteenth century, these *arteli* were increasingly organised from above by local government.[10] The increasing penetration of industry by the police and other agencies of the state made for atomisation rather than the segmentation that we shall see was more characteristic of Japan and China. As tax regulations were altered freeing the worker of his obligation to return to the countryside, the process of atomisation accelerated and the work-force began to resemble a proletariat in the Marxian sense. As labour-union, anarchist and socialist groups began to form, a concern for expressive goals which might have been satisfied by simulated-kinship structures, became inseparable from a wider need for working class solidarity aimed at fundamental social change.

Police penetration inhibited not only the development of simulated-kinship structures but also the development of labour unions. When unions were formed they were often suppressed or taken over by the police. By the end of the nineteenth century, it became clear that a simple policy of repression was ineffective, and there occurred that extraordinary phenomenon known as 'police socialism' – a process whereby police became leaders of labour unions. Labour unions controlled by the police sought to 'widen the rights of the workers by obtaining concessions from the bourgeois entrepreneurs but at the same time suppressing any challenge to the established order'.[11] By such action, police-controlled labour unions alienated not only the workers who perceived 'police socialism' to be no more than a covert means of control but also middle-class entrepreneurs who felt themselves forced to make economic concessions as a substitute for the government making political concessions.

Police control in Russia was carried out within a paternalist ideology that in other countries might have led to the widespread formation of simulated-kinship groups. The absence of a collectivity orientation at the basic level in Russian industry, however, meant that the paternalist ideology merely manifested itself in regulations governing industrial barracks.[12] An ideology of paternalism does not marry well with a policy of atomisation and all 'police socialism' did was to contribute to the revolution of 1905. In the period prior to the Bolshevik Revolution, large industrial concerns in Russia tended to be highly stratified but not segmented. Organisation tended to be of a simple vertical staff-line type intersected only by the intervention of external control agents such as factory inspectors and police. Apart from the existence of external police control, such concerns resembled their Western counterparts which is not surprising since many were modelled on Western prototypes and many were run by Western managers.

Right from the reign of Peter the Great, many of the entrepreneurs to whom state enterprises had been transferred were foreign and during the anti-middle-class reaction of the eighteenth century, such foreigners were able to gain ground at the expense of their Russian counterparts. After the 1840s, during the period of 'primitive capitalism', foreign capital became much more important in Russian industry due to a shortage of domestic capital, and foreign management became more important as the industrial revolution made headway in Western Europe. This period saw the rise of foreign capitalists such as Ludwig Knoop who came to control all the cotton mills in Central Russia. Knoop imported whole factories from England together with managers to supervise building, workers to install the equipment from Manchester and supervisory staff to run the factories once they commenced production.[13] The mid nineteenth century saw also the collapse of the old iron industry in the Urals and its replacement by a new industry between the Donetz and the Dneiper – exploited in large measure by foreign capital and by foreign management to the point that nearly half the capital invested in the coal industry in the Donetz basin prior to 1914 was foreign. Towards the end of the nineteenth century, when the largest individual industrial establishments in Russia were probably in the hands of Englishmen and Frenchmen, over 80% of the capital in iron mining, metallurgy and oil was foreign.[14] In such a situation, it is little wonder that factory organisation in the modern sector tended to resemble that of the West. There was however one crucial difference; stratification was frequently reinforced by ethnic considerations which impeded the growth of a real bourgeoisie in Cole's sense of the word and the development of a bourgeois hegemonic ideology, vital to any transition to a higher form of capitalism. The change that finally did occur as the First World War accelerated the revolutionary process was not to a new and more complex form of capitalism but constituted a major qualitative change – to socialism.

The socialist transformation of Russian industry following the Bolshevik Revolution was seen originally as a gradual process. Lenin spoke of the very early period as one in which 'the state power made an attempt to pass to the new social relationships, while adapting itself to the conditions then prevailing as much as possible as gradually as possible and breaking with as little of the old as possible'.[15] The Decree on Workers' Control of 14 November 1917 gave to newly created workers' councils supervisory but not managerial powers and nationalisation proceeded very cautiously.[16] There was division of opinion concerning the pace and nature of change and the process of take-over ranged from outright seizure of power by the workers to the establishment of vague control mechanisms to supervise foreign management. At one stage negotiations were even held concerning the establishment of 'mixed companies' in which foreign capital participated.[17]

With the advance of the White Armies in mid-1918, however,

extremely drastic changes in industrial organisation were undertaken. There was inaugurated a period of 'War Communism' which saw a wholesale programme of nationalisation and an attempt to administer industry bureaucratically. Industrial units became little more than extensions of a centralised state bureaucracy, although the apparently excessive centralisation of such a system was balanced by the continued existence of workers' councils. The power of these councils gradually diminished however as they came under the leadership of new labour unions organised on an industrial as opposed to craft basis.

The period of 'War Communism' has been the subject of many conflicting interpretations. Scholars disagree in their evaluation of the extent to which the radical changes undertaken during this period were forced upon the new regime by the Civil War and foreign intervention and the extent to which they were felt to be positive steps in their own right in the advance towards socialism. They disagree in their interpretations of the 'temporary' nature of 'War Communism' and consequently offer different evaluations of the 'retreat' from 'War Communism' in 1921.[18] We cannot go into the various arguments here, but it is worth noting that the current reinterpretation of the early years of the Chinese Peoples Republic to which this essay is a contribution poses very similar problems and is likely to give rise to a similar polemic.

An important feature of the polemic was the extent to which a policy of inflation was merely a temporary expedient to finance the war or an effective weapon to defeat the bourgeoisie. Whatever the answer, the organisational consequence of the inflation policy was for all production accounting to be conducted in terms of gross output. The result was the growth of a system of centralised bureaucratic control that was too cumbersome to respond quickly enough to the exigencies of war. Ways had to be found to by-pass administrative congestion and a number of 'shock' enterprises vital to the war effort were designated. Once this 'shock' category was established, there was constant pressure from the non-'shock' sector to have the former expanded and the ability of the 'shock' sector to overcome administrative congestion declined in direct proportion to its rate of expansion. By the time the 'shock' category had been expanded to include that branch of industry most suggestive of bureaucratic interests – office equipment – it was too big to be effective.[19]

Centralised bureaucratic control in an atmosphere of mobilisation for war led to a subordination of the labour unions to managerial control and a growing suspicion that many of the ideals of the Bolshevik Revolution had been sacrificed. The reaction took the form, on the one hand, of a 'syndicalist' tendency in the labour unions and, on the other, armed insurrection at Kronstadt. These two developments saw the end of the 'War Communism' period, and the defeat of the syndicalist tendency in the labour unions ushered in the New Economic Policy which involved a drastic decentralisation of industrial control. In 1921, attention was shifted from industrial to rural problems and, with the abolition of the policy of grain requisition, a rural market was allowed to revive. It was to be a short step from the re-creation of market relations as the link between agriculture and industry to the freeing of a large sector of industry from dependence on centralised supplies of materials and fuel and the granting of permission for economic units to engage in money transactions.

Prior to 1921, the greater part of modern industry was administered directly by the Supreme Economic Council through a number of *chief administrations*. With the decentralisation measures of the early 1920s, a strategically important sector of industry remained under the control of budgetary organs similar to the former *chief administrations* but the bulk of industry was now grouped into commercially autonomous units known as *trusts*. The primary principle for the formation of these *trusts* was horizontal (geographical proximity), although a few were integrated vertically where the concerns within them formed successive stages in a single production process. Although property rights remained vested in the State, trusts were defined as 'juridical persons' that could enter independently into contracts and negotiate loans; they were also obliged to pay tax. To facilitate such activities, the State Bank was reopened although its operations were constrained by the continuing inflation that was only brought under control with the currency stabilisation measures of 1924. In the meantime, the State and co-operative financial and trading organisations found themselves incapable of providing a complete commercial network for industries that had been decentralised at extraordinary speed and the 'Nepman' (private capitalist) stepped into the breech.

Although a sector of industry was not reorganised in autonomous *trusts*, all sectors of the economy, including that which was still subject to centralised allocation of supplies, were required to manage their affairs on a commercial basis. Thus, in state-run industry, whether under central control or not, an economic accounting system (*khozraschët*) was established stipulating the degree to which industrial units exercised autonomy in the use of funds either allocated from the state or borrowed from the State Bank.

The 'state capitalism' of the early 1920s had much in common with that earlier period of 'state capitalism' that lasted until the advance of the White armies and was seen by Lenin as a transitional step in the advance to socialism. It was, however, a period which saw a partial restoration of capitalism which was opposed by those in the Communist Party, prominent amongst whom was Stalin, who felt that this would hinder a long term socialist strategy. Stalin advocated a rapid process of industrialisation under central control with priority given to heavy industry. He was opposed on the 'right' by those who were unwilling to force the pace of industrialisation and on the 'left' by those who, whilst giving priority to heavy industry, saw the transition to socialism only in a global context.

With the advent of the Soviet Union's First Five Year Plan (which began in 1928) Stalin had won, and a complex centralised planning apparatus was re-established although this time within a money economy. Stalin was committed, above all, to vertical control and set about dismantling lines of functional supervision. By the early 1930s, the industrial hierarchy was headed by a Supreme Economic Council under which came a number of *chief administrations* responsible for particular spheres of industry. Under them were industrial *combines* which enjoyed a degree of financial autonomy as did the next level down, the *trusts*. Throughout the hierarchy both at levels above the *trust* and within it, the principal pattern of supervision was functional.[20] At the Seventeenth Congress of the Party in 1934, the principle of functionalism was formally abolished and in his key speech Kaganovitch upheld the principle of 'one-man management' which he defined as a process whereby the occupant of each level of line management was made an '*absolute*' leader.[21] In accordance with the principle of uninterrupted vertical control, *combines* were abolished, the number of separate trusts was reduced, the *chief administrations* were replaced by Commissariats (Ministries) although some did continue to exist as extensions of the latter, and a straight line of command established right down to the factory and beyond.[22]

In the new vertical structure, the role of the 'economic accounting system' changed. It was now something much more than a system of cost control and a success indicator.[23] It included almost everything that would be described in the West as 'business management' and represented the whole operational side of the planning system within the industrial enterprise. The 'enterprise' was gradually established as the basic unit in the industrial system, rather than trust or other organisations and, as such, it took on a new more precise definition. It was that unit of one or several factories that enjoyed a degree of financial independence prescribed by the economic accounting system. The actual degree of independence enjoyed by the enterprise director was, however, not always clear since he was subject to different degrees of control at different times. Such a situation could at least serve to keep him on his toes or at worst create an atmosphere in which managerial initiative suffered.

Thus a lack of unity within industry had been rectified by curtailing the powers of intermediate units at super enterprise level and what was left of the workers' representative bodies at enterprise level and the vesting of supreme power in the enterprise director. In a broad context, the 'economic accounting system' established *responsibilities* (however vague) of the enterprise director, whilst in the context of the enterprise itself, 'one-man management' (an extreme form of staff line system) established his power. As 'one-man management' and the Stalinist reformulation of 'the economic accounting system' were promoted, the so-called 'parliamentary system' of factory management declined and worker participation in management was confined to attending production conferences and worker and staff congresses which had no decision making power.[24] Although something of a representative conception of democracy remained, the 'democratic base' upon which one-man management was ideally to rest became defined increasingly in terms of 'making the will of the one man actualised in the voluntary actions of the workers'.[25]

The Japanese experience

The early industrialisation of Japan, which began in the second half of the nineteenth century, was more successful than that of Russia for three main reasons. Firstly, the class structure of Tokugawa Japan (up to 1868) was more closed than even that of Tsarist Russia which meant that not only were merchants not assimilated into the bureaucracy but neither were the minor nobility – the samurai. There began to develop an association between these two unassimilated middle-class groupings who together fostered a market orientation long before the Meiji Restoration of 1868 took place. Once the Meiji government embarked upon a policy reminiscent of Peter the Great, there already existed an assertive body of potential managerial personnel that was able to step into middle levels of administration in a way that had been impossible in early eighteenth century Russia. Secondly, the Meiji government took rapid steps to ensure centralised fiscal control. The land tax reform of 1873 established a uniform money tax which amounted to 25–30% of the total annual crop value and at the outset provided 94% of the central government revenue.[26] Thus the Meiji government was able to finance her early industrialisation without recourse to overseas and without allowing her industries to fall under foreign control. Thirdly, not long after the Meiji Restoration Japan joined in the scramble for China and by the beginning of the twentieth century had replaced Russia as a major imperialist power in Asia with all the economic advantages that such a position entailed.

State promotion of industry antedated the Meiji Restoration. Such large factories as existed in Tokugawa Japan were mainly owned, promoted and managed by the Shogunate or fief governments.[27] Industry was controlled by a traditional bureaucracy (dynastic élite) drawn from a class sharply demarcated from industrial workers and, as in Russia, this demarcation was frequently reinforced by the employment of a stratum of technically competent foreign experts at middle levels of administration. During the Meiji period, the central imperial government took over these industrial concerns and more and more senior management posts were filled by samurai-turned-bureaucrats who remained insulated from the workers by a stratum of foremen drawn from the workers' ranks.

As one might expect in industrial concerns run by traditional bureaucrats, managerial authority was potentially absolute though constrained by a collectivity orientation which required decisions to appear to be consensual. Status was defined but there was little delineation between authority and function. Vertical relationships were prescribed but little attention was paid to the horizontal relationship between functional units. Responsibilities were diffuse and individualism was discouraged. All these features of a traditional bureaucracy, which were ennumerated earlier had long been present in Japanese organisational life though they were strengthened considerably during the Tokugawa regime by restrictions on geographic and social mobility.

Many features of the above cultural pattern have continued down to the present day although industrial structure has changed considerably since the Meiji period. Towards the end of the nineteenth century, the Japanese government decided to sell all but a few of its factories to a handful of wealthy families, some of whom later became the controllers of huge industrial and commercial empires known as *zaibatsu*. The break with government was, however, less sharp than it appeared and a close relationship between government and big business persisted until 1945. The sale of government industries ushered in a period of 'primitive capitalism' very similar to that which occurred in Russia in the mid nineteenth century. The pace of industrialisation was accelerated, entrepreneurs became more ruthless in their pursuit of profit, working conditions deteriorated in the absence of any state regulation and large numbers of peasants were recruited from the rural areas who maintained close ties with the countryside. There were however two very important differences between Russian and Japanese 'primitive capitalism'. The former was characterised by growing foreign control; the latter was not, and, in fact, this period saw the virtual disappearance of those foreign managerial personnel who had remained in Japanese factories since the earlier period. Secondly, 'primitive capitalism' in Russia saw the beginnings of a process of worker alienation and atomisation whereas in Japan it saw the development of complex patterns of simulated-kinship structure.[28]

The simplest form of simulated-kinship system was the labour-gang. Gang-bosses were usually skilled workers, active in labour recruitment, who had come to control a body of workers which they placed at the disposal of management. Industrial labour gangs were not a peculiarly Japanese or Asian institution for such gangs had existed in British industry at the beginning of the nineteenth century[29] but what was peculiarly Japanese (and as we shall see later also Chinese) was that the internal solidarity of these gangs drew heavily on traditional patterns of simulated-kinship. Such patterns had existed since antiquity but the particular relationship of *oyabun–kobun* (superior–subordinate relationship modelled on that of father and son) which was central to labour gang solidarity dated probably from the beginning of the eighteenth century. As many different levels of gang-boss appeared, labour contracting networks became as complex as any real kinship system with different grades of fraternal relationship at each level. Membership of a labour gang was total in that the private and family life of both *oyabun* and *kobun* were drawn into the simulated-kinship network producing a fusion between ties of actual kinship and ties of simulated kinship.

The development of the gang-boss system was to a great extent a response to rapid social change and deteriorating labour conditions.

Under the preceding 'feudal' system, the industrial bureaucracy was committed to a value system which stressed 'benevolence' even though this quality may have infrequently manifested itself. Now, in the period of 'primitive capitalism', the entrepreneurial class was less concerned with such niceties. Labour gangs provided an elementary form of social security at a time when the state provided none and an alternative path of upward social mobility for the skilled worker at a time of rigid class division. But what is more important, they provided a sense of solidarity and identity for urban workers newly torn from rural families. In performing this function, the labour gangs resembled other simulated-kinship systems such as secret societies and blood brotherhoods and like them manifested a concern for ritual and the sacred. All such systems tend to be exploitative and the exploitation practised by gang-bosses often cancelled out the instrumental goals to which membership might first have been attracted. They may be understood best in the context of the expressive (concerned with group solidarity and identity in the face of social change). A necessary condition for their development is a segmental society where horizontal associations are weak and where higher authorities only communicate with the individual through a clearly defined superior whose position is legitimised by a paternalist ideology. Such a condition existed in Japanese industry but hardly existed at all in its Russian counterpart.

However functional the gang-boss system might have been in terms of narrow expressive goals, such a system was highly dysfunctional in terms of both managerial efficiency and working class solidarity. The gang-boss system led to a high degree of labour mobility between factories, prevented the development of horizontal cohesion between segments, hindered the control by management over a fragmented work force and perpetuated the rigid class division that had been inherited from the Tokugawa period. The degree of exploitation was such that gang-bosses extracted for themselves some 10–30% of the wages due to workers. Collective bargaining for the improvement of working conditions and for higher wages was prevented by a situation where workers were dependent upon the personal goodwill of a particular gang-boss. The development of trade-union organisations (typically characterised by horizontal relationships) was inhibited by the prevalence of vertical (superior–subordinate) relations and the development of a labour union ethos stressing rights and privileges was inhibited by a paternalist ethos stressing duties and obligations.[30]

Despite the above inhibitions on labour-union development, the second decade of the twentieth century saw the beginnings of organised labour in Japan. This was due in part to the extraordinarily rapid development of industry during the First World War which demanded an equally rapid process of labour recruitment. For the first time the labour force began to resemble a proletariat, though the continued existence of simulated-kinship networks made the labour force something other than the atomised proletariat described by Marx. The response of management to the challenge posed by the fledgling unions was an ideological one. The paternalist ideology which legitimised the simulated-kinship structure of the labour gangs was now projected on to the whole of industrial society and each industrial organisation was redefined as a simulated-kinship network. Such was the origin of what is now seen as the dominant distinguishing characteristic of the Japanese firm – its paternalism.

Much polemic surrounds the origin of Japanese industrial paternalism. The pioneer work of James Abegglen concentrates on the impact of traditional factors on workforce organisation which made for security of employment and a life-time commitment to a particular industrial organisation.[31] Following Yoshino, I have suggested above that political factors should also be given weight. A third and highly persuasive position has been put by Koji Taira who argues that a paternalist labour policy resulted from employers' 'rational' responses to labour market conditions characterised by acute labour shortage and high labour turnover.[32] These latter two arguments would suggest that paternalism should be considered largely as a new feature in the Japanese economy following the end of what I have described as the period of 'primitive capitalism'. If Taira is correct, then the utility of regarding Japan's industrial leadership in the early twentieth century as that of what Kerr and his school would call a 'dynastic élite' is open to question.[33] Indeed in adhering to capitalist 'economic rationality', Japan's paternalist leadership exhibited many of the characteristics of what Kerr would call 'middle-class leadership'.

This third period in Japan's industrialisation was ushered in with the factory act of 1911 and the gang-boss system which restricted quasi-kinship ties to relatively small units began to decline. Remnants of the gang-boss system persisted, however, right down to the labour reform of 1948–50. After 1911, attempts were made to assimilate the gang-bosses into formal management and to fuse together different work groups with loyalties to different gang bosses. This was done within a framework of human solidarity as opposed to technological solidarity and legitimised within a total ideology of *ersatz Gemeinschaft*, (the selective and usually bogus borrowing from traditional ideology of community). The challenge posed by the Bolshevik Revolution in Russia and its echoes in other parts of the world was frequently met by similar ideological defences, put forward by radical right-wing regimes and designed to limit class struggle.[34] The ideology of *ersatz Gemeinschaft* manifested itself eventually in the patriotic movement in industry[35] which stressed harmony in the face of external enemies. At the same time various institutions such as works councils were established by management offering bogus participation.[36] By 1932 the unions increasingly kept out of industrial disputes[37] and the new 'harmony' was increasingly capitalised on by employers who attempted to evade the provisions of factory legislation by hiring large numbers of temporary workers at lower wages.[38] As a consequence the old form of gang-boss organisation enjoyed a new lease of life. The economic determinist argument is very persuasive here. Paternalism owed its origin to a labour shortage. The easing of this shortage during the depression years produced a situation where employers made use of existing paternalist relationships to counter the power of the labour movement but at the same time responded 'rationally' to a labour surplus by reverting to earlier forms of labour recruitment. Such a situation was far from the picture of lifetime commitment portrayed by Abegglen. With the advent of full-scale war, however, demand for labour increased once again which led to the full flowering of paternalism and the ideology of *ersatz Gemeinschaft* came into its own.

Through each of the above periods, strategic industries (iron and steel, armaments, railways, telephones, etc.) remained under government control but the remainder of Japan's modern industry was in the hands of a number of *zaibatsu* mutually linked by complex cartel networks.[39] Taking advantage of low wages in the semi-modern and traditional sectors of industry, the major *zaibatsu* established subcontracting links[40] with that sector which resulted in huge sprawling networks of control which cut across different levels of ownership. Such unity as existed within these industrial empires was largely financial and considerable operational autonomy was enjoyed by their constituent parts.

During the 'liberal' period of the 1920s, diverse *zaibatsu* interests began to act as patrons of the politicians.[41] During the early 1930s, however, political initiative passed from the faction-ridden political parties to the military who were at first suspicious of the large *zaibatsu* empires. As a consequence, the military encouraged the formation of a number of new *zaibatsu* groups (*shinko zaibatsu*) which played an important part in the exploitation of North East China (the puppet state of Manchukuo after 1931)[42] but as time passed suspicion grew less and an alliance between the military and old *zaibatsu* developed. Finally, with the quasi-war economy of the 1930s, the government extended its control over a widened sector of strategic industries blurring the line of demarcation between the government and private sector. *Zaibatsu* became virtual branches of state economic administration[43] a situation which was to be referred to in a Chinese context as 'bureaucratic capitalism'. Thus the radical right-wing ideological response to the appearance of organised labour coincided with the convergence of government, military and *zaibatsu* as Japan went to war.

Japan's defeat in 1945 severed the link between government and *zaibatsu* but by that time over one third of the total paid-in capital in Japan was held by the ten largest *zaibatsu* of which the four largest produced 51% of all the coal, 60% of all aluminium, 69% of all locomotives, 50% of all pulp, 88% of all caustic soda and 43% of all sulphuric acid.[44] In the 1950s the *zaibatsu* were to revive around former *zaibatsu* banks and other financial institutions[45] demonstrating the congruence between financial and social networks that had been the basis of *zaibatsu* cohesion in the pre-war period.

The Chinese experience

There has been much debate about exactly when the 'sprouts of capitalism' first began to appear in China but most historians agree that her modern industrialisation began during the T'ung Chih Restoration which commenced in 1860 and paralleled the Meiji Restoration of Japan. As in Japan the initiative was taken by officialdom (dynastic élite) and most early industrial concerns were geared to national defence. The Japanese policy of '*Wakon Yosai*' (Japanese spirit and Western technology) found a Chinese counterpart in the doctrine which sought to preserve the essence (*t'i*) of the Confucian Imperial system through the instrumentality (*yung*) of Western technology.[46]

In Japan the initiative in industrialisation came largely from the central government which took rapid steps to ensure centralised fiscal control. In China however, official initiative was essentially that of *regional* government. The Kiangnan Arsenal (1865), the Foochow Shipyard (1866), the Tientsin Machine Factory (1870), the Lanchow

Arsenal (1872) and the Lushun Shipyard (1822), which were geared largely to military requirements at a time of actual rather than potential imperialist threat were set up on the initiative of governors and governors-general who exercised only regional control and did not have adequate capital resources at their disposal.

China's early industrialisation suffered not only from a shortage of capital but also from the effects of regional fragmentation exacerbated by imperialist intervention. The various governors and governors general, of whom the most famous in this context were probably Li Hung-chang and Chang Chih-tung, established, within areas under their control, military industrial complexes that depended directly upon their patronage. Industrial development within these complexes was adversely affected by shifts in the balance of power within the Empire and the changing relationship between central and regional government. With the fall of Li Hung-chang, for example, the military-industrial complex he controlled split into two parts – a network of military control headed by Yüan Shih-k'ai and a network of industrial and commercial control headed by Sheng Hsüan-huai. Just as the structure of military control in North China depended directly upon the personal fortunes of Yüan Shih-k'ai, so the pattern of industrial control and development in that area depended directly on the personal fortunes of Sheng Hsüan-huai. Both experienced alternating periods of fortune and eclipse. At various times in the last two decades of the Empire, Sheng managed to accrue to himself control over the Chinese Merchants' Steam Navigation Company, the Imperial Telegraph Administration, the Hanyehp'ing Coal and Iron Company, the Hua Sheng Spinning and Weaving Mill, the Imperial Railways Administration, the Imperial Bank of China as well as a collection of titles and official ranks. The 1911 Revolution, however, which had been precipitated by Sheng's attempt to nationalise the railways, saw the virtual collapse of Sheng's economic empire.[47] During the early Republic, Yüan Shih-k'ai inaugurated a despotic military regime which fragmented rapidly after his death in 1916. Just as Yüan was the prototype of what was later called 'warlord' (*chün-fa*) so Sheng was the prototype of what was later called 'bureaucratic capitalist'.

The industrial concerns which Sheng and others were instrumental in setting up were organised according to some variant of the formula 'official supervision and merchant management' (*kuan-tu, shang-pan*); this term was, however, very imprecise, a merchant being anyone in management who was not an official and the actual degree of official supervision varied from enterprise to enterprise. The *kuan-tu*, *shang-pan* formula was probably derived from the old government salt monopoly whereby the government appointed official supervisors who farmed out licenses to merchants giving them permission to manufacture, transport and sell the salt. Similarly, in the period of China's early industrialisation, a provincial governor or governor-general would appoint the head of a *kuan-tu, shang-pan* enterprise on the understanding that the latter would raise private capital to augment the official funds for its establishment which had been milked from any source available such as for example the military budget. The head of the enterprise (who went by a variety of titles such as *tu-pan, tsung-pan* etc) was not only an official with official rank granted by recommendation or purchase, but was also a semi-independent capitalist who would hold a number of shares in the company to which he had been appointed. He was responsible not only to his official patron (the governor or governor-general) whose protection he needed to ward off excessive government exactions, but also to a board of directors representing private shareholders. In a bureaucratic climate hostile to industrial development, he was suspected by his bureaucratic colleagues, with some justification, as a person who would help to undermine a Confucian ideology that rated land ownership as the only truly legitimate source of wealth and, with equal justification, as a person who would utilise his official position to gain more than his fair share of perquisites; in Confucian China graft was illegitimate only when it was felt to be excessive.

At the highest level, the *kuan-tu, shang-pan* enterprises were run according to the ethos of a traditional bureaucracy whose members considered themselves omnicompetent and who were reluctant to delegate authority. They were often run like the administrative *yamen* (government offices) without the advantage that those institutions had of having the *hsien* (county) magistrate on the spot, for *tu-pan* or other heads of *kuan-tu, shang-pan* enterprises who held concurrent official posts might be located hundreds of miles away from their enterprises. Decisions were made at the top of a bureaucratic hierarchy by officials with potentially absolute power but who were circumscribed by a collectivity orientation and bureaucratic channels of communication; a situation which frequently caused annoyance amongst foreign managerial personnel.[48]

The similarities between the traditional bureaucratic pattern of decision making in China and Japan will be apparent. There was, however, a major difference between China and Japan which lay not on the 'official supervision' side of the formula but on the side of 'merchant management'. The Chinese class structure in Ch'ing (Manchu) China was relatively more open than that in Tokugawa Japan which resulted in a process whereby successful merchants could be assimilated into an officialdom based on landed-gentry values in a manner that would have been impossible in Japan. Such a process inhibited the growth of an assertive middle-class except in areas under foreign control.

At middle levels of organisation in the *kuan-tu, shang-pan* undertakings, the *kuan* (officials) and *shang* (merchants) came together in three groupings.[49] First were the directors who represented the shareholders and who were concerned mainly with issues concerning financial policy. Second were the business and operational managers who were often foreigners and who effectively insulated processes on the work site from top levels of administration. Third were the 'official managers' who often held official positions but who were not so closely articulated to the bureaucracy as the head of the enterprise. This third category which combined both the principles of 'official supervision' and 'merchant management' had vaguely defined responsibilities, which led to a confusion between staff and line authority. As in Japan, it was not only the stratum of business and operational management that insulated the top of an organisation from its base; there was also a stratum of foremen who resembled very closely the Japanese gang-bosses. Before discussing the Chinese gang-boss system, however, some attention must be given to the various factors that made for the development of 'primitive capitalism' in China.

In sketching the early industrialisation of China, much has been made of the Japanese parallel. In one crucial aspect however China was nearer to the Russian pattern. There was an acute shortage of capital for the development of industry in all sectors except the rapidly expanding number of treaty ports where foreign industries, legalised by the Treaty of Shimonoseki (1895) enjoyed considerable advantages, such as the non-payment of internal customs dues, over their Chinese counterparts. According to one estimate, by 1910, 40 of the 156 firms in China employing over 500 workers were foreign.[50] By 1911 the domestic capital invested in modern factories amounted to only $U.S.19.3 million[51] compared with approximately $100 million of invested foreign capital.[52] One of the reasons why government initiative in promoting industrialisation took the form of *kuan-tu, shang-pan* was precisely to tap some of the funds accumulated by Chinese merchants in the treaty ports from their activities in foreign trade initially as adjuncts to foreign trading companies.[53] It was a short step from reliance on this 'comprador capital' (*mai-pan tzu-pen*) to the negotiation of foreign loans, which in a situation of growing political instability and increased imperialist pressure (particularly on the part of Japan during and after the First World War) might lead directly to foreign take-over.

Perhaps the paradigm case of foreign take-over was that of China's largest industrial undertaking, the Hanyehp'ing Coal and Iron Company which has been recounted by Albert Feuerwerker. The original plant at Hanyang (Wuhan) was set up by governor-general Chang Chih-tung with funds scraped together from sundry sources including the Kiangnan defence budget. Its first blast furnace was blown in 1894, two years before the Japanese government set up its first iron works at Yawata. From the start the Manchu court was unsympathetic to the official sponsorship of the project and, in 1895, ordered Chang Chih-tung to dispose of the iron works to private investors. The only taker was Sheng Hsüan-huai who only agreed to take on the headship of the concern in return for the directorship of the Imperial Railways Commission. He paid nothing for the company and merely promised to raise a levy on future production – a promise which he never had to keep. Finding it extremely difficult to raise capital, Sheng was forced finally into financial ties with the Japanese Yawata works and these ties became stronger after 1908 when the concern ceased to enjoy its semi-official status and became the Hanyehp'ing Coal and Iron Company. Attempts to halt the gradual process of foreign take-over such as that by Sun Yat-sen's provisional revolutionary government in 1912 which proposed joint Sino-Japanese control and by Yüan Shih-k'ai who sought to renationalise the enterprise, come to nothing and by 1913, the company was little more than a supplier of raw materials for the Yawata Works. Between 1900 and 1914, 61% of the iron ore used by Yawata came from mines owned by the Chinese company. By 1923, production of the South Manchurian works at Anshan (commenced operations 1919) and Penki (1914) which had been wholly Japanese-operated from the start, overtook Hanyehp'ing and by 1925 the Japanese had the whole field to themselves.[54] The impact of Japanese imperialism had been devastating but worse was to come. With the establishment of the puppet state of Manchukuo in 1931, China was to lose even the loose kind of political control she had enjoyed over the South Manchurian enterprises, and a few years later with the invasion of the rest of China, Japan came to exercise political control over the Wuhan area too.

The spectacular extension of Japanese control over Chinese industry was greatly facilitated by the First World War which gave Japan some temporary respite from the competition of other predatory imperialist powers. The war also gave indigenous Chinese industry the opportunity to make some headway. Nevertheless, by 1919, over 40% of the working class estimated by Jean Chesneaux to be some 1½ million[55] were employed in large foreign industrial enterprises concentrated in Shanghai, the Yangtze Estuary, Canton, Shantung, Hunan-Hupei, North Eastern Hopei and the southern portion of North East China (South Manchuria).

The development of modern industry and in particular foreign-controlled modern industry did much to weaken the semi-feudal relationships that had existed in industry hitherto. Although the system of wage payment still contained pre-capitalist elements such as the payment of gifts and the pattern of employment was something less than the rational exploitation of free labour, one can speak perhaps of the beginnings of primitive capitalist relations in industry. After the First World War, night-work became common. The introduction of shift-work in conditions of insufficient wages frequently obliged workers to work two consecutive eight hour shifts. The employment of children increased in both Chinese and foreign firms (particularly in textiles and tobacco) and where piecework remuneration systems were in force, the hours worked by child-labourers might be longer than adults.[56] The pursuit of short term profits led to an indifference to safety measures which resulted in appalling accident figures and the unconcern of China's fragmented political authorities produced that kind of immiserisation that Marx and Engels noted in the Europe of the nineteenth century. Certainly working conditions in nineteenth century Chinese industry were wretched, but in the opinion of Jean Chesneaux they reached their nadir in the 1920s.[57] Thus in the China of the warlords, there existed a form of 'primitive capitalism' similar to that of Japan at the turn of the century and Russia in the period 1840–80. In all three countries the development of this primitive capitalism followed the collapse or decline of the traditional dynastic élite and its replacement by a combination of bureaucratic capitalists, an indigenous middle-class and foreign imperialist interests. As was suggested earlier, the complexity of such a class structure cannot be brought out adequately by the Kerr-typology which, in the characteristic style of the late 1950s and early 1960s, concentrates more on élite–mass relationships than relationships between classes.

The period of primitive capitalism in Japan was characterised by the development of the gang-boss system. A similar development occurred in China. By the 1920s there were three main methods of recruitment into industry. The first method, apprenticeship under contract, was a pre-capitalist survival which had become divorced from its original function of merely training skilled artisans; in many sectors it had become little more than an excuse for the employment of child labour at low wages. Such a system of recruitment was more common in traditional industries, such as the carpet factories of Peking, with strong traditions of guild organisation, some of which employed nothing but apprentice labour. The system did however extend to some parts of the modern sector especially when workers were recruited from distant rural areas.[58] The second method of recruitment was free hiring of labour by the employer-factory. This method was preferred by the Japanese enterprises in the North-East who recruited labour from Shantung and Hopei and by other enterprises that were also expanding very rapidly. The recruitment of local free labour was often conducted on day to day basis at the factory gates. As one might expect there was an extremely rapid labour-turnover in this sector.[59]

The predominant form of labour recruitment was however recruitment through gang-bosses. Like its Japanese counterpart the gang-boss system (*pa-t'ou-chih*) was a system of contract labour (*pao-kung*) where various levels of contractor (*da-pao, er-pao, san-pao*) controlled bodies of workers which they placed at the disposal of management. Such a system was referred to as 'feudal' (*feng-chien ti*) in Chinese accounts because it was primarily an exploitative system that depended upon a network of human relations where the ties between gang-boss and worker were *personal* rather than the result of a capitalist labour contract. These personal ties often took the form of obligations stemming from indebtedness, not necessarily of the worker himself but frequently of his parents who tied their children to a gang-boss in settlement of a particular debt. Gang-bosses, for their part, went to great pains to see that such debts were never paid and that the worker remained a bond-man for life. Such was the root of the appalling labour conditions in textile mills and in the coal mines of Shansi where, in the 1930s, miners worked some twelve hours a day for a wage of ten cents.[60]

In the opinion of Jean Chesneaux, the gang-boss system in China probably dated back to the centuries-old organisation of the labour force under official supervision to undertake public works such as canals and dyke construction.[61] It was also related to traditional rural forms of organisation such as *cha-kung* (work gangs operating locally in the service of a patron (*kung-chu*) who was invariably a rich peasant or landlord and which was led by a boss (*kung-t'ou*) who acted as intermediary between workers and patron).[62] In the industrial sector, however, it was probably, as in Japan, a fairly new form of organisation that developed rapidly during the period of primitive capitalism. The gang-boss system might develop in an industrial concern without any rural influence whatever. Such is the impression given by the Nank'ai University economist H.D. Fong who, writing in the 1930s, noted that male operatives in a variety of industries developed a sense of temporary ownership of their job which entitled them to bring in assistants of their own choosing and such a practice became the main form of recruiting in Chinese industry. Many of those who were in a position to bring in assistants became gang-bosses who emancipated themselves from work and made a living on commissions which their assistants paid them for giving them a job.[63] Such a system developed considerably during the 1930s since it depended on increased labour requirements in an atmosphere of expanding production. This condition was essential since lowered production frequently forced the gang-boss back on to the shop floor, whereas an ever growing need for labour increased his personal income.[64] Such a situation, described by H.D. Fong, seems remarkably similar to that which pertained in Japan at an earlier date.

Traditional forms of urban organisation directed towards expressive goals took the form of guilds of local craftsmen (*kung-so* and *hui-kuan*) or secret societies. Since the former were concerned mainly with the recruitment of skilled workers, their association with the gang-boss system was slight. On the other hand, the latter category which included organisations such as the Shanghai Green Gang (*Ch'ing-pang*) with a long history of involvement in labour recruitment were frequently linked with the gang-boss network. The gang-boss network, therefore, might be involved in some of the activities of secret societies such as running protection rackets and the maintenance of brothels. An intermediate form of organisation between the gang-bosses and the secret societies were the mutual-aid groups (*pang-hui*) which formed to overcome the *anomie* of industrial life and which might turn into labour gangs if the opportunity arose.[65] The degree of simulated-kinship structure that pertained in this three-tiered form of organisation varied to the extent that expressive goals dominated instrumental ones and to the extent that elaborate secret society relationships and rituals were transmitted down the hierarchy.

We have seen that labour gangs might be generated from outside industrial enterprises (in the case of *pang-hui* which turned themselves into labour gangs) or from inside (in the case of a skilled worker who took on assistants). This second situation resulted from the fact that gang-bosses were not just responsible for labour recruitment but might also perform the function of labour supervision after recruitment. In such a case gang-bosses would appropriate a percentage of the wages due to workers under their control. Various estimates were made during the 1930s as to what this percentage was. Official figures for 1930 show that gang-bosses appropriated some 20% of the wages of mining workers[66] which was about the same as the earlier Japanese figure already cited. Some commentators, such as Lamson (1934), however, put the overall figure in mining as somewhere between 40% and 60%.[67] It is doubtful whether we shall ever be able to quantify gang-boss exploitation or even agree on exactly what constituted a gang-boss, for clearly the female textile worker who brought her daughter into the mill to help her out was in a very different category from the local despot with secret society connections who controlled several hundred men. The problem was compounded by the fact that, not only could the gang-boss network be a front for secret societies but also on occasion meshed in with the local government and Kuomintang Party apparatus. Describing an ideal career for the up and coming young ruffian in Tientsin, Kenneth Lieberthal pictures him using his connections with the warlords and the 'Black Flags' to muscle into a gang-boss network. Once established there he might enter the Green Gang in order to use that position to maintain control over the workers. From there he would try to seek some kind of understanding with each political group when they took power, the last of these being, of course, the Kuomintang.[68]

It was noted earlier that the Japanese preferred to recruit 'free' labour where possible but in certain sectors of the huge industrial complex, which they set up in Manchukuo, they were forced to perpetuate the gang-boss system since they felt 'little in common with the racial habits, customs and habits [sic] of the coolies'.[69] Gang-bosses were felt to be necessary to 'keep strict vigilance over morals and discipline'. The Japanese were, however, contemptuous of a 'feudal system' over which they did not have full control[70] and which was already on the wane in their own country. Nevertheless, whatever its defects as regards control, the gang-boss system was a convenient way of shifting the burden of dealing with the workers to a third party and in foreign firms, it was, as Chesneaux has observed, an exact parallel of the 'comprador' system which shifted to Chinese hands relations with the Chinese public; in some British firms comprador and contractor (a major gang-boss) was sometimes the same person.[71]

In the interests of efficient control, the Japanese in Manchukuo sought to limit the power of the gang-bosses. In the Fushun Mines, for example, pay scales for gang-bosses were worked out and a fixed allowance made according to the number of workers they controlled; further 'squeeze' was prohibited. Gang-bosses who supervised regular day-rate miners were granted allowances of 11.5% of the total wage paid to miners under their control and gang-bosses supervising other contract workers were paid 8%. In addition, management departments were required to appoint the greater and lesser gang-bosses to their position rather than accept self-styled gang-bosses as *de facto* contractors.[72] Such control was possible in Manchukuo because the actions of management were backed up by an efficient and ruthless regime. In parts of China not under Japanese control such as the mines of Shansi, no pre-liberation government was able to effect much control over the gang-boss system even if it had wanted to.

In Japan two factors contributed most to the decline of the gang-boss system. Firstly, the development of labour unions weakened segmental organisation and horizontal forms of association began to cut across traditional vertical ones. Secondly, the subsequent attempt to check class polarisation took the form of a paternalist ideology which focussed worker loyalty on to levels higher than the pre-existing industrial segments. In China, however, the survival of the gang-boss system in modern sectors of industry right up to 1949 would suggest that neither the formation of labour unions nor the development of an integrative ideology made much headway in the preceding period. To leave the discussion at that point, however, would be an implicit distortion of history. Attempts however pathetic, were made in the China of the 1930s to foster an integrative ideology and, for about eight years from 1919 to 1927, there developed a labour movement of surprisingly large proportions which came within an ace of effecting profound revolutionary change.

In the period before 1919, the segmental nature of Chinese industrial organisations with their vertical authority relationships hindered the development of labour unions. Many of the early worker organisations were undemocratic, vertically organised and mixed up with the secret society and gang-boss networks.[73] Much of the industrial labour force consisted of ex-peasants who responded to primitive capitalist *anomie* merely by Luddite activities.[74] After the end of the First World War, however, there began to develop a proletariat increasingly divorced from its rural origins and which was to be organised in the 1920s around the theme of anti-imperialism by the newly formed Communist Party and Chinese Labour Organisation Secretariat (both founded 1921).

In the face of clumsy attempts by the Hong Kong authorities to suppress a strike of seamen in 1922 and by similar action on the part of the Kailan Mining Administration in the same year, the working class anti-imperialist movement linked up with the parallel movement amongst intellectuals which had started in 1919.[75] Both Chinese and foreign authorities responded to this by alternating attempts at control and repression, perhaps the most famous example of which was that of the warlord, Wu P'ei-fu whose massacre of strikers in early 1923 turned the movement in on itself and left the way clear for a while for moderate reformist groups who sought labour protection regulations.

The various enactments of 1923–4 were extremely modest. The Peking government, for example, attempted to curb the power of gang-bosses in the mines by limiting the number of workers under the control of a single gang-boss to 200 and by insisting that gang bosses pay their workers in cash instead of in vouchers to spent in shops under their control. Some provincial regulations imposed limitations upon the length of a working day and proposals for ending child labour in the Shanghai International Settlement were considered; but little of the legislation and few of the proposals had very much effect in an atmosphere of intense competition and ephemeral warlord regimes.[76]

For a while it seemed that the Kuomintang, reorganised along Bolshevik lines and which had entered into an alliance with the Communist Party, was indeed an agent of revolution. It formed a Labour Organisations Army to counter the British backed Merchant Volunteers and passed a whole series of radical labour regulations.[77] The really decisive centre of activity in 1925, however, was not in areas under Kuomintang control. The coup d'état of general Feng Yü-hsiang in Peking in the autumn of 1924 resulted in a renewed toleration of labour-union activity in North China and renewed labour agitation in Shanghai.[78] Following the shooting of strikers by foreign troops in May 1925 there developed a nation-wide anti-imperialist movement which for a time was even supported by the Peking as well as the Kuomintang governments.

The effects of this 'May Thirtieth Movement' were varied. In Shanghai the General Labour Union, which had been created during the Movement, was able to survive the subsequent period of repression and remained strong enough to launch three armed uprisings during the Northern Expedition of the Kuomintang. In the North, however, feuding warlords came together in opposition to Communism, the labour movement, the growing Southern Regime of the Kuomintang and even the moderate warlord Feng Yü-hsiang, and established a government under the North Eastern warlord Chang Tso-lin, famed for maintaining factory discipline 'at the point of a sword'.[79] In the South, on the other hand, the May Thirtieth Movement led to a sixteen-month strike which was directed against the British and supported by the Kuomintang government. The Strike Committee, which resembled a 'Soviet' type workers' council organised its own armed picket corps (*chiu-ch'a-tui*) and actively campaigned for the abolition of the gang boss system and the development of industrial as opposed to craft unions.[80] In addition, the strike organisations helped produce large numbers of cadres who were subsequently active in the Northern Expedition which aimed at the reunification of the country.

By the beginning of the expedition, however, a number of smaller Chinese capitalists who had supported the anti-imperialist aims of the strikers now turned against the left as their own businesses were threatened and some of the craft unions which consisted largely of privileged skilled workers became vocal in their anti-Communism. As Chiang K'ai shek disarmed some of the worker pickets and as the Kuomintang Central Executive Committee revised some of its earlier radical labour legislation, a serious split developed between the right and left of the Kuomintang.

When fighting intensified during the expedition, differences were for a while submerged. The number of unions multiplied and worker organisations in the newly liberated areas of Hunan and Hupei resembled even more workers governments than the earlier organisations in Canton. Some unions demanded a share in management, appointed factory inspectors and, at the Anyüan Mines actually took over control after production had been halted following the arrival of the Nationalist forces. In Hankow and Kiukiang, unions played a major part in forcing the British to abandon their concessions in early 1927, and in other areas, managed to secure wage increases and a say in the hiring and firing of workers.[81]

The demands of the worker organisations were on the whole supported by the 'left' Kuomintang government which had been transferred to Wuhan, although that government attempted to apply a brake on what it considered to be excessive union demands and precluded the participation of workers or union representatives in management. In the East, however, dominated by forces loyal to Chiang K'ai shek much tougher restrictions were imposed upon the labour movement. As the Shanghai General Labour Union began to take armed action against the municipal authorities, the storm centre shifted in March 1927 to Shanghai at the same time as Chiang K'ai shek commenced a systematic suppression of the labour movement in areas under his control. As the armed insurrection led by the Shanghai General Labour Union got under way on 21–3 March, Nationalist forces under the erstwhile warlord Pai Chung-hsi occupied Shanghai and for about three weeks an uneasy truce existed between the worker pickets and the military. By early April, an odd collection of Green Gang adherents had been assembled and the worker pickets were ordered to lay down their arms. On 12 April armed bands led amongst others by underworld leader Tu Yüeh-sheng immobilised the worker pickets with the support of the nationalist forces and the strike which followed was crushed with great severity.[82] Within three months the 'white terror', as the repression was called, had spread to the Wuhan area too but such a policy could only be temporary: repression had to give way to control.

After 1928, the Kuomintang government pursued a policy of penetrating and controlling the labour movement in a manner not unlike that employed in the final years of Tsarist Russia. Although the government was not slow to suppress unions in which Communist influence was strong, the general policy adopted was to transform existing right-wing unions into agencies of government which would root out individual Communists. From 1929 a number of labour-union regulations were passed and amended and these took their final pre-liberation form in 1947. According to the Labour-Union Law of that year all factories above a certain size were required to organise a labour union in which membership was compulsory.[83] Although unions were not completely tools of government[84] they were subject to the jurisdiction of subordinate bureaux of the Ministry of Social Affairs (*She-hui-pu*) which was attacked by even the non-Communist 'left' as an organisation concerned with training secret agents. Unions were subject to control by local government which had the power to dissolve them. They were said to be infiltrated by agents of the Military Secret

Service (*Chün-t'ung-chü*) and would only mobilise workers in connection with rooting out Communists (for example when they formed 'work protection units' [*hu-kung-tui*]).[85]

The Kuomintang unions were not just vertically-organised control structures. Although union leadership was frequently appointed from above, it was occasionally elected (although from a slate of Kuomintang members).[86] Unions would concern themselves with welfare and labour protection and sometimes engage in bargaining with employers.[87] One is reminded of the Tsarist 'police socialism' that sought to 'widen the rights of the workers' by obtaining concessions from bourgeois entrepreneurs but at the same time suppressing any challenge to the established order. One might suspect that those who suffered most from such a policy would have been the small factory owners who did not have close ties with government. Just as the period of 'police socialism' in Tsarist Russia was one in which a series of moderate factory regulations were passed, so the period of the Kuomintang in China saw an attempt to regulate factories.[88] One might suspect that the Kuomintang government's Ministry of Social Affairs was motivated by much the same concern of the Russian Ministry of the Interior which pressed for factory regulation in the 1880s, but pending detailed research on this neglected area of modern Chinese history, we can only guess. What we can say with some certainty however is that much of the Kuomintang factory regulation was as disregarded as similar legislation in Tsarist Russia.[89]

As the control exercised by the Tsarist police increased in Russian industry, so did worker atomisation. In China the process of atomisation was impeded by the existence of simulated-kinship structures but one would have expected that union control over a long period would seriously weaken the gang-boss network. The gang-boss system was certainly not so strong in 1949 as it was in the 1930s[90] though it was still an extremely significant factor in Chinese industry. It is impossible without detailed research, to determine to what extent the decline of the system was due to growing unemployment and to what extent it reflected an effective policy of atomisation. It is doubtful that the policy of penetration and control was very effective since the Communist Party underground continued to operate within factories right up until 1949 and acquired a large amount of power for a time in 1945.[91] Furthermore, the instrument favoured by the right Kuomintang to suppress the labour movement in 1927 was initially not the military forces of Pai Chung-hsi but the motely collection of Green Gang adherents led amongst others by Tu Yüeh-sheng. A victory for the Green Gang meant also a victory for elements who upheld the gang-boss network and it is significant that Tu Yüeh-sheng continued to wield influence amongst sections of Shanghai labour right up to 1949,[92] which he would not have been able to do had an effective policy of atomisation been applied to his domain. Secondly, a fear of industry-wide labour agitation had become so ingrained in the Kuomintang after the events of 1925–7 that they were reluctant to foster the development of *industrial* labour unions.[93] They preferred instead the smaller craft unions which, being segmental in structure, were more easily susceptible to the operation of secret society networks (though probably not the gang-boss networks since craft unions were more characteristic of *skilled* labour whereas the gang-boss system operated largely amongst unskilled workers). It was much more difficult to atomise a collectivity of small groups than a large industry-wide organisation. Thus it is probable that a vertically organised, stratified, segmental union structure in which secret-society elements were not wholly illegitimate could not make much headway against a secret-society/gang-boss network that was similarly vertically organised stratified and segmental, particularly in a situation where political control was never effectively centralised.

The above is highly speculative since a history of Kuomintang labour unions has yet to be written. An attempt has been made, however, to indicate that the Kuomintang approach to crisis management was one mainly of control rather than the propagation of an alternative ideology as in Japan. One should note however that in China during the early 1930s when fascism enjoyed some popularity, the New Life Movement and the Blueshirts did attempt to create something similar to the *ersatz Gemeinschaft* we saw in Japan. It is doubtful that such an ideology had much impact on industrial workers, and the only research I have seen on the subject deals with intellectuals and students.[94] One can only conclude that if an attempt was made to foster a paternalist ideology within the context of the Chinese industrial enterprise, it was singularly unsuccessful.

China's experiment with fascism was undertaken during a relatively peaceful period in the history of the Kuomintang though, to be sure, Kuomintang China was hardly free from one kind or war or another throughout her entire history. Collosal military expenditure led to huge budget deficits and continued reliance on private bankers who in turn derived huge profits from their connections with government. The bureaucratic-capitalist empire of Sheng Hsüan-huai was the forerunner of the bureaucratic-capitalist empires of the 'Four Big Families'[95] whose financial stake in state-run industry had been institutionalised through the China Development Finance Corporation.[96] The huge budget deficits contributed also to continued foreign influence despite the various concessions the new government was able to obtain from the imperialist powers and despite the nationalism expressed by Chiang K'ai-shek.[97] By the end of the Second World War, there existed in China, huge sprawling industrial empires, many of which were controlled by the state though it was not always clear to what extent. Such industrial networks, characterised by multiple and weak lines of ownership and control, existed within a society riddled with corruption, ineffective administration and bureaucratic inertia. Pre-liberation China had many of the features of what Gunnar Myrdal has referred to as the 'soft state' – a state in which ineffective bureaucracy generates on the one hand corruption and on the other more ineffective bureaucracy to control that corruption. With Gunnar Myrdal, I am unconvinced that such a situation might be justified by the argument that corruption is socially functional where bureaucracy is weak, for corruption is not so much a necessary element in the functioning of a weak bureaucratic state as an element *consequent* upon increasing bureaucratic weakness.[98]

Thus the first most important feature of the post-war industrial situation was the huge size of the state controlled sector (however one defines the relationship between state and bureaucratic capitalists). Already by 1942, over 42% of the total industrial horsepower and 32% of the labour force of 242,000 workers in areas controlled by the Kuomintang government were employed by the state.[99] In 1945, following the Japanese surrender, the Chinese government took over more than two thousand industrial and mining establishments formerly under direct or indirect Japanese control in North East China, China South of the Great Wall and Taiwan.[100] These formerly Japanese-owned industrial concerns, valued at some $U.S.1.8 billion became state entèrprises under the control of the Kuomintang government's National Resources Commission (*Tzu-yüan Wei-yüan-hui*).[101] By 1949, this commission controlled 90% of the country's iron and steel output, 33% of its coal, 67% of its electrical power, 45% of its cement and all its petroleum and non-ferrous metals. Another huge state concern, The China Textile Construction Company (*Chung-kuo Fang-chih Chien-she Kung-ssu*) controlled 37.6% of spindles in the country and 60% of looms.[102] With the liberation of 1949, the actual extent to which these bodies were in fact national became academic since all former state property and the property of the four big families were taken over by the new government and uniformly classified as 'bureaucratic capitalist'. At that time, industries so classified accounted for more than one third of China's industrial output.[103] The point that is relevant to our discussion here is that a large sector of industry already under state control facilitated the process of nationalisation. Secondly, moves which were afoot to counter the bureaucratising effects of 'soft-state' management by transferring part of this state sector to completely private hands[104] were cut short by the victory of the Peoples Liberation Army.

A second important feature of the post-war situation was the fact that industry had been severely damaged. Damage to industry and transportation in China South of the Great Wall from 1937 to 1945 was estimated at $U.S.1.08 billion and in North East China at $U.S.2 billion.[105] A large part of this latter figure was accounted for by the removal of industrial equipment by occupying Soviet troops. It has been estimated (though I do not know with what accuracy) that during the 268 days Soviet occupation, the value of installations damaged or shipped away from North East China to the Soviet Union was between $U.S.635,640,000[106] and $U.S.845,238,000.[107] The damage to the steel industry was calculated at $U.S.204,052,000[108] (not counting invisible damage) and the steel production capacity had declined by over 60% when production was resumed.[109] In the immediate post-war years, rehabilitation funds, foreign loans, aid and Japanese reparations amounted to only 9.2% of the actual war damage.[110] In addition, hyperinflation and intensifying civil war did much to completely wreck the industrial economy. Thus, following the liberation of 1949 it was clear that rehabilitation of industrial equipment was to be given absolute priority and this priority inevitably affected programmes of social reform and revolutionary change.

A third feature of post-war industry was the continuing foreign domination of part of the modern sector. In 1936, 42% of the industrial capital in China was owned by foreigners.[111] In 1937, 61% of the total coal produced in China came from foreign mines and in 1936 foreign firms produced 86% of iron ore, 80% pig iron, 88% steel, 76% electric power, and owned 68% electrical generating capacity, 54% textile spindles and 40% of the looms.[112] As we saw above, the war and its aftermath changed this situation considerably as Japanese firms were taken over but, none the less, a foreign sector of industry remained and foreign capital remained invested in Chinese industry. The take-over of foreign interests was to be a major concern of the new government in the 1950s.

A fourth feature of post-war industry in China was a consequence of the decades of foreign domination. Foreign capital tended to be concentrated in the old treaty ports and in the former puppet state of Manchukuo. The distribution of industry, therefore, was quite uneven. Despite the fact that part of Chinese industry had been transferred to Kuomintang areas in the interior during the war,[113] in 1949 the coastal provinces, which comprise only 10% of the total land area of China South of the Great Wall produced 77% of that region's gross value of factory output.[114] Shanghai alone accounted for 54% of the number of factories and of the labour force.[115] In 1943 North East China produced over 90% of China's iron and steel.[116] Such a situation was very wasteful in terms of the supply of raw materials (at least as far as the coastal provinces were concerned) and eventually a strategy of industrial relocation had to be undertaken. In the period of our study however, which was one of rehabilitation, an overwhelmingly large proportion of China's industry was located in a small geographical area.

A fifth feature of post-war industry was again a consequence of long foreign domination. The bulk of aggregate production was located in the consumer industries. Prior to the war with Japan, 92% of industrial capital in China South of the Great Wall was invested in such industry.[117] The situation was of course different once the former state of Manchukuo became incorporated in China. What is of relevance to our concerns here however, is that, following liberation, China's leaders decided that there was an absolute priority to increase the producer goods industry and this was an extremely important consideration in their decision to look at that outstanding model of heavy industrial development – the Soviet Union.

A focus on large industrial enterprises would appear to preclude any consideration of industrial organisation in the war-time 'liberated areas' controlled by the Communist Party where there were no large scale organisations. At the end of 1941 in the Shen Kan Ning Border Region, for example, there were only 4,000 industrial workers distributed among some 84 factories.[118] Nevertheless the border areas cannot be overlooked for in them there developed a pattern of organisation of great relevance to post liberation China.

Together with the various movements of 1943 which were designed to combat bureaucratism, there evolved an organisational policy reminiscent of that centralised authority and decentralised administration that Alexis de Tocqueville so admired in the early American republic[119] known as 'centralised leadership and divided operations' (*chi-chung ling-tao fen-san ching-ying*).[120] Under this policy all key decisions were taken centrally but considerable operational leeway was granted to outlying parts of a dispersed industrial network. Dispersal was deliberately undertaken as a safeguard against enemy air attack and in order to facilitate the spread of industrial techniques to villages in which the basic level industrial units were located. Such an organisational pattern differed from the traditional sprawling networks of control in two very important respects. Firstly, the anti-bureaucratic movement which accompanied the decentralisation of industry was designed *inter alia* to prevent the growth of hierarchical barriers at middle levels. Secondly, policy formulation at the centre was not simply concerned with financial matters but endeavoured to devise concrete tasks to meet the requirements of war. A situation in which operational decision making was decentralised, where middle levels of organisation had been simplified or eliminated, where hierarchical barriers had been broken down but where the centre prescribed and checked up on the implementation of specific work tasks can only be characterised by some kind of functional leadership.

Such functional leadership, however, applied only to the relationship between centre and work units. The integration of conflicting instructions that might emanate from functional agents was effected at the basic level by that particular leadership type that is now seen as characteristic of the Chinese approach to development – the cadre.

As was described earlier, the 'cadre' was ideally highly politically motivated and policy conscious and committed to change within a network of human solidarity. Although one can not speak of the existence of an ideologically integrated functional model in a situation where the cadre exercised diffuse responsibility and where lines of functional supervision might not reach the individual worker, one can see the beginnings of a new approach to organisation, that was vastly different from the Soviet 'one-man management' or the traditional hierarchical organisation that characterised Chinese organisation at that time.

Of course there is a world of difference between a few isolated industrial undertakings or hand-looms linked to an up-country political centre and the Anshan Iron and Steel Corporation but such a difference would not preclude a consideration of the organisational perspectives inherited by the Chinese Communist Party from its most formative period. One is reminded of the 'War Communism' dilemma: to what extent was the Yenan model merely a product of circumstances and to what extent did it represent a pattern of organisation that could be applied to a different social and political milieu. In the early 1950s China's leaders tended to believe it was the former, but in the middle 1950s the latter.

The decision-making structure

The early industrialisation of both Tsarist Russia and China took place in a semi-colonial environment where a large foreign sector served as a model to be emulated by the domestic sector. Just as parts of Russian industry modelled themselves on the factories of Ludwig Knoop and his like, so Tawney observed:

> The disease of young China is its fever for imitation and in programmes of industrial reconstruction it rages unchecked. Designed for America, for Europe, for the moon, for anywhere except the unhappy country on whose attention they are pressed, they rehearse impossibilities with dreadful monotony as though mere persistance in repetition could convert fancies into facts.[121]

There existed in China a wide continuum ranging from blind imitation of the West to the perpetuation of traditional bureaucratic forms of organisation. Where the gang-boss system preserved organisational segmentation, whatever degree of functional specificity and delineation between staff and line applied at higher levels of organisation could not apply to levels below that of the labour gang. The most that one could expect was the gang as a whole might be characterised by specificity of function whilst its members were characterised by functional diffuseness.[122]

As far as I know, there has been no study of decision making structure in large pre-liberation Chinese industrial concerns, but an examination of the kinds of problems faced by the Chinese Communist Party in the 1950s has led me to the view that traditional bureaucratic patterns of decision making persisted in China, as in Japan, right into the 1940s. In the 1930s Tawney noted that the ideal *t'i–yung* dichotomy remained strong[123] and one of the key elements of *t'i* (Chinese essence) was the idea of an omnicompetent leadership unhampered by specific responsibilities.

A joint concern for hierarchy and collectivity, specificity of status rather than function, non-delegation of authority, the existence of bureaucratic filters and strong informal structure produced in Japan a decision making system known as *ringi* which required all decisions to appear to be consensual and to be promulgated at the top of an organisational hierarchy.[124] The *ringi* system, which required all potential decisions to be formulated as proposals, was extremely cumbersome since it required a long period of time between the initiation of a proposal and the authorisation of policy. It made prior planning very difficult since key decisions were dealt with on a piecemeal basis and it concealed gross incompetence at middle levels of organisation. On the other hand, this diffuse pattern of decision making did allow managers at middle levels to have a say in the formulation of policy even though their 'participation' might be constrained by a highly deferential ideology. Furthermore a consensual system, however constrained, offset the deleterious effects of a seniority based promotion system in which the most competent did not necessarily occupy the top hierarchical positions.

If, as I suspect, such a system also remained characteristic of Chinese industry, its application would have applied largely to policy decisions since the employment of foreign or foreign trained managerial personnel would produce a more Western type of decision making in operational matters. Difficulty in separating policy from operational decisions probably accounted for a great deal of the complaints voiced by foreign managers[125] in Chinese firms.

The Tsarist Russian decision-making pattern seems always to have been of a more orthodox authoritarian character perhaps because such traditional collectivity orientation as there had been did not apply to the serf-owning nobility nor the middle-class entrepreneurs and remained confined to the traditional village communities and *arteli*. Indeed a traditional bureaucracy in the Chinese–Japanese sense never really existed and the bureaucracy that developed after the reign of Peter was more 'modern' in the sense that it was directed to a technological conception of society.

The Bolshevik Revolution injected an important element into the decision making process that of 'Workers' Control' (in the sense of supervision) and although this atrophied under Stalin, it was to be taken very seriously by the Chinese Communist Party after 1948. Under the Stalinist system, line management took decisions on the basis of advice from specialised staff. In the case of proposals which came from lower levels of organisation, there existed mechanisms, absent in the traditional bureaucratic pattern, which were designed to prevent distortion. The Workers and Staff Congress was such a mechanism although it did not have any executive power. The enterprise Party structure was another although its power was severely constrained by the 'one-man management' system. Thirdly, a practice was instituted whereby workers discussed current and future plans; such a practice was designed to give ordinary workers a say in plan formulation but it was effective only when the consciousness of management was sufficiently elevated for them to listen to workers and when the Party organisation was willing and able to give moral support to worker proposals. Such conditions were infrequently present. The Stalinist decision-making pattern was potentially more authoritarian than that which prevailed in either the pre-war Japanese or pre-liberation Chinese industrial concern; any system which demanded 'absolute' leadership had to be. It was also potentially more democratic in a participatory sense provided that the participatory mechanisms were allowed to work. It was potentially more efficient in that status was closely tied to function and it was unlikely that senior management would be promoted on the basis of seniority alone. In fact there was a very high turnover of senior management and, at one time in the late 1930s, the role of senior manager in industry was a very precarious one indeed. Such a situation could, however, lead to conservatism, bureaucratic inertia and potentially far greater inefficiency. Such was to be the decision-making pattern prescribed for China in the early 1950s. Before long, many Chinese would criticise this Soviet model in terms reminiscent of the quote from Tawney above and were to re-examine the Yenan model of 'centralised leadership and divided operations'.

The relationship between staff and line

In any industrial organisation characterised by hierarchy, fragmentation and diffuse responsibility such as existed in Japan and Kuomintang China, a functional system is precluded. A functional system is inherently non-hierarchical for functional agents cut across middle levels of organisation and may even dispense with them altogether. The existence of organisational fragmentation militates against the effectiveness of functional agents who are unable to penetrate small discrete collective units and the very term 'functional system' implies that any agent required to issue instructions to the work site should have clearly defined responsibilities.

In Russia immediately after the Bolshevik Revolution, however, the functional principle was taken very seriously indeed. Such a principle was very appealing to revolutionary socialists. A technologically integrated functional model offers, on the one hand, a system which seeks to cut through bureaucratic hierarchy and on the other a glimpse of Engels' eventual administration by productive processes rather than administration by people. Nevertheless, however attractive it might seem from this point of view, its dehumanising effects outweigh its advantages. In human terms an *ideologically* integrated functional model would be much more attractive if only it could be made to work.

In the years immediately following the Bolshevik Revolution, it was the *technologically* integrated functional model of Frederick W. Taylor that came to the attention of Lenin, who whilst damning its dehumanising effects, spoke of adopting its better aspects.[126] It is very difficult to determine exactly what aspects of the Taylor system Lenin wished to save. If he really wished to advocate functional patterns of organisation, it is very difficult to understand why in the same report in which he offered faint praise to Taylor, he made the statement from which the subsequent advocates of 'one-man management' derive their inspiration:[127]

> . . . it must be said that large-scale machine industry – which is precisely the material source, the productive source, the foundation of socialism – calls for absolute and strict unity of will, which directs the joint labours of hundreds, thousands and tens of thousands of people. The technical, economic and historical necessity of this is obvious, and all those who have thought about socialism have always regarded it as one of the conditions of socialism. But how can strict unity of will be ensured? By thousands subordinating their will to the will of one.
>
> Given ideal class consciousness and discipline on the part of those participating in the common work, this subordination would be something like the mild leadership of a conductor of an orchestra. It may assume the sharp focus of a dictatorship if ideal discipline and class consciousness are lacking. But, be that as it may, unquestioning subordination to a single will is absolutely necessary for the success of processes organised on the pattern of large-scale machine industry.[128]

In insisting on unity of command and subordination to a single will, Lenin was quite clearly thinking of elements of the Taylor system other than the principle of functional supervision. On that question, Lenin seems not at all clear but, whatever his position, literature on Soviet management attests to the prevalence of functional patterns of organisation for at least a decade after the Bolshevik Revolution.

Japanese and Chinese organisation prior to 1949 tended to be based on the staff-line principle but although there was a formal distinction between staff and line the resemblance to the classic staff-line model did not go much beyond that. The classic model required that the criterion for attaching a staff member to a particular level of line management should be functional even though he did not enjoy any functional jurisdiction over lower levels. The Japanese and Chinese staff-line pattern, which was derived from traditional bureaucracy, required that the criterion for attaching a staff member to a particular level of line management should be *status* which was independent of function. Where the status of a particular staff member (as expressed in a formal title) was the equivalent of the line manager to whom he was attached, it was extremely difficult to prevent him assuming line authority. In a classic staff-line system, staff members may make proposals but only line managers may make decisions. In a situation however where there was no clear cut distinction between a proposal and a decision (for all potential decisions were initiated as proposals and gradually grew into decisions as they passed through various levels in the hierarchy), there could be no clear cut distinction between staff and line authority. One could not say that only the occupant of the most senior post made decisions for by the time a proposal reached him it was often already a decision that could only be ratified or rejected. According to the Japanese *ringi* system, both staff and line were in a sense decision makers and a ratified decision might be passed back to either for implementation. Although much research needs to be done before we can establish that the decision-making pattern in Chinese industry prior to 1949 was similar to the *ringi* system described above it is fair to hypothesise the similarity in the light of the complaints made by foreign management and the similar bureaucratic origins of industrial organisations in both countries. In any case the fact that the bulk of heavy industry in China by 1949 had recently been taken over from the Japanese would suggest a similarity.

Though I feel fairly confident in equating Japan and China above, there is one aspect of Japanese organisation, that I would hesitate to apply to China. The Japanese promotion system made the problem of staff-line relationships extremely complicated. In a non-paternalist system, it is possible to demote or dismiss an incompetent senior manager or at least to give him a 'golden handshake'. Within a paternalist system, however, where seniority was more likely than efficiency to be a determinant of status, it was extremely difficult to dismiss anyone.[129] It was of course possible to transfer an incompetent line manager to a staff post in the hope that he could do less damage than in a line position, though, as has been suggested, this was no guarantee that he would not continue to exercise line authority. One might surmise that the best way to get such a man out of harm's way would be to promote him to such an elevated position that all decisions were already formulated by the time they reached him. In that case, one had to wait until he was old enough and suffer his incompetence in the meantime. My reluctance to apply this to the Chinese situation, however, stems from the fact that at no time did China ever attain the organisational stability characteristic of the stage of advanced capitalism reached in Japan in the 1930s. Pending research on the organisation of Chinese pre-liberation industrial organisations, this question can only be left open.

In the Soviet Union, on the other hand, the relationship between staff and line, according to the principle of 'one-man management', was as near to the classic staff-line model as it was possible to be. Furthermore with the attack on functionalism which culminated with the Seventeenth Party Congress in 1934, functional overlay patterns at all levels of industry were severely weakened including that functional overlay pattern actualised in the Party organisation. The subordination of the Party network to line management reached such a point in the late 1950s that Khruschev was forced to engage in the creation of a different kind of Party with completely different relations with formal state administration.[130] He was to build a Party very different from the Chinese ideal but, at least, in both China and the Soviet Union there was eventually a recognition that the attack on functionalism severely diluted the power of the Party organisation.

Both the Japanese and Stalinist industrial organisations were capable of swift and effective mobilisation in times of crisis and such mobilisation was facilitated by vertical channels of command. In Japan, whenever competent people occupied the most senior positions and were not content merely to authorise decisions made at lower levels, they were capable of exercising considerable power which was effective so long as group unity remained strong as it did in the war years of the 1930s and 1940s.[131] Although a very different relationship between staff and line existed in the Soviet Union, effective mobilisation at times of crisis was also facilitated by vertical channels of command. Such mobilisation was possible because in both countries, there was an effective integrative ideology and because organisational segmentation had been overcome. In China, still in a stage of 'primitive capitalism', there was no effective integrative ideology and organisational segmentation continued in the form of the still powerful gang-boss system. The major shortcomings of the Japanese and Stalinist system applied to non-crisis periods. Some of the former have been mentioned and the latter will be examined later in terms of their applicability to a Chinese situation in which the Communist Party had developed a very different approach to organisation.

Remuneration and incentive

Much has been made in recent years of the work ethic and the role of religion (particularly Protestantism) in fostering a guilt culture said to be necessary for the development of capitalism. Though an element of coercion remained in the Soviet Union under Stalin, attempts were made to internalise a spirit of self denial and guilt measured against collective goals which were on the whole successful in promoting a work ethic in the Soviet Union. In Japan and China on the other hand, the traditional culture was shame-oriented rather than guilt-oriented and non-material incentive often took the form of allowing a worker to preserve face by not letting down his particular group. A guilt orientation stresses internalised commitment to group goals whilst a shame-orientation stresses external performance according to group norms. Both may be powerful factors in work incentive but the latter is usually incapable of transcending the limitations of the particular group. When, as in pre-liberation China, actual work groups were seen to be manipulated by crude exploiters, work incentive is low. On the other hand, when guilt-orientation is strong, the shortcomings of a particular group leader may be disregarded by a worker committed to collective goals of a higher generality – such, I would suggest was a more common feature in the Soviet Union.

Guilt-orientation is more common in an individually oriented incentive system. In the Soviet Union, the corollary of 'one-man management' was a system of individual responsibility which rewarded the productive individual and penalised the unproductive. The group orientation that might have developed out of the associations of the early revolutionary period were not reinforced by a collectivist tradition and were unable to survive the new tendency towards atomisation characteristic of the Stalinist system. The stress on the individual in an organisation held together by technological solidarity was reflected in the prevailing pattern of material remuneration. The ideal form of payment was by individual piecework which was measurable and therefore 'scientific' and justified according to the socialist principle of 'from each according to his ability, to each according to his work'. Though an important element of moral incentive existed in the system, material incentive was accorded an importance unparalleled in previous socialist theory. Model workers were designated with great fanfare and their commitment to socialism praised but much was also made of the bonuses they earned. Egalitarianism was held to be a petit-bourgeois phenomenon and a concentration on technical expertise and the over-fulfilment of norms led to huge wage disparities which were to be the target of a severe reaction after the Soviet model had been transplanted to China.

In Japan, on the other hand, the system of material remuneration that stemmed from a paternalist ethos stressed age, seniority and formal qualifications rather than job performance.[132] It took into consideration such factors as 'diligence' and 'seriousness' and included the provision of a whole range of services in addition to money wages. Wherever bonus schemes were adopted, they tended to be group-oriented rather than individual-oriented. Such a system has persisted down to the present day and as late as the 1950s, attempts to implement payment by type of work were unsuccessful. They were replaced by systems of payment according to ability though these were often little more than window-dressing for payment according to seniority; for seniority was frequently the most important factor taken into account when determining ability. A polemic exists on the relationship between ability and seniority similar to the polemic we noted earlier on the origin of paternalism. Abegglen argues that the post-war age-related wage system, like absolute job security for permanent workers, derives primarily from tradition whereas Taira, consistent with his anti-culturalist standpoint, argues that such a system derives from trade union insistence.[133]

Throughout Japan's whole period of industrialisation, there has always been firm opposition to any form of piecework and where piece-work systems have been introduced tentatively worker opposition to them, strong in all societies for good socio-economic reasons, was probably further strengthened by the traditional collectivity-orientation.

The Chinese pattern of remuneration was similar to the Japanese but was complicated by the existence of a very large foreign sector that was more prone to experiment with piecework payment systems[134] and by the continued prevalence of the gang-boss system which drained off a significant proportion of the wages due to workers. As in Japan, attitudinal factors were taken into consideration and a large number of traditional bonuses and obligations (e.g. to make certain gifts to the gang-boss) persisted down to the 1940s. Seniority and formal skill were the most important considerations in wage evaluation since these were the criteria that at one time separated those who were paid in silver or debased copper and those who were paid directly or through an intermediary such as a gang-boss.[135] As one might expect in a society that did not make the transition from primitive capitalism to any higher form of capitalism, wages were extremely low and pre-modern forms of payment (e.g. in kind) continued; in a situation of rapid inflation after 1937 such forms were very difficult to dispense with. Furthermore the perpetuation of traditional ideas about the artisan sometimes required a worker to provide some of his own tools and permitted him to appropriate part of his product.[136]

Low wages and the lack of an integrative ideology in Chinese industry made for poor worker morale. Finally, the element of patriotism which manifested itself in China during the 1920s was probably less strong in the 1930s and 1940s at a time when in the Soviet Union, patriotism proved itself to be a very important element in work motivation. In the 'liberated areas', however, where patriotism was a very important element in work motivation, it was combined with a form of egalitarianism which as we shall see in chapter 6 proved hard to eradicate once the Stalinist model was applied in the 1950s.

Egalitarianism in the sense of a theoretical commitment to equal payment regardless of work was, as far as I know, never a feature of official policy in any of the liberated areas. Such a doctrine had been condemned by Mao Tse-tung in the Kutien resolution of 1929 as the illusion of the small peasant producer in a situation where capitalism had not yet been wiped out. Equal payment which was practised in units of the Red Army at that time was said to derive from necessity rather than theory.[137] During the Anti-Japanese war, free supply systems for cadres had become prevalent as well as a grain ticket system for the payment of troops which related wages to the procurement of local tax grain.[138] Such systems, however, seem to have been the result of physical necessity rather than due to any theoretical commitment to immediate payment according to need. In fact Mao argued in favour of progressive piecework systems and against egalitarianism as early as 1942.[139]

The effect of such systems was to create more of an egalitarian ethos than an egalitarian ideology. The dividing line between the 'free supply mentality', which was the result of habit as the Chinese term suggests (*kung-chi-chih ti ch'ang-hsiang*) and a commitment to equality as an end in itself (*p'ing-chün-chu-i*) is, however a thin one, and there were some people who considered the ultra-egalitarianism of the 'peasant socialist' period of land reform should be applied to the industrial spheres.[140] Again one is confronted with the 'War Communism' dilemma; to what extent were 'egalitarian' systems of payment an unfortunate temporary expedient and to what extent did they represent an advance on the Stalinist system?

Part II

The political environment

2. The moderate phase (1949-50)

Policy during the civil war

From the beginning of the final civil war (1946) through to the establishment of the Chinese Peoples Republic (October 1949), the policy of the Chinese Communist Party towards taking over (*chieh-kuan*) industrial units may be characterised as a continuous move from radicalism to a moderate policy with rank and file cadres tending to be somewhat more radical than the centre. One might expect, therefore, that the earlier a particular city was liberated the more radical was the take-over of its industries likely to be. The de-radicalisation of policy was not, however, a steady process. Two watersheds can be discerned. The first came at the end of 1947 when it became clear that from then on cities would be occupied permanently.[1] Mao Tse-tung stated at that time that the policy to be adopted in 1948 was to ensure that the take-over of industries caused as little disruption of production as possible.[2] Throughout 1948 a number of articles appeared in the press urging cadres to concentrate on increasing production, condemning the importation of 'agricultural socialism' (*nung-yeh she-hui-chu-i*) into the industrial sector and opposing 'guerillaism', 'left adventurism' and a general ultra-left orientation.[3] It was during this period of moderation that the Sixth All China Labour Conference met in Harbin in August 1948. A deliberate effort was made to show continuity in the development of the labour movement from pre-Civil War days; hence the use of the ordinal number 'sixth', the previous five conferences being held back in the 1920s. The conference laid down the two principles that were to govern the reorganisation of industrial concerns – 'democratisation' and 'enterprisation'.[4]

There is little disagreement that Mao Tse-tung's pronouncement of a gradualist policy in December 1947 constituted a policy watershed. That there was a second watershed in April–May 1949 is somewhat more problematic. It has been argued recently in the Chinese press that the policies announced by Liu Shao-ch'i in his Tientsin Talks at that time ended the previous moderately radical policy in favour of a 'revisionist' policy which favoured the national capitalists in the private sector and precluded fundamental rearrangement of factory management in the public (*kung-ying*) (local government) and state (*kuo-ying*) sector. As such, it is claimed, this policy was a violation of the programme announced by Mao in his report to the second session of the Seventh Central Committee of the Party (5 March 1949).[5]

It is my impression that the implementation of reform in the spring and summer of 1949 was much less radical than in the earlier period and that the Tientsin Talks occupied an important place in the development of policy, but I am not convinced on the basis of available evidence that the Tientsin Talks constituted a total break with previous policy. The Tientsin Talks were only the culmination of the increasingly moderate policy dating from December 1947. This is not to say that I reject the charge that Liu's Tientsin Talks were opposed by Mao at the time. Some scholars have tended to question the Cultural Revolution assertions of disagreement between Mao and Liu on the grounds that Mao's speeches published contemporaneously said much the same thing as Liu's.[6] We have seen however instances where both Mao and Liu have contradicted their own deeply held beliefs in conformity with Party policy (for example Mao's attack on his own guerilla strategy in the guise of the Lo Ming line in 1934 and Liu's defence of the virtues of imbalance in 1958) and this question can only be left open. Suffice it to say that, if the record of the Tientsin Talks, printed in Taiwan recently, is at all genuine, then Liu's position certainly appeared more conservative than Mao's.

It was not however purely policy considerations that accounted for the different process of take-over in areas liberated before and after the spring of 1949.

Different patterns of take-over in North East China and elsewhere

Fighting in cities in the North East was considerably more severe than in cities south of the Great Wall which were not liberated until 1949. The result was that a considerable amount of industry was destroyed in the former region and many factories were not operational upon liberation.[7] In addition, as we have noted, the occupying Soviet troops had removed a large amount of industrial equipment after Japan's surrender. Furthermore, some damage had been done by retreating Kuomintang troops and Communist Party-led troops guilty of 'left deviation'.[8] The mammoth Anshan Iron and Steel complex which was to become the keystone of China's First Five Year Plan did not recommence production until 1947, after which, it changed hands no less than seven times between February and November 1948. When it was finally liberated on 3 November 1948 most of the mills had been reduced to debris.[9] Production recommenced only on 1 May 1949 but, in the first two years of operation, it has been claimed that production never exceeded 10% of the pre-war peak.[10] There was a shortage of spare parts and technical workers. In Manchukuo days the Anshan Works had some 120,000 workers. By 1949 the total population of the *city* of Anshan was only about 130,000 of whom 10,000 were workers and a little over 100 skilled. Many plants had only one skilled worker left upon liberation.[11] In most industries senior management had been transferred south by the Kuomintang military authorities before the Peoples Liberation Army (PLA) entered the cities and those that were left were under suspicion as Kuomintang appointees promoted to replace Japanese managers when Manchukuo industries were taken over by the state after the war with Japan.[12] In any case, even in 1947, it was estimated that there were only some 10,000 engineers of all types in China giving an engineer population ratio of 1 : 50,000 as against the current United States figure of 1 : 650.[13]

The increasingly mild policy reflected in the resolutions of the Sixth Labour Conference of August 1948 did not prevent the North East Bureau of the Party issuing a directive to the effect that Kuomintang members should not be employed in senior management positions for the time being.[14] It would seem, though, that the acute shortage of senior managerial personnel was due more to physical destruction and transfer of personnel than political reasons. Accounts of the take-over of industries in Shenyang[15] do not seem to be very different from accounts of the subsequent take-over of industries in Shanghai.[16] The main difference would seem to be that in Shenyang there were not so many managers that could be retained and Shanghai was not faced with such a large scale programme of industrial rehabilitation.

The North East People's Government and administration in older liberated areas were required, therefore, to appoint new people to many senior management positions. Middle level management, where it still existed, was largely retained;[17] but senior posts were filled by promoted personnel or more likely by people transferred from other parts of the country – often from completely outside the industrial sector.[18] There were, consequently, a large number of inexperienced people in senior positions. Press articles time and again bemoaned the fact that cadres were being despatched at random to serve as managers and accountants.

They sometimes brought with them the 'line of the poor peasant and hired hand' which paid no attention to costs and raised wages at will.[19] Insufficient attention was paid to the training and promotion of middle level cadres and, in some cases, the restoration of production meant that the proportion of skilled workers to unskilled went down.[20]

Tientsin was perhaps one of the last major cities where take-over proceeded according to the earlier North East pattern. It was an anomaly in that the actions of lower level cadres seem to have been much more radical than those in Shenyang liberated some months before.[21] Nevertheless the picture painted by Liu Shao-ch'i in his (alleged) report to labour unions reveals, in an extreme form, the kind of problems faced by Communist Party cadres in a situation where senior management had fled south. According to Liu, the 'bureaucratic capitalists' had vanished and the Communist Party cadres transferred from the countryside to replace them were sometimes less literate than the workers.[22] The extant documents may well be corrupt and should be understood in a context where Liu was trying to persuade workers and labour union officials not to hold the factory general managers in awe, nevertheless there is sufficient evidence from the North East to show that the experience of newly appointed factory general managers was often of a very different kind from that required by modern industry. I have, however, seen no assertion that any senior management in the North East was semi-literate.

The influx of new inexperienced senior management in the North East and parts of North China liberated before the spring of 1949 had three important consequences. Firstly their inexperience resulted in an enormous influence exercised by the joint Sino-Soviet enterprises in Lushun and Talien which were under Soviet occupation and where, in fact, senior management was largely Soviet; this will be discussed in Chapters 4 and 5. Secondly, since the North East and some other old liberated areas were starting the task of restoring production with large numbers of new personnel, the process of Democratic Reform could be accelerated. Thirdly, there was a tendency for some enterprise Party branches to take over the functions of technical management who were no more experienced than they.

As important as the lack of skill on the part of management cadres transferred to the industrial sphere, was the lack of experience on the part of the political cadres. Many Party cadres had been transferred directly from the Army and had little idea about how an industrial organisation operated.[23] It was not however just lack of *industrial* experience that caused concern, but also lack of administrative experience in general. According to Ch'en Po-ta, the Army could not afford to release personnel with great administrative experience whilst the fighting was still going on[24] and it might well have been for this reason that the administrative ability of both Party and management that Liu Shao-ch'i observed in Tientsin was almost unbelievably low.[25]

In such a situation 'left' excesses in the treatment of technical personnel were quite common.[26] In Tientsin, for example, Party personnel were engaged in struggles with technicians. Factories had been placed under an extremely low level of Party control – that of street governments.[27] At a time when 'take-over', 'democratic reform' and the restoration of production were entrusted to the leadership of *local* Party committees,[28] horizontal links were probably of far greater importance than vertical (ministerial) ones. In such a situation, the power of the Party-military organisation was extremely great. Party committees were sometimes in a position to absorb the newly formed factory management committees, take over their functions and exercise leadership themselves.[29]

Commenting on this situation in 1956, Li Hsüeh-feng, head of the Party Central Committee Industrial and Communications Work Department, whilst condemning the Party's usurpation of managerial position, looked upon this early period as one in which the Party did exercise correct leadership over industrial enterprises in striking contrast to the period of 'one-man management' which followed. Speaking at a time when the principle of collective leadership was reaffirmed, Li was particularly concerned at the erosion of the principle of collective leadership and individual responsibility practised by the Peoples Liberation Army during the war.[30] In this early period cadres still retained the tradition of collective leadership and individual responsibility that derived from the Yenan experience but it was mixed with an attitude of contempt for the workers amongst their least conscious members. In August 1951 An Tzu-wen, Deputy Head of the Organisation Bureau of the Central Committee noted that, not long previously, the prevalent opinion of members of a North China Party school was that since the revolution had been led by peasants and a few intellectuals not much attention should be given to the workers; after all they had made rifles for the enemy.[31] An observed even then, a widespread tendency for Communist Party cadres who had served in the countryside to resent the priviliged position of workers in the new society; their opinion of retained management could scarcely have been much better.

The volume of criticism directed at lower level cadres in North East and North China would indicate that the problem of excessive radicalism was greater there than elsewhere. As the Peoples Liberation Army swept south in the period following Liu's Tientsin Talks, much greater efforts were made to ensure the co-operation of former managers in the state sector. Managers now tended to remain at their post probably because there was nowhere for them to be transferred to and also because they were frequently prevented from being moved by worker picket organisations (*kung-jen chiu-ch'a-tui*).[32] Though the process of take-over of factories in the South was much less violent than in the North, some pressing reforms were carried out. Many accounts were published dealing with the struggle against secret agents (*t'e-wu fen-tzu*) and saboteurs. Yellow (Kuomintang) labour union officials were a special target since they were frequently identified with the *Chün-t'ung* (military secret service).[33] Nevertheless despite such actions, the internal organisation of factories south of the Great Wall remained much the same as it had been prior to liberation.

The process of take-over in Shanghai

In areas where a fairly strong Communist Party underground existed, worker picket organisations were formed to prevent sabotage by retreating Kuomintang troops and the removal of equipment and personnel to areas still held by the Kuomintang. In Shanghai, China's second major industrial centre, the Peoples Peace Preservation Corps (*Jen-min Pao-an-tui*) was formed by the Party and consisted of some 60,000 people of whom 60% were workers.[34] The corps maintained discipline whilst the fighting was still going on and undertook policing and patrolling duties.[35] Picket organisations assisted in disarming hostile units, confiscated weapons, unearthed hidden material, persuaded Kuomintang units to change sides and generally acted as intermediaries between the Peoples Liberation Army and enemy troops stationed in the factories.[36]

This was presumably how their predecessors saw their function in 1927 and 1945. On those two occasions, it will be remembered, worker picket organisations were formed in haste but soon suppressed by their erstwhile allies. This time they were to be absorbed into the Party and union structures they were instrumental in creating. Such picket organisations were to appear later in 1951 during the Democratic

Reform movement.[37]

The duties of the worker picket organisations were not confined to serving a quasi-military function. They also supervised the distribution of rations and tried to keep production going.[38] Some industrial units such as the Shanghai Power Company boasted that its workers remained on duty under enemy gunfire and that the supply of electricity was not interrupted for one day[39] and others resumed operations under the sound of gunfire.[40] It is impossible to assess how much more disruption of Shanghai industry would have been caused had there been no picket organisations; suffice it to say that, in the opinion of Jao Shu-shih, the newly appointed secretary of the East China Bureau of the Central Committee, their function was indispensible to the smooth transfer of power.[41]

The situation in Shanghai was very different from the devastation of Anshan and the ultra radicalism of Tientsin where, according to Liu Shao-ch'i, worker organisations often disregarded Party policy, took over factory management themselves and set up industrial co-operatives which very soon went bankrupt.[42] The smoothness with which take-over was effected depended very much on the efficiency of local military control commissions (*chün-shih kuan-chih wei-yüan-hui*). The function of these bodies has been succinctly described by Doak Barnett as similar to receivers in bankruptcy.[43] In Peking, where take-over was also relatively smooth, the control commission was assisted by a Joint Administrative Office consisting of Kuomintang officials and Communist Party representatives. The Kuomintang members of this office were required to reveal the assets of former government organisations and those of organisations designed as 'bureaucratic capitalist', whereupon the military control commission made an inventory and prepared to hand over control to the newly formed local people's government.[44]

The worker picket organisations did not take over the management of factories themselves, though they often formed take-over assistance groups (*pang-chu chieh-kuan hsiao-tsu*)[45] which co-operated with formal take-over groups (*chieh-kuan-tsu*) sent down by the local military control commissions.[46] Factory based take-over assistance groups were required to mobilise the workers to assist the formal take-over groups in stock taking (*ch'ing-tien*). Factories formed stock taking committees (*ch'ing-tien wei-yüan-hui*) which contained a number of worker delegates. For example the First Woollen Mill (formerly owned by the China Textile Construction Company) in Shanghai elected one man for every shop of 50 workers (30 delegates) and the Sixteenth Mill elected one delegate for every 30 workers (72 delegates). Ideally these stock-taking committees were to contain worker activists, white-collar workers and old skilled workers who were all enjoined to solicit and accept the opinions and suggestions of rank and file workers. Once formed, the stock-taking committees divided out work according to technical criteria, making sure that specialists were engaged in checking items within their speciality.

When stock taking was completed, military representatives (appointed by the original take-over group) and representatives of the take-over assistance groups were required jointly to affix their seals to a stock-taking record which was submitted to the local military control commission. In Shanghai the municipal military control commission designated a financial and economic committee to supervise this and other economic items and this sub-committee was empowered to send down work teams to factories that required extra help.

In addition to the above duties, the stock-taking committees also concerned themselves with restoring damaged stock and often emergency repair teams were formed. The Woosung Gas Works was cited as a model of stock-taking. The works had been damaged by retreating Kuomintang troops (evidently this was not one of the most successful examples of the work of the Peace Preservation Corps). They had burned the motor of the ammonium sulphate plant, broken the dying chamber and appropriated several hundred household gas meters. The workers worked night and day for 35 days and restored the damage. It was during this emergency repair stage that retained management and newly formed worker organisations such as the stock-taking/emergency repair groups had their first experience of co-operation, under the watchful eye of a military representative from the original take-over group.[47]

The role of the military representatives

The provision for a military representative in the new managerial organisation paralleled the organisational framework at municipal level. At that level military control commissions had been established as temporary bodies until local government and Party organisations were fully operative.[48] Within the industrial unit the military representative was the structural equivalent of a Party secretary and remained as interpreter of Party policy until a formal Party secretary was appointed.

The post of military representative was primarily a political rather than an administrative appointment. He was to supervise the implementation of Party policy rather than take administrative decisions himself.[49] At a time when horizontal (local) links were probably stronger than vertical (ministerial) links, his connection with local military control commissions was of great significance. Listing the duties of the military representative, Ch'en Po-ta, who was at that time Deputy Chairman of the Party Central Committee's Propaganda Department, made it quite clear that he was seen not only as a structural equivalent of a Party secretary but also as his functional equivalent. The military representative was not only to supervise the conduct of management but was also to serve as policeman and educator. He was to conduct research into technical and financial problems, eliminate waste, help organise labour union branches and consumer co-operatives and was to promote activists and cadres from among the white and blue collar workers.[50]

Faced with this rather impressive catalogue of the military representative's duties, it is perhaps strange, therefore, that the few accounts I have seen which describe the activities of military representatives do not reveal them as very dynamic and revolutionary characters, in striking contrast to later literature which is lavish in its praise of good Party secretaries. Accounts are confusing. Bearing in mind Franz Schurmann's observation that when horizontal links are strong there is tendency for Party secretaries (or, in this case, their equivalent) to take over administrative or managerial functions, it is not surprising that in 1950, Teng Tzu-hui, Deputy Chairman of the Central South Military Administrative Committee, was to warn against military representatives so doing.[51] On the other hand, Li Li-san, who in the early 1950s was Minister of Labour and first Vice Chairman of the All China Federation of Labour, was to remark that the military representative's power was simply that of ultimate veto.[52] One can only conclude that the policy of maintaining the status quo south of the Great Wall severely circumscribed the formal power given to military representatives. As a quasi-Party secretary without a Party organisation within his factory, his only power derived from his links with local military control commissions who were probably unwilling in this early period to precipitate conflict with retained management. This problem was probably not so acute in the North East for, by 1949, many of the functions of military control commissions had already been handed over to local government and military representatives had been replaced as more radical reorganisation was attempted.

The establishment of vertical control

The period of military control was to be only a temporary one. Municipal military control commissions were required to hand over authority to municipal peoples governments once they had full control over enemy assets. Similarly, take-over personnel (such as the military representatives) at lower levels were required gradually to hand over authority to structures equivalent to the peoples governments. At factory level these were the factory management committees. Peoples governments were set up soon after the military control commissions and coexisted with them for some time as authority was transferred.[53] Similarly, provision was made for the early establishment of factory management committees upon which a military representative would sit as an ex-officio member.[54] Chapter 7 will examine the operation of these committees; in the meantime one must note that, in accordance with the principle of democratic centralism, the establishment of representative bodies was to proceed alongside the establishment of vertical control.

In a situation where authority was fragmented throughout the country and where the only really effective body that could link up the various municipal, sub-municipal, productive and residential units was the Army, it was that organisation that had to provide the framework for future civilian administration. Once the Army had set about the task of supervising the election of representative bodies at various levels, attempts had to be made to draw up a plan for administration specifying what levels enjoyed what powers and what organisations what degree of autonomy. It was probably too mammoth a task to work out a scheme for the whole country and blueprints were worked out for each of six large administrative regions (*ta hsing-cheng-ch'ü*) which that of North East China was to serve as a model for the rest of the country with regard to industry.

In the very early days after liberation, the North East Peoples Government with easy access to Soviet advice in Lushun and Talien quickly worked out a model of administration based on the current Stalinist system of the Soviet Union. Other regions, however, were not at all sure how a general imperative to emulate the Soviet Union should be interpreted. After all, the establishment of factory management committees had little in common with the Stalinist system which vigorously condemned the 'parliamentary system' of management that had existed in that country in the early days of the Bolshevik

Revolution. To add to the confusion, labour union cadres were explicitly instructed to read material dealing with the Soviet Union's New Economic Policy of the 1920s since the relationship between the public and private sectors of industry in China during the period of New Democracy was felt to be similar.[55] Some people south of the Great Wall appeared to take the New Economic Policy parallel sufficiently seriously to advocate the establishment of basic level organisations remarkably similar to the NEP trust which, in the Soviet Union, had ceased to be the main basic level accounting unit in the 1920s. In the spring of 1949 Liu Shao-ch'i advocated the establishment of ten horizontally integrated corporations in Tientsin and the incorporation of sundry factories that did not fall into clearly defined production criteria into 'joint enterprises' (*lien-ho ch'i-yeh*).[56] Liu stated that private firms could enter these organisations, though it is difficult to imagine how this would have worked out in practice, and as far as I know no details have been published on the operation of such corporations or joint enterprises in this early period.

In the North East the major speeches in industrial policy were made by the regional chairman Kao Kang who throughout this period tended towards a Stalinist line, which is perhaps ironical in the light of the subsequent criticism that he had proclaimed himself the leader of the 'Party of the Revolutionary Bases and of the Army'.[57] The organisational blueprint that was adopted placed state run industry firmly under the control of an *industrial department* (*kung-yeh-pu*) which was divided into nine *administrative bureaux* (*kuan-li-chü*); coal mining (with nine *sub-bureaux*), machinery, non-ferrous metals, forestry, textiles, chemicals, metal mining (with four provincial *sub-bureaux*), military engineering and a bureau for other enterprises (including paper, cement, rubber, porcelain etc.). In addition, two *corporations* (*kung-ssu*) directly administered by the *industrial department* were set up; the Anshan and Penki Iron and Steel Works.[58] The various *administrative bureaux* were the counterparts of Soviet organisational forms (*glavki*) as were the *corporations* (*combines*). The *administrative bureaux* controlled a number of lower level *corporations* as did the Anshan and Penki complexes. Such corporations differed from the bureaux in that they were 'economic accounting organs' (profit making organisations) as opposed to 'budgetary organs'. With the exception of corporations, the basic economic accounting unit was to be the *enterprise*, which was similar to its Soviet counterpart except that it tended to be only one factory rather than several.

An attempt was made, therefore, to create a system of vertical control from the industrial department right down into the individual factory. Such verticalisation inevitably meant that the power of horizontal channels of command were weakened. Kao Kang was particularly concerned about the excessive power exercised by the newly formed Party structures that had taken over from the locally based military control commissions and their interference with the new vertical control structures in industry. He put the Party secretaries firmly in their place:

There are some comrades amongst us who consider that the secretary of the Party committee or Party branch can replace the system whereby the factory general manager enjoys overall responsibility. This idea is manifestly wrong. Party committees and Party branches are not administrative organs within the factories. They are the leading organs of the vanguard of the working class within the enterprise. They should call upon Party members to stand at the forefront of production and become models in fulfilling the production plan. They must supervise and advance the implementation of that plan. They may make timely suggestions when necessary but cannot replace the factory general manager or the system whereby the factory general manager enjoys overall responsibility. All members of the Communist Party in enterprises must know that each state enterprise must work under the economic plan for the whole country and that that plan is formulated by state organs under the leadership of the Party Central Committee or representative organs of the Central Committee. The responsibilities of the factory general manager are given him by higher organs of state and are determined not only by the needs of his own factory but also by the requirements of the coordinated national plan. If the factory general manager is made responsible not to leading organs of state or organs responsible for enterprises at a higher level but to a Party committee or party branch within the factory and if the production plan of a particular enterprise is made not to originate from higher organs of state or higher level organs responsible for enterprises but is formulated by the factory Party committee or Party branch, then there will be no longer any co-ordinated leadership [*ling-tao i-yüan-hua*]: Co-ordinated leadership will be split and shattered. We must understand that Party organs should not and can not replace state organs.[59]

The strengthening of the vertical component in the dual-rule scheme of control and the weakening of the Party's horizontal links was a far cry from the provisions made in Yenan in 1942 when the dual-rule scheme was introduced to counter bureaucratism and which strengthened the power of Party branches at the lower levels.[60]

Verticalisation and the formation of labour unions

When the All China Federation of Labour (*Chung-hua Ch'üan-kuo Tsung-kung-hui*), known in English after 1953 as the All China Federation of Trade Unions, was brought back to life in 1948 at the Sixth Labour Conference, it was mainly representatives of craft unions (*chih-yeh kung-hui*) that attended.[61] The Chinese Communist Party, however, strove to create industrial unions (*ch'an-yeh kung-hui*) whereby all white and blue collar workers in an enterprise belonged to the same union branch irrespective of job or trade and excluding only those whose class status or counter-revolutionary activities disqualified them.[62] Such a composition was reflected in the term 'white and blue collar workers union' (*chih-kung-hui*) which many unions were initially called[63] though later the simple term 'labour union' (*kung-hui*) came into wide usage. It was felt that the craft unions that existed in the days before liberation divided the work force and led to alienation between white and blue collar workers.[64] The literature cites with some justification but even more exaggeration, the fragmented work force in some British industrial establishments as an example of the pernicious nature of craft unions.[65] Secondly, industrial unions were more amenable to vertical organisation on a regional or national level. By 1950, ten national labour union hierarchies were under construction[66] linked at lower levels by general labour unions (*tsung-kung-hui*).

Membership of a labour union was voluntary[67] and, 90% of all industrial workers had been enrolled by 1952.[68] The main criterion for joining was 'membership of the working class' which took no account of class origin (at least formally), and a member of the working class was defined as anyone who derived his principal source of livelihood from hiring out his labour (mental or manual).[69] In the early years this broad definition of 'working class' led to a certain amount of confusion, as workers failed to understand the logic behind a senior manager being a member of the same union organisation as a part time auxiliary worker purely on the grounds that he worked in the same enterprise,[70] or why a peasant who let his land in order to work in a factory should be a union member.[71] The looseness of criteria for membership contributed to two phenomena which were considered highly detrimental to union development. Firstly, 'feudal elements' such as gang-bosses and runaway landlords were able to use their former influence and connections to be elected to union office and secondly, union leadership was often monopolised by people who held concurrent management posts.

It is my impression that the line of demarcation between Party and union organisation in both the liberated and 'white' areas in the period prior to liberation was not very clear. In the opinion of the reporter Chao Ch'ao-kou, who visited Yenan in June and July 1944, the Party committee was the nucleus of the union organisation in the factories he visited,[72] and an examination of the quite detailed material on the workers movement in Shanghai has led me to the tentative conclusion that the 'red unions' in the 'white areas' constituted a kind of outer Party with no clearcut organisational or functional distinction between the formal Party organisation and the formal union organisation.[73]

In the situation immediately following liberation where Party branches were able sometimes to usurp managerial authority, one might expect that the unions which were inextricably tied to the Party organisation would share in this process. Such a situation is suggested by Kao Kang in the following quote:

> There have been people who have caused the labour unions to take over some aspects of the administrative work of factory general managers. Everyone knows that this is wrong. The responsibilities and work of the labour unions are to unite and organise the broad masses of the workers, to educate them so that the whole body of the worker masses might understand their role as 'master', to enhance their consciousness of labour discipline, to foster their activism and concern for production, to exchange experiences one with another, to learn production management and furthermore to work for the protection of the working class. If labour unions are turned into ordinary administrative organs, they will consequently stand as rivals to factory management. Parallel administrative organs will stand side by side and it is quite manifest that this will impede the establishment of systems of responsibility.[74]

It is impossible to say to what extent the above phenomenon was a result of confusion between Party and union organisations, and to what extent it resulted from the fact that union officers sometimes held concurrent management posts. Whichever was the case, I know of no instance where the factory general manager was concurrently labour union chairman. I have, furthermore, seen no account of exactly how labour union branches came to usurp the functions of management and can only suggest that this phenomenon was, like the similar phenomenon of Party usurpation of managerial position, a result of the importance of horizontal linkages between local government, Party and union structures. In Tientsin, where the problem of left excesses was most serious prior to Liu Shao-ch'i's visit, labour union work was the direct responsibility of each group of five cadres who constituted a street government, and who tended to regard the labour unions in much the same way as did Poor Peasant Associations in the rural sphere.[75]

By mid 1950 the tendency for union branches to usurp managerial functions had come to an end. Paul Harper, who has written on the subject, argues that the 'traditional tendency of Chinese labour organisations' to serve as 'tails of management' had come to the fore in 1950. He notes that the various strikes of late 1949, together with the economic crisis of March–June 1950 caused the Party to step in with a firm hand, 'stressing compromise and ignoring class struggle'. The increasingly conservative tendency in the policy and activities of the labour unions in the first half of 1950 was dictated by a need to restore production as soon as possible; this stress on compromise and tendency towards conservatism was, Harper feels, particularly noticeable in the private sector, but also common in the public sector.[76]

In using the term 'traditional tendency', I feel that Harper confuses the nature of 'red' and 'yellow' labour unions of pre-liberation days. As we saw in chapter 1, the 'yellow' unions were basically control organs whereas the 'red' unions sought to mobilise the workers to act in concert with revolutionary military forces outside the cities and the literature is full of examples of red unions initiating strikes, even when there was formally peace between the Communist Party and the Kuomintang.[77] Attempts made by the old yellow unions to mobilise the workers such as, for example, when they formed 'work protection units' to root out Communists were rather ineffectual and cannot by any stretch of the imagination be compared with the mammoth work of mobilisation undertaken by the new Red unions in the early 1950s.

Secondly, I would disagree with Harper that the spring of 1950 was particularly significant in establishing a conservative line. As we have seen, such a line can be traced back to December 1947 or at least April 1949[78] and throughout this period the Party was constantly stepping in with a firm hand; it was not until 1951 that the policy of mass mobilisation radically changed the situation in urban areas. Thirdly, the strikes that occurred in late 1949 seem to have been largely in the private sector[79] and to have been a continuation of the left excesses that date from long before Liu's Tientsin talks. Indeed, in the state sector in the spring of 1950 the atmosphere, if anything, was a little less conservative, in that it was felt appropriate at that time to carry out some measure of Democratic Reform in North China.[80]

Bureaucratism in the unions

The tendency for labour unions to side with management was not so much due to any continuation of tradition as to the fact that union cadres often held concurrent management posts, that they were subject to repeated transfer leaving their branches in the hands of inexperienced cadres, that they were probably too busy with the sheer paperwork involved in establishing a union apparatus to give much constructive criticism to management. Finally, they were too busy studying technology to be anything but compliant.

In an article on labour union organisation in Kirin province in March 1950, it was noted that in some enterprise union committees, the majority of members held concurrent management posts. In the Shih Chü Tzu Copper Mine, for example, out of a labour union committee of six people, only two had no concurrent management post. In a match factory in the same province, a committee of seven contained only two members with no concurrent post. One labour union chairman held eight concurrent posts. In other places, workshop supervisors and one deputy Party secretary held union Posts. There was a tendency to promote workers who had proven their ability in labour union work to managerial positions. In the Shih Chü Tzu Mine, for example, nineteen labour union cadres were promoted to managerial posts from the emulation drive of May 1949 to March 1950 (an average loss of two cadres per month), which deprived the union of any degree of continuity and any effective power.[81]

The problem of transfer of cadres was made worse by the rapid expansion of industrial units as production was restored. During this process of expansion every effort was made to train large numbers of managerial personnel, for there was an unwillingness to rely for long upon retained personnel who, according to Kao Kang, were 'only able to master relatively backward techniques'.[82] In any case, there were insufficient retained technicians. Every means possible was used to bring forward new talent and the union became 'a school for management'.[83] By December 1950, 441 workers had been promoted to the rank of factory general manager in the North East, 484 to section chief and 2,247 to technician.[84] By April 1952, in the East China Region 7,962 people had been promoted to the rank of production management cadre, of whom 2,040 were to the level of factory general manager or deputy general manager. At that time in the coal industry over the whole country 1,583 white and blue collar workers had been promoted to the rank of factory or mine general manager or division chief (*ch'u-chang*).[85]

In a situation where the unions provided a vehicle for promotion to management, a rapid turnover of union cadres was inevitable. The more able cadres would be creamed off into management or into the Party (if their talents were more political than managerial), leaving the less able and inexperienced in union jobs. It is not surprising therefore that in 1951 such cadres complained that they were only treated as 'fourth class'.[86] In a climate where Party and union cadres were enjoined to learn all about production and study technology, there is little wonder that the more inexperienced union cadres would tend not to oppose those who did know about such things. It was probably because of a desire not to hand union work over to completely inexperienced personnel that union cadres sometimes retained their posts after promotion to management, as in the Kirin examples, and this could only add to their inclination to serve the interests of management.

The problem of subordination to management was not simply caused by rapid promotion and the holding of concurrent posts. Union cadres were frequently moved around even when they held no concurrent management post. This led to a situation, condemned by Li Li-san in June 1950, where large numbers of cadres existed in enterprise union organisations who had been sent in from the outside.[87] Such cadres were not familiar with their new place of work, and were not the best people to represent the interests of the workers in discussions with management, much less act as a check to the arbitrary actions of factory general managers.

Rapid transfer, and the holding of concurrent posts led to an alienation between union and workers which was described as 'bureaucratism'. The term, in itself, indicated nothing about how hard particular cadres worked, or how enthusiastic they might be about what they considered were their duties. In fact the term 'hard-working' bureaucratism (*hsin-hsin k'u-k'u kuan-liao-chu-i*) was employed to designate those cadres who lost contact with the masses precisely because of their enthusiasm for work.[88]

Perhaps the most important contributory factor in such bureaucratism was the sheer weight of paperwork that union cadres were required to undertake. The following figures for the expansion of union membership can give one some idea of the paperwork that must have been involved.

1948	1,448,228
1949	2,373,938
1950	4,904,408
1951	6,130,977
mid 1952	7,297,857[89]
end of 1952	10,000,000 (approx.)[90]

Investigation had to be carried out as to the class status of each applicant for union membership and labour insurance and there was seldom time to do this adequately. Indeed, one of the explicit items on the agenda for Democratic Reform was to persuade workers to correct their initial applications.[91]

The labour union law of June 1950 stipulated that the ratio of union cadres free from production work to total employees within industrial enterprises should be as follows:[92]

1 cadre for 200–500 white and blue collar workers
2 cadres for 501–1000 white and blue collar workers
3 cadres for 1001–2500 white and blue collar workers
4 cadres for 2501–4000 white and blue collar workers

In addition to the process of registration, union cadres were required to attend training classes and cadre schools, to organise training classes and literacy classes for union members, to supervise the initiation of various welfare projects, etc. It may well be that in this initial period, the volume of work assigned to an inexperienced labour union cadre meant that he had time only to concentrate on the paperwork assigned to him (for on this he would be immediately judged) and left his mass work unattended to. It would be very difficult indeed for a cadre in a large enterprise to keep his pulse on the opinions of up to 1000 workers.

Policy during this early period after liberation was to keep the number of full time union cadres to a minimum, and this was reflected in the labour union law. Many instances are cited of factories who employed too many union cadres, and official policy only permitted a large number of non-productive cadres during the period of initial registration.[93] After that period, the problem remained of what to do with the cadres appointed to conduct that registration. They could be transferred, which added to the problem of 'outside cadres' that I have mentioned above; they could be deprived of their union post (a most unlikely policy in the period following liberation), or they could remain where they were. In the Lung Feng Coal Mine in the North East, for example, they remained where they were. Sixty-three full time cadres were employed for a labour force of 18,000, which gives a ratio of 1 : 280. This ratio was said to be a contributory factor in alienating the union cadres from the masses.[94] Presumably just as too few union cadres meant that the burden of paperwork was excessive, thus alienating the cadres from the masses, too many tended to produce a union élite which likewise was alienated from the masses.

The problem here was how to determine the optimum number of union cadres. The prescribed formula was to adhere to the stipulations of the labour union law, which kept full-time cadres to a minimum, and employ a large number of union activists who engaged in union work in their spare time. In this respect, a model union organisation was the Plaster Works of the Far East Electronics Bureau in Talien, which had only two full time cadres (the branch chairman and secretary) for more than 1,100 workers, but a large number of activists who divided their union work into ten specialist committees.[95]

Activists, however, required a certain degree of administrative skill to sit on the specialised committees (wages, welfare, etc.) and although there might have been sufficient material in Talien, such skill was at such a premium elsewhere that such activists would probably be offered management posts. It is the boast of some British trade unions that their shop stewards have as much managerial skill as line management. This situation is only possible when either skilled labour is in plentiful supply or where union work offers as much satisfaction as management work. Clearly, in a situation where almost all considerations were becoming subordinate to questions of production, a skilled activist would prefer to lead production himself rather than fulfil an auxiliary role in the production process. A skilled activist would only be content with a union post if the tasks and goals of the union were significantly different from management. If they were not, he would remain 'fourth class'.

Bureaucratism in the Party

The growth of 'bureaucratism' as defined above applied equally to the Party organisation. Following the Second Plenum of the Seventh Party Central Committee in March 1949, when a decision was taken to shift the focus of Party work from the countryside to the cities,[96] an all-out effort was made to take into the Party large numbers of skilled workers and technicians. During the first of the major production drives known as the Movement to Create New Records, there was a rapid rise in Party membership and, in practice, a decline in the political qualifications for membership in the industrial sector. This process, which bore a remarkable resemblance to Stalin's 'Leninist Levy'[97] was designed to increase the proportion of industrial workers and technicians in the Party and enthusiasm for production began to be seen as a sufficient indicator of political consciousness.[98]

In the Raw Materials Department of the Antung Paper Works for example, Party membership rose from nine on the foundation of the Party branch on 1 October 1949 (4.8% of employees) to 53 by the end of November 1949 (26.5% of employees) and this expansion was directly attributed to the Movement to Create New Records.[99] In the North East Smelting Works, the proportion of Party members rose from 3.2% in August 1949 to 14% by the end of 1950 of whom two-thirds were skilled workers and the Youth League was expanded to comprise 45.3% of those whose age qualified them for membership.[100] By May 1951 the proportion of Party members in enterprises in the North East was said to be 11.4% of the total number of workers[101] and, at that time (when there were some three million industrial workers in the country as a whole) the Party Central Committee announced that it planned to recruit one-third of all industrial workers into the Party within five years.[102] In August 1951 An Tzu-wen reported that by that time 13,000 Party branches had been set up in industrial enterprises and 200,000 workers had recently been brought into the Party.[103] Such a rapid increase could not but have an effect upon the relationship between old and new cadres.

Perhaps the major reason by the Movement to Create New Records of 1949 was used to expand the Party was because the Party was heavily weighted in favour of its peasant component in a situation where the workers were held to be 'master' of society. There is, however, another dimension which must be mentioned, and that was that complacency was rife amongst the old cadres who had moved to the cities. In the opinion of Kao Kang in September 1949, there were very few old cadres in the North East who were hard working and who did not struggle for fame and material betterment.[104] The majority of cadres wasted time by convening unnecessary meetings because they did not know how to discharge their duties and although they tended to abide by higher directives were not always guiltless of trying to feather their own nests. A smaller group Kao characterised as bombastic showoffs obsessed by their own official classification or, if on a salary basis, the number of wage points they were earning. According to Kao Kang, the Party had been affected by 'the depraved ideology of remnant feudal elements and capitalists, petty bourgeois individualism and defects in ideological and educational work'.[105] Kao noted that cadres frequently rationalised their indolent attitude in political terms and when admonished for relaxing after entering the cities, they accused their critics of 'taking a rural viewpoint' and of not realising the importance of the united front between workers, peasants, petty bourgeoisie and national capitalists.[106]

Many old cadres did not take kindly to the rapid expansion of the Party and the employment of new cadres whom they felt to be their political inferiors, thus displaying a lack of political consciousness on their own part. The following extract from a letter to *Hsüeh-hsi*, the semi official theoretical journal of the Party,[107] refers not to industry but to government administration. It nevertheless speaks volumes about the decline in the political consciousness of the new cadres:

> In our organ [of government] there are very few old cadres. Many cadres have newly joined our work, the majority of whom are intellectuals straight from school. They have not been steeled in a life of struggle and in general their level of political consciousness is very low. I nevertheless have to do work similar to those new cadres and receive the same treatment. Some of these new cadres are even preferred by the leadership and are entrusted with even more important tasks than I. I feel that the higher levels have assigned to me work inappropriate [to my experience] and do not trust me sufficiently . . . Some people say that the old revolution[aries] are not [considered] as good as the new revolution[aries]. I too am of that opinion. When I conveyed my opinion to the higher levels, not only did they not accept it but criticised me for [displaying] the 'ideology of the meritorious' [*kung-ch'en ssu-hsiang*] saying that my feelings were backward, proud and complacent. They demanded that I cogitate on the matter but I have thought for a long time and am not convinced . . . Can one say it is fair treatment if the fruits of victory which we paid for with our flesh and blood are enjoyed by those who have not worked for them.[108]

Needless to say, this attitude was roundly condemned.

Within industrial enterprises, the friction between old and new cadres might take the form of conflict between cadres transferred from the rural sphere and new technocratic management, and such conflict was criticised as a manifestation of 'the ideology of power and prestige' (*ch'üan-wei ssu-hsiang*).[109] Friction, however, might occur between different levels of the Party organisation itself. In Cultural Revolution retrospect one might conclude that there was some substance in Kao Kang's alleged insistence that there were two parties, that of 'the revolutionary bases and the army' and that of the 'white areas'[110] which had developed with quite different organisational perspectives. Until the mass of Cultural Revolution material is fully sifted we will probably be unable to say to what extent friction may have occurred in the period following liberation between those cadres who were active in factories in the 'white areas' before liberation and those who were transferred from the rural areas and the Army. I have looked in vain for any contemporary account of, for example, how old Party members who had been active in Shanghai in the Peace Preservation Corps co-existed with Party secretaries transferred from outside the industrial sector. In this connection, it is most significant that the one top Party leader who was chosen to deal with the left excesses in Tientsin was a man who had considerable experience in both the revolutionary bases and the white areas.

In lieu of any contemporary evidence, one might get some idea of the problem from Ai Wu's novel *Steeled and Tempered*, where two levels of Party secretary are portrayed, one newly transferred to the Liaonan Iron and Steel Works and initially helpless in the face of a mass of complicated personal relationships and jealousies, and the other (a shop level secretary) who enjoyed a considerable amount of influence in the works due to the fact that he had been employed there for some years. The power and influence of the shop level Party secretary was not, however, matched by a high level of political consciousness, and he emerges as a rather slipshod, but not unsympathetic, character.[111] This novel was written during the Great Leap Forward and seems to have as its didactic purpose the portrayal of the wisdom of a transferred Party secretary who eventually came to understand the political situation in the Steel Works clearer than anyone else, and it may not be a completely true picture of reality. Secondly, there was no actual conflict between the two levels of Party secretary; nevertheless the novel does spell out a potential source of tension that further research might substantiate.

Bureaucratism, then, in the sense of alienation from the masses, was due, on the one hand, to the absorption of large numbers of people with a low level of political consciousness into the Party in the industrial sector, and on the other, to the decline of revolutionary fervour on the part of old cadres after entering the city which led to tension between different levels of cadre. A third source of bureaucratism, we have already noted when discussing the labour unions. Senior Party personnel transferred to the industrial sector devoted the major part of their energy to learning about problems of production before they felt confident enough to engage in reforming the technicians. In the Wu San factory in Shenyang, which later became a model for labour union work, almost all senior Party cadres and line managers came from outside the industrial sector whereas all the technicians were old factory personnel.[112] If the newly transferred personnel were to be in a position to influence the knowledgable technicians, they had to learn rapidly about the rules of production. The Party secretary of the factory, Liu Shih-hua, confessed in late 1952, that, after his transfer from the Army to serve as Party secretary of the factory following the liberation of Shenyang in the autumn of 1948, he resolved to spend all his time going around the shops learning about technology, to the detriment of his political duties.[113] So long as Party and senior management devoted all their energies to studying technology, they were in no position to penetrate the middle layers of administration that had remained from former times. In the North East, which experienced the highest turnover of senior management following liberation, due to the fact that managers had been transferred South and many factories were not operational at the time, some 70–90% of white collar staff were designated suitable for remoulding and immediate retention in August 1948.[114] If senior Party personnel neglected their technical studies to undertake this task of remoulding, what they gained in time, they might lose in respect. The abandonment of a radical solution to such a problem on the grounds that this would harm production resulted inevitably in the bureaucratic insulation of senior management and the perpetuation of a highly stratified form of organisation within the enterprises.

A final source of Party bureaucratism was a direct result of the logic of verticalisation itself. In the North East which set the pace for this verticalisation process, as the power of the industrial department grew, the significance of horizontal linkages declined. By mid 1951, Kao Kang noted that in sharp contrast to the previous situation, local Party and government organs had tended to abdicate all responsibility for state controlled enterprises.[115] Local Party and government tended to regard the production status of state enterprises as the responsibility of superior economic organs and were unwilling to interfere in their operation. Similarly, there was a tendency for the management of state enterprises to recognise only leadership from above. Such a situation isolated an enterprise management from its own Party committee, which was responsible in the first instance to local level Party committees and their own union committee which was responsible to the local level general labour union. Kao Kang demanded that leading personnel of all enterprises should take the initiative in obtaining the leadership and help of local Party committees and that they should educate the whole body of white and blue collar workers in how to obey the laws and decrees of local government. He laid the major responsibility directly at the feet of the local Party organisations which were to check up on how state enterprises in their area were carrying out central policies and their portion of the state plan. Local Party committees were to be directly responsible for mass work in all enterprises in their area and were responsible for the workers' political education. They were to correct any illegal behaviour on the part of enterprise cadres, to root out graft and to assume responsibility for security work.[116] Though economic departments of local government had certain responsibilities for state enterprises within their area of jurisdiction concerning supply and control of raw materials, the main link of a state enterprise with local government was via the Party organisation. The Party was also to involve itself in labour control,[117] for this was one of the major fields of tension between enterprises in the post-liberation situation. In 1951 problems occurred, such as the hijacking of personnel by government organs without any reference to local Party or government authority,[118] and offers of better living and working conditions were made to workers already employed in other enterprises.[119] In assuming duties concerning labour control, the Party was to overlap the local labour bureaux that were set up precisely to deal with such problems.[120]

Ever since 1942 the strengthening of vertical chains of command in China has been associated with the growth of bureaucratism.[121] The measures suggested by Kao Kang above to prevent the erosion of Party authority were in many ways the direct consequence of the establishment of vertical channels of command for which he was one of the most outspoken advocates.

The persistence of the gang-boss system

One of the principal reasons why Party and union organisations came under attack in mid 1950 was their inability to get rid of the old gang-boss system and implement effectively the policy of Democratic Reform. In the North East, the process of Democratic Reform had taken place immediately after liberation. This was probably partly due to the fact that the gang-boss system had already been restricted under the Japanese but was mainly due to the fact that there were fewer retained managers in that area and many factories which had been temporarily abandoned had to build up a managerial system from scratch. The political atmosphere at the time of the liberation of the North East was somewhat more radical than the atmosphere after the spring of 1949 and this meant that the struggle against gang-bosses and other reactionary elements could be launched immediately. An example of the early Democratic Reform Movement in the North East was that of the Wu San Factory in Shenyang. The factory was taken over in November 1948 and immediately a campaign was launched to educate the masses as to their new rights and duties. A 'speak-bitterness' movement (*su-k'u yün-tung*) was organised with much the same kind of objective as its counterpart in the rural sphere where land reform was in full swing. The movement consisted of a campaign of criticism and self-criticism in which both white and blue collar workers took part. At the same time as workers were registered for labour insurance, a register of members of reactionary organisations was compiled and feudal elements, enemy military policemen and counter revolutionaries flushed out. Upon this basis, steps were taken to rationalise the management and wages structures, restore production and take in new Party members. By October 1949, the factory was able to put the 'economic accounting system' into operation which indicated that such reforms were considered to have been completed satisfactorily.[122]

The model experiences of the Wu San Factory were rarely repeated south of the Great Wall. Sometimes surrogate organisations created by the Party to affect the abolition of the gang-boss system according to the principle of transformation from within were actually taken over by gang-boss organisations. The situation was especially bad in the mines. At a congress of mining unions, meeting in January–February 1950, it was reported that, apart from a few mines in the North East and North China, the policy of maintaining the status quo (*yüan-feng pu-tung*) was in force. In some mines management committees had not been convened or were formalistic and had incurred the hostility of the workers rather than their support. At the Ling Shan Coal Mine in Chahar, for example, the workers had dubbed the mine management committee (*kuan-li wei-yüan-hui*) the 'bureaucratic committee' (*kuan-liao wei-yüan-hui*) and many cases were reported where gang-bosses had just changed the names of their gangs to shifts or teams. In the Tsao Chuang Mine, twenty-two gang-bosses had been appointed team leaders and supervisors and were still engaged in their former practices. In the Hung Shan Mine sixteen former gang-bosses had been appointed team leaders or pit supervisors and many of these had adopted the philosophy that it did not matter who was currently in power, they would always 'get along' (after all they had experienced several changes of government).[123] In the construction industry, almost no change had been effected and here the problem was particularly difficult since it was virtually impossible at that stage not to depend upon contract labour. In some sections of the industry in Tat'ung in early 1950, there were as many as seven levels of gang-contractor who between them creamed off from 50–70% of the money paid to them leaving the workers 30–50% as wages.[124]

In the spring of 1950, China's leadership became more and more concerned about the effects of a policy which left old abuses unremedied and which permitted 'feudal remnants' to believe that they would 'get along' under the new government. A number of articles began to appear in the press which described the persistence of old exploitative forms of organisation and demanded that the process of democratisation and reform be speeded up. One such account dealt with the Yang Ch'üan State Coal Mines in Shansi which was traditionally the area where some of the worst excesses of gang-boss exploitation had occurred, and which in 1937 H.D. Fong had considered a 'living hell'.[125] Although it was an extreme case, it is narrated here as an example of what a moderate reform policy could lead to.[126]

When a reporter went down to the Yang Ch'üan Mines to investigate the failure to complete current production tasks, he was told that the gang-boss system had been abolished long ago. Nevertheless, bearing in mind the fact that the North China General Mining Bureau had issued several warnings to the mine about the persistence of the gang-boss system and that there were rumours currently circulating in Peking that these warnings had been unheeded, he pressed the matter further, only to be told that the gang-boss system was being maintained but that it was no longer exploitative.

After some further investigation the reporter discovered that after liberation all that had happened was that the various levels of gang-boss had changed their titles and continued as before. In the whole mine, out of a total of 38 senior level cadres at division (*ku*) level, 20 were some species of gang-boss who now rejoiced in the title of division chief (*ku-chang*), deputy division chief (*fu-ku-chang*) or unit leader (*tui-chang*). Under them came 55 group leaders (*ta-tsu-chang*), 90% of whom were former gang-bosses who did not work at all. Under each group leader were three team leaders (*hsiao-tsu-chang*) and a secretary. The secretary did no manual work and was responsible for wage payment and the team leaders worked, at the most, half time. The reporter calculated that out of the 3,556 white and blue collar workers in the mine, 2,498 were exploited by these 55 group leaders.

A group leader who did little or no work could earn 3,000–3,100 work points a month, as opposed to an ordinary worker's 1,320 points for a 22 day month, which in itself was not less than the former legal wage of a gang-boss. In addition, the group leader took his cut of the workers' wages, since grain payments were still paid in time honoured way to the team leaders rather than directly to the workers. This sometimes amounted to 5 out of every 20 *chin* of grain which was paid twice monthly. The group leader could also obtain illicit income by other means such as claiming bogus expenses or accepting payment for non-existing workers. As well as making automatic deductions from workers' wages, the group leaders received extra payment according to the amount of coal mined. There is little wonder, therefore, that the workers considered the democratic discussion of wage determination as something of a sham.

The acting manager felt that if he did not co-operate with the former gang-bosses, he would not be able to complete his production plan. It is ironical, therefore, that it was precisely the failure to complete the production plan that brought the situation to the attention of the reporter. According to him, Party and management personnel within the mine had not realised that the gang-bosses were in fact 'feudal remnants'. On the contrary, they were considered as 'skilled workers' and the main force that could be relied upon to develop production. Management was only concerned with receiving the coal once mined and was prepared to dismiss workers who objected to the system on the grounds that this attitude impaired productivity. The only way workers could protest was to write comments on the coal trucks criticising the stupidity of the acting manager for relying upon the group leaders. The reporter described such a situation as a 'commercial relationship' (*mai-mai kuan-hsi*) in which the only concern of management was the return they got for money paid to the group leaders.

The backwardness of Party personnel was explained by the fact that 13 out of 55 group leaders had been accepted as Party members and some of them were members of the Party committee. One such member of the Party committee managed to secure the demotion of a group leader who was not a former gang-boss and was concurrently a lower level Party secretary, because he had failed to donate to the wedding festivities of the committee member's son; as a Party committee member the former gang-boss was able to disregard the subsequent protests of the mine manager.

Party membership had expanded rapidly to a strength of 370 (10% of the total work force) and the group leaders had carefully controlled the acceptance of new members. As supervisors of education throughout the mine, the Party committee did its best to see that the gang-boss system was not criticised. When the reporter attended meetings of the Party committee which were discussing documents attacking the gang-boss system, he noted that they considered the mine a 'special case', and when the committee analysed the reasons why the mine was not fulfilling its production tasks, it could only conclude that insufficient reliance had been placed on the 'skilled workers' who were, in fact, the gang-bosses. The former gang-bosses had also formed the nucleus of the labour union organisation and many group leaders were concurrently leaders of union teams. Resenting this, the workers referred to union dues (*hui-fei*) as union tax (*hui-shui*).

It was in the interests of the former gang-bosses to see that planning did not work smoothly. The reporter noticed that none of the leading personnel seemed to know exactly what the size of the work force was. In this way they could continue to accept payment for non-working personnel. When management insisted that workers should be signed on and off work by a staff member, the union cadres declared that this was a 'bourgeois viewpoint' which placed no reliance on the working class. The workers were thus allowed to sign themselves in, which allowed group leaders to falsify records and maintain their own illicit income. Management was unable to exercise any discipline at all over the group leaders or their supporters. An attempt to discipline a union committee member who was absent longer than the period of leave granted him resulted in a protest by the labour union chairman and the quarrel which ensued caused a total breakdown of discipline.[127]

The maintenance of the gang-boss system in the mine resulted in considerable tension between the mine authorities and local government. In order to investigate the gang-bosses' control over the labour union, local Party and labour union organisations sent down an investigation team (*tiao-ch'a-tui*) which was frustrated by a parallel work team (*kung-tso-tui*) organised, ostensibly to help with the investigation, within the mine itself. When the investigation team called meetings, only minor cadres attended as observers and the team was unable to operate effectively. There was, furthermore, a lack of unity between Party, management and unions within the mine and this lack of unity was carefully fostered by group leaders who held posts in more than one body; every effort was made to prevent the formation of any group that could effectively oppose the gang-boss network.

The revelations of the situation at Yang Ch'üan led the North China General Mining Bureau to issue an order for the situation to be investigated and this order was published in the same newspaper as the above report. One would suspect that either the reporter or his editor had submitted his findings to the bureau before publication or that the reporter had gone down to the mine with explicit instructions from the Mining Bureau. In its order the Mining Bureau pointed out that the mine had already received two warnings (September 1949 and January 1950) and had done nothing about them, which clearly demonstrates the leisurely approach to Democratic Reform at that time. In its work plan for April 1950 the mine had put forward the abolition of the gang-boss system as its main task but was unwilling to call for 'self examination' meetings for fear that this would provoke the anger of the group leaders and thus harm production. Consequently the General Mining Bureau ordered the Yang Ch'üan mine to convene a conference of all cadres and with the participation of 'good' workers, conduct a movement of criticism and self criticism. The results of the self examinations were to be submitted to the General Mining Bureau together with a description of what measures were being taken to abolish the gang-boss system.

Such were the consequences of a policy which sought to subordinate political problems to the task of getting production moving again. The order of the Mining Bureau criticised an excessive concern for problems of production and its tone was more radical than any similar order that I have seen since the mild policy was confirmed in the spring of 1949. It was infinitely less radical, however, than what was to follow in the summer of 1951.

Control from above or mobilisation

Policy during the mild period after the spring of 1949 saw 'democratisation' and 'enterprisation' going hand in hand and the reform of old structures proceeding at a fairly leisurely rate. It was hoped that the newly created Party and union structures would carry out a gradual 'democratic reform'. What was probably not foreseen was a situation where 'feudal remnants' sought to take over the newly created Party and labour union organisations. During the spring and summer of 1950, following the publication of articles calling for a speed up in 'democratic reform', a series of administrative orders were promulgated formally abolishing the gang-boss system in various sectors of industry.[128] When lower level Party and union organs failed to respond adequately to this speed up, a rectification movement was launched.

It was suggested earlier that in this study two types of political movement will be discussed; those that involve widespread mass mobilisation and those that do not. In the period under review the various movements of late 1951 and early 1952 which will be discussed shortly were movements of the former type whereas the rectification movement of 1950 was a movement of the latter type. In 1950 the stress was on control from above. The Campaign for the Suppression of Counter-revolutionaries of late 1950 and early 1951 was described as a 'mass movement' and it required workers to denounce counter-revolutionaries within factories, but it did not involve anything approaching the degree of mass mobilisation of later movements. For this reason the Campaign for the Suppression of Counter-revolutionaries which exercised control from the top down was mainly concerned with the activities of active counter-revolutionaries rather than 'feudal remnants' such as gang-bosses. Some people argued, however, that it should have broadened its scope to include 'feudal remnants'.[129]

The preoccupation with control from above is demonstrated by the considerable attention that was given to the establishment of a formal control (inspection) apparatus. Attempts were made to build up such an apparatus as soon as cities had been liberated.[130] The regulations of May 1949 governing the establishment of factory management committees demanded that such committees institute a regular inspection within factories.[131] In January 1950, an emergency inspection was ordered for all publicly run enterprises in Peking, Tientsin, Shansi and Hopei, whereupon each factory and mine organised a control (inspection) committee (*chien-ch'a wei-yüan-hui*) consisting of representatives of Party, management, unions and Youth League.[132] Such control committees could not be very effective, however, so long as there was a danger that they might themselves be controlled by corrupt elements. Some eighteen months later, the 88th meeting of the

Government Affairs Council called upon municipal level Peoples Control Committees to extend their network down into the factories,[133] thus implying that despite the great attention given to control work, municipal level control organisations had not yet penetrated the factories.

The appearance of industrial kulaks

The revelations of Yang Ch'üan and other similar situations in North China resulted in attempts to press ahead with the policy of democratic reform in mid 1950. The removal of gang-bosses from above without widespread mass mobilisation, however, could lead to a situation remarkably similar to that of the rural areas where, following land reform, rich peasants came to exercise some of the power that formerly belonged to the landlords. Of course there was a considerable difference between the rich peasant and the retained middle level technician that I have chosen to call an 'industrial kulak', in that the former usually derived his power more from traditional connections than a knowledge of agricultural techniques whereas the latter derived his power more from a knowledge of technology than traditional connections, though as we have seen in the Yang Ch'üan example, traditional connections were by no means inconsiderable in the industrial sector.

To exemplify this point, let us consider the case of the Coal-Sorting Department of the Penki Iron and Steel Corporation.[134] Here, both Party and senior management were too busy working out the details implementing planned management to worry about the political consciousness of lower level cadres. One middle level manager, Hsia Chung-yü, had come to the fore in the Movement to Create New Records as an enthusiastic worker and had been promoted to a management position for which he lacked both technical and political qualifications. Hsia typified the new industrial kulak who had been promoted after the former middle level management had been removed during Democratic Reform. He was feared by the workers and had only a moderate level of skill.

At the end of 1949, a worker by the name of Ch'ang T'ai-tzu, who had been sent on a six month course to a workers' political university, returned to Penki to find that an old dust-collecting machine was working as inefficiently as in Kuomintang times and was polluting the atmosphere. Hsia Chung-yü had tried to mend it but, because he had not sought the advice of the workers, only succeeded in putting it out of action for a whole day, which cost the corporation a considerable sum of money. Ch'ang considered that the reason that the mending job had been botched was due to the fact that Hsia and the workers were more concerned with achieving new records than they were with safety and machine maintenance. On returning to the corporation, Ch'ang had been elected the chairman of a branch labour union and, in that capacity, forwarded a worker's suggestion for the renovation of the dust-collecting machine to Hsia Chung-yü. On receiving this, Hsia became furious because, after failing to renovate the machine himself, he had no confidence in an ordinary workers ability to do so. He refused to implement the suggestion on the grounds that a delay in production would have to be sustained, and accused Ch'ang of attempting to sabotage the Movement to Create New Records.

On hearing that a quarrel had developed between Ch'ang T'ai-tzu and Hsia Chung-yü, the Party secretary Chiang Ning, did not investigate the situation and decided quite arbitrarily that anyone who was attempting to slow down the attainment of new records must be politically backward. He removed Ch'ang from his position as branch union chairman and treated with hostility anyone who spoke on Ch'ang's behalf. The immediate result of this was that workers became alienated from the Party and lost faith in the idea of democratisation and putting forward rationalisation proposals, for even Ch'ang, a graduate of a workers' political university, could not get his voice heard. Ch'ang was not, however, to let the matter rest there. He wrote a letter of complaint to the North East General Labour Union, who forwarded it to the Organisation Bureau of the North East Bureau of the Party Central Committee. The Organisation Bureau sent down an investigation team (*tiao-ch'a-tsu*) consisting of two representatives of the Organisation Bureau, two representatives of the North East General Labour Union, one representative of the North East Coal Miners Union and one representative of the newspaper *Lao-tung Jih-pao* (*Labour Daily*). This team, under the leadership of the Penki Municipal Party Committee, conducted an investigation which lasted one week; after that the team instructed the Penki Party Committee how to deal with the matter and handed over the results of the investigation to the press.

The press comments were particularly interesting. Most blame was heaped, not on the industrial kulak Hsia Chung-yü who was felt to be a suitable candidate for remoulding, but upon the Party secretary Chiang Ning, who had apparently not only dissolved the labour union without investigating the matter, but had attempted to justify his action when the affair escalated by digging up circumstantial evidence that Ch'ang had been engaged in sabotaging the Party's underground military work during the war (again without investigating the true facts). Chiang's bureaucratic action in dissolving the labour union was considered by the North East Party newspaper *Tung Pei Jih-pao* to be a reflection of Party work in general in the Coal Sorting Department where 14 out of 17 Party members were unskilled and were in no position to decide whether the suggestion put forward by Ch'ang had been good or bad.

The above case has been recounted at length because it illustrates quite clearly the point that where the former 'feudal remnants' (gang-bosses etc.) had been removed and where considerable power resided at middle levels of management, the failure of the Party organisation to keep its grip on the actions of lower level cadres resulted in actions reminiscent of former gang-boss days. What is particularly worthy of note is that the official attitude seemed more concerned with the technical competence of lower level Party members than the high-handed actions of a new industrial kulak, and most blame was heaped on Chiang Ning, who had responded in time-honoured way to the possibility that he himself would be accused, by searching for historical evidence that his critic had always been politically questionable.

The rectification movement of 1950

As a result of dissatisfaction with the bureaucratism of Party and union cadres, their complacency, their failure to eradicate completely the gang-boss system and the dilution of Party spirit consequent upon the rapid expansion of the Party, a rectification movement got under way after the Third Plenum of the Seventh Central Committee in June 1950.[135] Launched by Mao, the movement focussed on the field of financial and economic administration and defined its targets as 'bureaucratism' and 'commandism' (much the same thing in this context)[136] and dragged on throughout the rest of 1950. As we shall see in the next chapter, it was not very effective and, in the case of the labour unions, led to quite the opposite situation to what was intended. The failure of the movement from above led to a complete reassessment of the conservative policy followed hitherto and the adoption of a new and far more radical policy in 1951.

3. From radicalism to stability (1951-53)

'Economism' in the labour unions

The process of union rectification in the second half of 1950 proceeded under the leadership of Party committees at the same level. In criticising 'bureaucratism' which applied equally to the Party, the rectification movement sparked off a debate within the labour unions on the precise difference in function between Party, management and unions within the enterprise. Launching the discussion at the end of July 1950, Teng Tzu-hui, Vice Chairman of the Central South Finance and Economics Committee, castigated labour unions for being alienated from the masses which he felt was due directly to the fact that they had confused their functions with management. In that work-posts (*kang-wei*) and work tasks were different, there was surely some difference in 'concrete standpoint' (*li-ch'ang*) even though their 'basic standpoint' was the same. It was the job of unions to see that the interests of the workers were not sacrificed to the goals of increasing production, though demands for increased benefits were to be based on greater productivity. Teng felt that the fact that so many union branches lined up with management meant that secret agents could hide behind left slogans and incite the workers to oppose both management and unions. There was a tendency for union cadres to talk high-sounding phrases about the glorious future and long-term benefits whilst ignoring the immediate demands of the workers. Some cadres had persuaded workers to take a cut in wages for the sake of long-term benefits and this only increased alienation. In Teng's view, savings could be generated by other means, such as economising on raw materials and fuel. Though the thrust of Teng's argument was to oppose the stress on long-term benefits at the expense of short-term ones, he did point out the dangers of the opposite policy, which was to become the main concern in the second half of 1951.[1]

In the debate which followed, constant reference was made to Teng's speech. What was particularly significant was his suggestion that there was a possibility that some differences in 'standpoint' could exist. In the terminology of the Chinese Communist Party, 'standpoint' was very important. Although people's work tasks and attitudes (*t'ai-tu*) might differ, their standpoint was a reflection of their class position, and any acknowledgement that there was a difference in standpoint between workers and management called into question the broad definition of the term 'working class', which comprised all those who hired out their labour for money. Teng Tzu-hui was extremely cautious in speaking of a difference between 'basic standpoint' (which was identical) and 'concrete standpoint' (which reflected differences in work position), though some of the participants in the subsequent debate were much less cautious. Teng's report was said to be instrumental in reforming union cadres in the private sector whose 'arses were sitting on the wrong side' (*p'i-ku tso-ts'o-le ti-fang*),[2] but in the public sector the issues were much more complex. With the fifteenth issue of the journal of the All China Federation of Labour, *Chung-kuo Kung-jen* (*Chinese Workers*) in April 1951, the whole question of standpoint was thrown open for discussion. *Chung-kuo Kung-jen* launched a correspondence column entitled 'Forum on the Question of the Labour Movement' (*Kung-yün Wen-t'i T'ao-lun-hui*), which was to discuss specifically the relationship of unions to management.[3] The first letter under this column was by a certain Li Nan-hsing, who declared that after Teng's report, debate started in his union branch. The majority of members agreed with Teng that the standpoint of unions and management was basically the same, though their different functions within the enterprise caused some concrete differences to appear. Some felt that management as the representatives of the state, served the interests of the four officially approved classes in the New Democratic Period, whereas the unions were concerned with the interests only of the working class. Others felt that since standpoints were basically the same, management should devote more attention to the welfare of the workers and their short-term interests.

Li's letter was highly theoretical and its function was to provoke a nation-wide debate in which concrete examples of differences in standpoint and identity of standpoint could be compared. In the index of the next issue of *Chung-kuo Kung-jen* (24 May 1951), however, under the heading of 'Forum on the Question of the Labour Movement' was just the cryptic remark 'temporarily suspended'.[4] This was the last issue of *Chung-kuo Kung-jen* to be published in 1951 and the magazine did not appear again until the height of the Three Anti Movement (January 1952) under a new title *Kung-jen* (Workers) and with a new format. A new editorial committee of *Chung-kuo Kung-jen* had been established in

December 1950 with Li Li-san as head[5] and doubtless the disappearance of *Chung-kuo Kung-jen* was connected with the charges of 'economism' made against Li Li-san in late 1951.[6] Until its suspension in May 1951 *Chung-kuo Kung-jen* reflected a policy which stressed the short term interests of the workers, and this inevitably had an effect upon the activities of union branches.

One way of linking welfare with increased productivity (in much the same way as current British productivity deals) was the conclusion of specific collective contracts between unions and management; in this way it was hoped that wage and welfare demands could be prevented from getting out of hand[7] but it would appear that this peaceful method of dealing with the problem of 'economism' was not very successful. In a survey of labour union work in the North East in July 1951, The North East Party newspaper *Tung Pei Jih-pao* observed that few union branches had made any serious effort to link welfare demands with increased productivity and there was rarely genuine co-operation between Party, management and labour unions.[8] Over half of all union branches were considered to be fairly skillful in organising production competitions and mobilising workers to fulfil plans, but were unable to co-ordinate welfare demands and productivity. Labour union branches were described as defective in organisation, unsystematic in work, as undemocratic and as having poor relations with Party and management. A number of cadres were merely passive and were concerned solely with articulating the demands of workers and complaining about the difficulties in their realisation. Finally, as we have seen, there still remained at this time a number of 'feudal elements' who had taken over union posts, though in the North East their numbers were small and were found mainly in the private sector. The following quote from the above article stands in direct contrast to the criticism that unions were excessively subordinate to management, made some twelve months before:

> Lacking a full grasp of the basic principle that the improvement of workers livelihood and welfare should be based on increased production, basic level unions easily waver, become isolated or counterpose production and welfare. Deviations occur easily with the result that they either alienate themselves from the masses or just follow the masses to stand against management . . . The unions have not done very well in organising the masses to unite with management in improving managerial work.[9]

By mid 1951 a number of cadres had switched from supporting to opposing management. The crisis of 1951 was not, as Harper suggests, mainly confined to the All China Federation of Labour centre,[10] as the above article makes clear, though there were several factors which made the problem of 'economism' less serious at the lower levels than it might have been. Firstly, as we have seen, vertical links within the All China Federation of Labour structure were comparatively weak,[11] which meant that the 'economist' line of the Federation could not be transmitted down the union hierarchies very effectively, especially after the suspension of *Chung-kuo Kung-jen* (the line of the All China Federation of Labour newspaper, *Kung-jen Jih-pao*, did not seem so markedly 'economist'). Secondly, the problem of rapid transfer of cadres was still important, as is shown by the following figures for length of experience in labour union work of cadres in 330 basic level union organisations in Shenyang:[12]

6 months experience	102 cadres
over 1 year	81 "
1½ years	55 "
Over 2 years	4 "

The fact that only four cadres had remained in union work within the enterprises since mid 1949 suggests one of two things. Either former union cadres had been promoted to higher level union posts which, according to the literature of the time, cut them off from contact with the lower levels, or they had been promoted to Party and management posts, which was not likely to lead to unions taking a constant stand against Party and management.

It is completely impossible to determine to what extent the rectification movement of labour unions that took place in the second half of 1951 was due to 'economism', 'bureaucratism', or the persistence of 'feudal elements'. The movement was extremely thorough. In Shanghai, for example, during the months of August and September 1951, 530 branches out of a possible 1,199 branches with over 100 members re-elected their branch union committee in entirety.[13] The problem of bureaucratism cannot be documented adequately because it was not until early 1953 that the full dimensions of the crisis were published.[14] Key documents such as Li Fu-ch'un's report to the Party fraction (*Tang-tsu*) in the All China Federation of Labour in December 1951, entitled 'Divergent Opinions on the Question of Labour Union Work', which attacked the Federation leadership for advocating labour union operational autonomy, have not been published. The official (1953) comment on the proceedings of late 1951 was that the majority of cadres had not followed the erroneous 'economist' line in the labour unions[15] but it should be remembered that the official comment was published at a time of stability after the mammoth Three Anti Movement of 1951–2 when many union cadres were found to be 'impure'.

In many ways the labour union crisis of 1951 was similar to the Soviet Union crisis of 1920–1,[16] and there were similarities between Tomsky and Li Li-san. Both the Chinese 'economists' and the Soviet 'workers opposition' saw the role of the unions in some way independent from the Party and in both cases the battle was fought out at higher levels within the Party. The differences are, however, more striking. In the Soviet case, the workers opposition often entered into dispute with peasant organisations, which was not the case in China. The Soviet crisis took place in a country exhausted by years of civil war when morale was low, whereas in China the civil war was well over and morale was soaring. In the Soviet Union the Workers Opposition advocated the transfer of control over industry to the unions. There is no evidence, however, that such a programme was put forward in China in 1951, nor were there any demands in China for the removal of intellectuals within the Party in 1951. In the Soviet Union the whole debate was aired publically in the press, whereas in China the principal journal carrying accounts of the debate was suspended. In the Soviet Union the crisis took place before the stress on Party discipline following the Kronstadt mutiny, and the stress on Party discipline was partly a result of that crisis. In China the stress on tight Party discipline not only preceded the crisis, but the anti-bureaucratic theme of the 1950 rectification campaign actually contributed to the tendency for the unions to seek autonomy. In China the crisis took place in an atmosphere of growing centralism of economic administration (even though the Three Anti Movement was to strengthen horizontal linkages for a time). In the Soviet Union, the crisis originated from an opposition to economic centralisation, but took place just before the widespread decentralisation of the New Economic Policy.

The acceleration of Democratic Reform

The labour union crisis of 1951 coincided with renewed attempts to carry through the process of 'Democratic Reform' and once and for all get rid of gang-boss and secret-society networks. It was quite clear that the policy of gradual reform was proceeding very slowly and the process of change from above was not very effective in dealing with Party and union branches that had been taken over by former gang-bosses. Finally, in May 1951, the Party decided that a policy of mass mobilisation was the only answer and it had great experience of such mobilisation in the rural sector. The Democratic Reform Movement of 1951 was described as a 'supplementary lesson' (*pu-k'o*) in that since liberation a certain amount of reform had been effected and the function of the 1951 movement was to make up for the deficiencies of these earlier attempts. Reform had been most thorough in the North East and least thorough in the Central South which bore the brunt of the 1951 movement.[17] In this latter area, former gang-bosses had found their way into the Party, the Youth League and the labour unions from which position they engineered strikes and go-slow resistance.[18] Some had achieved prominent positions in management[19] and others had even been elected model workers.[20] They were accused of having dealings with secret agents, of conducting sabotage and of taking their customary 'cut' of wages due to workers.[21] Although most accounts dealt with the activities of gang-bosses in transportation, on the docks, in the construction industry and in the mines, their activities were not confined to these areas, where for reasons of organisational diffuseness, control was particularly difficult, but were also found in other industries such as textiles.[22]

Although the main targets of the movement were the gang-bosses, there were others. The 1951 movement was to follow directly on the 'high tide' of the Campaign to Suppress Counter-revolutionaries and was to finish the work of that earlier movement.[23] The main target of the suppression movement had been secret agents (*t'e-wu fen-tzu*) who worked for such organisations as the Kuomintang Military Secret Service (*Chün-t'ung*) or the Nationalist Youth Corps (*San Min T'uan*).[24] Numerous accounts of their sabotage of industrial plant had appeared in the press since liberation;[25] now a mass movement was to disclose those who had escaped the net. Another target of the Democratic Reform Movement was the secret societies through which many of the gang-bosses had operated. A number of these societies were said to be still in operation, such as the *I Kuan Tao*, the *Chiu Kung Tao*, the *Kan Chu Erh Hua Tao*, the Green Gang (*Ch'ing-pang*) and the Red Gang (*Hung-pang*).[26] In addition to the large secret societies were the secret or semi-secret mutual-help organisations (*pang-hui*) which were sometimes little better than protection rackets.[27] Such organisations exercised influence not so much over the formal organisational network of factories (except where gang-bosses with secret society connections held formal managerial positions) but over the *informal* network.

It took a long time to persuade the Party that there was a need for a mass movement to implement the policy of Democratic Reform. Even in 1951 various non-radical alternative policies were put forward for consideration. One school of thought felt that the problem of flushing out feudal remnants and counter-revolutionary elements could best be undertaken gradually and indirectly by means of production competitions.[28] Presumably it was felt that once these elements took part in emulation contests they would either come to realise that they gained more prestige from this than their former activities or, if they failed to respond to such contests, would reveal themselves as indolent parasites, and be easily dealt with. This view was held to be wrong. Some 'depraved elements' had indeed become model workers but their activities had not changed. A *Ch'ang-chiang Jih-pao* editorial stated emphatically that not only were production competitions not useful for dealing with feudal remnants but that the Democratic Reform Movement was the *sine qua non* for holding production competitions in the future.[29]

Another school of thought felt that the Democratic Reform work could best be carried out through the introduction of labour insurance. Only people who could claim to be 'working class' were eligible (this included white collar workers and was not linked to family origin). People who derived a large part of their income from sources other than their own labour were not classified as working class and the sources of their income were subject to investigation. In this way it was hoped that undercover gang-bosses would be disclosed. During the process of democratic reform, however, false returns were submitted, for every concealed gang-boss could claim that his income derived from an official salary. *Ch'ang-chiang Jih-pao* declared that the registration of people for labour insurance could only be really effective *after* the Democratic Reform Movement had been concluded.[30]

A third school of thought saw no reason why the techniques of the Campaign for the Suppression of Counter-revolutionaries (which did not involve very much mass mobilisation) should not be continued. The official reply was that the fervour engendered by the suppression campaign would be useful in the subsequent mobilisation of the masses. The proper progress of any movement should be from the outside inwards and from surface to the depths, but in proceeding inwards and penetrating the depths, mobilisation was essential.[31]

Action was to be swift. After the Campaign for the Suppression of Counter-revolutionaries, it was felt that there was a need to strike whilst the iron was hot. In the period before May 1951, leading personnel considered that feudal forces within the factories had shown some sign that they were afraid and that their ranks were disintegrating. Now the workers' political consciousness had reached a level sufficiently high for them to be mobilised and leadership within factories had by now a fairly good idea as to whom the targets were to be.[32] Such was the mood in May 1951. The iron, however, was not always hot and exponents of guerilla warfare should not have confused disintegration with strategic dispersal. Many of the masses took quite a long while to be mobilised and some of the leadership did not realise that by the end of the series of movements of which this was the first, they themselves would in fact be the targets.

The literature is vague about how exactly the movement was to be led. The factory management committee was usually too weak to lead it and since retained management were suspect, management committees containing a retained factory general manager were, at least in one region, explicitly forbidden to assume a leading role.[33] In some cases union committees assumed leadership but they were frequently found to be 'impure' and to have connections with feudal remnants.[34] In general the Party committee led the movement according to the formula 'leadership by Party committee, call from management and response by the labour unions'.[35]

The Party committee usually exercised this leadership role through a specially created body such as a 'Committee for Studying Current Affairs'[36] or more probably a Democratic Reform Committee which consisted of Party and Youth League members, some management and labour union activists (preferably chosen from among the victims of a particular feudal remnant or group of feudal remnants). Such committees were ideally sponsored by the factory union committee or, if that body were corrupt, a higher level union committee.[37] The factory level Democratic Reform Committees were linked to municipal level Democratic Reform Committees which were united front bodies, led by the municipal Party committee but also containing representatives of the democratic parties, (non Party) democratic personages and worker (union) delegates.[38] Within the area under the jurisdiction of the South China Bureau of the Party Central Committee, Democratic Reform Committees (or their equivalent) at enterprise level were required to report to the municipal level Democratic Reform Committees once every two weeks and municipal level committees were required to report to the Provincial level Party committee once a month.[39]

The three stages of the 1951 Democratic Reform Movement

Three official stages were laid down for the movement – 'democratic struggle', 'democratic unity' and 'democratic construction'.[40] The first stage, 'democratic struggle', was launched at a number of mass meetings. At first, attacks were required to be of a very general nature (for example, against imperialism and the Chiang Kai-shek regime) and these general attacks would provide the starting point for 'initiation reports' (*ch'i-fa pao-kao*) which were usually made by cadres from outside the factory. The attack would then move nearer to the day to day concerns of the workers whose participation in the earlier meetings would have given them greater confidence to accuse people with whom they were in daily contact. Groups of activists would be formed within the shops whose task was to relate the discussion at factory level to their own particular circumstances and then submit their conclusions back to meetings at factory level. Then the whole process would be repeated, the content of the denunciations getting a little more specific every time. The leadership (Democratic Reform Committee) would utilise the material so collected to make a number of 'key point denunciations' for their propaganda effect and then the movement would be thrown wide open for denunciations to be carried on within small groups. After that, all the fragmented evidence would be collected together and 'speak bitterness' meetings (*k'ung-su-hui*) held.[41] At these meetings, the land reform experience was explicitly drawn upon.[42] Both land reform and the Democratic Reform Movement were aimed at 'feudal elements' rather than capitalists but in the latter, there was an element of caution far greater than in the case of land reform, even though 1951 was a relatively quiet period in the rural sector. Though I have seen accounts of gang-bosses being dragged through the streets,[43] I have seen no suggestion of any summary executions and the regulations governing punishment seem to have been adhered to. These regulations stipulated that the factory could only determine the nature of punishment if it fell within the category of demotion, reduction of salary, transfer of work, public surveillance or suspension of labour union membership. More serious cases were to be submitted to the Peoples Courts.[44]

In both movements, mass reaction tended to be similar. Workers were reluctant to denounce the accused through fear of retaliation[45] and the leadership was frequently accused of giving insufficient support to the accusers.[46] Once the process of accusation was under way, however, a psychological climate was created where accused people wished to put a speedy end to the agony and readily confessed.[47] Attempts were made to narrow down the number of targets and every effort made to avoid the persecution of technical personnel unless they were themselves active counter-revolutionaries or had links with secret societies.[48]

Instructions on how to conduct this 'struggle' stage of the movement stressed that the first battle must be fought with caution since it was vital to win it.[49] This caution was, however, not to be excessive and, after the first battle, the leadership of the movement was not to be fettered by demands to go slow for fear of harming production.[50] The press was eager to note examples where production actually went up in the course of the movement,[51] though in some cases up to 20% of the working hours for a whole month had been taken up by the movement and the effect on production must have been considerable.[52]

Progress was slow. Reporting to the Chengchow Party committee on an investigation into the progress of the movement in Honan in July 1951, the municipal Party secretary, Chang Hsi, noted that of the twenty-six publically-run enterprises in Honan, fifteen had been taken over from the bureaucratic capitalists upon liberation and eleven had been set up since. In both of these categories former gang-bosses could be found and some of them had usurped leading positions. Factories where any appreciable success had been recorded only constituted 10–20% of the total. Over half of the enterprises had carried out the initial mobilisation but impure elements remained in leading positions. The remainder (20–30%) had not responded at all to cadres who had been sent down to make 'initiation reports' and labour unions and other organisations were firmly in the hands of 'reactionary elements'.[53] The above type of analysis was the set form for summing up the progress of any movement in its initial stages[54] and was employed right down to the Cultural Revolution with much the same kind of percentage breakdown. This is not to say the figures were necessarily inaccurate, only that when initial reports of a movement's progress are published it tends to be at a point which shows a similar statistical breakdown. The crucial statistic here is that the report was delivered 2½ months after the commencement of the movement.

The struggle stage of the movement was in some cases to last right down to December 1951, by which time the Three Anti Movement was in full swing. It certainly set the stage for that movement. A whole series of problems were uncovered such as weak labour unions, bureaucratism in the Party branches and tension between white- and blue-collar workers. Directives instructed those carrying out the movement not to cover these up[55] for they were to be the basis upon which the subsequent movements would be built.

The second official stage of the movement was that of 'democratic unity'. Following the dismissal of the major targets, minor offenders, such as workers who had previously been forced to join 'reactionary parties', the Kuomintang military and police forces, the nationalist Youth Corps or various secret societies, were to confess their former activities and submit to criticism. In this stage, 'struggle' was to be avoided as the aim was to correct misunderstandings between white and blue collar workers, between labour union cadres and workers and between groups of workers in different departments and localities.[56]

It is very difficult to assess just how successful this stage of the movement was. Summing up progress in the movement in September 1951, Liu Tzu-chiu, who held a number of very important posts in the All China Federation of Labour, reported that many workers had come forward to confess their past errors and, in some factories, more than half the total number of workers had corrected the false information they had given when registering for labour insurance. He noted that the attitude of workers towards the Party and labour unions had changed. Union cadres were no longer eager to give up union work; it was no longer necessary to hold film shows in order to attract union members to a branch meeting and when Party and union cadres were sent down from higher levels, they were no longer treated with indifference by the workers.[57] All this may well have been true, but there were reasons other than Democratic Reform that made workers more interested in the activities of labour unions. This was the period in which labour unions were accused of 'economism' (where workers were mobilised to seek their own material benefit at the expense of wider goals). Would it be too cynical to suggest that this was at least a contributory factor to their new prestige?

September 1951 saw the beginning of the Three Anti Movement which was to reveal considerable bureaucratism (*kuan-liao-chu-i*) within industrial enterprises. Clearly the democratic reform movement had not gone far enough in closing the gap between workers and management. In view of this, one is tempted to be somewhat sceptical about Liu Tzu-chiu's optimistic report.

The third officially prescribed stage was that of 'democratic construction'. During this stage, systems of responsibility and production control were to be established, internal labour agreements signed, labour insurance re-registration carried out and a system instituted whereby there was provision for the regular re-election of labour union committees.[58] The extremely radical campaign against bureaucratism that took place at the end of 1951 meant that this stage was postponed until the second half of 1952 after the Three and Five Anti Movements had been concluded.

The Japanese parallel

The increased radicalism after May 1951 was probably due to many causes other than extreme exasperation with the slowness of relatively peaceful methods. Foremost amongst these other causes must surely have been the outbreak of the Korean War and the threat of imminent invasion posed by General MacArthur. National security questions became very important and the Movement for the Suppression of Counter-revolutionaries was in large measure designed to eliminate internal subversion during this critical period. The elimination of the gang-boss system, therefore, proceeded with a far greater sense of urgency than did the parallel elimination of the gang-boss system in Japan.

Prior to the radicalisation of 1951, Chinese official policy towards the elimination of the gang-boss system was not all that different from the policy of the occupation authorities in Japan. In that country, measures were taken to secure the legal prohibition of the gang-boss system but probably the most important measures taken towards that end consisted of institutional changes which directly or indirectly affected the motivations of boss-controlled workers. The provision of social security, the establishment of public employment centres in the major cities, the extension of the services of public welfare agencies and the provision of unemployment insurance surely did much to undermine a system already on the wane.[59] It has been pointed out that, in pursuing these policies, the American authorities, who displayed a characteristic lack of appreciation of non-American patterns of work motivation, were probably unaware of the effect of such actions on the gang-boss system.[60] In China, on the other hand, the Party was conscious of and devoted a lot of propaganda effort towards the effect of welfare policies upon social and political structure. Nevertheless the effect would probably have been the same had it not been for China's decision to speed up the process of reform, for both socialist and modern capitalist social relations depend upon the elimination of 'feudal' patterns of dependence. This is not to say that the radical measures adopted in China were not justified; for in addition to the security problem mentioned above, the existence of gang-boss networks hindered the establishment of a planning apparatus, served as a corrupting influence upon a Communist Party which had always striven to free itself of such influences, encouraged the 'get along' mentality and fostered a spirit of particularism which endangered policies of national integration.

The reforms of 1950 in Japan did not completely destroy the gang-boss system. Neither did the 1951 reforms in China, but it would seem that the process of destruction in the latter country was more thorough. I have seen no reference to the operation of gang-bosses in China after 1953.

The Three Anti Movement

The Movement to create New Records, which was launched in the autumn of 1949 grew into a movement to Increase Production and Practise Economy, which was formally launched at the end of August 1951,[61] also in the North East. This movement absorbed a drive for donations to help the Korean War effort which had been going on throughout 1951 and assumed a macro-political importance. The major aim was to eliminate waste, which was seen to derive from political as well as economic causes. It merged therefore with the three major political movements of 1950–1, the Democratic Reform Movement, the Party Rectification Movement and the Union Rectification Movement to form a Three Anti Movement, which took its name from its three major targets graft, waste and bureaucratism.

At first an attempt was made to examine the political factors that had led to waste. One of these was the rural viewpoint which continued to consider large-scale industry in much the same way as small-scale agricultural production. The cavalier attitude towards planning on the part of cadres of a rural orientation was likened to that of peasants who believed they could move seedlings at will from one place to another.[62] An attempt was made to involve the whole Party and all administration in a discussion of waste, the rural mentality and the economic consequences of bureaucratism.[63] The discussion then moved to a stage of great generality in which all the post-liberation targets for reform, such as the tendency to relax after victory, to feather one's own nest and tardiness in implementing democratic reform, were put forward. During this stage, principal suspect targets of the movement were entrusted with the task of leading it so that their own lack of zeal could provide an indicator of backward thought.[64] Once criticism started it moved closer and closer to the daily concerns of the workers and extended beyond the Party. In the course of this process the large number of activists who had been involved in disclosing cases of waste, graft and bureaucratism were taken into the Party.[65]

Formal leadership in the movement was usually vested in Increase Production and Practise Economy Committees (*Tseng-ch'an Chieh-yüeh Wei-yüan-hui*) at municipal level,[66] organised according to the United Front principle,[67] in much the same way as the Democratic Reform Committees discussed earlier. In practice, however, the Party organisation assumed leadership in the movement and acted through these bodies.[68] As far as industrial enterprises were concerned, leadership in the movement came from the local Party committee and this helped to counter the excessive growth of vertical chains of command, which had been condemned by Kao Kang in June 1951.[69] Within higher level vertically organised structures, Retrenchment and Economy Committees (*Ching-chien Chieh-yüeh Wei-yüan-hui*) were set up to flush out people guilty of bureaucratism at higher levels of economic administration.[70] Sometimes bodies of the same name were formed within industrial enterprises[71] though they were subject primarily to local Party control through the enterprise Party Committee.[72]

The initial stage of the movement was one of mobilising the workers within the enterprise. Teams, consisting of the factory general manager, labour union chairman and Youth League chairman, would go down into the workshops to propagate the ideas of increasing production and practising economy, and to help them formulate Increase Production and Practise Economy Plans.[73] Once cases of waste, graft and bureaucratism were discovered, enterprise Party committees would mete out penalties provided that the cases were not too serious. Serious cases were to be submitted to the local Party committee, or sometimes to Party committees in higher level economic organs (especially when the theft of economic secrets was involved).[74] In the initial stage, which lasted down until the end of 1951, the focus was on serious crimes, and statistics that were released dealt with the cases which had been handled by the courts. In the East China region, for example, higher level courts and organs of the Procuratorate (*Chien-ch'a chi-kuan*) had dealt with one hundred and seventy nine cases of graft by mid-December 1951, involving some ¥29 million and, according to the East China Peoples Control Commission (*Hua Tung Jen-min Chien-ch'a wei-yüan-hui*), the amount of money involved in cases of graft and loss of state property in the region from September 1950 to November 1951 was some ¥124,000 million. 650 people had been convicted by courts in the region, of whom 470 were employed in government departments or financial and economic enterprises. Of these 356 were retained personnel and 133 new cadres.[75] However impressive the above totals might sound, they were disproportionately low compared with the whole. According to the historian Ho Kan-chih, by the end of the movement, 4.5% of all state officials in China (including enterprise management and Party cadres) had received some form of punishment.[76]

In January 1952, the movement was accelerated and the range of targets widened. At that time Kao Kang observed that the Party had been corroded by bourgeois ideology and influence *in an increasing manner* during the recent past, and retained personnel (some of them by now Party members) were said to be attempting to turn the new state enterprises into private enterprises. Former capitalists now employed in the state sector were apparently using economic information to help their relatives and colleagues in the private sector and government officials were said to be taking bribes to treat former capitalists leniently. Kao Kang was particularly concerned about an increasing tendency to rehabilitate former managers, and prophesied that, unless an excessive reliance upon the bourgeoisie was corrected, the end of the Party was in sight. Kao criticised enterprise Party branches for not extending the movement down beyond a few obvious cases of waste and criticised those leading cadres who had allowed a considerable backlog of cases to pile up. It would seem that, by this time, the policy of placing targets of the movement in leading positions was beginning to reveal a situation where a movement designed to combat bureaucratism was being run itself with undue bureaucratism and Kao Kang was in a position to expose the guilty. Summoning leading cadres to a meeting under the North East Bureau of the Party on 10 January 1952, Kao demanded action on the backlog of cases within two days or immediately upon the return of such cadres to their units; otherwise they would be dismissed as guilty of bureaucratism.[77]

The Three Anti Movement saw a continuation of the Union Reform Movement begun earlier in the year. At the height of the Three Anti

Movement, on 7 January 1952, the All China Federation of Labour convened a conference of labour-union working personnel aimed at mobilising union cadres to participate in leading that movement. The conference concerned itself mainly with the persistence of bourgeois and petty-bourgeois ideology at higher levels in the union organisation and Li Li-san himself commented on the fact that higher level union officers rarely talked to labour union cadres at enterprise level. Li noted that the lack of working class thought among union cadres was due to bad leadership and called upon every labour union cadre to make a 'self-examination'.[78]

As we have seen, one manifestation of the result of the '*yamen* mentality'[79] at higher levels of union organisation was that lower level union cadres considered themselves to be 'fourth class' and one of the aims of the Three Anti Movement was to correct this over-concern for status and to 'give cadres a bath'.[80] Cadres were warned that unless this concern for status was ended, the nature of the unions would undergo a fundamental change.[81] This however was an old problem which had been noted by Liu Shao-ch'i in 1949,[82] and was probably due to the fact that the unions were training grounds for Party members and a 'school for management'.

Though the primary responsibility for leading the Three Anti Movement within an industrial enterprise lay with the Party committee, most leading personnel were involved in one way or another, often to the detriment of their production responsibilities. Many leading personnel were so busy investigating complaints that production declined.[83] The situation was made particularly serious by the fact that, as one might expect, graft was most prevalent in supply departments, and once personnel were flushed out of these departments there was no one to guarantee a regular supply of materials. A further factor which hindered production was a deliberate go-slow policy on the part of some management, who felt that their past was not unsullied.[84]

During the month of January 1952, the North East Bureau of the Central Committee reported that, out of a total of 49 planned product-targets in the Industrial Department's network, 29 had not been reached. In enterprises under the Light Industry Bureau, half had not completed their work for the month. None of the targets for principal products in the Textile Management Bureau had been reached. Other examples are given of the effect of the movement on production, such as a rise in the accident rate, failure to receive supplies, and a decline in the quality of products during the month of January 1952, the climax of the movement.[85] This fall in production, although only temporary, stands in contrast to the Democratic Reform Movement, in which it was claimed that production did not decline significantly. Failure to integrate successfully the political and economic movements meant that the Movement to Increase Production and Practise Economy continued long after the conclusion of the Three Anti Movement, which in 1952 changed into a Five Anti Movement[86] and moved from the public into the private sector.

Efforts were made in February 1952 to minimise the adverse effects of the movement by working out a concrete division of labour within enterprises. The factory general manager was, by that time, to concern himself solely with questions of production, and other management cadres were instructed to spend at least two-thirds of each eight hour day dealing with production problems. The remaining one third might be spent on the Three Anti Movement as well as part of their spare time. Immediate remedial measures were put forward to solve the problems of shortage of personnel in supply departments due to the removal of 'tigers' (principal culprits), and white and blue collar workers were instructed to work out ways of combining 'tiger bashing' (*ta-hu*) with emulation movements. The North East Bureau of the Party Central Committee demanded that enterprises guarantee not only to fulfil their production plan for March 1952, but also to make up for the decline in production suffered during the very active period of January and February.[87]

After March 1952, the steady rise in production in the state sector seems to have been resumed, and the whole focus of mobilisation within state run industrial enterprises switched to the Movement to Increase Production and Practise Economy, as the Three and Five Anti Movements were formally ended in various regions during June and July of that year.[88]

The movement to establish a responsibility system

We have seen that the Three Anti Movement arrested for a time the erosion of horizontal component in the dual-rule scheme of control. The movement gave a considerable amount of power to the enterprise Party branch, though no instances are on record, to my knowledge, of the Party taking over the functions of management, such as occurred in the period immediately following liberation.

Following the Three Anti Movement, the focus changed in a way reminiscent of 1949 from mass mobilisation to labour discipline, and the role of the Party changed from the mobiliser of the masses to an instrument whereby a sense of discipline might be inculcated. The change in atmosphere went together with a stress on national planning. In 1951 a regional planning commission for the North East had been set up[89] and this was followed in August 1952 by the establishment of a State Statistical Bureau (*Kuo-chia t'ung-chi-chü*) and a State Planning Commission (*Kuo-chia Chi-hua Wei-yüan-hui*) in preparation for the First Five Year Plan which began in 1953. The priority given to the establishment of a planning network was reflected in the fact that, on its establishment in November 1952, the State Planning Commission was given status equal to the Government Affairs Council (the cabinet) which meant that its head Kao Kang, who had been transferred from the North East, enjoyed status in the formal government apparatus equal to the Premier Chou En-lai (though his status in the Party organisation remained lower).[90] It was only after the demise of Kao Kang and Jao Shu-shih[91] that the State Planning Commission was brought under the newly created State Council (*Kuo-wu-yüan*) (1954) and made subordinate to the Premier. The State Planning Commission stood at the apex of a group of ministries each responsible for a sector of industry, each subdivided into administrative bureaux and modelled on the former organisation of the North East Industrial network described above. 'Rational' organisation and vertical chains of command were the order of the day.

The new stress on individual responsibility and 'one-man management' of early 1953, which will be discussed in Chapter 6, was a manifestation of this strengthening of the vertical component in dual-rule and was reinforced by the extension of external control organs down into the enterprises.[92] Now the Party organisation was no longer to be the organisation exclusively concerned with checking up on the bureaucratic actions of management. Commenting on the problem of bureaucratism in January 1953, An Tzu-wen noted that many of the errors and shortcomings repudiated during the Three Anti Movement had been '*revived or had assumed proportions even more serious than hitherto*'.[93] The prescribed solution this time was not another mass movement but an attempt to strengthen external control agencies (Peoples Control Commissions etc.)[94] which together with the stress on one man management, tended to reduce the role of the Party to one of political education.

In July 1954, the organ of the Party Central Committee *Jen-min Jih-*

pao (People's Daily) noted that:

In the past few years, each branch of industry was busy with Democratic Reforms and the restoration of production. Consequently, however correctly labour may have been organised within the enterprises, not a lot of experience was accumulated. It was impossible therefore to establish a comprehensive system for consolidating labour discipline. Today the situation must be changed. Labour discipline must be established *by means of legal forms.*[95]

The whole tradition of the Communist Party was one where discipline was fostered by education and group pressure, not by the force of law, and there was consequently a reaction to the above demand. Some cadres felt that the imposition of legal regulations encouraged passivity and was the 'working style of warlords'.[96] The official attitude was that the experience of the past few years had shown that the absence of regulations led to slackness and allowed individual bad elements to worm their way into People's organisations.

We must be clear that what threatens the normal progress of production and affects the labour activism of the masses is not that discipline is too strict but that it is too slack.[97]

The new stress on discipline of 1953 took the form of a movement very different from the Three Anti Movement. The Movement to Establish a Responsibility System of 1953 did not involve much mass mobilisation. Various articles noted that there was a tendency for workers not to denounce leading cadres out of fear of retribution and workers tended to show a lack of confidence in the effectiveness of discussions convened by the Party organisation. Some workers felt that the proper procedure for discussion should be 'officials to officials and people to people' (*kuan hsiang kuan, min hsiang min*),[98] which was a complete negation of the spirit of late 1951 and early 1952. What was even more serious were disclosures that the reluctance of workers to get involved in the movement sometimes resulted in the preservation of the gang-boss system as late as 1953.

On the building site of the Harbin Industrial University, for example, an investigation into the reason why workers were not getting their wages when there were work stoppages, started as an investigation into the phenomenon of a lack of responsibility for wage payment, and finished up as an anti-gang-boss struggle when it was found that the head of the reinforced steel girder team was a former gang-boss who was pocketing a cut of the wages in time honoured tradition.[99] The new stress on discipline had prevented the workers from denouncing their superior, though one might ask why he had not been denounced in the Democratic Reform and Three Anti Movements.

The initiative in the above anti-gang-boss struggle seems to have come from management rather than Party, which was characteristic of the Movement to Establish a Responsibility System. The movement commenced at the Harbin work site when management called a meeting of all technical personnel, at which a high-level Party cadre from outside the organisation spoke. This cadre reported on the differences between management in public and private concerns and pointed out that the aim of the Responsibility System Movement was 'not to rectify people but to improve work'.[100] After that the workers were encouraged to reveal examples of a lack of responsibility, and technical personnel were educated on the need for such a system.

In the movement which followed all sorts of examples of graft were revealed, where people had taken advantage of a system where no one had been specifically responsible for a particular work task. These ranged from deliberately falsifying accounts to using three inch instead of four inch nails.[101] The volume of complaints in the 1953 movement, however, was much smaller than in the Three Anti Movement of 1951–2 and, if in fact the shortcomings repudiated in the Three Anti Movement 'had been revived or had assumed proportions even more serious than hitherto', one can only assume that a movement that sought to improve work rather than rectify people was not the most appropriate one in the circumstances.

'Rectification', as used here, was a process whereby heterdox views were criticised and the socialist goal-values articulated by the Communist Party internalised. Such goal values were both long term and short term, political and economic, instrumental and intrinsic. They ran the whole gamut from increasing production and practising economy to the creation of a 'socialist man'. Since 1942, 'rectification' had been a major concern of the Party. Now in the early period of the First Five Year Plan, the keynote of political action was 'not to rectify people' (a major object of the Three Anti Movement) 'but to improve work'. The goals to be inculcated were thus restricted to the short-term, the economic and the instrumental. Those who still wished to promote the goal values of 1942 were to have a lean time.

Conclusion

As has been noted the gradualist policy described in Chapter 2 was remarkably similar to the original policy of Lenin after the Bolshevik Revolution, described in Chapter 1, when 'the state power made an attempt to pass to the new social relationships, while adapting itself to the conditions then prevailing as much as possible, as gradually as possible and breaking with as little of the old as possible'. As in revolutionary Russia, there was a division of opinion concerning the pace and nature of change. In Russia it was the advance of the White Armies in mid 1918 that led to a radicalisation in policy. In China the outbreak of the Korean War and the advance of latter day equivalents of the White Armies right up to the Chinese border bore some resemblance to the events of 1918 but there were also very strong domestic reasons for the adoption of a more radical policy. In China the persistence of the gang-boss system and the deterioration of 'Party spirit' called for a programme of mass mobilisation in which the Chinese Communist Party had great experience. Secondly, there was some impatience amongst admirers of the Stalinist system to create the conditions necessary for the implementation of a Soviet type planning system for which a blueprint existed in the North East with Kao Kang as its most notable exponent. In revolutionary Russia there had been, of course, no blueprint and the Stalinist system only emerged after many years of trial and error.

Nothing like the War Communism period existed in China and decisions were taken early on to emulate the Stalinist model of the Soviet Union. In the Soviet Union inflation was used as a weapon to 'attack the bourgeoisie in its rear'. In China the pre-liberation inflation had already achieved that object and the new government strove to bring inflation under control. In the War Communism period in Russia there was talk of the abolition of money, whereas in China the semi-monetary economy of the liberated areas was changed into a fully monetary one soon after liberation. Nevertheless both countries saw the growth of a syndicalist tendency; in Russia this was the precursor of a policy of decentralisation whereas in China it was to be the precursor for an attempt to create the centralised Stalinist model of economic administration. Both the Soviet New Economic Policy and the Chinese adoption of the Soviet model was to be short lived, for both in very different ways, seemed eventually to be harmful to the interests of socialism as defined on the one hand by Stalin and on the other by Mao.

Part III

Administrative rationality

4. Planning and accounting

Rationality

Although there was some confusion in various parts of China as to exactly which Soviet model was to be emulated, there seemed little doubt in North East China that the operational model was to be that of the Soviet Union in the late 1940s. We have seen that the network of the North East Industrial Department was a direct copy of similar Soviet network and the term 'enterprise' was defined in an administrative sense according to that network. To facilitate the implementation of Soviet organisational forms and industrial practices, a considerable amount of literature was translated from Russian and a number of articles appeared describing the 'rationality' of such forms and practices. The process of Democratic Reform, which has been described, was explicitly designed to pave the way for 'rational' administration. One is bound therefore to ask what was meant by 'rationality'.

The loosest definition of rationality is the 'selection of the appropriate means to achieve some end'.[1] For such a definition to have any operational significance, one must establish a definite hierarchy of ends and be in a position to predict the probable outcome of the means used to attain them. Since the determination of ends must be in accordance with a hierarchy of values, a conception of rationality is only operational when a convention as to desired values is established. It is impossible therefore to divorce rationality from ideology.

Within every society there is always a maze of contradictions between hierarchies of social and economic values, between human and technological values, between community and organisational values, etc.[2] Social scientists of a liberal persuasion who are concerned with assessing the 'rationality' of a particular action tend to abstract a single hierarchy of values and ends against which to measure that action, in the hope that other social scientists might abstract a different hierarchy of values and ends to measure the same action. The conclusion so produced is that the action in question is rational in terms of A but not in terms of B. Social scientists of a totalist persuasion on the other hand seek to measure action against a total integrated developmental process where individual ends are not abstracted. An action is therefore rational or irrational only according to that process.

The first approach to rationality all too easily leads to a situation where the process of abstraction becomes unconscious and the partial nature of ends becomes 'given';[3] what was hitherto a useful heuristic device becomes a reductionist ideology whose practitioners find it difficult to engage in interdisciplinary comparison. The second approach to rationality can only be successful when sufficient time has elapsed for the integration of theory and practice to produce a total plan related to domestic needs. The second approach all too easily leads to a failure to achieve a totally integrated hierarchy of values and ends and the employment of imported models rather than carefully worked out developmental strategies. One might well argue that those economists who bring to the study of China a view of rationality defined only in terms of 'optimum resource allocation patterns' may be guilty of the former, whereas those latter-day Weberian sociologists who bring to China a view of development in terms of stable behavioural models[4] might be guilty of the latter. In North East China in 1949, the term 'rational' tended to be equated with a prescribed stable Soviet model in much the same way as some of the (I believe illegitimate) heirs to Weber's 'legal rationality' measured rationality against a prescribed set of pattern variables[5] that were rooted somewhere in a stable 'mid-Atlantic culture'.[6] We shall note in this chapter and the next that the Soviet models of organisation and incentive were not all introduced all at once but the Movement to Create New Records of 1949–50 contained all the necessary ingredients of those models and the success of that movement was attributed to 'reliance upon the co-operation of allies and friends' (the Soviet Union) rather than the 'rationalism' (*sic*) of some Chinese equivalent of Frederick Taylor.[7]

Genesis of the Movement to Create New Records

After the Democratisation of Management and Democratic Reform, the New Record Movement was the third of a trinity of movements carried out simultaneously within North East industry in 1949. The movement was to have a significance far wider than just beating pre-war records and my impression is that it was considered to be of far greater significance than the other movements. Li Fu-ch'un Vice Chairman of the North East People's Government, described its political significance as no less than 'the consolidation of the material foundation of the

People's Democratic Dictatorship' and its economic and administrative significance as no less than 'laying the foundation for enterprisation by raising the level of output, improving quality, determining norms, practising 'economic accounting' and improving systems of production management'.[8]

The movement originated in the joint Sino-Soviet enterprises in Lushun and Talien where Soviet experts were at hand long before the conclusion of the Sino-Soviet Treaty. In the North East as a whole, the movement dates from June 1949 when the North East Industrial Department conducted an investigation into the work of factories in each of the administrative bureaux that had been set up some six months before. The investigation discovered that waste was very serious and this was attributed to the inexperience of management. Quite naturally the Industrial Department turned to the one region where management was not inexperienced (Lushun and Talien) for guidance as to how to overcome this problem. The answer given by the Soviet experts was that the 'economic accounting system' (*khozraschët*) should be implemented as soon as possible and, in July 1949, the Industrial Department decided that the economic accounting system would be introduced or strengthened in all factories under its jurisdiction. From July to September 1949 considerable discussion was held as to how such a system could be implemented and again Soviet advice was sought. The Soviet experience had shown that the implementation of the economic accounting system could only be effectively undertaken once an efficient system of norm determination had been worked out within enterprises and the best way to do this was to hold production competitions according to the Stakhanovite system of the USSR. Consequently in September 1949, the Movement to Create New Records began formally, with the primary aim of establishing norms through labour emulation competitions. Upon these norms a system of planning and accounting could be built.[9]

In October a number of directives were published by the North East Bureau of the Party Central Committee and the Industrial Department establishing the scope of the movement[10] and linking it with the policy of implementing the economic accounting system.[11] In addition each bureau chief, corporation director and factory general manager under the jurisdiction of the Industrial Department attended a mobilisation conference so that the movement could proceed in a uniform manner.[12]

As a result of the introduction of the New Record Movement, it was claimed that in the three months from October–December 1949, the labour productivity rate in enterprises under the jurisdiction of the North East Industrial department went up by 13% on the September rate. In the first five months of the movement (October–March 1950), over 50,000 workers in two thirds of the 170 principal factories in the Industrial Department's network were involved in creating new records either individually or collectively and this amounted to 19,940 items. Of these 116 factories, 36 had already arrived at a new set of norms by March 1950, and 16 had partially done so. In the North East as a whole, output of enterprises under the Industrial Department doubled in the second half of 1949[13] though this is also attributable to many other factors not the least the repairing of war damage.

In the Introduction to this book the Movement to Create New Records was broken down into three parts. In this chapter we shall consider the first of these parts – norm determination and the establishment of a planning and an accounting system, and carry the discussion through until 1953. We shall return to the other two in subsequent chapters.

Early norm determination

Norms were to be determined on the basis of new records and technical standards. At first there was a tendency to decide norms arbitrarily, upon the basis of abstract theory or according to international standards. International standards tended to be higher than Chinese standards at that time and this resulted in the setting of norms which were too high and which dampened the workers' ardour. For example, the Antung (now Tantung) Paper Works began to establish norms in August 1949 upon the basis of international standards and the current production of the factory. A monthly target of 12 tons of a particular type of paper was fixed for the whole factory but, by October, the highest monthly target reached was 9 tons. In November the factory general manager was forced to lower the target to 11 tons. In that month the Movement to Create New Records was initiated in the factory and this resulted in a record output of 12.632 tons. The target (an aggregate of lower-level output norms) was raised accordingly to 12 tons. In December an output of 15.92 tons was recorded which brought the average monthly output up to 12.67 tons and, in January, the target was raised to a point just above the average (13 tons).[14] This clearly demonstrates a policy which sought to keep targets (and lower-level norms) closely tied to average production over a period of time and to actual increases in production rather than purely technical or normative criteria.

Output norms were not the only kind of norm. Originally there were three others (quality, time and labour) which were collectively known as the *four fixed* (*ssu-ting*) but, as the movement was developed, ten norms were prescribed. First a quality norm was determined and, after that, nine other norms were determined in the following order: norm for utilisation of raw materials, labour norm, time norm, output norm, equipment norm, expenses norm, cost norm, capital construction norm and technical norm; the first eight of these were aid to form a system since the last two categories were to a greater extent independent variables.

After the workers had been mobilised to create new records, technical cadres went down into the shops to fix quality and technical standards against which to measure the above norms. On the basis of these standards and records which had already been achieved, discussion was organised at all levels.

Individual norms were fixed according to an individual worker's achievements. Once he had established a tentative record, workers engaged in the same job would discuss his achievements and if they felt that they could realistically achieve the same themselves, would propose the formal adoption of this record as a norm. If they felt they could not achieve the record, a different worker did the same job of work and a new discussion was started. The initial norm could only be set once there was no more disagreement.

Once initial norms were determined, they were submitted to the factory management committee for adoption and then to the appropriate administrative bureau or corporation for ratification. Once such ratification had been obtained, the norms could not be altered for a period of six months during which time new records would be set which would provide the basis for new norms for the second six month period. During this process or norm determination, factory general managers were warned not to concentrate solely on output and technical norms at the expense of others.[15]

The student of Soviet management will perhaps be surprised at the relatively low priority given to output norms, the degree of flexibility in norm determination and the degree of worker participation in their formulation. One should remember, however, that in 1949 the process of norm determination was carried on in an institutional atmosphere very different from that of the Soviet Union. Factory management committees were still operative and what is more important was that, although rudimentary regional plans for the North East had existed since 1947,[16] norms were worked out not in response to the requirements of a centralised planning structure but as precursors of the establishment of such a system. It was not until after the Movement to Create New Records had laid the basis of a planning system that the net flow of information switched from bottom to top to top to bottom.

The establishment of a planning network

As the Movement to Create New Records developed, concern was expressed by managers that the movement could become too 'democratic' in the sense that labour activism might lead to confusion and the shelving of responsibility in the drive to achieve new records.[17] What was feared was democracy in its participatory sense in much the same way as the policy of mass mobilisation was often feared in the democratisation movements.

In the first five months of the movement not a lot of attention was paid to labour discipline and the establishment of definite chains of command and information, for the movement was felt to be like water which in the end would flow along defined channels.[18] Presumably if one dug the channel too soon the water might dry up. By the end of February 1950, however, attempts were made to implement a system of responsibility and following an authorative decision of the North East Industrial Department,[19] a number of articles appeared in the press specifying what the establishment of such a system would entail.[20] The requirements of the Industrial Department revealed a very tight conception of control indeed.

The problem was that regional plans were not linked to a control network that would ensure their implementation. I do not know what operational planning documents looked like before the New Record Movement or whether anything more than just broad policy documents existed. By the beginning of 1950, however, the operational planning period for factories under the jurisdiction of the North East Industrial Department was set at ten days. By that time each administrative bureau had set up a planning department and the heads of these departments were required to hand down a ten day plan to each factory general manager in the first two days of each ten day period giving details of the day and night operation of equipment within each factory. On the basis of these ten day plans, each factory general manager was to hand down daily plans to the workshops giving concrete instructions for each worker and each piece of equipment.[21] The head of each bureau and corporation was required to report daily to the Industrial Department on how far the current plan had been fulfilled in enterprises under his jurisdiction, whether machines had been stopped and on the state of equipment, supply of materials and distribution of products. The Industrial Department was required to analyse the opinions and suggestions of the bureau chiefs and corporation directors and to make periodic summaries. To this end the department published a journal *Tung Pei Kung-yeh* which was the forerunner of the many ministerial journals that were to appear in the years that followed.

Every week, bureau chiefs and corporation directors were required to collect summaries from the heads of each sub department and each factory general manager and mine general manager within their network. These summaries were to be based upon the reports made by factory general managers to work conferences or production conferences within their own units; they were to deal with work over the past week showing how the resolutions of previous conferences had been implemented.[22]

The regulations governing the establishment of the planning system were accompanied by regulations governing the establishment of a responsibility system within the shops. We shall examine these in Chapter 6. In the meantime, one might note that these regulations were probably too ambitious. By 1953, there were revealed many examples of simulation and plan evasion which would make one suspect the effective implementation of the very tight measures of 1950.

Financial control

The above detailed regulations designed to establish tight physical control were felt to be particularly necessary in a situation of price and currency instability and where the supply situation fluctuated. As one might expect, they were accompanied by the establishment of a banking system which was given particularly wide powers.

The People's Bank of China, which was set up on 18 November 1948[23], was an extremely important control organ and has remained so throughout the past twenty-five years. It is the one organ of government that has remained highly centralised throughout the history of the Chinese People's Republic, even at times when other financial organs such as the Ministry of Finance, were decentralised.[24] The establishment of the People's Bank was followed by a series of regulations limiting the amount of money in circulation. Following the registration of assets, every enterprise was required by law to open a bank account and to deposit with the bank all cash over three days' normal expenditure (or in the case of enterprises in places where there was no branch of the bank, one month's normal expenditure).[25] The bank was expected to have a complete picture of the operations of every enterprise in the country and to practise strict financial control.[26] It was to ensure that the financial operations of enterprises were in accordance with the stipulations of higher levels plans, to make deductions for industrial and commercial tax, to control the amount of above-plan profit that might be retained by the enterprise for investment purposes and to control the amount authorised for retention as working capital or in the form of bonus funds, welfare funds, etc.[27] The bank was also empowered to make loans for purposes of capital construction, though, until 1953, these were channelled through central bureaux and ministries and only made directly to enterprises after that year.[28] In 1954 a People's Construction Bank was set up which took over much of this function.[29]

The scope and duration of plans

So long as inflation was rampant and prices had not been brought under control, the major focus of planning work centred on operational plans of short duration (10 days). Plans of longer duration had been in existence, however, since before the Movement to Create New Records. We have noted that the first annual construction and financial plan for the North East was put forward at the end of 1947 and in the years which followed, as the currency situation became more stable, attempts were made to link short term operational planning with the formulation of annual plans.

The aim was to create an integrated Soviet-type planning network and to this end the various planning bodies described in Chapter 3 were set up but in the area of planning, as in many other areas, the contradiction between policy and resources was a glaring one. So long as allocation problems restricted the proportion of the market supply of products controlled by the state, the scope of planning would be restricted. By 1952 only 28 commodities were distributed by the state in a 'unified' manner, rising to 96 in 1953, compared with over 1500 in the Soviet Union.[30] Planning was frustrated by wide cost disparities between sections of the same industry[31] and a continuing erratic relationship between planned and actual output due to supply difficulties. Annual targets continued to have a limited operational significance right through until the period of the First Five Year Plan and, in 1953, overall production targets were revised three times in one year. In the view of one economist who has written on this subject, Dwight Perkins, such a situation was inevitable in a situation of under-development where more sophisticated planning techniques were on the whole not very important.[32]

As a result of supply difficulties, annual plans often appeared quite late in the year. Even though general control figures might be set as early as August and September of the previous year, some seven to nine months might elapse before a definitive plan went into operation.[33] Such a situation led to the phenomenon of 'storming' which has always been a bugbear of Soviet management.[34] In situations where only the latter part of the year is covered by definitive targets, the pace tends to speed up towards the end of the year, with a deleterious effect on the quality of production and worker morale. Overtime becomes common and difficulties occur in adhering to wage targets. In China during the New Democratic period, this phenomenon seemed to be most marked in the construction industry[35] which is quite understandable in a period of rapid rehabilitation of industrial plant. Many articles appeared in industrial journals condemning tardiness in putting plans into operation[36] and regulations were imposed governing the amount of permitted overtime. In September 1950, for example, the North East Industrial Department limited overtime to two hours per day and 48 hours per month and demanded that unions check that this regulation was being adhered to.[37] It was, however, frequently violated. Sometimes workers' rest days were taken up by production duties[38] and workers were occasionally coerced into working extra shifts in connection with movements such as the Korean War donation drive.[39] Complaints about such practices continued throughout the period. The problems, however, could not be tackled effectively by dealing only with the symptoms (overtime, etc.) when the root cause was tardiness in planning due to supply difficulties exacerbated by continuing warfare and military blockade.

Planning and the participatory conception of democracy

It was not only irregular supplies and the rudimentary nature of planning that caused the late publication of annual and quarterly plans. Another important factor which caused delay was the requirement that workers be involved in the process of planning. The formulation of plans was ideally to proceed according to the formula of 'two down and two up'. The relevant ministry, industrial department or management bureau would issue control figures which were sent down to the enterprise. The enterprise would then work these figures into a draft plan which would be sent back to the higher level. After making necessary amendments, the higher level would send the plan down once again whereupon the enterprise would organise detailed discussion of its provisions and draw up concrete work plans for each of its subdivisions (staff departments, shops, sections, etc.). Finally, the resulting document would be sent back to the higher level for approval. This whole process might, in the case of an annual plan, take as long as eight months and involve a tremendous amount of discussion.[40]

In the early period following liberation, factory management committees upon which worker delegates sat, were required to discuss and approve plans submitted to them by the factory general manager. Where the committee system was effective, matters of importance would be discussed at factory level and matters of detail discussed at shop, section or team level. This detailed discussion proceeded according to subdivisions worked out by the standing committee of the factory management committee which met daily in what was known as a 'head knocking session' (*p'eng-t'ou-hui*).[41] The democratic discussion of the plan proceeded here according to both the representative principle and the participatory principle discussed earlier. We shall discuss at length the workings of factory management committees in Chapter 7. Suffice it to note here that by 1951 such management committees were all but defunct and their decline resulted in one of two possibilities. Either discussion would proceed only at shop, section or team level and become inordinately long or all the key decisions would be taken by management at factory level. This latter course gave rise to criticisms of bureaucratism.

In bridging the gap between workers and management in the discussion of plans, the role of the Party organisation was crucial. The Party organisation was required to ferret out all ideological obstacles in the way of plan fulfilment and to keep management informed about worker opinion. It was, on the one hand, to control any tendency towards bureaucratism on the part of management and, on the other, to educate the workers as to their role in completing plans.[42] In performing a liaison function between management and workers, the Party organisation was to steer a middle course between acting as the representative of the workers and as an agent of management which might invest administrative commands with moral force. The growing tendency towards that latter end of the spectrum has already been noted and will be discussed further in Chapter 7.

By 1953 the slogan 'the state plan is law' had been advanced and the educative role of plan discussion was given particular stress. The process of 'education' was, however, as time consuming as the process of consultation. The Anshan Iron and Steel Corporation, for example, submitted its 1953 draft labour plan to the Ministry of Heavy Industry (under whose jurisdiction it had passed following the abolition of the North East Industrial Department) at the end of 1952 and this was sent back to the corporation with the demand that the total number of employees be reduced by 10,000. An amended plan could only be sent back once the various departments in this huge industrial complex had been mobilised to conduct discussion and educated in the need to reduce the originally planned number of personnel. The procedure took a considerable amount of time and it was not until much later that the planned figure for personnel reduction was worked out at 10,288 with a corresponding planned rise in the labour-productivity rate. A summary of the planning process was not published until October, when the corporation reported that by the end of the year, the total number of employees would be 2,067 less than the revised plan approved by the ministry.[43] The mind boggles at what would have happened if the ministry had objected that the new planned figure had been too great a reduction.

The contradiction between the process whereby workers took part in the formulation of plans and the process whereby they were educated by higher levels on how to fulfil previously determined targets will be familiar to anyone who has examined the dynamics of the Chinese approach to participatory democracy known as 'the mass line'. The 'mass line' which took its final form during the Yenan rectification movement of 1942–3 demanded careful balancing of local initiative and centrally determined policy.[44] Its success in Yenan days was dependent upon a system whereby cadres were required alternately to go down to the 'basic level' to participate in ordinary manual work and then up to the centre to participate in a process of 'rectification' whereby they received the prescribed policy orientation. If they were too bureaucratic, then their integration with the masses would be reported as inadequate and they would be criticised for 'commandism'. If, on the other hand, they just drifted along with popular sentiment it would be their 'tailism' that would be criticised. As policy changed, then the dividing line between 'commandism' and 'tailism' shifted and this occasioned a new round of 'rectification'. When the mass line was successful according to the Yenan model, it was only where it was accompanied by the process of 'rectification' and where leadership was of the 'cadre' as opposed to the 'managerial' type according to the formulation of Franz Schurmann discussed earlier. As the Soviet model was implemented in China in the early 1950s the stress was on managerial leadership according to a technological conception of solidarity and, in such a situation, one might expect that the original mass-line concept would atrophy.

To evaluate how democratic the whole process was, one must be in a position to examine not only the discussion of amended plans during the second 'down' stage but also the discussion of the initial control figures sent down by the higher levels, for it would be in this first stage that matters of principle were considered. Articles on the discussion of plans, however, seem to deal almost exclusively with the second 'down' stage and were published for the guidance of cadres engaged in organising discussion.

One might be tempted to suspect that the discussion of initial control figures did not take place at all but there is another reason why discussion of the first stage of the planning process was not described in industrial journals. Discussion of control figures might contain information classified as 'economic secrets'. A particular concern for economic secrets was manifested as early as 1949 when some managers went so far as to advocate not informing workers about the planning process, though such advocacy was sharply criticised.[45] During the Three and Five Anti Movements at the end of 1951 and beginning of 1952 the 'theft of economic secrets, was considered to be a major crime[46] and some former capitalists, then employed as managers in the state sector, were accused of utilising information gained by virtue of their new position to help private concerns which were still under their own or their relatives' control.[47] Although a curb on the publication of planning information would not do much to rectify this, it would at least restrict the amount of information directly accessible to the private sector and to other parts of the state sector eager for their share of scarce resources. The 'up' and 'down' process of planning was very similar to the process whereby official documents (such as Party and

State constitutions) were approved and it is significant that, although examples of these have found their way out of China, no similar economic document, to my knowledge, has. I suspect that one will only be in a position to examine the discussions of initial control figures once it is possible to talk to managers in a way similar to Joseph Berliner, who was able to construct a detailed picture of Soviet management from interviews.[48]

It is my impression that as the planning system took shape after 1951, very little worker-initiative entered into the first stage of plan formulation. The slogan 'the state plan is law' was taken very seriously and any attempt to alter control figures seems to have been resisted. In his report on the activities of the Party branch at the model Wu San factory in Shenyang the Party secretary Liu Shih-hua is quite unequivocal:

> There can be no disagreement, amendments [to the plan] or lowering [of targets]. This is because the state plan is law. It is sacred and may not be violated. It is the concrete manifestation of the Party's policy for industrial production within the factory. If it is amended, this could affect the whole [nation's] economic construction and national industrialisation.[49]

This was a far cry from Yenan days. It was even a far cry from the situation in 1949. After the liberation of Shanghai, it had been possible, in a few cases, for workers to take the initiative in determining not only planned targets, but what factories should produce. After the take-over of the Shanghai factory of the Coca-Cola Company, for example, workers were in a position to resist a demand that production be switched to making confectionery and to demand that the machines be used for producing soy sauce.[50] Three years later worker initiative had been restricted to matters of operational detail.

Figure 2 shows in some detail a scheme put forward in 1952 by the Machine Industry Management Bureau of the North East Industrial Department,[51] for discussing the formulation of the two major enterprise level plans (during the second 'down' stage). These two plans were the *production, technical and financial plan* and its technical counterpart the *plan for technical and organisational measures*, which provided the basis for the drawing up of concrete work plans (*tso-yeh chi-hua*). Figure 2 shows who was to take the initiative in formulating a particular plan (level 1), what other staff departments it should discuss this plan with (level 2), the name of the plan (level 3), who was required to

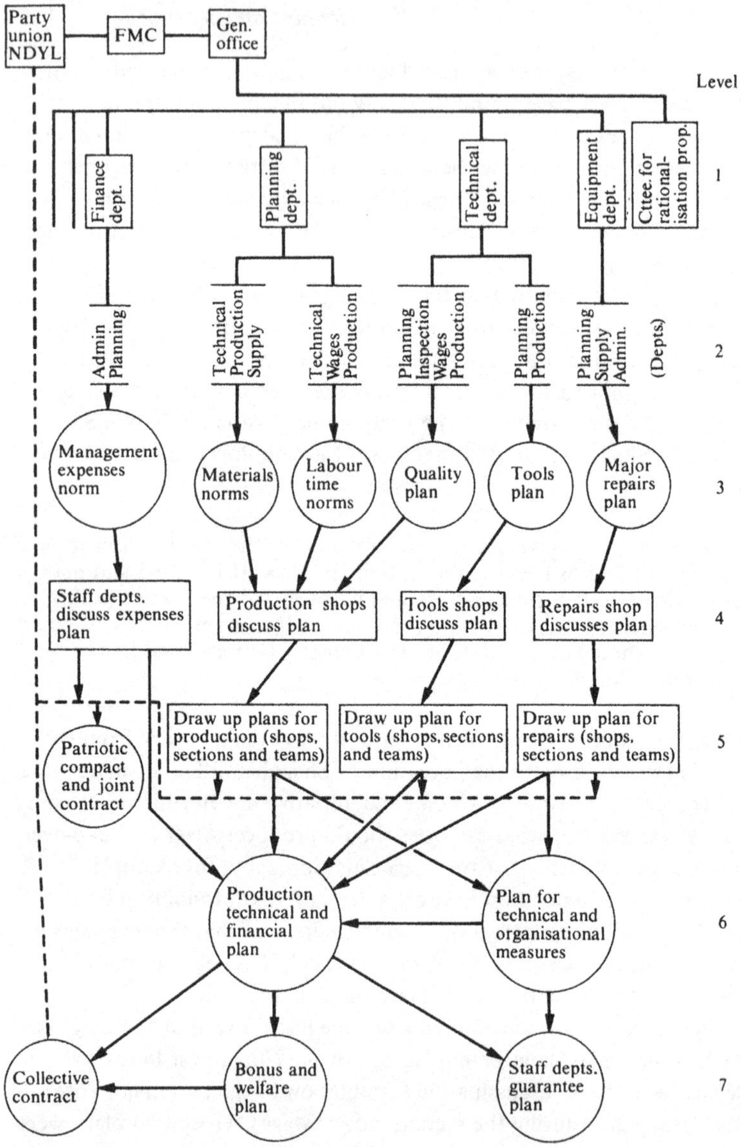

FMC = Factory Management Committee
NDYL = New Democratic Youth League
Source: *Tung Pei Kung-yeh*, No. 94, 11 May 1952, p. 7.

Figure 2. Specimen chart for mass discussion of enterprise plans. (Put forward by the North East People's Government Industrial Department, Machine Industry Management Bureau)

discuss the terms (level 4), the resulting plans at shop, section and team level (level 5), the incorporation of these partial plans into the *production, technical and financial plan* and the *plan for organisational and technical measures* (level 6) and plans and contracts deriving from these two key plans (level 7). Intermediate guarantees might be formulated in the form of *joint contracts* and *patriotic compacts* (level 5) and these will be discussed in Chapter 5. The whole process was to be supervised by the Party, union and Youth League organisation, who were to involve themselves actively in the formulation of a *collective contract* which tied the stipulations of the plan to working conditions, agreed wage-rates, etc. It would be difficult to imagine how such a scheme, which demanded a considerable degree of co-ordination, could deal with anything other than matters of detail.

Priority of targets and the growth of conservatism

Policy demanded that workers participate in basic level management and yet the growth of a planning system restricted the scope of their participation to matters of detail. Similarly, policy demanded that management give full vent to their creativity and yet the nature of the planning system resulted in what was described as 'conservatism'.

We noted earlier in this chapter that during the Movement to Create New Records, ten norms were prescribed. Of these, policy assigned priority to the quality norm, though gradually output norms tended to carry the greater weight, with the result that waste increased. As attempts were made to spread the planning network over the whole country, twelve targets became mandatory. Five of these were physical targets; output, total number of employees, trial manufacture of new products, total number of employees at the end of the year and certain technical-economic norms. The remainder were money targets; gross value of output, cost reduction rate, cost reduction quota, total wage bill, average wage, labour productivity rate and profits. The most important of these targets tended to be in practice the gross value of output, which in the opinion of Perkins was determined by the very nature of materials balance planning, since funds for future investment and bank loans were dependent upon the gross output value target to the detriment of other targets.[52]

It took some time to determine which elements of the Soviet model were inherently contradictory and which were temporary contradictions caused by shortages of the necessary resources, and it was not until

1957 that published accounts appeared indicating that the excessive stress on output targets was due to systemic causes. In that year, the stress on the gross output value target was vehemently attacked by the economist Sun Yeh-fang (subsequently labelled as 'revisionist'), who argued that it had nothing to do with value and was merely an accounting device for measuring physical volume.[53] The primacy of this gross output value target led to considerable waste, which was one of the main reasons for the periodic drives to increase production and practise economy (which began in 1951).

During the New Democratic period many articles appeared criticising the neglect of other targets and the tendency for management to take increased production as the sole success indicator,[54] but such a practice was not described as due to systemic causes. Such a practice led not only to waste but also to 'conservative thinking'. Management was unprepared to switch to new products that required a trial period of manufacture or which required modification of equipment, because such actions would slow down the rate of production.[55] A second tendency was to concentrate solely on overall output figures without attempting to break them down into their constituent parts. In the sector controlled by the Ministry of Heavy Industry during the period January–April 1953, for example, the overall production figure was in excess of the plan, but when these figures were broken down it was found that in January 54% of enterprises had not met their targets, in February 45%, March 30% and April 46%.[56] Such a practice concealed inefficiency.

'Conservatism' in this sense indicated a reluctance to listen to any new ideas in pursuing a success-indicator easily measurable by higher echelons. In such a situation rationalisation proposals would not be listened to since they would require testing. One might well argue that the stress on output targets contributed to the isolation of management from workers and was thus a contributory factor in the growth of bureaucratism.

Controls and the growth of illegality

The primary mechanism of physical control was the centralised system of allocating raw materials, machinery, etc., which was backed up by formal contracts between enterprises selling and purchasing these materials.[57] In 1950 such contracts were seen by Kao Kang to be essential prerequisites for the establishment of a planning system.[58]

Physical control was also exercised by the formal control apparatus and the statistical system. As has been indicated, the main instrument of financial control was not financial targets as such, but controls over the sources and use of enterprise funds exercised by the banking system.[59] Such controls seem only to have been moderately effective. The provisions for controls over planning did not prevent a situation where, during the Three Anti Movement, enterprise managers came under attack for attempting to turn state enterprises into private concerns.[60] Nor did such controls prevent new supply problems developing in the wake of the Three Anti Movement, resulting from the removal of large numbers of people in supply departments who had been accused of graft.[61]

Even after the Three Anti Movement, enterprise managers continued to break through the controls that were imposed upon them by delaying payment and purchasing on credit.[62] Such activities were technically illegal, though insignificant compared with the charges that were made during the Three Anti Movement. One commentator on Soviet management, David Granick, has pointed out that the one area in which Soviet and American managers are similar lies in their ability to break the law to get things done. In fact, Granick goes so far as to say that the only way in which Soviet managers could achieve what was expected of them in the period of very rigid controls was to break the law.[63] Economic law-breaking was always much easier in China than in the Soviet Union because there was always a substantial section of top Party leadership who winked at people who disregarded unreasonable regulations.[64] This difference may well stem from a different conception of the role of law in the two countries, but more probably it reflected growing dissatisfaction with the inflexibility of the Soviet model. In the period prior to 1953, there was probably a greater concentration on the need to adhere to state regulations on the part of senior Party personnel than later. By the second quarter of 1954, however, despite the regulation of 1950 prohibiting the obtaining of credit from sources other than the Peoples Bank, 17.2% of the total working capital of enterprises under the five industrial ministries derived from illegal sources (such as other enterprises).[65]

The overwhelming emphasis in this early period was on getting production moving again and the pragmatic approach to problems that characterised the New Democratic Period meant that, when necessity demanded it, the introduction of certain features of the Soviet model was postponed. It is understandable, therefore, that once what were felt to be serious cases of law-breaking were dealt with in the movements of late 1951 and early 1952, minor infractions would not be considered all that seriously. In a situation where the establishment of contracts was seen primarily as precursors of an effective planning system and only secondly as guarantees of plan-fulfilment, one would not expect to find that curiously ambivalent attitude towards the 'fixers' (*tolkachi*) that characterised Soviet management at the time.[66] In the Soviet Union the institution of the 'fixer' arose out of a highly bureaucratised planning apparatus where someone was needed to cut through red tape. The flexibility of planning during these early years in China when managers were able to conclude supply and sales contracts fairly freely, probably meant that such a role was unnecessary. Even during the middle 1950s when tea-house transactions and the activities of unofficial brokers began to resemble Soviet practice, enterprises were able to employ purchasing agents quite legally.[67]

The economic accounting system

We have seen that the term 'enterprise' was defined according to the 'economic accounting system' (*ching-chi ho-suan chih*). A state-run industrial enterprise was that unit of industry which maintained its own bank account and which enjoyed a certain degree of autonomy in the use of funds either allocated by the state or borrowed from the bank in accordance with the stipulations of the state plan. In the Soviet Union the economic accounting system (*khozraschët*) originated at the time of the New Economic Policy, when the basic economic accounting unit was more frequently the horizontally integrated 'trust' than the much smaller enterprise.[68] We have noted that in China following liberation, trust-like organisations were occasionally advocated though the prescribed form of basic level organisation in the North East, which provided a model for the rest of the country, was usually a unit of one factory, except in the case of vertically integrated corporations. The economic accounting status of constituent elements of corporations is by no means clear.

The economic accounting system was interpreted in primarily Stalinist, as opposed to New Economic Policy terms, although Chinese material explaining the economic accounting system described the NEP version in some detail and spelled out the contradiction between central planning and self-reliance (*tzu-li keng-sheng*)[69] which was fought out in the Soviet Union in the 1920s and was to become salient in China in the middle 1950s. The Stalinist version of economic accounting was something more than mere cost control. It included almost everything that would be described in the West as business management and represented the whole operational side of the planning system within the enterprise.[70] One may document the fluctuation within China of economic accounting defined as such and defined merely as a method of providing success indicators measurable in monetary terms. This latter definition, which was advanced in the early 1960s, was associated with those 'revisionists' who advocated a return to something more like a market economy.[71] In the early 1950s, however, the term 'economic accounting system' was inextricably associated with the planning system.

The first step in the implementation of the system was the registration of assets, which was the responsibility of the various take-over organs and proceeded immediately after liberation. This was no mean task in a situation of regional price variations and currency instability.[72] Following the registration of assets, directives were issued calling for the establishment of economic accounting systems, which was described as the 'central task of management'[73] in a situation where waste was considerable. Writing in February 1950, Cheng Hung-su noted considerable success in implementing the economic accounting system in the North East,[74] though in the light of the scathing criticism of waste made by Kao Kang in the autumn of 1951 at the beginning of the Three Anti Movement,[75] one might perhaps qualify Cheng's enthusiasm.

Articles explaining the system went to great pains to demonstrate that the prescribed view of an industrial enterprise was of an organisation that took as its objective 'the rational pursuit of profit'; it was not that traditional bureaucratic office the '*yamen*'. Fixed capital and part of working capital was part of the state budget and the remainder of working capital was to derive from bank loans or ploughed back profits. Once fixed and working capital were determined, the enterprise was to act independently in pursuit of planned targets. Within the enterprise, control mechanisms were set up as part of the system, of which the most important was the provision of an independent accountant who had the right to examine and supervise accounts without interference from line management or staff departments. The economic accounting system included a system for periodic planning, procedures for the acceptance of draft plans, inspection systems, the accounting of purchases, the storage and requisition of materials and the submission of accounts for approval. Systems for the periodic submission of statistics, the determination of norms, cost calculation and book keeping, the accounting of goods in transit pending sale and regular summaries of work done were established. Also included under the rubric 'economic accounting' were provisions for establishing the rights of creditors and liquidation of debts and a system for strengthening labour discipline and punishing cadres.[76]

Though the main elements of the economic accounting system described above were the provision of systems for accounting production purchases and sales, the scope of definition was wide enough to be co-terminous with management itself. In that it concerned itself with labour discipline and punishing cadres, the system had a very significant political as well as economic dimension. The close association of graft, waste and bureaucratism which were the 'Three Antis' of 1951, existed right from the time of liberation.

In that the economic accounting system embraced the whole of management, various contradictory elements in the Soviet model had inevitably an effect on the working of this system. An obvious contradiction was between the demands of 'one-man management' and that accounting be practised at all levels in an enterprise with the accountant as an independent control officer. Where 'one-man management' was effective, the role of the accountant was circumscribed and it was not until the early 1960s that he eventually came into his own and was in an effective position to refuse the payment of unauthorised funds.[77] A more important contradiction, however, resulted from the low level of education of junior line management. In 1950 cadres were instructed to be flexible in implementing the economic accounting system and not to copy everything from the Soviet Union regardless of the concrete situation.[78] At the same time a large amount of material appeared in the press describing in considerable detail the operation of *khozraschët* in the Soviet Union.[79] Articles demanded that economic accounting be practised not only at enterprise and shop level but also at work-section or team level and at the level of the individual worker, and all production activities be expressed prominently and clearly in charts (*piao-pao*).[80] This involved a considerable amount of paperwork and depended for its success on the existence of an adequate system for communicating statistics.[81] It depended even more on a literate and highly skilled body of foremen. Perhaps the sector of heavy industry where foremen were least literate was the construction industry. In examining the contradiction between policy and resources therefore, let us look at the provisions for team level economic accounting in that industry where one would expect the procedures to be the most simple.

Economic accounting at team level in the construction industry

In the construction engineering corporation under the ministry of Heavy Industry, the highly complex accounting procedures were replaced in July 1953 by a 'simplified' procedure. This procedure involved the production of an 'economic accounting handbook' consisting of 14 forms. Three days before the commencement of a particular job of work, the production order (*tiao-tu*) team concluded a *piecework contract* with a team of workers which was based on the *work plan.* Four copies of this were made, and sent to the work team in question, the statistics team, the wages team and the work supervisor/inspector (this latter constituted an *engineering-work allocation form*). At the same time, the production order team filled out two copies of a *form limiting the amount of materials that could be drawn* (from stores), one copy being sent to the work team in question and one to the materials team where it constituted a *materials allocation form*. In addition, the production order (*tiao-tu*) team filled out a *tools allocation form* according to the requirements of the job, and this was forwarded to the tools team. In accordance with the allocation form, the tools team prepared tools and made appropriate entries in a *tools requisition handbook*. After discussion, the relevant work regulations, quality standards and responsibility systems were determined (and entered on paper).

During the course of work, the work team in question could draw upon tools held by the tools team by applying a seal to the *tools requisition handbook*. Materials could be acquired when the head of the work team applied his seal to the *card limiting the use of materials for the particular job* and the materials despatch officer applied his seal to a *materials requisition form*; this procedure would be followed as and when necessary and was designed to avoid the situation where teams acquired more materials than they actually needed and correspondingly wasted them. The leader of the work team was required to keep a *daily log* even when the team was not working, and this would be submitted daily to the statistics team which would draw up a '*form showing the daily use of labour time*'. This form showing the daily use of labour time would be compared with the *work plan* and thus would serve as a guide to the implementation of the latter. If an accident occurred during the work process, the safety technician would fill in an *accident report form* and if a work stoppage occurred or a situation occurred where work needed to be repeated, then a statistician would fill in a *work stoppage form* or a *form showing work having to be done again*. If the contents of the *piecework contract* or stipulations regarding materials' quality or quantity underwent change, then the production order (*tiao-tu*) department would fill in a '*document showing changes in the contract*' or '*a document showing changes in the stipulations regarding materials*'.

When the work was completed, that is when the work team had completed the tasks stipulated in the contract, the work supervisor and the technical inspector would inspect the quantity of materials used and the quality of the finished work, and would fill in a '*slip requesting release of wages upon inspection of completed work*'. This would be handed to the statistics team and the wages team. They would compare the contents of this request form with those of the '*form showing the daily use of labour time*' and a previously completed *attendance record*, and upon this would make payment. After that, all the statistical information contained in these various forms would be scrutinised by higher levels when determining accounts according to the procedure of economic accounting.[82]

The above was described as a 'simplified' procedure and applied only to team level. One can imagine what might happen at higher levels when faced with an emergency construction job and indeed the above description contributed to a process described in detail in Chapter 6, the growth in the ratio of non-productive to productive personnel.

The account of how economic accounting procedures should be carried on in the construction industry appeared before a number of articles which, in late 1953, expressed disquiet about the general level of skill and literacy of foremen in that industry[83] and one might suspect that the detailed procedures were rarely put into operation. According to the economist Tso Ch'un-t'ai, writing in 1958, the lower level economic accounting systems were only tried out experimentally in a few enterprises[84] and one may well imagine why. There can be no clearer example of the contradiction between policy and resources than this.

Conclusion

Of all the various contradictions listed in the introduction to this book, that between policy and resources was probably the most marked in the field of planning and accounting. In the very early period of price fluctuation and currency instability,[85] any form of planning would probably have seemed utopian. In a situation where costs were sometimes expressed in single figures for a certain period, sometimes according to various stages in a production process, sometimes in relation to each batch of finished products and sometimes for each individual product,[86] any system of planning and accounting would have to be highly flexible until some kind of uniform procedure was adopted.

At a higher level, sophisticated planning techniques were probably not very important. In the early period, contracts were precursors to the development of a planning system rather than deriving from it. Bearing this in mind, the degree of precision with which planning and accounting systems were prescribed for lower levels of administration (and in particular by the North East People's Government) were probably quite unrealistic, especially in a situation where levels of skill and literacy were low.

Although the policy–resources contradiction was probably the most important, certain intrinsically contradictory features of the Soviet model were quite apparent during the period. For example the tendency for output targets to be given priority might result in conservatism and inefficiency. Secondly a highly centralised planning system that demands full discussion of plans might produce plans which are either too late to be of much operational use or result in that bugbear of Soviet management 'storming'.

The contradictions between the stipulations of a Soviet model and the wartime experiences of the Chinese Communist Party were also extremely important. The Chinese Communist Party was not accustomed to any form of strict centralised control and probably adopted the Lushun–Talien experience with so few reservations because it did not know what it was letting itself in for. Throughout the Movement to Create New Records, however, there seemed to be a reluctance to impose too much discipline from above and it was not until after the Three Anti Movement that one sees physical controls becoming more important than financial controls. As China entered the period of her First Five Year Plan, the attempt to control productive activity by formal rules and regulations produced such absurdities as team level economic accounting procedures. Such was alien to the anti-bureaucratic tradition of the Communist Party and was to be repudiated in the middle 1950s and 1960s.

5. Incentives and labour agreements

We noted earlier that the Movement to Create New Records of 1949 sought to promote the breaking of records in order to establish norms as a prerequisite for the operation of the economic accounting system and the wider planning network. It sought also to foster *rationalisation proposals* which were to play an important part in norm determination and to create *incentives* for workers to engage in production competitions and break new records. The new production targets, wage systems and labour regulations were to be combined together in the form of *labour agreements and contracts* so that the worker knew exactly where he stood and what he could gain by setting new records. In this chapter we shall examine rationalisation proposals, incentives, production competitions and labour agreements as they were propounded in 1949 and trace their development through to the first year of the first Five Year Plan, 1953.

Rationalisation proposals

The creation of new records was closely associated with the fostering of rationalisation proposals which would serve to raise the level of quality control and technical standards upon which norms could be established. A 'rationalisation proposal' may be defined as anything which improved labour productivity and lowered costs – in fact anything which contributed to the determination of higher but realistic norms. Such proposals might deal with cutting down on useless operations, eliminating waste, reducing losses, aiding inter-departmental co-ordination, improving the working environment, new designs for equipment, measures to save time, etc. All such proposals could in theory be accorded a cash value. Rationalisation proposals were divided officially into three categories – inventions, technical improvements and other rationalisation proposals and the cash value of each proposal was an estimate of the annual amount of money saved by its adoption. Bonuses were awarded in direct proportion to the cash value according to a set scale (see Fig. 3).[1]

Right from the start there was a tendency for technical and

Value (annual savings)	Inventions	Technical improvements	Other Rationalisation Proposals
under 100	20–25%	15–20%	5–10%
100–500	15%+10	12%+8	6%+4
500–1,000	12%+25	8%+28	4%+14
1,000–3,000	10%+45	5%+58	2.5%+29
3,000–6,000	8%+105	4%+88	2%+44
6,000–10,000	6%+225	3%+148	1.5%+74
10,000–30,000	5%+325	2.5%+198	1.25%+99
30,000–60,000	4%+625	2%+348	1%+174
60,000–100,000	3%+1225	1.5%+648	0.75%+324
100,000–300,000	2%+2225	1%+1148	0.5%+574
300,000+	1%+5225	0.5%+2648	0.25%+1324
	not to exceed 15,000	not to exceed 8,000	not to exceed 4,000

Source: Tung Pei Jen-min Cheng-fu, Kung-yeh-pu: 'Kuan-yü Ch'uang-tsao Sheng-ch'an Hsin Chi-lu Chiang-li Chan-hsing T'iao-li' ('Temporary Bonus Regulations for Establishing New Records'). *Tung Pei Kung-yeh*, No. 20, 16 April 1950, pp. 50–3.

Figure 3. North East peoples government industrial department temporary bonus scale for rationalisation proposals 5 April 1950. In units of JMP(NE) ¥10,000. (JMP = *Jen-min pi*, People's Currency)

managerial personnel not to give sufficient weight to rationalisation proposals that were put forward by ordinary workers.[2] As early as October 1949, it was noted that some factory general managers disregarded rationalisation proposals that did not offer spectacular results, and this prompted official instructions that general managers think of benefits of the order of only 5–10% and discuss all proposals at the regular production conferences that had been instituted as part of the Soviet system.[3] General managers were required to work out concrete procedures for dealing with such proposals and their submission to higher levels for approval. Such procedures were not always worked out very well and we shall note in Chapter 6 that where staff-line tension existed there was a real danger that technical staff personnel would disregard rationalisation proposals coming up the line.

Despite the above tendency, the figures published for the advancement and adoption of rationalisation proposals are very impressive. As one might expect, the drive began in Lushun and Talien before the remainder of the North East and within Talien enterprises in 1948, 1426 proposals were recorded of which 449 were considered to have definite technological value. The estimated value of these proposals was ¥61,000 (*Kuan-tung* currency) equal to 15% of the overall value of production in the city of Talien.[4] In the country as a whole during the years 1949–52 almost 400,000 rationalisation proposals were recorded, of which 241,000 were adopted.[5] I have, however, seen no nation-wide bonus scales for rationalisation proposals promulgated before May 1954.[6]

The Lushun–Talien wage system

The principle whereby workers were rewarded for making rationalisation proposals was one of individual material incentive. This was in line with the current Soviet model and was the principle which informed the establishment of the industrial incentive system first in Lushun and Talien and later in other parts of the country.

The prescribed system for enterprises in Lushun and Talien was a seven grade system for blue collar workers with a progressive differential between grades. For example, if one takes grade one as 100, grade two would be 120, grade three 145, grade four 175, grade five 215, grade six 260 and grade seven 320, thus giving differentials of 20, 25, 30, 40, 45 and 60 between successive grades. The lowest grade was initially calculated as just enough for a single worker to live on according to the 1946 cost of living index in Talien which amounted to a wage of ¥2,400 (*Kuan-tung* currency).[7] In 1948 the Sixth Labour Conference decided that the lowest basic wage should be calculated as the lowest possible wage for *two* people to live on[8] and as the Lushun–Talien model was implemented in North East China as a whole, the prescribed seven grade system tended to be replaced by an eight grade system. Throughout this period, workers in heavy industry enjoyed a higher wage scale than workers in light industry which was the exact opposite of the situation that had prevailed in pre-liberation Shanghai.[9]

People not principally involved in manual work on the factory floor (managers, technical-staff, clerks, etc.) were referred to by the Chinese term *chih-yüan* which I shall translate hereafter as 'white collar workers'. I am, of course, conscious that much has been written on exactly how one defines the term 'white collar worker' and indeed, that the term conjures up a totally inaccurate sartorial image but am anxious to avoid using the term 'staff' which will be used later in discussing staff-line relationships. Such white collar workers in Lushun and Talien were not paid according to the seven or eight grade system but ideally according to a separate 15 grade system (see Fig. 4). This was not a progressive system since it was felt that workers directly engaged in manual productive tasks needed a greater incentive.[10]

According to the Soviet model described in Chapter 1, the best method of payment was considered to be piecework which was justified according to the socialist principle of 'from each according to his ability, to each according to his work'. In its most rudimentary form this meant no more than a *progressive bonus system for overfulfilling norms*. For example, if a worker over-fulfilled his output norm by 5%, he would get a 10% bonus, whereas if he over-fulfilled it by 75%, he would get not a 150% bonus but a 200% bonus, the principle being the more the norm is overfulfilled, the greater the bonus. This was hardly a piecework system.

A more sophisticated version was the *simple piecework system* which by 1949 was the main system in force in Lushun and Talien (and was said to be enjoyed by 80% of Soviet workers at that time). According to this system the basic wage was fixed at the stipulations of the seven grade scale plus 10%. If, for example, a glass cutter was required to meet a norm of 280 square metres per day and his normal working day was eight hours, his time norm for every metre would be 1.7 minutes. Thus for every metre he cut, he received payment for 1.7 minutes according to his particular grade scale plus 10%; if he cut 2 metres every 1.7 minutes, his wage doubled.

The ideal system was a progressive piecework system which was the same as the above except that, when norms were exceeded, the extra payment was on a progressive scale. Thus, if the above worker cut 2 metres in 1.7 minutes, he would get more than double his pay and if he cut three metres, he would get considerably more than treble his pay. According to the progressive system, the bonus graph is curved rather than a straight line, though the degree of curve may vary.

Grade	Grade one enterprise (heavy)	Grade two enterprise (light)
1	3,500	3,200
2	4,500	4,000
3	5,500	5,000
4	6,500	5,800
5	7,500	5,600
6	8,500	7,700
7	9,000	8,200
8	10,000	9,000
9	11,000	10,000
10	12,000	11,000
11	13,000	12,000
12	14,000	12,500
13	15,000	13,500
14	16,000	14,500
15	17,000	15,000

Note: I cannot understand why a grade five white collar worker in a grade two enterprise should earn less than a grade four white collar worker. This is probably a misprint though I have seen the same pattern elsewhere (in the collective contract for the Glass Factory of the Lushun–Talien Electronics Bureau (Appendix II)).
Source: Chu P'u, 1950.

Figure 4. Fifteen grade salary scale (monthly) for white collar workers in Lushun and Talien – early 1950. (*Kuan-tung* currency)

According to the Lushun–Talien system, white collar workers were to get bonuses in proportion to the progressive bonus system of workers on the seven grade system if the particular factory overfulfilled its target by under 40%. If the factory overfulfilled its target by more than 40%, white collar workers were to get a bonus of 70% but that was the ceiling.

Although the seven grade system was fully operative in Lushun and Talien by the autumn of 1949 and that, by the spring of 1950, 78% of all workers in this area were in receipt of payment according to the piecework or progressive piecework systems,[11] the model spread very slowly to other areas. Outside Lushun and Talien in 1950 piecework systems were found mainly in light industry (especially in textiles) where they had survived from the pre-liberation period.[12] In heavy industry the progressive bonus system for overfulfilling norms remained more common than piecework systems at least until 1954.[13] Though strenuous efforts were made to introduce the seven or eight grade systems during the Movement to Create New Records, once norms were formulated, very little success was recorded even in the North East in establishing unified differentials.[14] The Lushun–Talien experiences are valuable only as a model.

The elimination of the supply system

The Lushun–Talien wage system was expressed in monetary terms. In other parts of the country, however, the chronic inflation that lasted until 1950 was compensated for by assessing wages according to a system of points known variously as *hsi* or *fen* in different places.[15] Each point was the equivalent of a certain quantity of consumer goods (rice, wheat, coal, oil, salt and cotton cloth)[16] and payment might be made in these goods or in their monetary value at current prices. The prices of the constituent elements of the wage point were all controlled and an attempt was made to allow for the greater degree of fluctuation of uncontrolled prices by tying wage payments to a cost of living index in a way similar to the Lushun Talien model described above.[17] Though the wage point system was phased out in various places in the years after liberation, it was not formally abolished until 1956.[18]

Soon after liberation, attempts were made to standardise the constituent elements of wage points, though the wage reforms that followed proceeded on the assumption that there would be no immediate changeover to payment in monetary terms. The major task of wage reform was the much more difficult one of standardising wage grades. Various wage reforms had taken place in the liberated areas prior to 1950 but their provisions varied one from another.[19] Even after liberation, wage reform took place in different areas at different times according to a pattern with which we are now familiar – the North East in 1950, the North in 1951, the East in 1951–2 and the Central South in 1952.[20] Wage reform commenced in the North East as soon as inflation had been brought under control, though, in the rest of the country, the commencement of wage reform depended upon the completion of Democratic Reform; the existence of gang-bosses who took their customary cut of wages would have frustrated any attempt at uniform wage grading.

The first task of wage reform was to eliminate the element of free supply that had remained from civil war days. Studies have been undertaken on exactly how this was achieved which I shall not reproduce here. My aim is to discuss the contradictions arising from the introduction of Soviet industrial practices. I shall concentrate therefore on the effects of persistent 'egalitarianism' and the cleavages resulting from the introduction of highly progressive incentive systems.

We have already discussed some of the shortcomings of cadres transferred to the industrial sphere following liberation. As far as incentive systems were concerned, what was particularly serious was that, although liberated areas such as the North East had established wage scales for management cadres in state run factories as early as 1948,[21] many cadres retained what was described in Chapter 2 as the 'free supply mentality' (*kung-chi-chih ti ch'ang-hsiang*) and resented a system of payment that sought to measure their contribution (*kung-hsien*) to production. In the opinion of Kao Kang, this type of cadre manifested the lack of a sense of responsibility and whose attitude he caricatured as '*kan pu kan i-chin-pan*' ('whether I do the work or not, I'll still get one and a half *chin* of grain as wages').[22]

The free supply system for cadres was to survive wage reform, but I have seen no instances of any managerial personnel remaining on this system. In the light of my own observations in the middle 1960s when transferred Army cadres remained on Army pay scales after they were transferred to other walks of life, it is not inconceivable that some Party personnel transferred to factories remained on this system, but I have seen no account that discusses the salary of enterprise Party secretaries in the period under review.

Grading

I suggested in Chapter 1 that one definition of the term 'egalitarianism' was a belief in free supply for its own sake. This was not, however, the definition that was most commonly used. What was usually meant by the term in the industrial sphere was the maintenance of very small differentials between wage grades even though the number of these grades might be enormous.[23]

It is virtually impossible to generalise about the nature of wage grade systems that were in operation in the period immediately before wage reform. Not only were there variations between areas, but even within the same local industrial network a number of different grading systems might be in operation. The Ta Chung coal mine under the T'aihang Mining Corporation, for example, revealed in 1948 a uniform wage of 7.2 *chin* of millet for carpenters regardless of work-skill, whereas other units under the corporation had three wage categories (9 grades), four categories (12 grades) or even five categories (15 grades).[24] As early as 1948 this lack of uniformity was explained as the result of the free supply mentality and other *erroneous* modes of thought.[25]

The process of wage reform reduced the ratio of highest to lowest to something of the order of 3 : 1.[26] Though this ratio might be lower than that which had prevailed hitherto, it was considered to be less 'egalitarian' because a reduction in the number of grades made the differentials between grades much steeper. The ideal was now seven or eight grades such as pertained in Lushun and Talien. Wherever possible, grading was not worker-oriented but job-oriented. A number of work points was assigned to specific activities on the basis of required skill (*ying-hui*), required knowledge (*ying-chih*)[27] and working conditions, in accordance with prescribed ranges laid down by regional government.[28] The ranges prescribed for heavy industry were higher than those prescribed for light industry[29] (the reversal of the pre-liberation situation) and those for state-run industry higher than for provincial or municipally-run industry.[30]

A model for wage grade determination during the 1951 North China wage reform was the Power Plant of the Shihchingshan Iron and Steel Works near Peking. This thirty-year-old plant had inherited no less than 110 wage grades with very small differentials. Not only was the grading system 'egalitarian' but, in some cases, skilled workers were paid less than unskilled workers; for example a highly skilled worker had been graded at 309 *chin* of millet whereas an old forge hand received 460 *chin*. A wage reform committee (*p'ing-tzu wei-yüan-hui*) was set up in July 1951 to carry out wage reform. The committee consisted of cadres (presumably management, Party and union officers) and skilled workers who had been in the plant for some time. The committee worked out a grading plan which was submitted to the shop floor and discussion was held at plant, shop and team level. Pilot teams were selected, their experiences propagated, and within three days every member of every team had been assigned to a definite position in the eight grade scale.[31]

The above exercise in participatory democracy depended to a very large extent upon the political consciousness of the workers involved. In the days when factory-management committees were operative cases are on record of workers voting themselves a wage rise without much concern for the size of the wage fund nor productivity.[32] A worker was required to have sufficient political consciousness to realise that political factors should determine his attitude towards wage grade determination but not the grades so determined. In the liberated areas prior to wage reform 'labour attitude' was frequently an important factor in grade determination.[33] At the time of the 1950–2 wage reforms, however, the employment of political criteria in grade determination was strongly opposed. It was felt that, on the one hand, such a practice might cause resentment between old workers who were highly skilled but politically not very conscious, and young political activists whose level of skill was very low, and on the other hand that it might act as a disincentive for young activists to study technology.[34] Evidently at this stage the political consciousness of the young political activists was not considered in itself a sufficient motivating factor.

The contradiction inherent in a process of political education which demanded that political consciousness be discounted in grading, is an example of a contradiction between medium and message that we shall meet again in Chapter 7. It was a contradiction which was only to be partially solved. Even after the major wage reform of 1956 which reinforced the doctrine that no payment should be made for 'labour attitude', the campaign against the employment of political considerations continued[35] until policy was reversed in 1958; this would indicate that such a practice was difficult to eradicate.

Whatever difficulty might have been experienced in discounting political attitudes when evaluating blue collar workers, the problem of cadres was much more complicated and caused far greater difficulties, since political attitude was the *raison d'être* of the Party cadres, vital in line managers who were required to concern themselves with personnel, and could only be discounted in the case of technicians.

In the early 1950s, the prescribed qualities of a cadre were summed up in the three concepts *ts'ai, te* and *tzu*. They are usually translated as 'ability', 'virtue' and 'qualifications'; a lot however is lost in the translation.

In 1949 Kao Kang defined *ts'ai* as one's capacity to complete tasks assigned by the people, *te* as one's loyalty to the cause of the people and *tzu* as one's experience in 'struggle' and the degree to which one is close to the people.[36] Each of these concepts has ideally a technical and a political dimension. One's capacity to complete work tasks depends upon having the right attitude (political) and the required skill (technical). Despite Kao Kang's wide definition of *tzu*, in the early 1950s, *tzu* tended to be defined in terms of paper qualifications and did not achieve the theoretical importance of the other two concepts.[37] *Ts'ai* tended to be defined as knowing how to do things and having the talent to do them and *te* as showing why such things need to be done. Throughout the past twenty-four years writers on *ts'ai* and *te* have condemned any attempt to counterpose the two concepts. Within an industrial enterprise both the factory general manager and the Party secretary were required to possess *te* and *ts'ai* in great measure, the difference being that a Party secretary was required to concern himself with other people's *te* whereas the factory general manager was to concern himself with other people's *ts'ai*.

In the early 1950s there was a tendency to give greater stress to *ts'ai* than to *te*. An Tzu-wen, Deputy Director of the Party Organisation Bureau and Minister of Personnel, condemned this tendency and answered those cadres who had declared that it was impossible to combine a great deal of *ts'ai* and *te* in one person. Some cadres had put forward the idea that those with *te* and no *ts'ai* should run Party affairs and those with *ts'ai* and no *te* should do administrative work. Some even tried to lay down criteria for administrators and managers on the basis of 30% *te* and 70% *ts'ai*, which was criticised by An as 'the simple business viewpoint'.[38]

If it was impermissible, therefore, to separate out political and technical qualifications, then political attitude would of necessity figure in all evaluations not only of Party cadres but also line management. Technical cadres, on the other hand, were much easier to grade and, for this reason, separate grading systems were worked out for staff and line cadres,[39] the former appearing usually long before the latter. In the North East, for example, a comprehensive system of grade standards for technical personnel were worked out for the whole region in 1952,[40] whereas grading schemes for line management in some sectors of industry were not formulated until much later. In the construction industry, for example, a nation-wide grading system was worked out only in 1955,[41] which was the year in which a comprehensive national plan was put forward for grading all cadres, both in state administration and in the industrial sphere, and the year in which what was left of the free supply system was finally brought to an end.[42] Significantly the national grading schemes for line managers were not put forward until after the abolition of the large administrative regions into which China was divided until June 1954, which meant that sometimes technical personnel were graded according to the former regional standards, whereas line management were graded according to a national standard. In the Anshan Metallurgical General Building Corporation, technical personnel remained until 1957 on the North East standard for 1952, whereas line managers found themselves, after 1955, on the national standard for the construction industry, which was lower than the North East standard.[43]

The payment to technical personnel of salaries higher than line management was a violation of the Soviet model and the provisions for wage reform of 1950–2 had stressed that line managers should be graded at a higher level than staff officers.[44] Although it would appear that the problem of technical personnel paid at a rate higher than line managers was particularly salient after the nation-wide grading systems were put forward in 1955,[45] it is my impression that this process was a natural consequence of the policies of not alienating technical staff, the relative ease in grading technical personnel and the fact that, at the beginning of the Five Year Plan, the engineer enjoyed a prestige higher than the administrator.[46] In 1957 one critic went so far as to say that the phenomenon of higher pay for technical personnel resulted in a situation where managerial recruits into industry tended to be engineering graduates rather than graduates in economics (business management).[47] One can indeed demonstrate that the number of engineering graduates increased out of all proportion to economics graduates (see Fig. 5), but I feel that this was more a consequence of copying the Soviet pattern than the consequence of its violation; and in any case, in a situation where provision for higher education was planned, it is doubtful that higher pay for technical personnel could influence the number of university places for engineering students.

One can show fairly conclusively that the provision in the Soviet model of higher pay for line management was frequently violated at the higher levels. I am not so sure about the lower levels. One of the bones of contention of lower level staff officers in the construction industry was that they were paid at a lower rate than junior line management whereas their technical qualifications were higher.[48] This kind of question can only be solved definitively after very detailed research into the mass of material on wages that exists for the early and middle

Year	Graduates in finance and economics (including business management)	% of all graduates	Graduates in engineering	% of all graduates
1949–50	3,305	18	4,711	26
1950–1	3,638	19	4,416	23
1951–2	7,263	23	10,213	32
1952–3	10,530	22	14,565	30
1953–4	6,033	13	15,596	33
1954–5	4,699	8	18,614	34
1955–6	4,460	7	22,047	35
1956–7	3,651	6	17,162	31

Note the considerable decline in the number of graduates in finance and economics after 1953 when the Soviet model was fully operational.

Figure 5. Relative increase in the numbers of graduates in economics (including business management) and engineering

1950s. The very limited aim of the above discussion is to show that there was a remunerative dimension to that perennial problem of staff-line tension to which we shall return. I have tried to show also that the wage reforms which took place in our period of study were least effective in dealing with managerial staff. The result was that there was a lack of homogeneity between the various systems for grading line managers and the uniformity that was achieved in grading technical staff in the North East was itself a contributory factor in staff-line tension.

Piecework

We have already noted that the prescribed Soviet model demanded systematisation of salary scales for management and provision of higher pay for line managers. These elements were contradictory in a Chinese context and the need for systematisation resulted in an uneven pattern which gave technical staff higher salaries than line management and was a violation of the prescribed Soviet model. A second contradictory pattern which we shall explore here is between a demand that piecework systems of remuneration be introduced and the pressing need to raise the level of technical education.

The prescribed method of wage calculation was a progressive piecework system which, we have seen, was considered to be the best way of adhering to the socialist principle of 'from each according to his ability, to each according to his work'. Piecework related wages to productivity and thus was felt to provide a very good incentive for technical education.[49] The relationship between technical education and piecework, however, can be seen in two ways, *dialectically* or in terms of a *vicious circle*. In the New Record movement, records were to be broken and rationalisation proposals submitted in order to establish norms. Upon these norms piecework systems were to be created and the continued desire to overfulfil one's norm was to lead workers to study technology to improve their efficiency. Thus new rationalisation proposals could be put forward and new records broken which would provide the basis for new and higher norms. Such was the dialectical view which saw the contradiction between education and wages solved repeatedly at ever higher levels. One may look at this contradiction however in another way. The ability to establish new records and put forward rationalisation proposals depends in the first place upon a worker's level of technical education. If this is low he will not break records and not put forward the rationalisation proposals upon which norms might be established and piecework systems built and thus not have sufficient incentive to raise the level of his education. In such a situation the arbitrary imposition of norms and piecework systems will result in a situation where the worker feels he is exploited. The worker may only break out of this vicious circle once he feels that his technical competence is sufficient to break new records and put forward rationalisation proposals. This must be in a situation where technical staff do not despise worker-suggestions and where the development of production competitions is not too erratic, as it was in the early stages of the Movement to Create New Records.

A certain amount of time was necessary therefore before educational levels were sufficiently high, technical staff sufficiently humble and production competitions sufficiently stable to introduce piecework systems. The implementation of piecework systems depended too upon the satisfactory completion of wage reform and, apart from the North

East, such reforms were only deemed to have been satisfactorily completed after the wage reform of 1956.[50] In fact over most of the country piecework systems were just introduced in time for them to be subject to the most severe criticism in 1957–8,[51] when the doctrine of strict payment according to work began to be reconsidered.[52] In striking contrast to the optimism which was recorded during the Movement to Create New Records, it was reported that by 1952 only 34.5% of the production workers in state enterprises were pieceworkers; and even in 1956 they did not constitute the majority.[53] In the North East, where a campaign was launched as early as the spring of 1950 to introduce piecework systems on the grounds that time work encouraged slackers, there was an atmosphere of caution. The advanced 'technical norms' of the Soviet Union which required a complicated method of calculation were considered too difficult to introduce. A system of 'average advanced norms' (*p'ing-chün hsien-chin ting-o*) was adopted and these norms were determined by selecting a point between the overall average target for output and the levels of production which workers commonly reached. Factories were warned not to proceed too quickly, to designate a trial period and not to alter initial norms for a period of six months.[54]

There were three main reasons for this caution. Firstly, as has been mentioned, education levels were low and a premature stress on piecework might dampen enthusiasm. Secondly, workers frequently did not understand the complicated methods for calculating piecework and, thirdly, inexperienced management might have recourse to manipulating norms to balance the books, which might have bad repercussions on workers' morale.

Grade and norm determination were to be conducted according to the participatory principle of democracy. It was comparatively easy to assign work points to a particular task but the determination of norms and piecework systems was particularly complicated. The Leninist conception of participatory democracy was very closely linked with the degree of consciousness and understanding of the participants, and in the campaign to abolish piecework in 1958 the existence of piecework systems was held to be a contributory factor to the failure of workers to participate effectively in basic level management.[55] Whilst accepting this, I feel that the failure of workers to participate effectively in basic level management during the first five year plan period was attributable more to the structure of command and control than to the existence of piecework systems especially since, in the period under review, piecework systems were only operative in one third of industry and I have seen no definite evidence that worker participation was any more effective in factories that had not yet adopted piecework systems. In fact factories which had not yet adopted such systems were usually those where political consciousness was considered to be lower.

The creation of the degree of consciousness and understanding necessary to make piecework a success was the function of the Party[56] and more particularly the labour unions. The unions were to organise discussion of grades, norms and systems. They were to combat egalitarianism, make certain that every worker understood the way his grade was determined and the way piecework norms were formulated and how to calculate his wage. They were to play an active part in the examination of apprentices and the promotion of workers who had improved their skill. They were to make certain that norms were realistic and could be attained by the majority of workers. In fact, they were to supervise the whole process of wage determination and payment. During the wage reform in the North East in 1950, the head of the Wage Department of the North East General Labour Union, Chou Shu-k'ang, was none too complimentary about the way basic level unions had carried out these tasks. In fact, Chou noted that union cadres often did not participate in the discussions of wages, let alone organise them, but just handed down gradings determined previously by management.[57] We saw in Chapter 3 that during 1951 criticism switched from the unions' bureaucratism to their 'economism', where apparently the increase in discussion did not lead to an increase in consciousness, at least in the way the Party defined it. However successful the unions might have been in stimulating discussion during 1951, it is unlikely that the understanding of workers was raised to any new height, since piecework systems were not introduced on a large scale until after 1954.[58]

Norm manipulation

What was perhaps more significant than the lack of democracy in lowering workers' morale and engendering their hostility to piecework was the fact that the regulations for maintaining norms for fixed periods of time were frequently violated. This was partly a consequence of a contradiction between two other elements in the Soviet model, the wage fund system and production competitions.

The size of the enterprise wage fund was determined by the current plan. When norms were greatly surpassed, as in the case of successful production competitions, more funds would be needed than the wage fund made available. Management could either get funds from unauthorised sources or raise norms in anticipation of further production increases.[59] To prevent this, unions were required to make certain that the size of the wage fund was appropriate for the fulfilment of production tasks,[60] though what they might do if they found that it was not is not clear. Unions were also required to make certain that norm revision took place at the planned intervals.[61] This was probably not a very great problem when planning was relatively flexible in this early period and when a large proportion of enterprise funds derived from unauthorised sources. Later, however, as economic control became tighter, worker criticisms began to appear in the press to the effect that norm manipulation was like 'turning a screw'.[62]

Equally common was the opposite tendency, that of lowering norms, which was described as 'economist'.[63] Students of Soviet management will be familiar with a situation where norms are kept low in order that a larger bonus might be generated for management who overfulfilled them. It was stated during the middle 1950s when the Soviet model of incentive came under criticism that workers were infuriated with the huge bonuses that were paid to factory general managers for overfulfilling their targets (sometimes ¥300–400 in post 1955 currency) and themselves had to be paid bonuses as bribes to keep quiet.[64] I have, however, no data on bonuses paid to management in the period under review. Sometimes the 'economist' tendency manifested itself in a situation where norms assigned to workers were kept proportionally lower than the targets assigned to management. In this case workers might receive wages higher than management which made for resentment on the part of white collar workers.[65]

Appropriate norm determination was therefore essential if piecework systems were not to cause tension. It was not only norm manipulation, however, that led to tension. In 1957–8 when piecework systems were being dismantled it was noted that workers not on piecework were frequently jealous of those that were, and some pieceworkers refused to be assigned to jobs for which they were paid on an hourly basis.[66] From an economic point of view piecework led to waste and even when workers were penalised for waste, they often did not care because they knew they could gain back all they would lose through increased production.[67] This was to be the culmination of a process begun in Lushun and Talien in 1949, spread to the North East in the period under review and implemented in other parts of the country after 1954.

Production competitions

We have seen that the formulation of wage systems was closely associated with the development of production competitions. Competitions were used to formulate norms which would provide the basis for piecework and bonus systems. During the early stages of the Movement to Create New Records, the irregularity of these competitions caused imbalance between output and other norms, with the result that attempts were made in early 1950 to regularise the whole process.[68] During 1950 the stress was on working out stable norms and commencing wage reform, and it was not until the Korean War donation drive of 1951 that the development of production competitions was given new impetus. The fervour of production competitions continued into the movement to Increase Production and Practise Economy of September 1951 which was to be the precursor of the Three Anti Movement. As that movement drew to a close, further efforts were made at regularisation.

The character of the 1951 campaigns became heavily influenced by the Movement to Resist American Imperialism and Aid Korea with which they coincided. The terms of the competitions were frequently incorporated into patriotic compacts and widespread use of military metaphor was made. Teams might issue 'challenges to combat' (*t'iao-chan k'ou-hao*)[69] to other teams within the same enterprise. Competitions might be concluded between enterprises producing similar goods, between enterprises within the same locality producing different goods,[70] or even between enterprises in China and the Soviet Union.[71]

After the experiences of the Movement to Create New Records, particular stress was laid upon planning. Municipal general labour unions laid down guidelines for competition plans[72] and each competing unit would work out its own plan with the consultation of relevant Party and union personnel. After group discussion, work tasks would be assigned to each individual, who would work out his own plan. Success in fulfilling the terms of these individual plans would determine who would be designated a model worker (or advanced producer). The whole process of planning was to be supervised by the labour unions which, as we have noted, were frequently under criticism for bureaucratism in 1950. Municipal directives condemned those union cadres who did not bother with competition plans due to a distaste for detail and those who rejected plans without bothering to explain why. In striking contrast to the autumn of 1949, the Harbin General Labour Union in December 1950 forbade the holding of competitions unless planning had been adequately carried out.[73] The 'economist' tendency in labour unions in 1951 was equally non-conducive to production competitions and it was not until after the Three Anti Movement that labour unions began adequately to fulfil their role in supervising the planning of labour competitions.

In these early labour competitions, it was not only the unions that were found wanting. The problem of technicians, which we discussed in this chapter in connection with wages, applied equally to the sphere of production competitions. Technicians were instructed to examine whether competition targets were realisable or not and to work out their own individual plans specifying what help they would give to the competitors. Many technicians, however, were unwilling to be so tied down,[74] which added yet another dimension to staff-line tension.

In the early 1950s the stress was very much on the individual rather than the group. Individual bonus systems were preferred to collective bonuses. Individual piecework was preferred to collective piecework and where it was impossible to avoid giving a collective bonus, the recipients were required to divide out the proceeds according to which individuals made the greater contribution. At all costs 'egalitarianism' was to be avoided.[75]

The feats of the individual model worker were given great publicity. Although charts were displayed showing unit (team, shop, etc.) progress,[76] it was the individual who was given the most kudos during the production competitions of this period. Photographs of advanced workers were displayed, rolls of honour compiled and articles describing individual achievements displayed in house organs and the local and national press.[77] Although model workers received considerable cash bonuses for their exploits, great efforts were made to promote individual fame as an element of non-material incentive, as is graphically portrayed in Ai Wu's novel 'Steeled and Tempered'.[78]

The kudos given to model workers dates right from the start of the Movement to Create New Records. In its formal decision to launch the movement, the North East Industrial Department singled out a number of labour models in the Machinery Bureau's network who had established new records upon which norms could be determined.[79] Considerable publicity was given to their exploits and soon other factories began to publicise the achievements of workers who had successfully emulated them. In the space of one month seventy workers were designated 'advanced producers' within factories under the Machinery Bureau. All of these workers received large bonuses but there was also a significant element of non-material incentive in the propagation of their achievements. The selection of model workers was defined as an anti-conservative measure, but this conservatism could be defined in three different ways. Some people were conservative in the sense that they thought that the former Manchukuo standards could not be improved upon. Others feared that machinery might be broken in the movement and others were conservative in the sense that they still clung to a collectivist ethos and disliked the development of a belief in 'individual heroism'.[80]

The people who seemed to get most kudos were the team leaders of successful teams and such teams were known by the name of the team leader. One of the most famous of the team leaders who achieved prominence in 1950–1 was Ma Heng-chang, of the Fifth Machinery Works in Shenyang under the North East Bureau of Machinery. His team, consisting of 10 workers and three apprentices, surpassed its production targets every month from April 1949 through to 1951 and met all the quality control specifications. During that period the team invented 15 different kinds of tools, set up 25 new records and received three banners for advanced production (one from factory management, one from the North East General Labour Union and one from the North East Industrial Department). Every member of the team established some kind of record and in September 1950 Ma Heng-chang was elected a delegate to the All China Congress of Model Workers and Combat Heroes[81] (a similar body to the Soviet Congresses of Stakhanovite Workers);[82] at the same time the team was designated a national model.[83] In the final quarter of 1950, 678 model teams and over 7,600 advanced workers, 92 advanced shops and 123 advanced staff sections had been designated in Shenyang, though there was an increased accident rate of 0.9%.[84]

In January 1951, the Ma Heng-chang team issued a challenge to the whole country[85] and this gave rise to a movement designed to catch up with and surpass its achievements. Throughout the early part of 1951 the press published a mass of statistics showing the numbers of teams who had accepted Ma Heng-chang's challenge. By March, 1,008 teams in Peking,[86] 244 teams in Shanghai[87] and 583 textile mill teams in various parts of the country[88] had taken up the challenge, and in some places municipal general labour unions convened conferences of teams who were in competition with the Ma Heng-chang team.[89] By the end of June 11, 159 teams had accepted the challenge.[90] In the course of this movement Ma Heng-chang reported several times to Chairman Mao[91] and achieved a reputation as great as many an old Central Committee member.

After such a sudden rise to fame Ma Heng-chang fell ill from overwork in August 1950[92] (though he modestly attributed his illness to an old complaint)[93] and did not return to work until April 1951. He was, therefore, spared the gruelling life of many of the other model workers (of less prestige than himself).

Various articles appeared in the press throughout 1951 complaining about the excessive duties of model workers. It would appear that, up to a certain point, a model worker gained in prestige amongst the workers as he achieved new production records, but beyond that point his prestige might decline sharply. The case of Juan K'ai-li illustrates this point most clearly. During the 'Red May' production drive of 1950 when the Movement to Create New Records was extended to Shanghai, Juan put forward a number of rationalisation proposals that made it possible for his mill to double its monthly steel output. His prestige became very great and he was elected as a delegate to the National Congress of Model Workers and Combat Heroes held in Peking. Upon his return, his workmates went on to increase steel output threefold (as compared with the output figures prior to the 'Red May') but Juan had very little to do with this achievement, since a large part of his time was spent attending meetings (only some of which could be classified as involving the spreading of advanced experiences).

Within the mill, Juan's concurrent duties were to act as a team leader, a member of the factory labour union committee, a member of production committees, and a member of the factory management committee. He was required to carry out the duties of a Party propagandist and to serve as deputy director of the factory committee for the suppression of counter revolutionaries. Outside the mill, Juan served as a worker delegate to the Shanghai Peoples Congress, was Vice Chairman of the Consultative Council of his ward and was required to serve as representative to meetings of his residential district. The number of meetings he had to attend was very great indeed. They included various meetings called by management, the mill workers and staff congress, meetings of the labour union committee, propagandists' meetings, mill management committee meetings, meetings of local government at residential district, ward and city level, meetings called by the Shanghai General Labour Union and the Shanghai Metal Workers Union and forums called to launch each mass movement in the political and economic sphere. In addition, he was required to address other organisations on subjects such as conducting propaganda concerning current affairs, the enlistment of young workers in training institutions for military cadres, the movement against the American rearming of Japan, the suppression of counter revolutionaries and national celebrations such as 7 February (the anniversary of the 1923 massacre of strikers) and 1 July (the anniversary of the founding of the Party).

These meetings involved one third of his working time and almost all of his spare time. On one occasion he had to participate in a series of meetings after his twelve hour shift which lasted until the beginning of the next shift. From December 1949 to May 1951 he averaged 3–5 hours sleep per day and sometimes fell asleep at work. Each month he was given five injections of glucose to keep him going. He complained that he felt dizzy at work and spent most of his working time thinking about what to say at meetings.

As a consequence, the production of his team fell below that of other teams and his prestige declined. Workers jeered him, declaring that 'He was a model in attending meetings'. He was therefore 'alienated from the masses' and useless as a model worker. The Shanghai Party newspaper, *Chieh-fang Jih-pao*, declared that the case of Juan was not an unusual one. The newspaper carried out a survey and found that almost all model workers complained of too many duties and this shortened their life as models. *Chieh-fang Jih-pao* noted a general decline in the prestige of model workers and a tendency for workers to hold them in contempt as they manifestly did not continue to live up to their initial records. The slogan 'Protect the model workers' was advanced.[94]

There were two possible answers to this problem. Either the whole idea of labour models could be given up, or the number of labour models greatly increased so that the duties of the few would not be so burdensome and the whole process fall into disrepute. In mid-1951 Li Li-san sharply criticised the tendency for model workers to get bogged down in meetings and repeated the call that production competitions should become 'a regular form of labour and a regular form of life for the broad masses of the workers'. He condemned most strongly 'worker sectarianism' (which may have been partially the result of production competitions) and, as we noted earlier, advocated collective heroism instead of individual merit.[95] During 1951 the number of model workers multiplied, which was partly a reflection of the fact that the number of workers involved in production competitions went up from 683,000 in 1950 to 2,380,000 in 1951, rising to 80% of all workers in the second half of 1952, but was also a reflection of the fact that the best way to protect model workers from excessive attendance at meetings was to multiply their number. By 1951 over 86,500 model workers had been designated.[96]

Internal collective contracts

We have considered so far the various elements of the 'enterprisation' process individually. We shall now turn to the process whereby all these elements were brought together into formal documents which specified the responsibilities of individuals and units, established terms of service, wage scales and bonus systems, made provision for the day to day settlement of labour disputes and integrated such provisions with labour regulations and the current plan. These documents which existed right from the time of liberation were known as collective contracts (*chi-t'i ho-t'ung*). They varied considerably in duration and scope and might be anything from a charter of employment to a short-term productivity deal. We shall consider first two general types – annual contracts and those of shorter duration.

As one might expect, the earliest examples of collective contracts may be found in the joint Sino-Soviet enterprises in Lushun and Talien and, in the light of our discussion so far, one might expect that such contracts would be highly ambitious and not suitable for application elsewhere. In Appendix II, I have summarised one of the more comprehensive annual contracts that appeared in the Lushun–Talien area in 1949 – that of the glass factory under the Far East Electronics Bureau.[97]

The glass factory contract reflected a situation which hardly pertained elsewhere. In Lushun and Talien, social security provisions had already been worked out, production was relatively stable, wage payment was made to a very large extent in money terms (though there was still a subsidy element in wages) and, in the glass factory, initial norms had already been worked out. Nevertheless the glass factory contract, which was put forward as a model, was rare even for Lushun and Talien and was concluded only one month after regulations governing collective contracts were put forward for that area;[98] only one other factory in Lushun and Talien, the paint works under the same bureau, was able to conclude a contract in so short a time. I know of no industrial unit outside Lushun and Talien that was able to conclude a contract of such comprehensiveness as the glass factory and even in Shenyang where production was rapidly restored and where there were many advanced industrial enterprises, it was felt that the Lushun–Talien model was too comprehensive and of too high a standard to serve as a model for its own collective contracts. The contract is summarised in this essay because it was a national model, as is made quite clear by some of its stipulations (such as those for grade 2 factories) which had no relevance for the glass factory and were only appended for the guidance of other enterprises basing their own collective contracts on the Lushun–Talien model.

Within factories in Lushun and Talien during this early period there were usually three important documents at factory level upon the basis of which action concerning production, employment, working conditions and welfare were taken – the production plan, the collective contract and the internal factory regulations. The production plan dealt with measures taken to fulfil the various targets described in Chapter 4. The collective contract dealt with production competitions, wage and bonus payments, guarantees and compensation, working hours, holidays, labour protection, the disposal of the social insurance and culture and education funds and the settlement of labour disputes within the factory. The internal regulations which usually appeared as an appendix to the contract dealt with such matters of detail as internal security regulations, procedures for requesting leave, procedures on entering and leaving the factory, the issue of identity cards, etc.

These latter two documents were usually combined into one but in mid 1949 the provisions of the collective contract were not usually integrated with planned targets. This is probably because contracts of the Lushun–Talien type were worked out on an annual basis and it is doubtful whether annual plans had much operational force at that time within the enterprise; furthermore the relevance of annual targets for a contract that was concluded in July could not have been very great. For the integration of production targets into the terms of the contract, the duration of the contract must be co-terminous with the operational production plan.

The terms of the contract which appear in Appendix II are fairly self-explanatory though one point deserves mention here. Provision was made in the contract for the establishment of a conciliation committee (*t'iao-chieh wei-yüan-hui*) and, if necessary, the convening of arbitration conferences (*chung-ts'ai hui-i*) at a higher level to settle labour disputes. One would like to know the relationship between the Party organisation,[99] the unions, the conciliation committees and the local labour bureau (when established),[100] which were all explicitly charged with the settlement of internal disputes but I have seen no specific account of the process of arbitration and conciliation during the period under review.[101]

A more common type of contract employed in the North East in late 1949 and thereafter was the monthly or bi-monthly contract into which the stipulations of the short term operational plan were written. For example, the collective contract of the Shenyang Third Machine Building Factory for November and December 1949 stated precisely the planned targets down to the last machine.[102] It specified in what way costs were to be reduced and called for the establishment of certain management systems such as a system of personnel management, a costing system, a statistical system, a work schedule system, an inspection system, a system of individual responsibility, an accounting system, etc. Precise stipulations were made concerning the time machines were permitted to be in operation (not less than 96% of working time). A planned attendance rate was agreed upon (97%). Provision was made for schools and training classes, master apprentice contracts, the examination and re-assessment of wage grades, regulations governing the treatment of rationalisation proposals and agreements to reduce the injury rate. The Machine Building Factory also attempted to write into the contract the precise responsibilities of staff sections involved in planning. Whereas the Lushun–Talien contract was more like a charter stipulating terms of service, the Shenyang contract was a cross between a charter and a productivity deal concluded between management and unions. Though the Shenyang contract was less comprehensive than the Lushun–Talien contract it was more detailed in terms of its immediate goals. The fact that these short term contracts were an integral part of the planning procedure and concerned themselves with explicit production targets was reflected in the fact that they were sometimes called 'production contracts'.[103]

The short term Shenyang-type contract was much less detailed than the Lushun–Talien contract on the question of wages and this type of contract was deemed to be appropriate for plants where norms and wage scales were still in the process of being formulated. The implication was very clear that, in future, longer term contracts such as the Lushun–Talien type would become the norm, though in fact the opposite was to be the case. As the planning machinery became more consolidated, the contracts of the Lushun–Talien type were not to reappear, especially since many of their provisions were later taken care of by regional or national agreements (on social security, etc.).[104] The terms of the contract came more and more to reflect specific measures for plan fulfilment.

In the model Wu San Factory the collective contract which was drawn up quarterly at the same time as the factory work plan, was described as 'a step in the direction of planned management'. It was a way of linking not only welfare provisions with the production plan, but also of linking production tasks with each of the major and minor movements that were launched in industry throughout this period. For example, in the second, third and fourth quarters of 1951 three successive movements were given priority in the industrial sphere in the North East. These movements were to improve quality control (2nd quarter), to increase production and practise economy (3rd quarter) and to strengthen workshop work (4th quarter) and provision for each of these was made in the three collective contracts concluded by the Wu San Factory during these nine months.

In the Wu San Factory the collective contract had by 1951 almost the force of law. It was seen as a kind of mini 'Common Programme' (the provisional state constitution) for Party, management, labour union and Youth League.[105] Later the analogy between collective contracts and constitutions became more explicit and in the 1960s actual 'constitutions' for industrial enterprises began to appear. In this earlier period, however, collective contracts appeared more like productivity deals than constitutions, and were explicitly linked to planned targets.

Collective contracts at sub-enterprise and supra-enterprise levels

Normally collective contracts would be concluded only at enterprise level, though in the very early period contracts were sometimes concluded at lower levels. In the Wu San Factory, for example, a mini collective contract existed at team level until 1951 when it was replaced by a team compact (*hsiao-tsu kung-yüeh*) (a kind of patriotic compact which will be discussed later in this chapter). By 1951, however, the existence of bi-partite agreements at lower levels was seen to be inappropriate and lower level contracts were replaced by patriotic compacts which reflected the determination of a unit to fulfil certain tasks and did not involve bargaining between two parties.[106]

Although collective contracts and contractual agreements between the enterprise and supply and marketing agencies were usually quite separate, some overlap occasionally occurred. When, for example, it was felt necessary to tie down some planning or supply agency, a collective contract might be concluded at a level higher than the individual enterprise. For example, the Third Machine Building Factory in Shenyang could get no support for its September 1949 contract from the Municipal Machinery Bureau. The account does not say why or in what form this lack of support manifested itself, but one might imagine that the bureau could not guarantee a supply of raw materials and was reluctant to ratify an agreement that might over-commit itself. This problem was dealt with by the Machinery Bureau initiating a collective contract that covered a number of factories and which formed the basis for individual factories to draw up their own contracts.[107] In such a case the freedom of action of unions and management in the individual factories was probably considerably restricted.

The imposition of a contract from above was a violation of the general principle that contracts should be concluded by negotiation between union and management at enterprise level. Occasionally, however, the situation demanded that contracts be concluded at levels above the enterprise and attempts were made to secure full consultation and agreement at lower levels in much the same way as in the case of periodic plans which we discussed in Chapter 4. Perhaps the most famous example of this was the collective contract of the Ch'angch'un Railway network of mid 1951 which covered all the workshops and construction units under its control. The sixty-two clause contract was only concluded after eight revisions, nineteen full days of discussion and the sifting of 6,074 suggestions which took four months.[108] Such a contract seems however to be the exception rather than the rule.

Pao-kung and Shih-kung contracts

A major theme of this essay had been the modification of the prescribed Soviet model in conditions of inadequate resources. The rudimentary nature of planning meant that the prescribed Lushun–Talien type collective contract was not implemented very widely. Similarly, where vertical control was weak and where traditional contractual relationships were still strong as in the construction industry, there appeared a peculiar type of document known as a *pao-kung* contract. Such a contract contained clauses very different from the ideal exemplified in the Lushun–Talien-type.

The term *pao-kung* is extremely difficult to translate. It is used normally to signify the process whereby a factory employs workers through an external contractor which in former days, as we saw in Chapter 1, would be some species of gang-boss. Such a contract, which continued to be concluded throughout the 1950s, is an external contract and is not discussed here. There was however a form of internal collective contract which also went under the term *pao-kung* contract.[109] Such a contract would be concluded in factories engaged in rehabilitation of plant and undergoing emergency repairs and represented a transitional stage during the process of abolishing the gang-boss system.[110]

Under the old gang-boss system, wages and bonuses would be paid to the gang-boss and he would decide on their distribution. When the gang-boss system was abolished in the manufacturing industries, wage and bonus systems were established whereby the enterprises paid workers directly without going through any intermediary. In the construction industry, however, such systems were extremely difficult to institute. When construction work was undertaken by a state construction corporation, an external *pao-kung* contract could be concluded (*wai-pao*) and workers could be paid directly by the construction corporation. Such a process was theoretically very simple, though in practice state construction companies came under very heavy criticism for graft during the Three Anti Movement.[111] Where construction work was an internal matter, however, although wages could now be paid directly to the workers, the weak control exercised by the factory for which the work was being done in a situation where construction tasks and repair tasks were constantly changing meant that an individual bonus system was particularly difficult to put into operation. Collective bonus systems were introduced, therefore, by which a lump sum was made over to a group of workers and divided out amongst its members according to criteria which the group itself decided.[112]

In drawing up a *pao-kung* contract which formalised this process, the workers engaged in construction tasks were frequently represented not by the labour union, which being of an industrial as opposed to a craft nature represented everyone within the factory or mine, but by a 'committee for emergency repairs (*ch'iang-hsiu wei-yüan-hui*) elected by the construction workers themselves.[113] Such contracts consisted simply of an undertaking by management to provide the necessary materials and to make individual payment and collective bonus payment in return for the completion of specific construction tasks.

The simple *pao-kung* contract was a temporary expedient in the period of rapid reconstruction after liberation resulting from weak vertical control following the abolition of the gang-boss system. In certain situations which will be explored in Chapter 6, a system of control from above was superimposed upon what was left of the existing segmental structure following the abolition of the gang-bosses. The result was that workers at the basic level were required to respond to commands from two sources – foremen belonging to the traditional segmental structure and work-supervisors (*shih-kung-yüan*) belonging to the new superimposed command structure. In such a situation a contract between the traditional work gangs and representatives of the work supervision network would be concluded known as a *shih-kung* contract.

In certain situations, new work gangs were formed out of existing factory departments for a specific task and subordinated to a new factory department specifically created for that task and fulfilling much the same kind of function as the work supervisors above. In this case too, the newly created gangs would enter into a *shih-kung* contract with the supervisory body for as long as the specific task remained.

In the Chin Hsi Cement Works, for example, an inspection was carried out at the end of 1950 when it was found that some 270 items of construction work had to be undertaken, which was more than could be handled by the works basic construction department (*chi-chien-k'o*). Production units and technical departments were required to provide labour to undertake these production tasks, but workers in these units were unwilling to involve themselves with building work which they considered was not their concern. To overcome this problem cadres and workers were deputed from all departments and amalgamated into a construction engineering department (*kung-ch'eng-pu*), which was divided into a number of specialist sub-departments and teams. A small amount of the construction work to be undertaken was contracted out (*wai-pao*) to an external construction corporation, and the remainder handed over to this newly formed construction engineering department, which was required to make plans for each item of work.

After plans were formulated stipulating the numbers of workers necessary for each construction task, the labour union organised the ordinary production workers into teams, each of which entered into a *shih-kung* contract with the relevant subsection of the construction engineering department. Such teams were placed under the functional leadership of each subdivision of the construction engineering department responsible for a particular type of construction work at the basic level. Bonus payment was paid to the teams according to the degree to which they fulfilled the stipulations of the *shih-kung* contract. Because the bonus payments were determined by the particular construction jobs undertaken, such a system was called 'the internal *pao-kung* piecework system' (*nei-pao-kung chi-chien-chih*).[114]

In concluding normal collective contracts, the workers were represented by the labour union, whereas in concluding simple *pao-kung* contracts, the workers were represented by no-one and participated directly in the process themselves. As such the *pao-kung* contract was praised in 1950 for giving workers an opportunity to participate in the democratisation of management. Workers were in a position to divide out the bonus payment for themselves and were not bound by the union hierarchy. The official attitude was ambivalent, however, for warnings were issued that *pao-kung* contracts did not have universal application[115] and the *shih-kung* contract described above represents a step in the direction of greater control over the exercise of participatory democracy on the part of the workers. In concluding the Chin Hsi *shih-kung* contracts, the role of the union was much greater than in the case of a simple *pao-kung* contract. The process whereby teams of workers were formed was described as 'proceeding spontaneously under the leadership of the labour union'[116] and whatever degree of spontaneity this implied, it was much less than in the case of a simple *pao-kung* contract where the role of the gang-boss was replaced by a committee, elected directly by the workers. Such a difference in formulation would seem to indicate the first stage in a process whereby direct worker representation was replaced by indirect union representation.

The joint (co-ordination) contract

One further type of bi-partite agreement that must be mentioned is the joint contract (*lien-hsi ho-t'ung*), which was designed to achieve co-ordination between the various workshops and staff departments within the enterprise. Like the collective contract, joint contracts appeared immediately after liberation and were considered to be one of the most important organisational forms employed during the early stages of the Movement to Create New Records.[117]

The most important stipulations of such contracts concerned the quality and quantity of raw materials and semi-finished products supplied by one part of the enterprise to another or the frequency of supply. Such contracts were seen to be particularly important in effecting co-ordination between the various staff departments and production units, which tended to focus on different targets (for example, between an accounting department concerned with cost reduction and production units concerned with gross output) and in preventing wide disparities in quality control standards and norms between one part of the enterprise and another.[118]

Joint contracts were considered to have a political significance which it was the duty of the labour unions to propagate.[119] Such contracts were felt to be particularly useful in preventing ill feeling between one sub-unit and another. For example, in the Shenyang Wool Weaving Mill a contract was drawn up between the wool sorting team and the wool blending team stipulating the proportion of lumps of small broken pieces the former was permitted to send down to the latter and thus, it was hoped, avoiding mutual recriminations.[120] Concluding such contracts was one of the first tasks of fledgling union organisations during the Movement to Create New Records and such a task was useful in recording on paper how successful the union was in overcoming tension within factories. Joint contracts were also seen as useful in specifying the responsibilities of one sub-unit to another, but it was anticipated that they would gradually be assimilated into collective contracts.[121]

The Korean war donation drive and the genesis of patriotic compacts

The above forms of 'internal contract' were so called because they were the product of negotiation between management and union (or emergency repairs committees in the case of simple *pao-kung* contracts). We shall now consider a different kind of document which appeared later than the contracts and was only integrated into the planning system in late 1951, the 'patriotic compact'. The strict terminological difference between a contract (*ho-t'ung*) and a compact (*kung-yüeh*) lies in the fact that whereas the former is the product of bargaining between two parties, the latter is an undertaking to fulfil a certain obligation which might be unilateral. In the case of the patriotic compact that obligation was, at first, a general commitment to support the Korean War effort though later its terms became more specific. In fostering such compacts the role of the union was not one of workers' representative in negotiations with management, but the propagandist of Party and management.

I have so far suggested three factors in work motivation – material gain, prestige accruing to model workers and guilt deriving from inadequate fulfilment of internalised group-norms. To these a fourth element must be added – patriotic fervour. Right from the time of the Yenan Production Movement through to the movement to support the front in the latter days of the Civil War, an attempt was made to add a patriotic dimension to work motivation. The movement to draw up patriotic compacts which arose out of the Movement to Resist American Aggression and Aid Korea of 1951 was, however, more sophisticated than these earlier movements in that it attempted eventually to integrate patriotic motivation with the system of planning and responsibility.

A donation drive to support the Korean War effort commenced in the first half of 1951. During this drive individuals, families and units of production, residence and administration undertook to donate specific sums of money to purchase armaments for Korea. Contracting individuals or groups would make a donation plan, which could be expressed either in monetary terms or more probably in terms of armaments. To facilitate this, an official conversion table was published as follows (JMP = *Jen-min pi*, People's Currency):[122]

JMP ¥ 5,000 million = 1 bomber
JMP ¥ 2,500 million = 1 tank
JMP ¥ 1,500 million = 1 fighter aircraft
JMP ¥ 900 million = 1 piece of artillery (field)
JMP ¥ 800 million = 1 anti-aircraft gun

Every effort was made to achieve identification between the donating unit and the front and weapons purchased would be frequently named after the donating unit.[123]

The movement was as much political as it was economic. It aimed to integrate macro-politics with the day to day concerns of ordinary individuals[124] in much the same spirit in which Committees for the Study of Current Affairs took a leading role in the Democratic Reform Movement. Cadres whose over-zealous desire to meet donation plan targets resulted in coercion were vehemently denounced on the grounds that they negated the role of political education, which was of the utmost importance.[125]

In the early part of 1951 the donation drive was not linked with the process of planning and units of all shapes and sizes contracted to make donations. Contracting units might be anything from province, municipality or *hsien* right down through production team or family to the individual.[126] Such agreements might either express a guarantee to make a direct donation or a contribution to the war effort through economy and increased production. In the latter case, the size of the donating unit was very important. The political aims of the donation drive would best be served if some degree of congruence could be achieved between the donating unit and the group with which the individual made the strongest identification. In the case of a worker making a direct donation, this unit might well be the family, but in the case of an agreement to increase production and practise economy in support of the war effort, this group would normally be the work team or work section. If the donating unit were too large,[127] it would be extremely difficult to achieve congruence between the various elements of work motivation, and if the unit were too small, agreements might cut across normal lines of group orientation and control would be particularly difficult.

Attempts were made, therefore, to achieve congruence between donating units and work units. In Peking, for example, during the early part of 1951, the donating unit was often the urban ward (*ch'ü*) or a particular segment of society (business circles, etc.). After May Day, however, attempts were made to restrict the size of the donating unit in industry to the workshop or team and the role of Party and government at urban ward level changed to a co-ordinating one. Periodic 'Resist American Imperialism and Aid Korea Congresses' were held at that level to achieve standardisation in the donation movement and to provide some element of competition.[128]

Whereas in early 1951 the size of a donating unit might vary, patriotic compacts tended to coincide with work units right from their very inception at the beginning of China's involvement in the Korean War in November 1950.[129] At first such patriotic compacts did not include the specifications of donation plans and were just declarations of intention to meet production targets as a contribution to the war effort, to maintain vigilance against spies and saboteurs, to conduct patriotic propaganda, and study current affairs.[130] The procedure for developing the movement to draw up such compacts was exactly the same as that of the Democratic Reform Movement. Party and union cadres would organise a general programme of denunciation of the pre-liberation crimes of the Japanese and American imperialists and then, on the basis of this initial mobilisation, the focus of the movement was moved nearer to the daily activities of the workers. Off-duty time was used to educate workers on the need for such compacts. Forums were held at which the compacts of model teams were examined, and these provided models for the formulation of compacts within the remaining teams.[131]

In early 1951 compacts were frequently so vague as to be unworkable and the specific contribution to the war effort was stipulated in a separate donation plan. In the patriotic compact of the Chen Huan (World Shaking) Spinning Mill in Wuch'ang, for example, clauses appeared such as 'Support the Communist Party' and 'Get a grip on production' without any indication of what this meant in concrete terms and how one could check up on the fulfilment of these clauses.[132] To achieve greater specificity handbooks were published showing what patriotic compacts ought to look like.[133]

In one such handbook published in September 1951, the models of specificity which it quotes seem to me still to be rather vague. Two of these compacts of April and May 1951 are translated in Appendix III. They show that by the spring of 1951, the terms of compacts had not yet been integrated with physical contributions to the Korean War effort and actual planned targets. There appeared to be some confusion between a demand for specificity and a demand that compacts reveal a higher degree of political consciousness. For example one production team had written into its patriotic compact an undertaking not to listen to the 'Voice of America'; this was revised as an undertaking not to listen to any reactionary radio station[134] which, however laudable from a political point of view, must have created problems of definition and was hardly a move in the direction of specificity. These early compacts were most specific in their provisions for patriotic education. For example, compacts included undertakings for collective study of newspaper articles, though the time devoted to this end was usually very short (sometimes only five minutes daily).[135] This may reflect a low level of literacy or the fact that workers were too busy with production duties.

It was perhaps because the terms of the patriotic compacts were so general and that they were not closely integrated with concrete production targets that the charge of 'formalism' was frequently made. For example, an investigation of 16 units (13 factories, one harbour district, one municipal ward and one communications corporation) carried out by the Lushun–Talien municipal committee of the Party in July 1951 noted that only three of these units had anything like a good record in compact fulfilment, the remaining units being characterised by formalism. In some cases the leadership could not remember the stipulations of the compact and had not transmitted their provisions downward, let alone adhered to the principle of voluntarism and spontaneity.[136] Demands were made for strict inspection of the fulfilment of compacts and their periodic revision, lest they fail to reflect current production capacity or were not renewed after completion.[137] Such demands would indicate that, in some cases, compacts had by that time been integrated with production tasks, but I have seen no examples of any compact which showed such integration as early as August 1951.

Before any really effective method could be devised to integrate patriotic compacts with concrete donation agreements and production plans, an effective system for checking up on the implementation of such contracts had to be devised, and this was particularly necessary in a situation of growing bureaucratism on the part of Party and management and 'economism' on the part of labour unions in the period prior to the Three Anti Movement. In addition to the routine publication of blackboards and posters showing the current state of compact fulfilment,[138] three methods of checking up progress in compact fulfilment were put forward.

Firstly, an inspection group might be organised in each unit that had concluded a patriotic compact to mobilise the workers to ensure its daily fulfilment. This inspection group would organise periodic forums to discuss the current implementation of the compact where criticisms and self-criticism might be practised. The ideal frequency for such forums was weekly, and at the weekly meetings the inspection group would deliver a summary of its daily inspections. Secondly, compact fulfilment might be investigated by higher level labour union organisations, such as was undertaken by the Shanghai General Textile Union in April 1951. Thirdly, the periodic 'Resist American Imperialism and Aid Korea Congresses' might investigate the compacts, though this would be applicable only for larger units (factories) since it would be impossible to listen to reports about compacts made in every production team in every factory in a whole urban ward or *hsien*.[139]

By the autumn of 1951 the donation drive had grown into a major movement to 'Increase Production and Practise Economy' which was justified in terms of its contribution to the war effort. By that time, many of the original donation targets had been met and the donation drive as such drew to an end in December 1951, showing contributions to the tune of JMP ¥ 4,617,800 million, which was said to be sufficient to purchase over 3,000 armoured vehicles or over 5,000 pieces of artillery.[140] At that time precise figures showing the expenditure of funds were not given and no specific associations were made between a particular donating unit and a particular tank or aircraft.

During the last few months of 1951 various regions formulated 'Increase Production and Practise Economy Plans' which were expressed in millions of tons of food grain, and the purchasing power of these economy targets in terms of military equipment was often stated in the propaganda.[141] Similar plans were also formulated at enterprise level[142] and below; at team level their terms were incorporated into patriotic compacts.[143] As the compacts became more specific in terms of production targets however, their specifically patriotic element became more generalised.

The Wu San factory – an example of the integration of the patriotic compact and the planning apparatus[144]

As the donation drive grew into the major economy drive at the end of 1951, so patriotic compacts became linked to the planning apparatus. This point may be best illustrated in the case of the model Wu San Factory in Shenyang.

At the beginning of 1951, in addition to a team plan (*hsiao-tsu chi-hua*), three other documents existed at team level – the 'team compact' (*hsiao-tsu kung-yüeh*), the 'team contract' (*hsiao-tsu ho-t'ung*) and a team 'declaration of determination' (to fulfil production goals) (*hsiao-tsu chüeh-hsin-shu*). As we have indicated, the difference between a contract (*ho-t'ung*) and a compact (*kung-yüeh*) lies in the fact that the former is an agreement between two parties, whereas the latter might be a unilateral agreement to fulfil a certain task; the difference between a compact and a declaration of determination (*chüeh-hsin-shu*) lies in the fact that the former is an on-going document that is constantly revised, whereas the latter is only related to one specific temporary end. After much discussion at the Wu San Factory, it was decided that the conclusion of bipartite agreements (*ho-t'ung*) at team level was inappropriate and such contracts should be concluded at factory level between management and unions. Similarly, declarations of intention were temporary documents that could be done away with in 1952 when there was felt to be a need to 'rationalise' internal agreements. This left the team compact which, being the concern of everyone in the team, was renamed the 'collective compact' (*chi-t'i kung-yüeh*).

We have seen that the relationship between the team plan which specified concrete production tasks and the patriotic compacts in the period prior to the autumn of 1951 was not very close. In the Wu San Factory, the team compact (which was not called 'patriotic' but which contained clauses concerning production, livelihood, ideology, education, etc., and was to all intents and purposes the same as a patriotic compact) was changed into a 'collective compact' which only contained guarantees of fulfilment of quantity and quality targets, guarantees that principal obstacles to plan fulfilment facing the team would be overcome, and concrete measures to unite the terms of the compact with the main current political or economic movement. The collective compact was now closely tied to the team plan and was an integral part of the planning apparatus.

Once the compact was tied to the plan, it was subject to the kind of problems discussed in the last chapter. Both plan and compact had to be discussed together at the beginning of each planning period. In the Wu San Factory the basic operational plan was a monthly one, and discussion had been streamlined to the point that, by 1952, the plan could be issued at the beginning of the month. It was sometimes not until the tenth of the month, however, that the monthly compact was concluded. Just as a delay in putting a plan forward resulted in 'storming' at the end of the planning period, so a delay in putting a compact into operation was said to result in shoddy work at the beginning of every planning period when workers had not made agreements as to quality. The model Wu San Factory was able to overcome this by working out a system whereby the factory's planned production targets were handed down on the 15th of the preceding month, submitted to the shops on the 20th, discussed in the teams on the 25th, incorporated into compacts by the 30th to go into operation on the 1st of the next month. On the 1st and 2nd of the month, progress in implementing the preceding compact was summed up and compared with other teams. In the case of a team that undertook a number of different work processes, time was saved by appointing mutual aid groups to examine each individual process during the summing up period. In the light of our discussion in the last chapter, it would seem that few factories were so fortunate in being able to plan so far in advance.

Even at the model Wu San Factory, the vice of 'formalism' existed. Frequently during the summing-up period at the beginning of each month, workers apologised for not fulfilling certain tasks which they promised to do the following month but never did. Clearly there was a need for some additional control mechanism to check up on the implementation of compacts while they were in operation and team leaders were given instructions in how to conduct 'focal-point investigations'.

Conclusion

Underlying all the many contradictions we have discussed, between the desire for systematisation in grading and the prescription of higher wages for line management, between the level of technical education and the development of piecework, between the fostering of model workers and a desire to propagate their experiences, between the demand that the labour union *represent* the workers and the continuance of participatory *pao-kung* forms of organisation, there existed the contradiction that determined all others – that between policy and resources.

If there were insufficient criteria for evaluating the required political qualities of line management, there could not be a unified grading system for both staff and line; if facilities were inadequate for training workers, piecework systems would not get off the ground; if there were insufficient model workers, the few would be overburdened to the point of causing alienation between them and the many; if gang-bosses were not replaced by mechanisms whereby control might be exercised over the basic level, then management would have recourse to *pao-kung* contracts, the persistence of which might act against the policy of individual incentive; if the prescribed forms of contractual relationship derived from an area which was comparatively rich in prescribed managerial resources, the other areas would have great difficulty in adhering to them. In the period under review one may trace the steady growth of the required resources but it was not until after the First Five Year Plan was under way in 1953 that the various elements of the prescribed Soviet model began to be implemented really effectively. Only after some experience in their implementation could one determine what elements were in contradiction because of inadequate resources what elements were intrinsically in contradiction and what elements were in contradiction with what Mao and the Party considered to be creativity and rationality.

In this chapter, one may perhaps begin to see that there was something intrinsically contradictory about a system which maintained a fixed wage fund and yet demanded the holding of production competitions and something intrinsically inflationary (in a very restricted sense of the word) about the selection of model workers. There was also a sharp difference between the individual orientation of incentive policies which derived from the Soviet Union and the former group-orientation of the Communist Party. The new individual orientation in wages policy led to divisiveness which was to be sharply criticised during the middle 1950s but the new individual orientation in production competitions never really eclipsed the importance of the group as a competing unit; even Ma Heng-chang would have been little without his team. Here sectarianism was probably a more serious shortcoming than individual discord. One cannot create an individual ethos overnight, especially when ideological prescriptions condemned 'individualism' as a bourgeois phenomenon. Just as one might contrast an egalitarian ethos which resulted from circumstances and 'egalitarianism' which was the product of conviction, so one may contrast the individual focus of incentive policy during this period with a desire for individual betterment at the expense of other individuals. Similarly, as an egalitarian ethos may change into an egalitarian conviction, so an individually focussed incentive policy might change into what was described as 'bourgeois individualism'.

A preference for the free supply system, *pao-kung* forms of organisation, and taking into account political attitude in grading were not just to be temporary phenomena that would disappear once human and technical resources improved. These issues surfaced again in the mid 1950s and at least one of them (that of political attitude in grading) in the mid 1960s. One of the 'logic of industrialism' school would probably say that they surfaced again because resources were *still* inadequate. There is of course no answer to such a classic untestable statement.

6. A discrete command structure

An advocacy of the functional principle

In the Introduction, we discussed the three traditional forms of organising an industrial unit and, in Chapter 1, noted that by the late 1940s the Soviet model that was emulated in China prescribed a very rigid form of staff-line system known as 'one-man management'. It is quite clear, however, that the alternative organisational models considered earlier were also considered in China at the time of liberation. In the first two issues of the unofficial industrial journal *Chung-kuo Kung-yeh* which appeared either side of the liberation of Shanghai,[1] an extensive discussion of organisational models by a certain Yin Ku was published.[2] I have seen no reference to what effect his advocacy of functional patterns of organisation had, but the fact that his articles were published in a journal that supported the liberation of Shanghai[3] meant that some retained managers must have considered the possibility that liberation would not mean the automatic adoption of the Soviet model in all its detail.

Tracing the history of various types of factory organisation from the military or line type (*chün-tui-shih-ti huo hsien-ti tsu-chih*) (single line type) through the staff-line type (*hsien-ti chien ts'an-tsan-shih ti tsu-chih*) to the functional type (*chuan-chih-hua tsu-chih*), Yin Ku concluded that the functional type was the most advanced. Such a type of organisation could be implemented in China since, by the 1930s, China had reached the stage of development comparable to the United States at the turn of the century when Frederick Taylor had first put forward the idea of functional supervision. Yin Ku felt (erroneously) that China need not fear confusion arising from workers receiving instructions from different sources since this had not been a great problem in the West. One could help the process of integration by the provision of a strong committee system (*wei-yüan-hui-chih*) and specify the degree of stratification by locating functional supervisors at two levels, in a production control department (*sheng-ch'an k'ung-chih-pu*) at factory level and in similar departments at a lower level. The committee system would ensure not only lateral integration of conflicting instructions on the shop floor but also vertical integration between instructions originating from functional supervisors at these two levels. As such, Yin Ku's prescribed system was really a mixture of staff-line and functional systems (*hun-ho hsien-ti chien ts'an-tsan-shih-ti chi chuan-chih-hua ti tsu-chih*) with real functional leadership being operative at the lower levels.[4]

Yin Ku acknowledged that there would be a tendency for specialist workers not to understand the comments of members of other departments and to show a lack of interest in committees. He felt, however, that frequent meetings of the appropriate committees would help to overcome this problem. He realised that, in the case of divergence of opinions, specialisation might militate against a successful conclusion but this was a fault of the men not of the system. Yin Ku also called for appropriate supervisory organs to be established to pinpoint difficulties, and advocated the establishment of a separate system of personnel management to pay attention to the human factor (*jen-ti yin-su*).[5]

It was suggested earlier that the process whereby integration is achieved between conflicting instructions may be technological (as in the Taylor model) or ideological. The particular stress given by Yin Ku to the problem of men as well as system may be interpreted as a call for ideological integration and certainly a separate system of personnel management which paid attention to the human factor could be seen as a mechanism through which such ideological integration might be effected. Yin Ku's prescriptions are in many ways similar to the kind of pattern that was elaborated in Yenan in 1943 which has been described in Chapter 1. This pattern which was put forward again during the Great Leap Forward was characterised by unified policy which could best be achieved through a staff-line system at the highest level and 'divided operations' (*fen-san ching-ying*) at the basic level. It was a system in which functional agents might intervene at any level except the very top and where the Party was responsible for ideological integration.

The establishment of responsibility systems in the Movement to Create New Records

Although it is conceivable that retained management south of the Great Wall considered their options to be quite wide, we have seen that, at the same time as the above article was published, the official journal of the North East Industrial Department, *Tung Pei Kung-yeh* explicitly drew on the experiences of Lushun and Talien and contained many articles advocating the current Soviet system of organisation.

As the Movement to Create New Records developed, it was felt that the need to establish a responsibility system was a particularly urgent one since the movement was becoming too 'democratic' in the sense that labour activism might lead to confusion and the shelving of responsibility in the drive to achieve new records.[6] Although many new records had been set in the last quarter of 1949, overall production targets were sometimes not achieved due to faulty systems of management.[7] The Movement to Create New Records had been designed primarily as the first step in introducing the economic accounting system which was above all aimed at minimising waste. In the course of the movement however, waste had sometimes increased due to a stress on quantity at the expense of quality, a preoccupation with finishing work in record time, insufficient attention paid to inspection procedures and the large-scale testing of rationalisation proposals which often went wrong. The enthusiasm of the workers had led to their participation in extra shifts and night-shift workers frequently worked through the following day shift thus endangering their health.[8] The time had come to give greater stress to discipline and, for discipline to be effective, precise responsibilities had to be prescribed and a discrete chain of command established.

A number of articles appeared in the press highlighting the lack of a sense of responsibility. It was noted that in some factories there were no technical regulations at all and in others some people came and went at will without any regard to the work-post to which they had been assigned. Demands were made therefore that the Party, management and labour unions carry out all measures necessary to define responsibilities and enforce labour discipline even to the point of compulsion.[9] When the movement began, policy had been to 'let the water find its own channel'.[10] By the summer of 1950 the new order of priorities was reflected in the fact that press accounts of the movement were sometimes included under the heading 'Establish a Responsibility System'.[11]

The original policy for the Movement to Create New Records had been one of discipline on the basis of creativity. In early 1950 this changed to one of creativity on the basis of discipline and it was at this stage that the movement spread to the rest of the country. The successful implementation of a drive to create systems of labour discipline and responsibility depended on the elimination of gang-bosses and the prior completion of 'Democratic Reform'. We have seen, however, that although this was achieved in North East China by 1950, democratic reform was not very thoroughly implemented south of the Great Wall in the period 1950–1. Nor indeed was the development of labour emulation competitions, for they too depended upon a policy of mobilisation which was not to appear in any significant way until mid-1951.

In that year, the Movement to Create New Records was given a new lease of life and it subsequently developed into a Movement to Increase Production and Practise Economy as mass mobilisation became more thorough. As late as July 1951, Li Li-san warned against precipitately imposing disciplinary measures upon workers engaged in production competitions even though such competitions might harm their health and so affect production. Li felt that the intense vigour engendered by such competitions could not last for long and only when movements began to lose their vigour was one to lead them 'from their temporary shock nature into becoming regular campaigns'.[12] Li's remark was an echo of the 'water' analogy that had been applied to the North East at the height of the Movement to Create New Records.

Since it was impossible to routinise production competitions until after the completion of 'Democratic Reform',[13] the stress on labour discipline and the creation of Soviet type responsibility systems which occurred in the North East in the spring of 1950, did not take place with anything like the same degree of thoroughness in the rest of the country until after the conclusion of the Three and Five Anti campaigns of 1951–2.

We have already discussed the measures taken in the North East to establish a tight system of control and a short-term planning system. The system of responsibility that was adopted was a corollary of those systems. Just as the planning system established the responsibilities of the factory general manager to higher echelons, so the internal responsibility system was an extension of that process into the factory. Before beginning work every day, meetings of technicians, shift leaders, foremen and team leaders were to be held in the shops to determine work posts for the day (or shift) and after every shift a fifteen minute meeting was to be held in every shop to analyse difficulties encountered in the shift and shortcomings in the work done. One person was to be assigned responsibility for each piece of equipment and responsibility for shift-change, supply, safety and the resolution of different kinds of technical problems located. A regular inspection procedure for every item of equipment was to be instituted and, in the case of work stoppages due to equipment malfunction, the bureau or corporation concerned was to call a meeting to determine who exactly was responsible; these meetings were to submit reports to the head of the Industrial Department.[14] The instructions on responsibility were supplemented by a directive on safety[15] following which, each bureau conducted an investigation into safety measures throughout its network. The Industrial Department organised four inspection teams to carry out spot checks. In addition, each factory was required to set up its own safety inspection system, the provisions of which were to be ratified by the appropriate factory management committee.[16]

One-man management

The key element of the responsibility system laid down for North East China in early 1950 was the provision that *one man* was responsible for each work task and responsible only to his immediate superior. Staff was subordinated completely to line and, if anything went wrong, one could always locate the individual responsible for it. This was the negative counterpart of the positive individualised incentive policy described in Chapter 5.

One-man management was an extreme form of staff-line system and lay at the core of the Soviet model that was imported into China. In an article in *Chung-kuo Kung-yeh* one year after Yin Ku had put forward his defence of functional systems, Cheng Hung-su, an exponent of the Soviet model, reflected very clearly how the three possible organisational principles were now viewed.[17] His translation of the single line, staff-line and functional principles are contrasted with those of Yin Ku as follows:

	Yin Ku	*Cheng Hung-su*
Single Line System	Military or line organisation *chün-tui-shih-ti huo hsien-ti tsu-chih*	System of hierarchical leadership *chu-chi ling-tao-chih*
Staff-line System	Line and staff organisation *hsien-ti chien ts'an-tsan-shih ti tsu-chih*	One-man management *tan-i ling-tao chih*[18]
Functional System	Functional (specialist job) organisation *chuan-chih-hua tsu-chih*[19]	Functional (divided job) system *Chih-wu fen-kung-chih*

As far as organisation theorists in China were concerned, a staff-line system was now synonymous with 'one-man management' and descriptions of functional management described not the way it employed expertise but the way it *divided work*. Needless to say, Cheng Hung-su was most contemptuous of this functional system.

During the early period in which the Soviet model was propagated in China, many works were translated from Russian explaining in some detail what was meant by the term 'one-man management' and its application in the Soviet Union.[20] Though the term was applied to descriptions of Chinese organisation, there seemed to be a reluctance to use it. In fact the Soviet term *edinonachalie* (one-man management) was translated in a number of different ways (*i-chang-chih, tan-i ling-tao-chih*) and frequently not used at all but subsumed under the general term 'managerial responsibility system' (*hsing-cheng tse-jen-chih*).[21]

Perhaps the main reason why the principle of one-man management was not given prominence in the early New Democratic period was that its implementation was to be combined with the establishment of factory management committees which were not very different from the 'parliamentary system' (Chinese translation: *i-hui-chih*) which, in the Soviet Union, one-man management had been designed to replace. Again we return to the problem of exactly which Soviet model was to be implemented. If it were really the Soviet model of the late 1940s, as official pronouncements indicated, there could be no place for 'parliamentary forms'. If however, it was the Soviet model of the early 1920s, there was a place for management committees and some precedent for recognising a contradiction between such committees and the principle of unity of command.

It is my impression that the rigid staff-line system involved in one-man management was only incompletely implemented. I have suggested why it was extremely difficult to implement the system in China south of the Great Wall before the Three and Five Anti Movements of 1951–2, and it must have been even more difficult to implement it during those movements which strengthened horizontal lines at the expense of vertical ones.[22] It was not until 1953 that a campaign was launched to implement the system over the whole country[23] and not long after that campaign began, accounts appeared in the press covertly attacking the system on the grounds that it was being interpreted wrongly.[24] It was formally abolished at the Eighth Party Congress in 1956 when Li Hsüeh-feng, the head of the Party's Industrial Work Department took the unusual step of praising those comrades who had persisted in the tradition of the Communist Party and refused to implement the one-man management system.[25] Even in the North East during the New Democratic period what was described as 'one-man management' seemed only a very incomplete version of its Soviet parent as I shall attempt to show later in this chapter with reference to the Anshan Iron and Steel Works, the largest and most advanced industrial complex in the country.

The superimposition of the Soviet command system

The Soviet principle of organisational command demanded that staff-line patterns of organisation replace existing patterns and that the insulation of senior management from the shop floor resulting from the gang-boss system be ended. Until democratic reform was fully effected, gang-bosses were frequently sufficiently resilient to place themselves in line management posts and perpetuate the highly stratified form of pre-liberation organisation.[26] In such a situation, the adoption of a single-line command system would only strengthen the power of the gang-bosses.

Following democratic reform the Soviet model could best be implemented by the *replacement* of all former line managers, for only this way could one be certain of breaking down existing patterns of solidarity. Such a policy was impossible, however, in a situation where managerial talent was scarce. The most practicable policy for implementing the Soviet model, therefore, was one of *superimposition*.

Chapter 1 noted that in pre-liberation China there were two ways in which an individual could become a gang-boss. He could utilise connections with organisations outside his place of work, as in the case of people who made use of the Green Gang network in Shanghai or Tientsin to become gang-bosses;[27] or he could place himself in a position to control the number of assistants taken on to help him, as in the situation described by H.D. Fong.[28] In view of the terms of reference of the Democratic Reform Movement, one would imagine that gang-bosses of the former type were more easily dealt with than those of the latter type. This latter type of gang-boss depended upon technical skill to be in a position to take on assistants in the first place, and for this reason it is understandable that some Party and management personnel had great difficulty in differentiating between gang-bosses and skilled workers.[29]

The Democratic Reform Movement tended to define gang-bosses in terms of their actions rather than their function; consequently there is every reason to suppose that minor gang-bosses who had not completely 'emancipated themselves' from labour remained as foremen after democratic reform was completed, in much the same way as rich peasants remained in the rural sector. In Chapter 2 we discussed the political implications of this process of industrial *kulakisation.*[30] Let us now discuss the organisational implications.

Multi-headed leadership in the construction industry

We shall consider here two sectors of industry – the construction industry which tended to retain old forms of organisation longer than many other sectors due to the necessity of maintaining a system of contract labour, and the iron and steel industry, which was given priority in this early period and might be expected therefore to show the greatest degree of change. We noted in Chapter 4 that in the construction industry, the contradiction between policy and resources was one of the most glaring for this was an area in which detailed economic accounting was practised and yet where literacy levels were very low. We saw also in Chapter 5 that instead of creating a new command structure in the construction industry following the abolition of the gang-boss system, a system of control from above was *superimposed* upon the existing segmental structure resulting in the institution of *shih-kung* contracts.

The process of superimposition was necessitated by the fact that foremen had a very low level of literacy and were not responsive to commands coming down the line.[31] Blockages in line communication could be overcome by replacing such foremen by more literate workers but these were in extremely short supply. The only way to maximise the ability of existing foremen therefore was to create a *shih-kung* system whereby workers were expected to respond to the functional supervision of work supervisors (*shih-kung-yüan*) as well as the foremen. Such work supervisors were linked to the site manager (*kung-ti chu-jen*) by a parallel command structure which exercised functional leadership over all levels of line management.[32] Thus the process of strengthening the pattern of command which the Soviet model demanded resulted not in the development of one-man management systems but in the growth of new patterns of functional supervision. There is a similarity here with the pre-liberation relationships in some Chinese factories between the 'long-gown' foreman linked to the formal management structure and the gang-boss responsible for the operational supervision of the workers.[33] One should stress, however, that the *shih-kung* system was not just a carry-over from the past but the result of a process whereby the Soviet command system was superimposed over the existing structure. This is demonstrated in the following diagram.

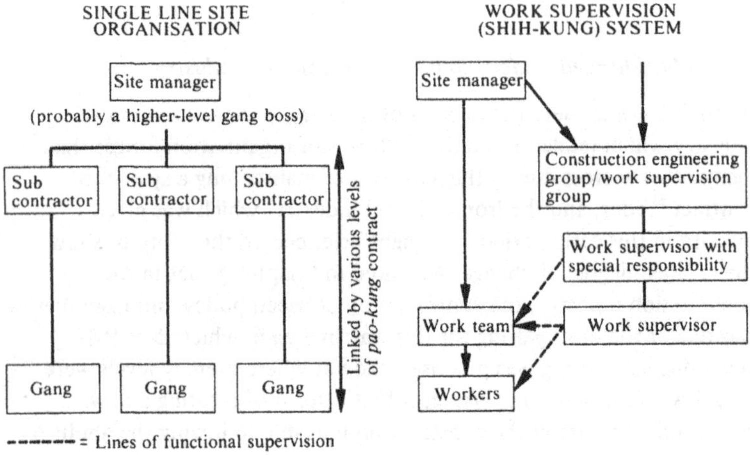

Figure 6

Such a system caused considerable staff-line tension which was exacerbated by the fact that section (gang) leaders were skilled but not very literate, whereas work supervisors were literate but not very skilled.[34]

The quasi-functional leadership exercised by work supervisors was the complete opposite of that prescribed by Taylor. The Taylor system demanded that functional agents be not only responsive to the demands of a central planning department, but also have an intimate knowledge of basic work processes. For example, a certain skilled bricklayer who was appointed work supervisor in 1951 noted that he had under his functional jurisdiction scaffolders, concrete workers, metal workers, bricklayers, carpenters etc., and the nature of his particular skill was such that he could give useful guidance only to bricklayers.[35] If he had been a line foreman in a staff-line system he could have called upon staff experts to help him supervise these other jobs. As it was, he was required to give guidance to line foremen who knew more about their own jobs than he did. The cardinal point of any functional system is that work processes at the basic level determine the scope of functional supervision. Once the scope of functional supervision is determined by a work supervisor's relationship to a planning department, confusion will ensue.

The lack of knowledge of basic work processes on the part of work supervisors led either to a situation whereby they moved work sections around from one job to another, which made the responsibilities of individual workers very diffuse, or where they were too cowed to do anything in the face of line foremen who were more skilled than they and submitted all questions great or small to an overworked site manager.[36]

Under the *shih-kung* system a work section might receive instructions from a lower or higher level work supervisor or directly from the site manager himself. These orders frequently conflicted and there was no mechanism to achieve integration. The result was that frequently workers became alienated from all management and held the work supervisors in contempt. Such a situation was referred to in the Chinese press as multi-headed leadership (*to-t'ou ling-tao*)[37] rather than 'functional leadership' (*chuan-chih-hua ling-tao*) for clearly a work supervisor who was required to intervene in the line in areas beyond his expertise was not exercising functional leadership as understood by Taylor and his successors.

The growth of patterns of functional leadership in the construction industry resulted from the superimposition of the *shih-kung* system over the single line organisation of the work site. We have so far considered the system only from the point of view of the construction corporation undertaking the work. There were, however, other networks of command which might issue instructions to the site. In the case of an external corporation undertaking construction work, there was frequently a problem of conflicting orders emanating from the enterprise for which the work was being done and the construction corporation doing the work. In mid-1952 a number of directives were issued by the North East Industrial Department which specified that, when construction work was being undertaken for a particular enterprise by organisations external to that enterprise, the primary channel of command should be that of the enterprise for which the work was being done.[38] Despite these directives, confusion remained even to the point of one cadre writing to the very journal in which the directives had appeared asking for advice on how to deal with the problem of multiple chains of command.

The cadre had to deal with four chains of command (excluding the

Party network). First there was the factory for which the work was being done, which maintained a representative on the work site. Secondly there was the construction corporation undertaking the work, which was represented by the site manager and an inspector (*chien-kung-yüan*). Thirdly there were technical inspectors from an industrial design (*she-chi*) corporation, and fourthly there was the labour union organisation affiliated to the local general labour union apparatus. The construction corporation was responsible for the quality of the work; the factory for which the work was being done was responsible for examining and approving the work done; the labour union was responsible for training workers and the design corporation was responsible for technical direction. The perplexed cadre had no idea how this process might be unified. In practice, the organisation which assumed the major responsibility was the construction corporation, since it had signed a contract and was responsible for the quality of the work, but the cadre felt that the primary initiative should have been taken by the factory for which the work was being done. He suggested that liaison meetings should be held, though he was not clear which party should be responsible for convening them nor who should be responsible for conducting political education. The editorial comment castigated the cadre for not reading the relevant directives which had laid down that all forms of 'parliamentary system' were wrong since they only led to responsibility being passed on. The initiative should clearly have been taken by the factory for which the work was being done, which would lay down the specifications of the work and not be subject to any inter-corporation haggling.[39]

A number of points emerge from the above account. Firstly the cadre had clearly not read the relevant documents of the Industrial Department, which makes one wonder just how effective the mass of detailed instructions emanating from that source was. Secondly, it would appear that the Party organisation had been completely eclipsed in a situation where the cadre in question was not sure who should take the initiative in liaison and who should be responsible for political work. Thirdly, the attack on the very idea of a liaison committee indicated an attitude of considerable rigidity, which might have been permissable within units under the jurisdiction of the North East Industrial Department but in other areas which were required to emulate the North East and where vertical communications were much weaker could have been highly counter-productive.

Multi-headed leadership in the iron and steel industry

It was not only in the construction industry that the phenomenon of multi-headed leadership was noted. Most other sectors of industry revealed examples of strong functional patterns which overlay the formal structure. In the T'angshan Steel Works, for example, the General Machinery Department and the Machine Electrical Power Department frequently both concerned themselves with the same problem on the shop floor, or took action in a particular shop without informing the shop supervisor.[40] Such functional confusion stemmed from the weakness of vertical chains of command and may well have been a carry-over from pre-liberation days. There were some areas, however, where, as in the construction industry, the growth of patterns of functional leadership was a direct consequence of post-liberation organisational reform.

An example of this in the iron and steel industry would be the production order (*tiao-tu*) system. In the larger enterprises, various levels of production-order-officer were established after liberation to ensure that each production-department and shop adhered to the enterprise work plan (*tso-yeh chi-hua*) and that the disposition of labour was carried out in a uniform way. In the Anshan Iron and Steel Works, production-order officers were directly subordinate to staff (*chih-neng*) departments and were constantly entering into disputes with the line managers. In the iron smelting plant, for example, production-order officers were subordinate to the Plant Production Department (a staff department) and such officers at shop level frequently refused to subordinate themselves to shift managers (*chih-pan-chang*): this situation was condemned as a violation of 'one-man management'.[41] The functional power of such officers is illustrated in the diagram on the following page.

The above examples demonstrate that the partial implementation of the Soviet model frequently resulted in the growth of functional patterns that were the very antitheses of the 'one-man management' principle which was prescribed. By 1953, however, the consequence of stressing controls from above at the expense of single chains of command were felt keenly and a campaign was launched to attack the phenomenon of 'multi-headed leadership' under the rubric of establishing a responsibility system. Let us now discuss how the above problems were dealt with.

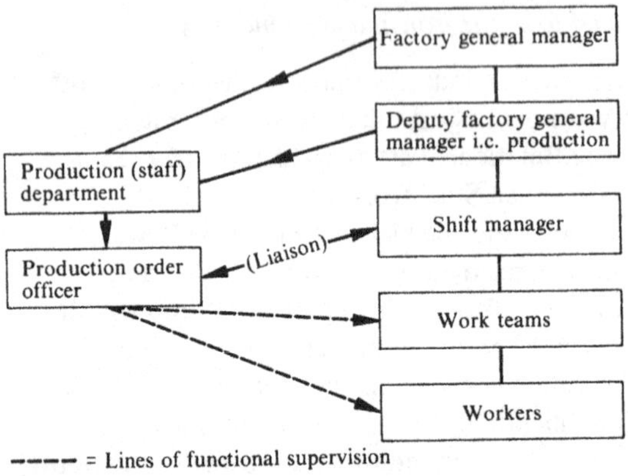

Figure 7

The 1953 reforms in the construction industry

The confusion occasioned by the superimposition of a work-supervision (*shih-kung*) network on top of the old building-gang system was the subject of much debate in the early part of 1953. Some people argued that it was essential to keep work sections (gangs) separate from work-supervision units, since work-supervision units (or construction engineering units) (*kung-ch'eng-tui*) were able to organise technical training, provide welfare facilities and act as general overseers of construction work, without getting bogged down in the actual details of construction. Foremen could devote all their energies to the job in hand without bothering with problems such as technical training for which their level of literacy rarely equipped them. The work supervision unit specified the work tasks to be undertaken and entered into contracts with the work sections with regard to supply of labour. Thus the system not only facilitated cost accounting but also ensured that there were not large numbers of workers in the sections with no work to do. In addition, it was felt that mutual supervision on the part of both unit and section would facilitate plan fulfilment.

Others argued that these advantages were merely theoretical. In fact, as we have noted, the result of such a system was acute staff-line tension; sections and units engaged in mutual recriminations and, in the words of one commentator, there were 'too many officers and not enough men'. As a result of this experience, the units and the sections were amalgamated in accordance with another feature of the Soviet model which up to 1953 had not been given very much prominence in the construction industry, the 'production territorial system' (*sheng-ch'an ch'ü-yü kuan-li-chih*).[42]

Just as one-man management stipulated that one man was to be in charge of each level of administration, the production territorial system stipulated that, as far as possible, all work being carried on in a particular place should be under unified command.[43] Accounts which described the confusion on building sites were specifically designed to prove the superiority of this production territorial system and so staff-line tension was described as a direct result of organisation separation. This is by no means self-evident. Staff-line tension will occur in any situation where the educational level of staff members is higher than the educational level of line managers. I suspect that the issue at stake was really one of a conflict between two different types of expertise, theoretical knowledge on the part of work supervisors and practical knowledge on the part of work-section chiefs. A recurrent problem was the tension occasioned by the promotion of trainees to staff posts at the expense of skilled workers. The existence of such tensions is essentially a political problem that can only be effectively solved by political means, and there is no reason to suppose that the tension between work supervisors and section chiefs was any the less once the former were stripped of their functional power.

The new post of foreman (*kung-chang*) was to be filled wherever possible by former section chiefs, provided that they could read charts, fill in forms, that they had some experience in work supervision, that they had the ability to work according to plan and were 'good at uniting with the masses'.[44] Work-section chiefs were said to be rather poor at the first three requirements and rather good at the fourth, whereas former work supervisors were said to have opposite virtues. Under the new system, if a section chief were appointed as foreman, the work supervisor was to become his deputy and vice versa.[45] One might imagine the tension that would ensue when a semi-literate section chief was transferred to a staff post in a situation where senior staff looked down on their juniors[46] or when a relatively competent work supervisor was made deputy to a less literate foreman. The logical answer to such a problem would be to demote redundant personnel to the level of ordinary building worker, and one which management would have no compunction at arriving at in the middle 1950s. In 1953, however, redundant personnel were given staff appointments. This was the beginning of a bureaucratic cycle where surplus staff personnel were beginning to accumulate at the middle levels, and to this problem we shall return at the end of this chapter.

The 1953 reforms at the Anshan Iron and Steel Works

We have seen the superimposition of the production-order system at the Anshan Iron and Steel Works prevented the effective establishment of staff-line systems of organisation according to the principle of one-man management. In the early 1950s Anshan was held up as a model of advanced Soviet experiences and the inability to establish one-man management systems there did not suggest the successful implementation of such systems elsewhere.

As a result of the drive to press ahead with the implementation of Soviet organisational forms in 1953, the production-order system, which was held to be the principle obstacle standing in the way of 'one-man management', was considerably modified. The new organisational chart within the iron smelting plant at Anshan was as follows:

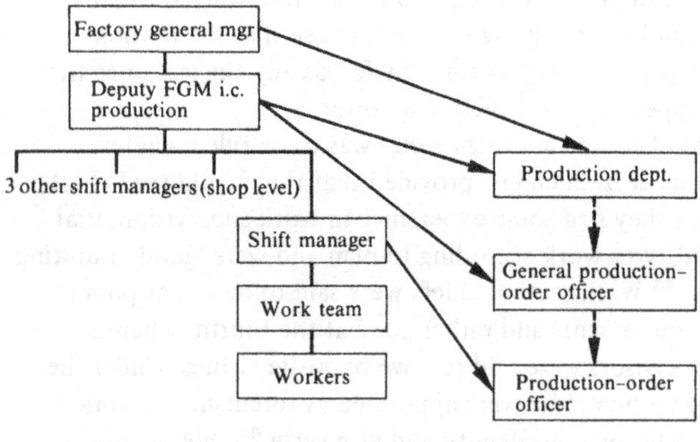

Figure 8

The plant was reorganised according to a four-shift system and the post of general production order officer (*tsung-tiao-tu-yüan*) established directly under the deputy factory general manager in charge of production. Lower level production-order officers were made subordinate to each of the four shift managers. Nevertheless, although production-order personnel were now placed firmly under the command of line management, there was still scope for them to exercise functional leadership over the lower levels. The general production-order officer was still to be responsive to instructions emanating from the production department (a staff department) if they concerned professional/ technical work (*yeh-wu*) and lower level production order officers were still responsive to instructions emanating from the general production-order officer if they concerned such professional/technical work.[47]

Though this was a considerable step in the direction of one-man management, it was not a rigid staff-line system. A perfect staff-line system (if such a system were possible) would only allow the production department to issue instructions to the general production-order officer through the factory general manager and would normally only provide reference materials for line management to consult. Similarly, such a system would require the lower level production order officers to receive all directions through the shift managers and the deputy general manager in charge of production *including* those concerning professional/technical work. Such would be very cumbersome and the system adopted probably reflected the fact that, whether one liked it or not, some functional patterns would exist. The effectiveness of the system would depend directly on how clear a line of demarcation could be drawn between instructions concerning professional/technical work on the one hand and administrative orders on the other. Such articles that I have seen seem to assume that the distinction was self-evident, which is doubtful to say the very least. Suffice it to say that the system adopted in 1953 was only a partial realisation of the principle expounded by Kaganovitch in 1934 and described in Chapter 1.

Movement to establish responsibility systems on a national scale

The attempts made in 1953 to overcome the problem of 'multi-headed leadership' were part of a much wider process to extend the drive to create systems of responsibility begun during the Movement to Create New Records of 1949–50.

We have seen that the earlier movement did not extend much beyond North East China and even there the atmosphere was not the most conducive to discipline. In early 1950 Kao Kang noted that cadres who had been transferred to the industrial sphere showed a marked unwillingness to bother with organisational detail. Compared with the demands of war (or what old soldiers imagined the war to have been), the details of industrial construction were boring and transferred cadres did not seem to take to heart Kao Kang's injunction that the best test of a Party member's revolutionary enthusiasm lay in his sense of responsibility concerning matters of detail.[48]

Throughout the next three years the press contained numerous accounts of accidents, waste and failure to fulfil planned targets, due to the fact that 'everyone is responsible and yet no-one is responsible'.[49] The system of detailed individual responsibility which the Soviet model prescribed was frustrated by three factors. Transferred cadres were unwilling to have the scope of their initiative restricted; stable patterns of organisation were difficult to implement in a period of rapid organisational change which did not come to an end until after the Three and Five Anti Campaigns. Thirdly, the very idea of individual responsibility contradicted both traditional Chinese patterns of solidarity and the organisational ethos of the Communist Party. Solidarity in traditional China had always stressed *group* responsibility. Such was the result of a pattern of solidarity which was as valid for the guerilla band as it was for the family or the traditional work-gang and one might imagine that Soviet advisors were as annoyed as were their Western counterparts three quarters of a century previously for precisely the same reasons. An organisation characterised by a technological conception of solidarity was an alien creature and one which was to be severely modified during the Great Leap Forward.[50] In the early 1950s, however, the Soviet view of modernisation was no less insistent on the need for specificity of role and function than Talcott Parsons.

Responsibility in a staff-line system is determined not only by the nature of the work done but also by the physical location of the workers. A functional agent supervises all those who perform the same function regardless of where they are, whereas a line manager supervises all those workers who are located in a particular place. It was for this reason that by 1953 the adoption of the production territorial system, which attempted to locate all the workers engaged in the same job in the same work area, became closely associated with the principles of unity of command and individual responsibility. These three principles were embodied in a Ministry of Heavy Industry Directive of May 1953 which was to launch a full scale nation-wide movement to implement the Soviet model.[51]

The directive began by noting that many attempts made in the past to establish systems of responsibility existed merely on paper. In many cases no specific person was responsible for ensuring that adequate conditions existed for plan-fulfilment, for ensuring inter-shop and inter-team cooperation, for the supply and handling of raw materials, for quality and production control, for ensuring the adherence to technical regulations, for the timely solution of technical problems and for the care and maintenance of machinery. When accidents occurred, no-one could be held responsible. Accounts were kept by a number of people, which made it difficult to correct mistakes; costs were incorrectly assessed and charts not produced on time. In conditions such as these no matter how perfect a plan might be it could not be completed.

The directive demanded that the production territorial system be implemented and a three-tiered level of management established; the factory (*kung-ch'ang*), the shop (*ch'e-chien*) and the work section (*kung-tuan*) with one man in full charge of each.[52] In addition, seven types of responsibility system were prescribed:

1. the system of sole responsibility by management (under the factory general manager).
2. a technical responsibility system (under the chief engineer, who was usually also deputy general manager in charge of production).
3. a responsibility system for production order (*tiao-tu*).
4. a responsibility system for equipment maintenance and repair.
5. a responsibility system for safety technology.
6. a responsibility system for supplies.
7. a responsibility system for production costs and finances.

The first of these systems affirmed the principle of one-man management but carefully avoided using the term. In case anyone should have any doubts on this score, however, the propaganda material explaining the details of the movement dealt explicitly with the principle of one-man management.[53] Articles dealing with individual enterprises talked quite freely about the principle of one-man management, but official pronouncements talked merely about the system of 'sole responsibility by management under the factory general manager' and I can only interpret such an approach as indicating disagreement within the Party Central Committee as to the desirability of one-man management.

The second of these systems assigned technical personnel to each piece of equipment and the third established measures for coordination and shift change and a control apparatus to ensure the implementation of the enterprise work plan.[54] The remaining systems are self-explanatory. As a whole, the responsibility systems enumerated above were not only a faithful copy of current Soviet practice but were themselves probably drawn up by Soviet experts.[55] They were supplemented by a number of other different types of system and sub-system, depending upon the nature of work undertaken in each branch of industry and were even accompanied by responsibility systems for propagating advanced Soviet experiences[56] which amounted to responsibility systems to implement responsibility systems.

The chief engineer and the responsibility system

The new responsibility system attempted to specify in detail the responsibilities of technical personnel. This was particularly important because it was usually in the field of technical supervision that functional overlay patterns were strongest. In the very early period, this problem was exacerbated by the fact that ministerial departments maintained the contradictory desires, on the one hand, to extend tight control over the technical network within enterprises, and on the other, to prevent the excessive growth of line power as a result of one-man management. Such contradictory desires are shown in the regulations published by the North East Industrial Department in early 1951 which gave the chief engineer (*chu-jen kung-ch'eng-shih*) full command over the whole technical network in enterprises within its jurisdiction but made him answerable in the final analysis not to the factory general manager but to the head of the relevant bureau or corporation.[57] The chief engineer was required to exercise leadership over the whole technical network and yet technical personnel under his command were not permitted to interfere in the line except in areas specifically designated by the appropriate line manager.[58] One might wonder how the chief engineer was able to exercise the function assigned to him short of violating the prohibitions against 'multi-headed leadership'.

The considerable power given to the chief engineer in 1951 was partly a result of complaints that technical staff had been reduced to an advisor (*ku-wen*) status where they had responsibility but no power (*yu-chih wu-ch'üan*) and were treated as 'guests' (*tso-k'o*).[59] By 1953, however, the stress had changed from deploring the lack of power of technical personnel to deploring the growth of this 'multi-headed leadership' and an attempt was made to remedy the situation by placing the chief engineer (now usually referred to as *tsung kung-ch'eng-shih*) under the direct authority of the factory general manager as a *line manager*. The chief engineer was now frequently also the deputy general manager in charge of production (according to Soviet practice) with power over both the shops and the whole planning and engineering apparatus within the enterprise. His main function was to supervise the drawing up and implementation of the work plan (*tso-yeh chi-hua*)[60] which specified the concrete tasks for each unit (and each individual) in the enterprise according to a more general enterprise plan which had been derived from centrally determined control figures.

According to the principle of one-man management (sole responsibility by management under the factory general manager), the chief engineer was required to consult the factory general manager on all important matters[61] and the degree of line power he exercised depended almost entirely on the personality of the factory general manager. Sometimes the chief engineer seemed to be exclusively in charge of the production and technical networks at the expense of the general manager. At the Paotow Iron Works, for example, the factory general manager was reported to be interested in neither production nor technology, and when an investigation team was sent down by the Suiyüan Provincial Office for Patriotic Competitions to Increase Production and Practise Economy[62] to investigate the works, the general manager told them he did not know anything about production and they had better ask the deputy general manager in charge of production.[63] In other cases, the factory general manager just handed over routine business to the chief engineer, leaving the latter very little scope for initiative. Some chief engineers appeared not to be very interested in planning or technology and just stuck their oar in factory general affairs departments when they felt like it. Others were too busy studying technological research that they neglected to do any. Still others were reluctant to accept a system which gave the chief engineer a considerable amount of power on the grounds that this was a Soviet system and was an inevitable result of her being a technologically advanced country; some five or ten years would be necessary before China reached that stage.[64] One could argue equally that precisely *because* China was a technologically backward country, she needed a system which gave the chief engineer considerable line power; I feel that some essential logical links in the argument have been omitted from the account.

The net result of placing the chief engineer in a line position directly under the factory general manager seems not to have defined his power but to have made it conditional on the personality of the general manager. As the above examples show, the chief engineer's power could have been very great or very small. To clarify matters, various management bureaux published detailed lists of instructions for chief engineers in enterprises under their jurisdiction. One such set of instructions, that of the Chemical Management Bureau under the Ministry of Heavy Industry, even went so far as to stipulate how he should divide his day and at precisely what time of day he should read what kind of directives, convene what kind of meetings, etc. According to the Chemical Management Bureau the chief engineer was to be something of a polymath. He was not only to draw up the work plan, supervise production-order work, organise stable production, supervise the formulation, amendment and implementation of technical regulations, supervise the control maintenance and repair of equipment, take charge of safety technology, supervise labour protection work, organise experimental work and the trial manufacture of new products, ensure the implementation of suggestions from (foreign) experts, foster and ensure the implementation of technical rationalisation proposals, formulate and implement measures for technological operations, improve technical organisation and ensure that the level of technical skill of white and blue collar workers was raised, participate in drawing up the factory's annual plan, long term plans and plans for new construction and rebuilding, supervise the work of capital construction, but also supervise technical education. He was to share an educative function with the Party secretary (politics) and the labour union (culture-literacy). He was to promote the integration of politics, economics (business management) and technology and to ensure that the workers had the right frame of mind to study advanced Soviet experiences. He was to make sure that line management was not 'divorced from technology'. He was to work out and supervise the implementation of separate responsibility systems for each staff department. He was to determine the organisation of shops and was to examine all regulations, work norms, organisational charts of lower levels, work graphs, production order reports, etc.[65] Such were the consequences of responsibilities determined geographically rather than functionally.

Staff-line tension

I have suggested that the considerable degree of staff-line tension resulting from the superimposition of functional patterns of supervision over existing organisational structures would probably not be eased by tying staff members to fixed points on the line. This suggestion is more than confirmed by accounts of the progress of the movement to establish a responsibility system of 1953. Technical personnel frequently refused to submit themselves to line leadership and were held to be guilty of petit-bourgeois 'libitarianism' (*tzu-yu san-man*). Sometimes technical personnel felt that the new system which gave them responsibility without power required them to do nothing but work to rule, which was criticised as 'the mentality of the hired hand' (*ku-yung kuan-tien*). Line management frequently did not utilise the expertise of staff management, which was criticised as the 'methods of handicraft management' (*shou-kung-yeh kuan-li fang-shih*).[66]

The process of tying production order personnel more closely to line management did very little to enhance their function or their popularity. Line foremen still considered them ignorant of basic level operations and senior engineering staff looked down on their limited expertise.[67] These production-order personnel, who were required to fulfil a co-ordinating role, were caught in the middle of staff-line conflict. Many of them were of worker origin who had managed to get a little technical education, which as far as senior engineers and technicians were concerned was little better than no education at all. The lenient treatment accorded to engineers and technicians during the various political movements of the early 1950s and their privileged salary structure probably made them the one group in authoritative positions in Chinese society who were least affected by revolutionary change and, as old intellectuals, they did not take too kindly to the co-ordinating function of the production-order personnel. Many of these technicians refused to attend production order conferences on the grounds that production-order personnel just made trouble[68] and, as we have seen, many others refused to listen to rationalisation proposals put forward by the workers on the grounds that such ill-educated people had nothing to offer.[69]

Problems such as these could not be solved only by organisational means. It was naively hoped in 1953 that some of the tension could be lessened by the regular convocation of production conferences and production-order conferences. A directive of the Anshan Iron and Steel Corporation demanded that production conferences should be held every month at factory level and every 10–15 days at shop, section and team level. At these conferences the relevant staff manager was to make a report and receive mass criticisms. Such conferences could serve to bridge the gap not only between workers and management but between staff and line management.[70] Another form of conference introduced during the movement to establish responsibility systems of 1953 were the joint forums of senior staff and line management (shop level and above).[71] The problem, however, was far wider than bad coordination and was a reflection of the whole problem of intellectuals which China has had to face during the whole twenty-five years since liberation. It could only be effectively solved by a whole change in the educational system.

The most immediate remedial measure that was to be undertaken was to raise the educational level of junior line management so that they were more equal in expertise to technical staff. The logical end of this process would be to make all management personnel into engineers and technicians. By the 1960s the Soviet Union had gone a long way towards this goal and indeed, in that country, many enterprise Party secretaries have engineering qualifications.[72] In the China of the early 1950s however all that could be done immediately was to convene training classes at factory level[73] to explain to foremen and shop supervisors how to draw up plans and to impart some of the theoretical knowledge which had hitherto been the monopoly of staff management. The external educational system was of no immediate use since, in the early 1950s, its engineering graduates tended to follow the same path as graduates in most developing nations; they moved into high prestige staff jobs, leaving lower level line positions to be filled by promoted workers.[74]

The command system at shop level

The responsibility system prescribed for the North East during the Movement to Create New Records indicated a process of extending control from the top down and paid consequently little attention to the determination of responsibilities at middle enterprise level. It was followed in late 1950 and early 1951 by a campaign to strengthen the power of the shop supervisor in accordance with the principle of one-man management. The immediate consequence of this downward process of determining responsibilities was that vesting greater authority in line management at higher levels resulted in the growth of patterns of functional leadership at lower levels.

At the Seventh Rubber Factory under the North East Industrial Department for example, the campaign to strengthen workshop work enhanced the power of the shop supervisor to the point where intermediate levels between shop and team were abolished and the post of foreman ceased to exist. Foremen were transferred from the line to staff posts and, as inspectors, exercised functional leadership over the team.

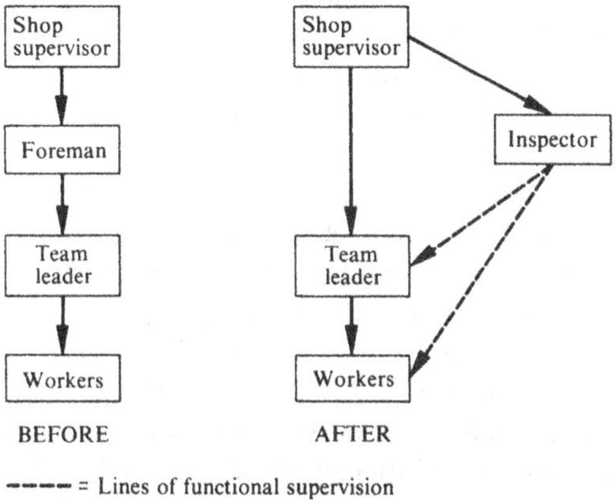

Figure 9

The rubber factory claimed that such a system increased productivity, but a *Tung-Pei Kung-yeh* editorial comment revealed that the North East Industrial Department was a little worried about the growth of mini-functional systems. The editor declared that the success of this system had been possible because the factory in question was small; some of the old foremen had in fact only exercised leadership over one team and were redundant since they only duplicated the function of the team leader. Further research was necessary before any decision could be taken on the wider applicability of this system.[75]

A second consequence of the growth of line power at shop level and above was that, now shop supervisors were under the direct line leadership of the factory general manager and his deputy (the chief engineer) as opposed to the functional leadership of senior staff officers, members of the production department found themselves with little to do. Such personnel were required to concern themselves with professional/technical work (*yeh-wu*), which may have been somewhat difficult to define.

A third consequence of the new power located at shop level was that some shop supervisors felt that they were independent (*tu-li*) and did not inform higher levels about what they were doing. Factory level leadership was considerably worried about the ability of the factory general manager to control the shops without the functional supervision of a production department, for the burden placed upon a general manager, who was required to integrate all the advice of factory level staff departments and process it into operational instructions, was quite considerable. We have already seen the considerable list of duties assigned to the chief engineer once he was made deputy general manager in charge of production. Those of the factory general manager were greater.

Not only was concern expressed about the burden placed upon the general manager, but some disquiet was felt about the experience and ability of the shop supervisors to undertake the responsibilities which were assigned them. The suggestion here was that the existence of functional patterns of supervision in the early post-liberation situation were a direct consequence of the low level of technical competence of junior line management, who could not be trusted with increased line power. To overcome this problem special training classes were to be set up for shop supervisors.[76]

The strengthening of line power at the level of shop supervisor was the first step in a process whereby staff functions were decentralised. Staff-line systems tend to produce a situation where, as one proceeds down the organisation, each level of administration is a miniature version of the preceding level. Consequently, as we have seen, each level in an enterprise was required to work out its own work plan, to maintain its own accounts (internal economic accounting), and (to all intents and purposes) the shop supervisor was a mini factory general manager.[77]

The decentralisation of staff functions was said to be designed to improve contact between staff members and the shop floor[78] now the principle of functional intervention was given up. Figure 10 shows the organisation of a workshop at the Fushun Steel Works, where the downward transfer of staff functions was carried to the point of assigning a technician to each work section and locating responsibility for shift change at work section rather than shop level. Most staff functions, however, were located at shop level and were placed under the control of vice-supervisors.[79]

Figure 10 is a very clear example of the implementation of the production territorial system. The size and organisation of the work section was determined by the number of men required to operate two furnaces (three shifts of thirty men, fifteen for each furnace). One technician was assigned two furnaces and one engineer was placed in charge of all the furnaces in the shop; thus there was perfect congruence between the network of technical competence and the network of administrative

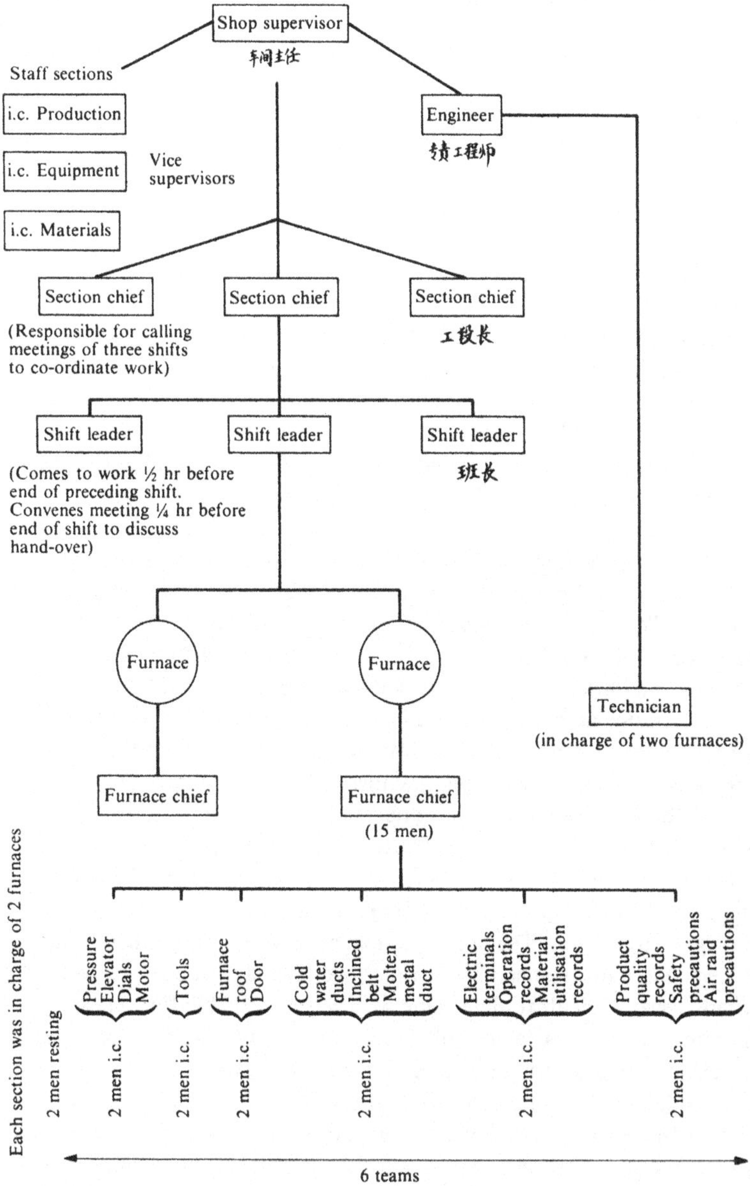

Note: One man could not be assigned to each of these 16 functions as some were fulfilled at one stage of the heat and others at different stages

Figure 10. Organisation of a workshop at the Fushun Steel Works

command. It was comparatively easy therefore for the shop supervisor to determine the relationship of a technician to the work section. At the lowest level the production territorial system made for very clear and specific relationships between staff and line. At higher levels, however, as we have noted, a geographically-determined field of concern led to the situation where the responsibilities of senior line management were excessive.

In factories operating a shift system, the shop supervisor was to appoint shift managers and shift leaders, who were to be in full charge of operations during their shifts. A responsibility system for shift change was to be determined and each person (whether worker or line or staff manager) was required to hand over to a clearly-defined opposite number.[80] In some factories, meetings of shift leaders at work section level were convened to co-ordinate shift change,[81] though how this was possible when the factory was operating 24 hours a day is difficult to determine.

Shift change offered perhaps the severest test of the criterion of individual responsibility. In his novel about the fictitious Liaonan Iron and Steel Works, Ai Wu narrates in great detail the life of three furnace-chiefs (one on each shift) and the conflicts between them.[82] The hero, a young and impetuous furnace-chief, was deeply resented by the other two chiefs, one an old experienced worker of considerable skill and the other a lazy and inefficient man. The old skilled worker felt that the hero was producing steel at temperatures which were too high in order to gain the prestige for producing heats of steel in record time, and when the roof of the furnace collapsed there were mutual recriminations. It turned out that no-one was free of guilt, though the real villain of the piece was a counter-revolutionary who was trying to sabotage production. The point was made, however, that under a shift system where heats of steel sometimes overlapped shift changes and where it was difficult to determine who was responsible for the care of the furnace, the doctrine of individual responsibility did not hold. The novel was written during the Great Leap Forward when the doctrine of strict individual responsibility was being reconsidered, and it may well be that the author was influenced by a political climate which gave greater weight to group commitment than individual responsibility. I feel, however, that in a situation where three shifts operated the same relatively fragile equipment, the doctrine of strict individual responsibility could not but give rise to recriminations, regardless of the good will or dedication of the people involved.

The foreman

I have suggested two factors which led to the growth of patterns of functional supervision in the period after liberation – the superimposition of new chains of command over pre-existing organisational structures to facilitate control and the fact that low levels of technical expertise on the part of junior line management precluded the complete transfer of power down the line. Clearly the existence of gang-bosses made impossible the immediate implementation of a Soviet model which sought to establish one or two levels of management below that of shop supervisor. In Chapter 2 we saw instances where gang-bosses were appointed to junior line posts with disasterous results. After democratic reform, however, some progress was recorded, although the lack of technical expertise (and sometimes even literacy) on the part of foremen made necessary such systems as the work supervision system and the production-order system.

The Soviet model of organisational command saw the work-section (*kung-tuan*) as the basic level of administration with its head the foreman (*kung-tuan-chang* or *kung-chang*) as the lowest rung of management, who was in Stalin's term 'the junior commander of production'.[83] There was frequently an even lower level, the team (or brigade) (*hsiao-tsu*) and in Chinese terminology its head the team-leader (*hsiao-tsu-chang*) might be referred to as a 'basic level cadre'.[84] The principle of one-man management (sole responsibility by management) placed the foreman in exactly the same relationship to his work section as the shop supervisor to his shop or the factory general manager to his factory or enterprise. No staff organ at factory or shop level had the right to issue orders directly to him and he was responsible only to the shop supervisor. He was responsible for his section's portion of the work plan, care and maintenance of machinery, the adherence to technical regulations and quality-control specifications, the organisation of production competitions, the promotion of advanced experiences, cost accounting within the section and was required to act as the workers' spokesman concerning wages and bonuses.[85] Such duties required a considerable degree of literacy and technical competence, which took a long time to achieve. In late 1953, even at the advanced Anshan Iron and Steel Works, complaints were still voiced about the technical skill and literacy of foremen, which was said to be a major contributing cause to the phenomenon of 'multi-headed leadership', since technicians continued to take direct action on the shop floor without bothering to go through the tiresome process of explaining everything to the foreman.[86] Occasionally additional labour was sent down to the teams without any reference to the foreman, and this led to resentment.[87] Some foremen echoed technical staff in complaining that they had 'responsibilities but no power' (*yu-chih wu-ch'üan*).[88] Others felt that their teams were too large to control and in effect technicians exercised control in their place.[89]

The educational gap between foremen and technical staff led to urgent campaigns to institute training programmes for foremen[90] and to campaigns to restrict the functional power of technical staff. Strengthening of line management, however, often resulted in the same problems that we noted in the case of shop supervisors. Foremen began to act independently and wallowed in the ideology of 'departmentalism' (*hsiao-pen-wei ssu-hsiang*) where they just 'did their own thing', provided the shop supervisor was happy.[91] Not that line channels were always very effective. Sometimes workers were appointed to the post of foremen when they had no work sections to take charge of[92] and redundant foremen who had been deprived of their position due to administrative reorganisation, as in the case of the amalgamation of construction engineering units and work sections, found themselves in staff jobs which only contributed to the process where surplus personnel accumulated at the middle levels of administration.

The effectiveness of a Soviet staff-line type organisation at the lower levels therefore depended to a very large extent upon the effectiveness of factory-organised training programmes. The problem, however, was not just one of technical training and organisational reform. Not only was the technical and literacy level of foremen to be raised so that they would be more equal to technical staff, but technical staff had to be persuaded that the trained foreman and line manager was in fact their equal. This political problem took a very long while to solve.

The bureaucratic cycle

We have observed that in a functional system, technical and other staff tend to concentrate at the top of an organisation, whereas in a staff-line system, technical staff tended to concentrate at the middle levels of organisation due to the decentralisation of staff functions. We noted also in the Introduction that where the staff-line principle is followed, there is a greater likelihood that chains of command might elongate, the number of levels of organisation increase and the personnel engaged exclusively in communication proliferate. In China this pattern has occurred several times in the past twenty-four years and has always resulted in anti-bureaucratic campaigns which seek to shorten channels of command and abolish middle levels of organisation. I shall call these patterns *bureaucratic cycles*. In the period under review the decentralisation of staff functions was only really effective after the conclusion of the Three Anti Movement, and consequently it is only realistic to speak of a bureaucratic cycle in terms of the period 1952–7. In the period prior to 1951 the superimposition of new forms of organisation on to pre-existing structures led to a growth of non-productive personnel which was the focus of a retrenchment policy during the Three Anti Movement.[93] We have noted however that in 1953 junior supervisory staff who were made redundant were transferred to staff posts. This was characteristic of a new bureaucratic atmosphere in which the ratio of non-productive to productive workers in enterprises grew. In a Kwangtung sugar refinery, for example, the ratio of white collar workers to blue collar workers grew as follows:[94]

1951	47 : 100
1952	52 : 100
1953	65 : 100
1954	66 : 100

It is probable that the Kerr school would regard the above as an inevitable consequence of the 'logic of industrialism'. Many people in China, however, did not see such a development as inevitable and attributed the ratio directly to the introduction of one-man management; the figures were published as a part of an intensifying critique of that system.[95]

Conclusion

The fact that Soviet models of organisation were only partially implemented, was due in large measure to what has been constantly referred to here as a contradiction between policy and resources. In Chapter 4 we noted that the contradiction between sophisticated planning techniques and a changing economic environment resulted in something less than the ideals of the Soviet model. In Chapter 5 we noted contradictions between the provision of piecework systems and facilities for training workers and between the creation of a small number of model workers and a desire to propagate their experiences. In this chapter we have seen a similar contradiction between a desire to establish control over the basic level and to maximise such leadership talent that existed at that level. The inadequacy of foremen and lower-level managerial personnel resulted not just in the continuation of functional overlay patterns but in their strengthening as Soviet forms of organisation were implemented.

'One-man management' and the system of individual responsibility was the 'stick' that accompanied the 'carrot' of the individualised material incentive system. It ran counter not only to the diffuse traditional patterns of organisation discussed in Chapter 1 but also the collectivist ethos of the Communist Party. It was quite clearly resisted and the implementation of 'one-man management' in China was slow. It tended to be more effectively introduced in North East China where democratic reform had been completed earlier, where there were fewer retained personnel and where Soviet influence was stronger.

To be sure, the centralised system described in this chapter was ideally balanced by various committees designed to prevent excessive authoritarianism. In the next chapter we shall examine just how effective these committees were and how effectively a synthesis was achieved between democracy and centralism.

Part IV

Checks and balances

7. Checks on managerial bureaucratism and authoritarianism

Chapter 6 noted that Soviet 'one-man management' structures were liable to give rise to the proliferation of personnel at middle levels of organisation and so insulate the top of an organisation from its base. An excessive stress on discipline was liable to minimise the activism of ordinary workers and an individualised system of incentive and responsibility was liable to make for that very alienation that socialism was to overcome. An awareness of this grew within the Chinese Communist Party in the middle 1950s but, in the period under review, all the implications of adopting a Soviet model of organisation, planning and the incentive, were probably not foreseen. It was hoped that the one-man management system might be balanced by structures which would prevent blockages in communication identified earlier as principal features of 'bureaucratism'. It was hoped also that ordinary workers would identify with these structures and, through them, participate in decision-making.

In this chapter we shall examine extensively three of these structures – the factory management committees, the worker and staff congresses and the Party organisation and touch briefly on a fourth structure that had anti-bureaucratic potentiality – the labour-union organisation.

The factory management committee

Of the above four structures, the factory management committee had no Soviet counterpart at least in the late 1940s. As we have noted, it was organised more in line with the 'parliamentary system' long abandoned in the Soviet Union and reviled by Stalin. Provision for the establishment of these committees was made by the Sixth Labour Conference in August 1948[1], at a time when the Soviet influence was less strong than later and detailed regulations appeared in 1949 governing their formation.[2] The various regulations and directives are summarised below.

In addition to the military representative discussed in chapter 2, the following personnel were to be ex officio members, the factory general manager (or in the case of corporations the director (*ching-li*)), the chief engineer (or principal engineer), the labour union chairman (once the labour union organisation had been formed) and the deputy general manager or director (who, as we have seen, was often also chief engineer). The remaining members (from five to seventeen) would be elected from a meeting of all white and blue collar workers (*ch'üan-t'i chih-kung ta-hui*) or, in the case of large enterprises, a congress of white and blue collar workers (*chih-kung tai-piao ta-hui*) (hereafter workers and staff congress) which would be convened by the labour union. The elected members were to submit to re-election once every six months.

The factory general manager was to be chairman of the factory management committee and also of its standing committee which would consist of the chairman of the labour union and the military representative (ex officio) and one other member elected by the factory management committee. In large factories and where there were branch factories, management sub-committees might be organised, their method of organisation being the same as general committees. The general committee was to meet once every two weeks and branch committees once every week. Standing committee members were required to be in constant communication with each other.

The factory management committee was defined as the 'administrative organisation exercising unified leadership within the factory or enterprise, under the leadership of higher organs'. Its task was to relate the directives and production plans of higher organs to the concrete situation in the particular factory and to discuss and decide all important questions concerning production such as plans, operations, management systems, production organisation, appointment and dismissal of personnel, salaries and welfare. It was required to carry out periodic investigations into how economic plans and its own resolutions were being implemented and make summaries of work done.

The standing committee was to handle day to day work concerning all the above matters in the spirit of decisions taken by the factory management committee. Branch committees were to have no decision making power beyond the application of the decisions of the general committee to their particular branches. They were, however, required to put forward suggestions on any topic.

The principle of unified leadership demanded that all decisions taken by a factory management committee would only become effective when they were promulgated as administrative orders by the factory general manager or director. If a decision were taken by a majority of the committee which the general manager considered to be against the

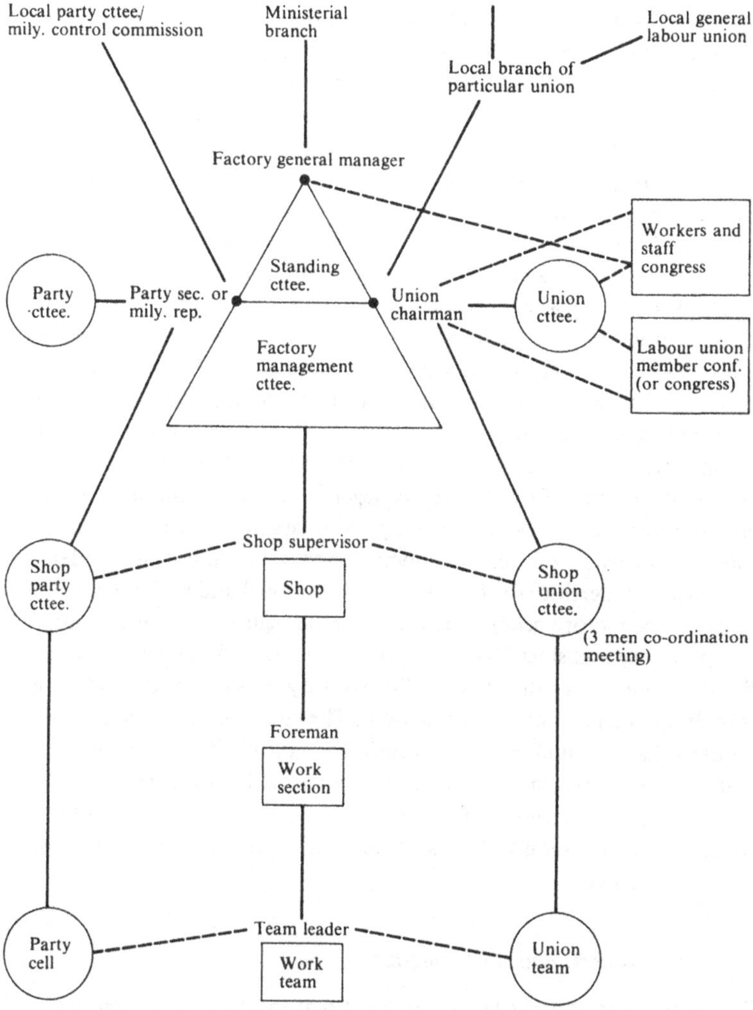

Figure 11. Factory management committee and workers and staff congress

best interests of the factory or not in accordance with higher directives, then he had the right of veto but was required to report the reasons for his veto to a higher level for ratification. Similarly, if a majority of the factory management committee considered that the general manager had acted wrongly in applying his veto or if they disagreed with the report which he was required to submit to each of its meetings, they likewise could submit their views to a higher level. Pending a directive from the higher level, committee members were required to abide by the decision of the general manager. If a matter of urgency arose which the factory general manager did not have time to submit before the factory management committee, he might act without reference to the committee provided that he subsequently inform that body for its approval. Such a formulation gave the general manager considerable leeway to disregard democratic procedure. His arbitrary actions would be checked so long as the higher level valued the principle of democratic decision making, so long as there was adequate contact between basic and higher levels in a ministerial chain of command and so long as there were effective political control personnel within the factory who were willing and able to supervise the factory general manager's conduct. As one might expect, concern was expressed about the potentially undemocratic nature of the general manager's veto and handbooks for labour union workers went to great pains to assure the sceptical that there was really no danger.[3] Democracy was to be 'democracy under centralised leadership' for only this way could will and action be unified. The factory general manager was the highest responsible person in the factory and since 'the higher levels understand the whole picture better and represent the views of the majority, this power of centralism is built upon a democratic foundation'. The veto was justified on the grounds that it would prevent confusion arising when the general manager and management committee were at odds. If the general manager's decision were wrong, one could expect the higher level to rectify it.[4] It was soon to be discovered that such a faith in bureaucracy was a trifle naive.

The workers and staff congress

The regulations of early 1949 stipulated that in addition to a factory management committee, there was also to be organised a factory workers and staff congress in factories employing over 200 people. This body was to be convened by the chairman of the labour union and was to meet once or twice per month, preferably on a public holiday or in the workers' spare time, each session not lasting more than half a day. Delegates to the congress were to be elected from each basic unit (production teams, shifts, etc.) and each delegate was to be directly responsible to the unit he represented. Elections were to be held annually unless a delegate was recalled by his constituents. In particularly large factories, the congress might divide into two levels, delegates to the higher level being elected from the lower level.[5]

The congress was not authorised to make authoritative decisions and its resolutions had to be ratified by the factory management committee and promulgated by the factory general manager before they took effect. Its main function was to expose the general manager to a fairly large representative body which would listen to his report and offer criticisms and suggestions concerning his management of the factory. Factory general managers were frequently required to make a public 'self-examination' (*chieh-t'ao*), the importance of which should not be under-estimated. Managers were considered as 'intellectuals' (*chih-shih fen-tzu*), preoccupied with questions of 'face', and the management-worker gap was, to a far greater extent than in the West, reinforced by class and cultural distinctions. In the past workers and management were often very carefully insulated from contact by the gang-boss system. Managers were not used to direct contact with the workers and many of them felt, therefore, that a system which demanded the factory general manager report to a factory congress would harm their prestige, especially if they were required to make 'self-examinations'. The official view considered questions of 'face' a characteristic of a petty-bourgeois outlook and that the process of 'self-examination' would enhance the prestige of the general manager for the workers would treat a sincere self-examination with respect and 'regard the general manager as a member of the same family'.[6] One cannot but observe that workers and senior management often came from very different kinds of family and the official view confused petty-bourgeois 'liberalism' (in Mao's sense of the word) and the legacy of a traditional shame culture.

It has been argued that China is experiencing a process of transition from shame culture to guilt culture. In the former the fear of public humiliation acts as an incentive to prescribed conduct. In the latter there is an active desire to confess one's faults in public in order to lighten the burden of guilt unshared. In this early period 'intellectuals' such as factory managers were greatly afraid of public humiliation and for this reason attempts were made to expose such managers to the criticism of workers. So long as this criticism is constructive, the fear of humiliation may be lessened and one can proceed to develop amongst managers an activist-guilt pattern of motivation.

The function of self confession was not only to lay the foundation for psycho-cultural change, but was also the first step in the process articulated in Yenan which sought to transform 'organisation', which is characterised by a network of interconnected roles and structures, into 'community', which is characterised by a network of interconnected human relations.[7] The closure of the élite–mass gap lies at the core of Mao's view of community,[8] and if one wishes to effectively close this gap and prevent the development of 'bureaucratism' there must be a free flow of information through an organisation.

Prior to liberation, management was not concerned with explaining policy to workers and later, as a result of the obsession with secrecy that characterised the period of China's First Five Year Plan, many crucial policy decisions were not communicated to them. We saw in Chapter 4, however that in the early New Democratic period, any attempt to hide economic secrets from factory workers was strongly opposed. Fears were expressed by management that once workers knew about the current state of enterprise profits they might ask for higher wages and some managers advocated concealing certain information from factory management committees for reasons of security. At this stage any such advocacy was denounced.[9]

The communication function of the congress would probably be better served if the congress were not tied to any formal organisation since formal organisational ties tend to produce formalised procedure. In the Soviet Union, for example, the establishment of formal ties between workers' councils and labour unions resulted in the latter swallowing up the former, only to be devoured themselves by the State.[10]

In China the regulations of early 1949 governing the establishment of management committees and congresses indicate that a very close connection between the labour union and the congress was envisaged. The labour union committee was to organise the congress and was obliged to carry out all its resolutions (unlike the management committee which was only required to listen to its advice) and the labour union committee was not empowered to alter the resolutions of the congress without the permission of a higher level labour union organ.[11]

Reading the resolutions of early 1949, one might have supposed that the worker and staff congress was a part of the labour union structure and its relationship to the union committee was much the same as a Party Congress to its Central Committee. This, however, was not the case. In reply to a query as to whether the congress had the right to elect the union committee and to amend the factory labour union constitution, a handbook for labour union cadres entitled *One Hundred Questions on the Workers Movement* declared that the congress should not have that right which properly belonged to a Labour Union Member Conference.[12] The congress was to be organised by the labour union but remain outside the union structure. This distinction was probably stressed because, when the regulations governing worker and staff congresses were drawn up in early 1949, most of the country had no basic level labour union organisations and, indeed, much of the country had not been liberated. It was probably in recognition of this fact that the *One Hundred Questions* (published in December 1949) stated that congresses should be organised jointly by the factory general manager and labour union chairman[13] rather than the labour union chairman alone as was laid down in the regulations of May 1949. Furthermore, congress delegates were frequently not union members which irked labour-union committees who were required to carry out congress resolutions. In answer to a question on this point, the *One Hundred Questions* could only reply that if some congress delegates were not union members, they ought to be, since the very fact that they had been elected showed that they had the confidence of the masses and were ideal labour-union material.[14] Within a few years of liberation, however, over ninety per cent of people eligible for union membership[15] had joined and this could no longer have been a source of tension. By that time, however, the congress system was all but defunct.

The process of democratisation: a case study – the Tientsin Third Textile Mill

The above description of the formal institutional structure of the 'democratisation' process tells us very little about how 'democratisation' worked in practice. The following account deals with one textile mill in Tientsin from liberation (January 1949) through to early 1950 and, although the situation in Tientsin as a whole was hardly typical, the process of 'democratisation' in the Third Mill was fairly smooth and its experiences were propagated for other factories to study.[16]

On 15 January 1949 the PLA occupied Tientsin and a take-over group was immediately assigned to the mill, which had formerly been owned by the Chinese Textile Construction Company and was therefore subject to confiscation. No details are given as to who comprised this group though it may be assumed that it was sent by the local military control commission. It proceeded to impose controls over the top management and consolidate control from the top down; the impression one gets from the account is that top management remained unchanged though it became subject to military supervision. The take-over group formed a work team (*kung-tso-tsu*) whose task was to mobilise workers to elect delegates who would assist the take over group in stock taking which was completed in two days.

Production recommenced on the third day but due to a shortage of raw materials the machinery could only run from three to four days per week and it was not until April that all the machines could be operated for a full week. The atmosphere in Tientsin during the first three months after liberation was quite revolutionary. No attempts were made at the Third Mill, however, to effect any radical reorganisation, and no changes were made in jobs or wages. Nevertheless, the revolutionary atmosphere in Tientsin did have some effect upon the workers. They expressed dissatisfaction with their jobs and wages and wished to engage in a struggle with the white collar workers. The white collar workers, for their part (presumably fearful of what was going on elsewhere in the city), considered that the question of wages and jobs was just being used as a means for fomenting strife between white and blue collar workers to secure their replacement by former blue collar workers. Needless to say, tension and bad labour discipline affected production and caused waste.

In April 1949, Liu Shao-ch'i visited Tientsin and delivered his Tientsin Talks. With regard to policy in the public sector, his major theme was the need for unity between white and blue collar workers. Whatever truth there was in the charges that Liu sought a 'capitalist restoration', after his speeches there was less stress on instant democracy within Tientsin factories and tension between white and blue collar workers at the Third Mill lessened. As a result of Liu's speeches, the Tientsin General Labour Union put forward a mild policy for the democratisation of factory management within the city and the only elements that continued to be prosecuted were former 'yellow' labour union officials. It became clear that management was to be subjected to 'democratic control' through a factory management committee which was formally set up on 25 April. This was not long after Liu's arrival in Tientsin. It was before his authoritative speech to labour union cadres[17] and I have only found reference to one of Liu's Tientsin speeches which antedates the establishment of the factory management committee (that of 24 April).[18] I suspect that the account gives too much credit to Liu Shao-ch'i, especially since it states that changes in personnel organs were effected, a worker and staff congress set up and a labour union preparatory committee organised *after* Liu's speech and *before* the establishment of the factory management committee.[19]

The account is very vague about how the management committee was elected. Elections were supervised by the take-over group whose work had finished in the middle of January and since it is difficult to imagine that this group was still in the mill, I can only assume that the members of the management committee were the very people who had been elected to help out the take-over group in the three days after liberation, especially since the account tells us that, at the time of election, some workers had not much idea as to what a factory management committee was even after three days' propaganda.

The take-over group had very little idea about the nature of factory management, how to conduct elections or how to conduct preparatory work prior to the elections. Furthermore, the formation of the management committee was undertaken before the detailed regulations on the formation of factory management committees in North China were promulgated.[20] I assume that all the take-over group had to go on were the vague formulations of the Sixth Labour Conference and perhaps some concrete examples from the North East where factory management committees were already in operation.

The inexperience of the take-over group, together with a distrust of white collar workers on the part of blue collar workers resulted in the majority of elected members consisting of unskilled workers with no technical knowledge. Some members were clearly unsuitable on political grounds; for example, the delegate of the cloth mill, Liu Tso-hsiang, proved his unsuitability when discussing wages by proposing to increase his own bonus. Other members did not say anything at all fearing, on the one hand, to say anything which the leadership might find 'incorrect' and, on the other hand, to say anything which would incur the anger of their constituents. Still others concerned themselves with petty trifling questions. The picture, presented here, reveals a combination of fear and indecision remarkably similar to the early stages of land reform in the rural sector.

Because of its manifest incompetence, the factory general manager did not treat the committee very seriously. He either failed to carry out conscientiously the committee's resolutions or exercised his veto. The military representative, for his part, tended to side with the general manager. The general manager vetoed a majority proposal for the establishment of a cooperative store. He refused to entertain a proposal calling for the abolition of the system whereby workers were searched when leaving the factory, even though such a system had long been attacked in Communist Party propaganda and refused to authorise the release of labour to the labour union for the construction of an air raid shelter at a time when North Chinese cities were being bombed.[21]

Then something happened to change the factory general manager's mind, though the text does not make it very clear exactly what this was. His changed attitude was ascribed to the persistence of the Party, the military representative and the labour union. I am not clear exactly what was meant by 'the Party' in this context since no reference is made to the appointment of a Party secretary; the subsequent account, however, does indicate that there were some Party members in the mill so presumably some cell organisation existed. The management committee now felt sufficiently confident to make proposals concerning the training of workers for participation in management and the promotion of skilled workers to supervisory posts. Acting on a committee proposal, Party members and the labour union preparatory committee organised an eight term training class in which six hundred and forty-five workers enrolled. The curriculum stressed the fostering of a new labour attitude and the role of the workers in management and the graduates of this class were to form the backbone (*ku-kan*) for a subsequent movement to increase production. The first skilled worker to be promoted was a certain Yü Shih-hui who had 'dealt a blow to a management that had no confidence in the masses' by carrying out improvements on twenty-three machines. He had formerly been underpaid and discriminated against. Now, as a shift leader, he secured for his department the first 'red flag commendation' in the factory and became one of Tientsin's first thirteen model workers.

The management committee once again accepted a proposal that the search system be abolished and this time there was no veto. It delegated this task to the labour union which organised over two hundred and ninety-nine workers. Those who were cleared as trustworthy displayed exemption certificates (or badges) (*mien-chien-cheng*), but by February 1950 there were still some workers who were subject to search and the article demanded that this situation be rectified. Following the organisation of these groups, four or five surprise searches were carried out and no stolen property was discovered.

In addition to the exposure of the factory general manager to the workers at the periodic meetings of the workers and staff congress, the committee endeavoured to establish a regular system of 'self examination' at lower levels in the factory. Workshop self examination meetings were organised at which technicians and other personnel guilty of alienating themselves from the workers were criticised. The first such meeting dealt with the case of a certain technician by the name of Liu Hui-t'ang who was charged with beating ordinary workers before liberation and of not having reformed in the period since. The workers wished to expel him from the factory but it was decided that he should be given a chance to confess and undergo criticism. Following his 'self examination' his relations with ordinary workers underwent a change for the better.

The mildness of the treatment given to Liu cannot be contrasted too strongly with the methods of land reform in the rural sector which, although milder than before, were much more severe than in the factories. At the Third Mill it was 'responsible people' who launched the criticism and there was no attempt at total condemnation from all levels. One may also contrast this period with a later period (1951) when corrupt cadres were given short shrift in the Three Anti Movement. Even during this mild period, however, some dissident elements were expelled from the mill; for example, Chao Chen-chiang, a former KMT 'thug' (*ta-shou*) who took opium and had continued to attack workers after liberation. One might suspect that the difference between the above two cases stemmed from the fact that Liu was a technician and valuable to the mill whereas Chao was an ordinary worker, for Liu Shao-ch'i had demanded that every effort should be made to avoid struggles against technicians. We have insufficient evidence to confirm or deny this suspicion.

The management committee was required to conduct propaganda among white collar workers with the aim of developing their reliance on the masses. Propaganda was later seen as mainly a Party and union function. At this stage, however, resolutions on propaganda were taken by the management committee which authorised reading lists for white collar workers. In addition, practice workshop self-examination meetings were organised so that white collar workers would learn how to carry out criticism and self criticism before being exposed to the real thing. The reason for this kind of exercise (*yen-hsi*) was that white collar workers were still unsure of their position and feared to speak out.

We are told that the case of Chao Chen-chiang prompted the workers spontaneously to organise mutual-aid groups to investigate problems concerning production and technology and, at the same time, the electrical supply plant and repair shop set up technical research groups. We are not told, however, how exactly the dismissal of a rowdy worker was able to bring about a demand for technological improvements, nor is it at all clear why something that occurred spontaneously should be listed as one of the great achievements of the factory management committee. In the opinion of the military representative these mutual aid groups were to serve as a form of cell organisation (*hsi-pao tsu-chih*) for receiving mass opinions on the democratisation of management until labour union teams (the lowest level of labour union organisation) could be formed. If the activities of these groups were confined to matters concerning production and technology, one might suspect that the military representative had a rather restricted view of what democratisation meant, and indeed what the function of labour union teams was to be once they were formed.

Despite the above achievements, at the end of August 1949, the mill leadership (undefined) were still concerned about the predominance of unskilled workers on the factory management committee and demanded that some skilled workers and personnel with managerial skill be elected. The text does not make it clear whether a new management committee was elected or whether extra members were elected to serve on the old committee. In any case, the first management committee of the mill had served some two months longer than the period stipulated by the regulations governing factory management committees which had been promulgated whilst it was in office.[22] The second management committee contained three new members, the newly promoted shift leader Yü Shih-hui, Ho Feng-kao, a skilled fitter, and Chang Ching-yü, an old maintenance worker of thirty years standing. White and blue collar workers throughout the mill were reported to be happy with this choice which had been made after a lengthy period of propaganda and fermentation (*yün-niang*), unlike the election of the first committee.

From the convening of the first meeting of the second committee (9 September 1949) to the time the account was written (probably February 1950), twelve meetings were held, which was about the frequency stipulated by the official regulations. The most important task of these meetings was to collect and assemble the one hundred and thirty 'rationalisation proposals' that were put forward. Ninety-nine proposals were submitted to the nine meetings that were held between September and December and of these ninety-five were adopted. They may be classified as follows:

Proposals concerning		
	production planning	5
	technical matters	9
	management	54
	personnel	12
	welfare	13
	other matters	6

The fact that over 80% of these proposals concerned management and technology as against 13% concerning welfare is taken by the author of the article to demonstrate how much the workers cared for production, though he subsequently criticised the committee for paying insufficient attention to welfare. The factory general manager did not exercise his veto at all. Once these proposals had been accepted by the management committee they were submitted to the engineering personnel for testing and implementation.

The management committee was now strong enough not only to avoid the factory general manager's veto, but also to censure the general manager for what they considered high-handed action. For example, at the twelfth meeting of the factory management committee, the general manager was censured for taking on extra labour without consulting the management committee or its standing committee. The employment of this labour was only put on the agenda of the committee after the action was taken. According to the formal regulations, the factory general manager might well have been within his rights if this could be defined as 'emergency action'. Nevertheless, he apologised to the committee and promised that such a situation would not occur again. Another worker complained that the general manager had employed a large number of trainees (*shih-hsi-yüan*) who, after their period of training, became white collar workers. This lessened the promotion chances of blue collar workers. The committee submitted this complaint to the military representative in his role as interpreter of Party policy and, after an investigation, he declared that the promotion rate for blue collar workers to staff status was not high enough. This example is of particular interest in that, during the middle 1950s, personnel matters were considered the prerogative of the Party, whereas, in the early 1950s, where the Soviet model was implemented, management tended to take the initiative in personnel matters. This appeal to the military representative, as substitute Party secretary, shows how matters of promotion were viewed before the adoption of the Soviet model really got under way.

Meetings of the factory management committee were held every other Friday. On the Wednesday before each meeting, every member would hand his proposals to the secretary of the committee (it is not clear from the text who the secretary was) who would sort them out, tabulate them and hand a list to each member and to the chairman of each branch committee (*chih-hui chu-jen*). After receiving the list it was the duty of each committee member to go out among the workers and seek their opinions. On the Thursday evening the labour union chairman would convene a preparatory meeting which each elected delegate (though not the other *ex officio* members) would attend in order that everybody should have a clear idea of the implications of the proposals and thus prevent discussion at the main meeting becoming too trivial. The preparatory meeting could also be used to bring forward new proposals. It does not take too great a stretch of the imagination to see how the preparatory meeting might be used to throw out proposals of too contentious a nature in order that more time at the main meeting could be spent getting through other proposals that stood a better chance of success and how a factory general manager could persuade the labour-union chairman who convened the meeting to exercise what was to all intents and purposes a veto. To gauge how democratic the whole procedure was, we need to know not only what happened to proposals made to the main meeting, but also to proposals submitted to the preparatory meeting and no account of this is given. It would seem that a preparatory meeting would serve the interests of rank and file workers so long as labour-union chairmen were prepared to take a stand against management. As far as we know, they were rarely prepared to do this in 1949.

The management committee's standing committee met for one hour every afternoon in a 'head knocking session' (*p'eng-t'ou-hui*); a session where Party, management and union representatives put their heads together. It concerned itself mainly with solving problems handed to it by similar workshop level 'head knocking sessions' where the detailed implementation of committee resolutions was worked out. In addition to these, workshop meetings (*ch'e-chien hui-i*) which were particularly useful in acquainting white collar workers with shop floor conditions, shop level 'self examination' meetings continued to be held and a system of shop production conferences (*sheng-ch'an hui-i*) concerned with technical problems was instituted.

A meeting of the workers' and staff congress was held every month and its principal content were reports by the factory general manager and labour union chairman on production work and labour organisation. When first set up, some discussion was allowed at this meeting though later there was no time for this as meetings only lasted one hour. Self examination was now carried on at shop level meetings (which probably exempted the factory general manager) and detailed topics raised by the congress were discussed by labour-union teams (which had been formed by February 1950). This would seem to be the first stage in the fusion of the congress with the labour-union organisation and the reinsulation of the factory general manager which became a feature of factory organisation during the First Five Year plan period.

The great increase in production during the latter part of 1949 was attributed to this process of democratisation and the experiences of the Third Mill were considered relatively successful. By February 1950, however, there were still considered to be a number of serious shortcomings. The management committee had paid insufficient attention to the problem of mobilising women workers to take part in management and no woman had been elected to the committee (though one was subsequently co-opted). The committee had not gone far enough in soliciting the suggestions of rank and file workers and had been dilatory in its transmission of resolutions (for example, the resolutions of the 11th session were passed on at the preparatory meeting for the 12th session). The factory general manager was still slow in carrying out committee resolutions and some workers still felt him not to be conscientious. Not enough cadres had been promoted to managerial posts (only two workers had been promoted to the position of foreman [*kung-t'ou*]). There was still some mutual antagonism between white and blue collar workers and welfare matters were not given sufficient weight.

The failure to implement the democratisation of management

The fact that the Third Mill's modest catalogue of achievements should have been held up as a model suggests that the democratisation movement was not particularly successful and the suggestion is confirmed by the publication of a number of articles in early 1950 describing this lack of success and calling for an end to the policy of maintaining the status quo.[23] The publication of these articles was followed by a partial Democratic Reform Movement in North China which as we have noted spread to the Central South region after May 1951. During the course of this movement, material was published describing why the management committees were not functioning as they should.

The root cause of the lack of success of management committees, noted in early 1950, lay in the fact that the principles of democratising management had been poorly propagated.[24] This was partly the function of the management committees themselves[25] but was more properly the function of Party and labour union organisations.[26] We saw in Chapter 2, however, that there was a tendency for Party committees to be complacent which led to a major Party rectification movement in the spring of 1950. The responsibilities of the labour unions were far greater. As 'transmission belts' between Party and masses, they were to solicit the opinions and suggestions of rank and file workers as to unpopular systems of management and to educate these workers on their role in management.[27] We noted, however, that many union branches 'lacked democratic spirit' and 'were not able resolutely and correctly to represent the interests of the workers nor conscientiously to organise and lead activists among the white and blue collar workers to take part in democratisation and struggle against bureaucratism'.[28] We have noted also that a situation where unions were 'tails of management' is not surprising when such unions were in the process of formation and were not clear about what their functions ought to be.

In the absence of effective propaganda and a spirit of participation, 'democratic' structures were just seen as rather tiresome committees that wasted everyone's time.[29] Not enough notice was given before meetings of management committees and inadequate preparatory work done. Having failed to solicit mass opinions and suggestions, delegates tended to represent no-one but themselves and in such a situation, neither management nor workers took them very seriously. Not wishing to waste time listening to the comments of unrepresentative and uneducated delegates, the factory general managers and labour-union chairmen tended to devote more and more time at meetings to their own reports, often to the point of precluding any discussion at all. In many cases sessions of the management committee became merely 'meetings where responsible management passed on job assignments'[30] or 'audiences for management' (*t'ing t'ing hui*).[31] Many worker delegates, tired of just raising their hands and ratifying decisions taken previously by management, stopped attending meetings. Delegates, upon transfer to other departments or units frequently left vacant their seat on the committee and in one case, that of the power plant of the Peking Shih-ching-shan Iron and Steel Works, this process led to the management committee just consisting of one man – its head.[32]

Management usually complained that, although they warmly supported the policy of democratisation, they were too busy to waste time on discussions that were either too abstract or too trivial.[33] In the North East, where the political vocabulary of senior management had reached a level higher than their political consciousness, some very interesting political rationalisations were made. For example, some managers justified their bureaucratic attitude by saying that the workers were politically backward for they were fuilty of viewpoints which were, on the one hand, 'economist' (*ching-chi-chu-i-ti*) (i.e. they stressed only self interest) and, on the other that they were 'ultra democratic' (*chi-tuan min-chu-ti*) (i.e. they were undisciplined). Others claimed that as the representatives of the state, they were the representatives of the working class and, as such, commanded the unquestioned obedience of the workers. One manager made play on the word 'democracy' which consists of two characters, *min* (people) and *chu* (ruler) by saying: 'What is *min-chu*? You are the *min*. We are the *chu*.'[34]

The attitude of management toward the workers and staff congress was, if anything, worse than their attitude towards the management committee. The management committee could, after all, serve the useful function of training managerial talent. All the congress did was to embarrass management. In many cases congresses were convened at irregular intervals and sometimes not at all. In Peking, four month intervals between congresses seemed to be the rule rather than the exception.[35] Congresses were frequently convened to pass on work assignments for a particular movement (such as the Movement to Create New Records) and then did not meet again.[36] The congress was supposed to be a 'bridge between the factory management committee and the masses' organised by the labour union. Presumably labour unions felt that one 'transmission belt' was enough.

The above complaints about the attitude of management in the North East shows that even in this area, where the process of 'democratisation' had commenced somewhat earlier than the rest of the country, factory management committees were not faring very well. According to the statistics of the North East General Labour Union for January 1951, only 683 (39.3%) of the 1647 factories and mines under its jurisdiction had set up management committees and the majority of those that had been set up suffered from 'formalism'.[37] Reporting on an investigation of over twenty committees in Shenyang, Chang Li-k'o, the chairman of the Shenyang General Labour Union, reported that the majority were organisationally defective. Some contained only half the required number of elected members. Standing committees and congresses were not performing their function and there was a general lack of democratic spirit. Chang attributed this failure to incorrect leadership on the part of the Party and a general lack of experience.[38] This part of China, it should be remembered, was the first area to implement the democratisation policy and the one with the most experienced urban Party organisation.

Sometimes the standing committee of the management committee usurped the functions of the full committee on the grounds that the knowledge (and even the literacy) of members of management committees was of a very low level. Condemning this attitude, the Industrial Department of the North East Peoples Government stated that the general management level of cadres in industrial enterprises was also very low, and for that reason such cadres were to listen to the informed comments of worker members of management committees.[39] Should one conclude from this that once the managerial skill of cadres was higher, there would be no more need for factory management committees? Similarly if factory management committees were schools for training managers, what would be their fate once the need for managerial talent was less acute?

Herein lies a crucial problem which is also relevant to that other organisational structure that, as we saw in Chapter 3, was described as a 'school for management' – the labour unions. Was the factory management committee to train workers to *become managers* or to train workers with administrative skill to participate in management *as workers*. In other words, should education be seen in a *selective* sense or in a *creative* sense? Ideally it should be both but, in practice, as the case of Yü Shih-hui of the Third Mill shows, the former was a more probable outcome.

The short life of the experiment with management committees, however, does not permit us to come to any definitive conclusion on this point. One year after the regulations governing the establishment of factory management committees in North China were promulgated, the All China Federation of Labour noted in its annual report that 'no remarkable record' had been achieved.[40] Various remedial measures were advocated during 1950 such as setting up tripartite (Party, management and union) inspection systems to check up on the implementation of committee resolutions, provision for meetings of committees where no reports were made so as to allow for greater discussion, fixed meeting schedules[41] but without much success. If there was to be a structure within industrial enterprises which effectively countered the authoritarian tendency of management, it was to be something other than the factory management committee.

The functions of the Party organisation within the enterprise

The above discussion will have made it clear that the factory management committees were not very effective instruments in combating bureaucratism and curbing a tendency toward authoritarianism on the part of management. We saw in Chapter 2 that, in the period immediately following liberation, there was a tendency for the Party organisation also to be ineffective. The Party organisation did however go through a number of rectification campaigns which gave it a new lease of life and so we must ask to what extent the reformed Party organisation was able to achieve what the management committees were unable to achieve. We will examine what I feel to be the three major functions of the Party branch within the industrial enterprise – structural liaison, control and propaganda–education. Official Chinese descriptions of the functions of the Party branch talk about 'leadership', 'supervision', 'education' and 'guarantee' as its principal functions. With the exception of education, these terms are somewhat confusing and will be integrated with the first three headings in the following discussion.

The structural liaison function

We saw earlier that in conditions short of perfection, both staff-line and functional systems of organisation depend for their effectiveness upon co-ordinating structures, which, in the former, cut across vertical chains of command and, in the latter, ensure that the functions of technical agents do not overlap. In addition to structures which perform the function of horizontal co-ordination, any organisation that wishes to minimise alienation between structures at its top and bottom must make provision for mechanisms that effect vertical liaison. In Chinese terminology, leadership that proceeded according to the first principle was referred to as 'co-ordinated leadership' (*ling-tao i-yüan-hua*)[42] and the system whereby vertical liaison was effected was included under the rubric 'democratic centralism' and the 'mass line'.

In the immediate post-liberation situation, the factory management committee was to fulfil both the function of horizontal co-ordination (between military representative/Party, labour union and management), and vertical liaison between management and workers. In the words of Kao Kang, 'our factory management committees are both democratic and centralist institutions'.[43] Of slightly more importance as a horizontal co-ordinating structure was the standing committee of the factory management committee where the factory general manager, the Party secretary and the labour union chairman met in daily 'head knocking session', and who were ideally linked vertically with the workers through the Party and union structure. Similarly, the main liaison structure at shop level was the 'three-man joint meeting' (*san-jen lien-hsi hui-i*) of similar composition appropriate for this lower level.[44] Such liaison structures were to be responsible not only for day to day co-ordination and vertical liaison, but also for the formulation and implementation of collective and joint contracts stipulating the interdependency of the constituent parts of the enterprise.

We have seen, however, that the problem of horizontal co-ordination and vertical liaison was not solved effectively by the provisions of the Democratisation Movement and that bureaucratism continued to be an important problem. Commenting on the confusion in enterprises in the North East in July 1951, Chang Li-k'o noted that up to that time liaison had been very bad and everybody 'did his thing' (*ko hsing ch'i shih*). Unless liaison was strengthened, there would either be complete confusion of function, or rigid specialisation of function in which 'the labour union concentrated on "democratisation" and management concentrated on "centralism" and carrying out one-man management'.[45] In situations where the above structures were not very effective, the role of the Party as an agent of horizontal co-ordination and structural liaison was very important.

Where liaison is impossible, a body entrusted with this function either becomes utterly powerless and subordinates itself to one of the bodies between which it is maintaining liaison, or takes over leadership from both of the bodies and treats liaison as direction. Both patterns could be discerned in this early period. The Antung Machinery factory provides us with an example of the first extreme. Here the Party committee was unable to maintain liaison between management and labour union, with the result that the labour union was taken over by corrupt elements and a 'saboteur' became union chairman. This drove the Party to the side of management, from which position it 'helped the labour union to sort itself out' during the Movement to Create New

Records.[46] The Wu Erh factory, provides us with an example of the second extreme. Here the Party committee took over the functions of the factory management committee and turned that body into an enlarged Party committee.[47] Such a situation was the subject of attacks by Kao Kang, which we quoted in Chapter 2. A third possible permutation, also attacked by Kao Kang, was where the Party took a syndicalist line and backed the labour union in its usurpation of the functions of management.[48]

If the Party was not to take everything on to its own shoulders, what exactly was meant by the Party 'exercising leadership'. In the ideological sphere the exercise of leadership by the Party committee indicated the total responsibility for creating an organisation ideology and for macro-political education. In the field of organisation, I take it to mean exercising control over liaison structures which were to effect horizontal linkage and to unite the principles of democracy and centralism. As an independent organisation the Party was, in the early period, to carry out this aspect of leadership through channels other than its own organisation. It was to act through the factory management committee and three-man meetings where it brought management and union together, and its mass work was to be conducted through the medium of the labour unions. It was to exercise control over the formal and informal network of communication in the enterprise and to initiate joint discussion at those points where there was a blockage in communication. Party committees could, however, only act effectively through other organisational structures when those structures were performing properly. In a situation where labour union committees might be corrupt and where bureaucratism was rife, the Party committee might cut through formal liaison and co-ordination structures and exercise direct leadership over the basic level. Such power exercised by the Party committee was not direct line power, for the Party committee occupied no position in the line, but *functional* power.

We have noted that functional power may be defined as power that stems not from status or position in a formal hierarchy but from the nature of the work performed. We have seen also that technical cadres frequently exercised such power in a situation where the technical level of line management was low, and that attempts were made in 1953 to restrict such functional power to matters that were described as technical/professional work (*yeh-wu*). Ideally the Party was to exercise such power in the non-technical sphere, but since 'politics was the lifeblood of economics',[49] it was very difficult to define what exactly the non-technical sphere was. In the Wu San factory, for example, the Party organisation was expected to organise research into problems of production, supervise the writing of teaching material on norm determination, and guide discussion in such work.[50] So long as the Party was to exercise such leadership effectively, the phenomenon of 'multi-headed leadership' (*to-t'ou ling-tao*) could not be avoided, and any attempt to implement staff-line systems of command could not but dilute the power of the Party organisation.[51]

As regards democracy, the functional role of the Party was extremely important. Some organisational theorists maintain that the prevalence of functional contacts minimises the tendency towards authoritarianism, since they impose restraints on the exercise of power throughout an organisation.

It has been argued that the greater specialisation and the consequent growth of functional networks which overlay formal patterns of authority helps to explain why organisational absolutism has been less prevalent since the industrial revolution.[52] Modern organisational absolutism attempts to deal with the problem of functional overlay by increasing the number of functional agents performing a given function at any level and by the creation of a number of parallel hierarchies, any one of which may be by-passed by the hierarchy that communicates best with the leadership of the organisation at any given time.[53] So long as Party leadership did not share its functional jurisdiction over a particular level of work, then the existence of the Party organisation could offset the authoritarian tendency of management. In the Three Anti Movement, for example, Party committees were in a position to combat bureaucratism at any level of organisation. In 1953, however, the attack on multi-headed leadership reached a new height and the Party was joined by a number of parallel hierarchies (external control apparatus, etc.) which diluted its power, resulting in a pattern of single-headed leadership and multiple control (in the Schurmann–Chou Fang sense of the word, which signified checking up after the event).[54]

In the light of the criticism of the dilution of Party power, which grew in direct proportion to the growth of other parallel hierarchies, it would seem that the following hypothesis was confirmed: 'For any given level of functional importance in a system, the power residing in a functional agent (functionary) is inversely proportional to the number of other system functional agents' performing the function.[55] In a situation where a number of weak control organs co-existed with a very strong chain of vertical command (one-man management), intra-enterprise communication tended to move along that strong chain of command with the growth of what industrial sociologists term 'noise entropy'.[56] Since the volume of information passing from top to bottom is greater than the information channel can cope with, various levels in the organisational hierarchy tend to screen out a certain amount of the information. As this happens, parallel control organs find they are too weak to influence this screening process. Perhaps the classic example of such screening in modern China was the way central directives on the Socialist Education Movement in the early 1960s were seriously distorted as they passed down a national chain of command.[57] What is particularly important in the context of the present discussion, however, is that people at lower levels within industrial and other organisations screened messages to the leadership of the organisation in order to present their own performance in the best possible light. Attacking this tendency, An Tzu-wen noted in early 1953:

> What is especially serious and most harmful to the Party is the fact that when reporting on work to the upper levels, only the achievements and not the shortcomings, only the good news and not the bad news, only the merits and not the failures are told.[58]

This was precisely the bugbear of traditional Chinese administration that we noted in Chapter 1 and was one of the problems that the Party organisation within vertically organised administrative structures was supposed to prevent.

One wonders whether An, as Deputy Head of the Party's Organisational Bureau, realised that the continuance of this phenomenon was the direct result of diluting the functional power of the Party organisation. One might wonder too whether Kao Kang realised that the decline in lateral liaison with local government was due to exactly the same cause.

The control function of the Party organisation

In the Introduction we considered some of the problems associated with the word 'control'. In examining the control function of the enterprise Party organisation here, I shall confine myself to Schurmann's somewhat over simplified distinction between *chien-tu* (supervision) and *chien-ch'a* (监察) (control) in the sense of checking up during the after the event.

In a lengthy document published in September 1951, the North

East Bureau of the Party Central Committee attempted to define the function of the Party organisation in the industrial enterprise as follows:

The Party is the highest form of working class organisation. It is an independent political organisation. It has total responsibility for the ideological leadership of the factory or mine and has the responsibility for supervising the production work of management. According to the laws and decrees of the state, the plans of higher level economic organs and the directives of higher level Party committees, the factory or mine Party committee unifies thought and guarantees that the thought and actions of Party, management, labour unions and Youth League are in accord. This is done by strengthening ideological leadership and taking the implementation of the economic plan as its central task.[59]

Supervision (*chien-tu*) in this sense allowed the Party organisation to interfere in the implementation of policy at the basic level when it felt that the laws and decrees of the Party and state were being violated and, in the Three Anti Movement, the scope of this intervention was very wide indeed. In the period prior to that movement, organisations other than the Party were usually only involved in checking up on activities at lower levels when the Party was found to be bureaucratic or corrupt. Such ad-hoc investigations need not necessarily involve the formal control apparatus (Peoples Control Commissions). We saw in Chapter 2 that the Yang Ch'üan case, the formal control apparatus was not involved at all and the initial investigation was carried out by a newspaper reporter. In the case of the Coal Sorting Department of the Penki Iron and Steel Corporation, the investigation team (*tiao-ch'a-tsu*) was only sent down when the Party organisation was charged with being bureaucratic and again the formal control apparatus was not employed.

The problem of control from organs outside the enterprise was complicated by the fact that Peoples Control Commissions usually dealt only with people who did not hold Party posts, as illustrated in the following example.[60]

In the 24th North East Military Engineering Works, the factory general manager was responsible for demolishing a building near the works in order to use the building materials to expand his own factory. The building in question had changed hands several times since 1937, and its last owner had handed it over to the Military Engineering Works for a token sum of money which had never been paid. At first the Military Engineering Works had tried to get rid of the building, and offered it to the *hsien* government, who could find no use for it.

Finally, in January and February 1950 the general manager secured the agreement of the former *hsien* magistrate and former *hsien* Party secretary to demolish the building and use the materials for refurbishing the Military Engineering Works.

As soon as demolition commenced, the workers joined in a free-for-all gutting of the building and helped themselves to materials such as lead from the roof. Someone sent a letter describing this situation to the Party newspaper *Tung Pei Jih-pao*, who, instead of publishing it, forwarded it to the new *hsien* Party secretary. The *hsien* Party secretary should have conducted an investigation into the matter through the factory Party apparatus, but instead he just drafted a report on the basis of the letter which had arrived via the newspaper and sent it on to the Provincial Party Committee. Eventually the matter came before the North East Peoples Control Commission, who appointed a control officer to investigate the situation. The control officer organised an investigation group, which eventually presented a report to a special meeting, at which the Head of the Military Engineering Department made a self-confession about his dilatoriness in controlling what went on in his department. On the recommendation of the Peoples Control Commission, the factory general manager was dismissed his post and the former *hsien* magistrate and current Party secretary censured. The former *hsien* Party secretary, however, who had authorised the destruction of state property in the first place, was not punished by the Peoples Control Commission, but handed over to disciplinary organs of the Party.

Thus we see a fairly clear example of control being exercised by the formal control structure only after the Party authorities had shown that they were incapable or unwilling to deal with the problem in hand. Nevertheless, although control was exercised by organisations other than the Party, the punishment of Party officers was in the final analysis held to be the function of the Party itself (except in the simple case of censure). Secondly, we see another example of the tremendous importance exercised by the Press as a control mechanism. As in the Yang Ch'üan case, the press took the initiative in bringing the matter before the appropriate authorities, and was reluctant to publish anything unless the material had gone through the proper channels. In fact, *Tung Pei Jih-pao* published its own self-confession on 8 April 1950, stating that its initial account of the value and description of the property concerned had been inaccurate.[61]

Thus control during this early period might be exercised by all kinds of structures above the enterprise when the Party organisation in question was defective. In some cases, the fact that structures other than the Party had to be employed was explained as due to the fact that there were not enough Party members in the enterprise in question. In the Shihchingshan Iron and Steel Works, for example, the director (*ching-li*) and military representative were held to be guilty of 'hard-working bureaucratism' and had failed to notice that equipment was lying about the works in heaps exposed to the elements. This time an inspection corps (*chien-ch'a-t'uan* 检查团) was sent down by the Central Finance and Economic Commission and the Enterprise Department of the North China Peoples Government, which rectified the situation and gave impetus to the rapid expansion of the Party to stop such a situation occurring again.[62]

The rapid expansion of the Party was, however, no guarantee against bureaucratism, as the Three Anti Movement demonstrated. During that movement, control over the bureaucratism within the enterprises was exercised by the Party organisation through the local Increase Production and Practise Economy Committees. Paradoxically, it was partly as a consequence of the fact that the enterprise Party committees were expected to exercise detailed control over the implementation of plans that they were made subject to such stringent controls from local Party committees. In September 1951 the North East Bureau of the Party Committee noted that, in the years since liberation, the Party organisations in the North East area had been remarkably successful in learning managerial and technical skills;[63] they were thus able to control plan-implementation. Some three months later, however, the head of that bureau, Kao Kang, noted that certain Party cadres were overlooking political questions in pursuit of production and that they considered being asked to do Party work as 'taking advantage of honest men'.[64]

This was the old question of *ts'ai* (ability) and *te* (virtue). As cadres were transferred from the rural sphere following liberation, the criterion of *te* demanded that they achieve *ts'ai*, and in achieving *ts'ai*, they neglected *te* and were criticised during the Three Anti Movement. In late 1952, after the Three Anti Movement was concluded, an attempt was made to steer between the two extremes of subordination to management and interference in everything. In the words of the Party secretary of the model Wu San Factory:

In short when the Party committee is engaged in political and ideological leadership, when, with production as its central task, it is unifying operational measures to guarantee and supervise the implementation of higher directives and the state plan, under no circumstances may it interfere with the management work of the factory general manager. Of course it cannot descend into routine practical work and thus be indistinguishable from management.[65]

As the power of the external control agencies grew and the horizontal component in the dual-rule chain of command withered, the control function of the Party committee was restricted to convening meetings to discuss political obstacles standing in the way of plan-fulfilment and reporting to the factory general manager on how the plan was being fulfilled. Such was the description of Party work at the model Wu San Factory made by its Party secretary at the end of 1952, in which the function of the Party as 'guarantor' of plan-fulfilment was given great stress. The enterprise Party committees remained, however, answerable in the first instance to local Party committees and the fact that their independence of action was not totally eclipsed was attested to by Li Hsüeh-feng at the Eighth Party Congress.[66]

The propaganda and education function of the Party organisation

Although the Party organisation was required to act as a co-ordinating and liaison structure and was required, for a time at least, to control the bureaucratic behaviour of management, most of the literature on the functions of the Party organisation in the enterprise deals with its educative and propaganda function.

During the Movement to Create New Records, as we have seen, there was a tendency for the Party organisation to take everything on to its own shoulders, and this was most noticeable in the fields of propaganda and education.[67] Instructions of early 1950 urged Party branches to share these tasks with management and unions and an attempt was made to draw local Party committees into the task of co-ordinating propaganda work, at a time when the horizontal links were growing weaker. We have seen that in the early period there was a tendency for Party cadres to concentrate solely on technical work to make up for their own inadequacy, and cadres frequently complained that this did not leave them enough time to conduct propaganda. The focus of educational work was on technical matters and improving literacy rather than political education.[68] Various methods were suggested to overcome this one-sided stress on basic skills and discussion of these methods became a major topic of the various propaganda conferences which were held in enterprises at that time.[69]

In organising propaganda work the Soviet experience was explicitly drawn upon, and a distinction was made between 'propaganda' and 'agitation'. 'Propaganda' consisted of explaining to workers the logic behind a certain policy and *systematising* their thoughts, whereas 'agitation' was defined as the promotion of a single course of action and *unifying* thought. In theory, 'agitation' spelled out what a worker should do and 'propaganda' explained to him why he should do it. It was pointed out that 'propaganda' without 'agitation' would make it impossible to unite the workers to pursue a common goal, and 'agitation' without 'propaganda' would make it impossible to persuade workers why the goal was worthwhile in the first place.[70] The Soviet distinction between 'propaganda' aimed at Party members and worker activists and 'agitation' aimed at the masses does not seem to have been made. The two extremes, therefore, were conscious confusion and unconscious unity. The task of the Party was to steer between these two extremes.

Initially a distinction was drawn between higher level 'propagandists' (*hsüan-ch'uan-yüan*) with a good grounding in Marxism, Leninism and Mao Tse-tung's thought, and lower level agitators (*ku-tung-yüan*) who understood government policy and had close ties with the masses.[71] Later, however, a more common distinction was to be between lower level 'propagandists' (*hsüan-ch'uan-yüan*) and higher level 'reporting officers' (*pao-kao-yüan*).

It was this second distinction that was put forward as an attempt was made to establish a propaganda network on a national scale after the Central Committee decision on Propaganda of January 1951. This decision called for the recruitment of large numbers of Party propagandists to explain to the masses current domestic and international developments (and thus to link production with support for the Korean War), to publish Party policy and the policies of the Peoples Government, to publicise the duties of the masses, and in particular those duties directly related to the period of time (i.e. the current political or economic movement) and the locality in question, to narrate model experiences in production and other fields, to refute reactionary rumours and mistaken ideas, to assist the Party in its choice of propaganda material, and to make regular reports to Party committees on the state of the people's consciousness.[72] Much of the source material for this essay derives from such material, for precise instructions were given on each of the major movements of the time and on political and economic organisation. The numerous pamphlets issued during this period have provided us with what is, in my opinion, the richest source of information on basic level policy from liberation until the Cultural Revolution.

Within each factory, propagandists were appointed and their duties were determined by the enterprise Party committee. Representatives of these propagandists were to attend regular propaganda meetings at *hsien* level and above and as many as possible were to attend special training classes at Party schools. In addition, higher level Party committees were required to send down reporting officers to the factories to give speeches on major issues.[73] To help propaganda work in the factories, journals were published[74] and regional posts for disseminating propaganda set up.[75]

It is very difficult to make any generalisation on the ratio of propagandists to workers in the factories. At the beginning of 1951, the ratio at Anshan was 1 : 20–5[76] (mainly Party members), whereas by the end of 1952 the ratio at the Wu San Factory was something of the order of 1 : 10 or 1 : 5–6 if one includes the even lower level of propaganda-activist, which compares with a Party membership ratio of 1 : 11.[77] These figures are, of course, much higher than for urban areas in general, where in Shanghai, for example, in September 1951 the ratio was 1 : 326.[78] In the model Wu San Factory there were either 248 or 316 propagandists (from two different undated accounts around the end of 1952), 157 propaganda-activists, 7 reporting officers, 12 broadcasters, who together organised 30 broadcast-listening groups (with 500 people taking part), 60 newspaper-reading groups (with 500 people taking part), 8 art groups, one cultural-workers' team (*wen-kung-tui*), 11 smaller cultural-workers' groups (*wen-kung-tsu*) and one band.[79] Unfortunately, we are not told how many workers there were in the factory, but I estimate some 2–3,000 people.[80] The Wu San Factory did not pretend to be typical, but it illustrates the kind of propaganda organisation that was aimed at.

The one striking thing about the propaganda material for the early 1950s is its sheer detail. Pamphlets appeared on every conceivable subject, right down to the layout of a meeting hall.[81] As far as I know, nothing so detailed existed before or after, at least for general consumption. This is, of course, a very subjective impression, for one cannot judge a question like this without having been there in the period in question. It was certainly more detailed than the material available in bookshops during the middle 1960s, about which I can speak from personal observation. Many of the propaganda handbooks of the early 1950s resemble military basic-training manuals, and the contradiction between this type of literature and macro-political propaganda, such as on the Korean War, was a glaring one. It was all too easy for the old rural cadres, whom Kao Kang described as unwilling to bother with administrative detail,[82] to overlook the former and it was all too easy for worker cadres of a low level of literacy not to understand the latter. We saw earlier that in the very early period political consciousness did not always go together with a high level of literacy, at least in the immediate post liberation situation, and the Party secretary of the Wu San Factory noted that the keeping of propagandists' diaries was a useful way of raising their literacy level.[83] Furthermore, one of the major arguments in favour of radio propaganda was that many workers were illiterate.[84]

The Party branch was to achieve some kind of appropriate mix between the two types of propaganda and to devise a way of maintaining revolutionary fervour and a concentration on detail. In the early 1950s, it would seem that the Party believed that enthusiasm could coexist with administrative detail. We have seen however that a concentration on detail led frequently to 'hard-working bureaucratism', where whatever enthusiasm a Party cadre might have was not much use if there were no time for him to communicate it to the masses. We noted that the prescribed attitude was one not of enthusiasm per se but of 'activism', which was infectious and, having looked at the detailed cost accounting manuals of the period, my mind boggles at the thought of an activist cost-accountant. During the Great Leap Forward, this problem could only be dealt with by an insistence that Party cadres did not encumber themselves with administrative detail, and both the Great Leap Forward[85] and the Cultural Revolution[86] were most inconoclastic in their treatment of detailed regulations.

Not only was there a potential contradiction between activism and attention to detail, but also between medium and message. For example, the Party was to propagate the attack on functional leadership, and yet in so doing it exercised itself a kind of functional leadership. If the Party ceased to exercise functional leadership, it would no longer exercise any leadership at all and would become only the adjunct of management, with scarcely any more power than personnel management in a traditional western factory.

The role of the union branch after the Three Anti Movement – the Wu San model

We saw in Chapters 2 and 3 that the union organisation within industrial enterprises were never particularly effective as a check on management. In the very early period following liberation, overworked union branches experiencing rapid turnover of personnel were criticised for being 'tails of management' and when, in late 1950, they did show a greater degree of independence it was frequently in the direction of 'economism'. As the union rectification movement merged into the other mass movements of 1951–2, the Party organisations strove to bring union branches under their control. The Three Anti Movement, as we have seen, took as one of its targets, 'bureaucratism' and 'economism' in labour union branches and by 1952 the unions were considered to be sufficiently under Party control for them to play a major role in the Five Anti Movement which extended the Three Anti Movement into the private sector and initiated a struggle with unreformed capitalist elements.[87]

Following these major movements, we saw that the control function of the Party declined and since the union organisations were now effectively tied to the Party organisations, one might expect that the chance that the unions might exercise any independent control function was even bleaker. To illustrate this point let us conclude with an examination of the role of the labour union in the model Wu San factory in Shenyang after mid 1952.

In the public sector, we saw that after mid 1952 there was an increasing tendency to relate everything to matters of production. Indeed, the union branch at the Wu San Factory was praised precisely because in all its activities it 'took production as its central point of reference'.[88] In such a situation any discussion of differences in standpoint between management and labour union was precluded. The main function of the union was to ensure adherence to the terms of the collective contract and team compacts, to make provisions for patriotic, cultural (literacy) and technical education, to foster rationalisation proposals and check up on their implementation, to organise labour competitions, to aid the Party in propaganda work, to help management in welfare and safety work, to organise the ratification of bonus payments, and to conduct research into technical problems.[89]

Of all these functions, the educative/propaganda function was perhaps the most important, and in performing this the union seemed not to serve the function of 'transmission belt' between Party and workers but between management and workers. At the Wu San Factory for example, the union branch was required to study each document or directive sent down by higher levels of economic administration as well as documents from higher level union and Party structures. Joint discussions were held between management and the heads of each labour-union team regarding the political and economic significance of such documents and how to implement them within the shops and teams. The union was then entrusted with the task of communicating the conclusions to the workers (and if need be to visit their homes).[90]

In accordance with the principle of relating everything to the production, efforts were made to create parallel union structures, not only for line organisation but for staff bodies also. For example, the enterprise wage section would be paralleled by a union wage committee. (See Fig. 12.)

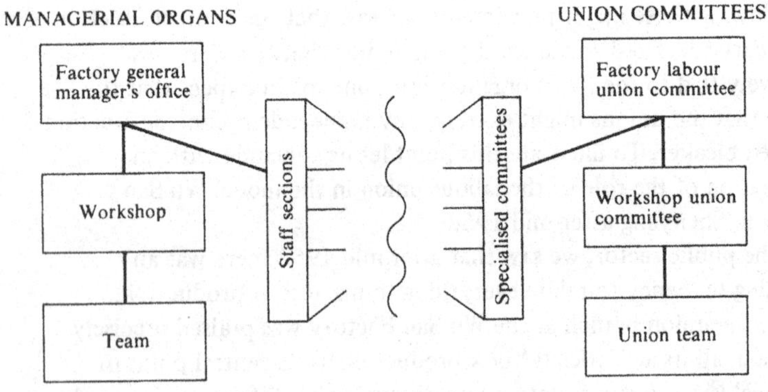

Figure 12

In the early period when functional patterns of control were more common, not only was there overlap between management personnel in staff organs and union personnel in parallel union committees, but such committees might issue instructions directly to the shop floor without informing any union structure attached to the line. For example, the Cultural Committee at the Wu San Factory directed culture and education work at team level, often without informing the labour-union chairman. As the staff-line system of command was strengthened after the Three Anti Movement, the 'one man' principle was applied to union work also. Henceforward specialist union committees could only issue advice to the factory union committee, which exercised direct leadership over the shops and teams. In the case of routine work, such as directing regular training classes, each specialist committee was required to draft a plan for the approval of factory committee and shop committees specifying the scope of functional direction.[91] Thus the adoption of staff-line systems of management was reinforced by the organisation of the labour union with the consequent attenuation of channels of command and the growth in the number of restrictions imposed upon union committees.

The whole process of union work in industrial enterprises became highly formalised. The model Wu San Factory worked out a very complex meeting schedule, specifying not only when general meetings were to be held but the scope of the agenda for standing committee meetings for each of its thrice-weekly meetings. Detailed provisions were laid down for the convocation of 'head knocking sessions' at factory and shop level. Provision was made for the inspection of the diaries of shop committee chairmen and heads of union teams which contained production records and a summary of the problems confronting particular union members, and a detailed curriculum for evening study was established.[92]

In the mass of committees that were exemplified in the model Wu San Factory, the role of the factory management committee had shrunk considerably. I have seen very few accounts of the existence of such committees after the conclusion of the Three and Five Anti Movements. Indeed, the account dealing with the Wu San Factory is the last account I have seen that mentions the existence of a factory management committee. By that time the committee seemed solely concerned with matters of production and planning. Its great virtue was held to be its role in co-ordinating the work of Party, management, union and Youth League, which was exactly the same function as the weekly factory-level head-knocking session of factory general manager, Party Secretary and labour union chairman.[93] In the various articles praising the achievements of the Wu San Factory, scant reference is made to the actual activities of the factory management committee and far more attention is given to the factory level 'head-knocking sessions', the membership of which might be enlarged to include members of relevant staff sections and appropriate specialist union committees. I can only conclude therefore that all that was left of the factory management committee were these 'head-knocking sessions', enlarged to include a few union delegates who had no official position.

After mid 1952, managerial initiative was stressed in all matters that required consultation. Cadres were urged to give weight to the opinions of the labour union but 'not to lean excessively on it'. When drawing up the collective contract at the Wu San Factory, for example, there was no longer any joint discussion in the preparatory stage, but both sides prepared a draft and, after discussion and amendment, the union draft was modified to supplement the draft of management.[94] There can be no doubt which draft carried the greater weight.

Conclusion

In terms of our policy–resources contradiction, one reason for the lack of success in establishing factory management committees was that the political consciousness of management and workers alike was inadequate. In addition the new Party and union structures were not strong enough to perform adequately the educative functions required of them.

A more important reason for their lack of success, I feel, is that their very existence could not be reconciled with one-man management forms of organisation. The attempt to impose discrete chains of command, strict systems of responsibility and the production territorial system could only effectively be undertaken according to what I have described as the Stalinist principle of imposed change from without. In the period immediately following liberation, however, it would seem that the policies of rectification and democratic reform proceeded according to the Yenan principle of change from within. One of the results of this contradiction was that factory management committees, Party and union committees sometimes contained unregenerate elements who were perhaps the last people to be imbued with a democratic and anti-bureaucratic spirit. As democratic reform speeded up, factory management committees showed themselves incapable of taking a lead and when an outside body stepped in, the very idea of factory management committees lost its credibility.

When, for example, the large-scale mass movement was launched in South China in 1951 to carry out once and for all the Democratic Reform Movement, formal leadership was assigned to the factory management committees and labour unions except where the factory general manager was a retained person or the union was felt to be 'impure'. In such cases 'democratic reform committees' were set up.[95] As we have seen these committees were under Party leadership and were the major form of organisation for the Democratic Reform Movement of 1951. There were many retained managers in South China and many instances of union branches dominated by former gang-bosses as the movement disclosed. In such circumstances the factory management committees were brushed aside. In the radical political movements of 1951–2, workers participated as individuals in effecting change rather than rely on elected deputies to carry out the changes on their behalf. Management committees were not revitalised after the 1951 Democratic Reform Movement and very few survived the Three Anti Movement for, by that time, democracy was seen more in a participatory than a representative sense.

The factory management committees had proved themselves ineffective as a counter to bureaucratism and the arbitrary actions of management by the end of 1950. In the period which followed, enterprise Party committees found themselves exercising this role alone and this they were able to do so long as the mass movements of 1951–2 lasted. After mid 1952, however, the role of the Party organisation in industrial enterprises declined to just that of another (although very prestigious) functional agent.

Although the major decline in the role of the Party organisation dates from mid 1952, there were some people who wished to ensure that its power was restricted right from the time of liberation. Commenting on the relative lack of success in implementing one-man management in the Soviet Union prior to 1940, Cheng Hung-su attributed the cause directly to the interference of the Soviet Communist Party, the labour unions and local government,[96] implying that such a situation ought to be avoided in a Chinese context. We saw in Chapter 2 that Kao Kang was most insistent in his demands that Party committees confine their leadership to the sphere of ideology and such a situation could only lead to a diminution of their power.

In examining the role of the Party organisation as an agent of liaison and control, we have seen that an increase in the number of control structures diluted its effectiveness as a check on the arbitrary actions of management and the doctrine of one-man management made such actions possible. In such a situation 'democracy' however defined, could not but be weakened. As a result of the growth of one-man management, the major persisting role of the Party was one of propaganda. Ironically, in the period of greatest Party independence, Party members were frequently too busy studying technology to exercise this role effectively and it was only after the power of the Party organisation had been restricted that the propaganda role was effectively exercised. By that time propaganda did little more than reinforce the directives of management.

We have seen that the rapid expansion of the Party resulted in a somewhat different membership composition by the beginning of the First Five Year Plan. The change in membership composition must surely have been an important factor in the change in organisational perspective from one which stressed a combination of collective leadership and individual responsibility to what in practice was more one of single leadership and multiple but weak control.

Finally we have noted that the labour union organisations within Chinese industrial enterprises were never very effective as anti-bureaucratic and anti-authoritarian structures. The only time that they showed any independence during the period under review, they were held to be guilty of 'economism'. Closely tied to the Party organisation after mid 1952, they were to share its fate.

Conclusion

A major theme that runs through this work has been the attempt to graft upon Chinese industry a model of organisation and incentive which derived from the Soviet Union. This model was very different from the pattern of organisation and incentive that existed in pre-1949 China both in areas under Kuomintang and Communist Party control. Conscious of the current polemic concerning the origins of Japanese industrial paternalism, I have tried not to assert categorically that these differences *determined* the way the Soviet model was received for quite clearly another important reason why the Soviet model was not accepted in its entirety was that human and technical resources were inadequate. In conclusion, therefore, I shall first summarise what has been formulated as a contradiction between policy and resources, defining resources very widely to include anything from a stable currency to political consciousness. Additionally, before entering into a final discussion of the above major theme, I must specify the extent to which the received Soviet model was unclear.

One of my major tasks has been to discuss the leadership types that existed in Chinese industry both before and after 1949 and their attitudes to decision making, worker participation and conflict management. The question I have posed is how did various leadership types influence the pattern of leadership prescribed by the Soviet model and through what structures did they best operate. These different types of leadership articulated different values and different goal structures, and it is against these that I have attempted to evaluate the 'rationality' of the Soviet model rather than some external abstract criterion.

My discussion of the rationality of the Soviet model has centred on planning, incentive and organisation. In discussing incentive, I have attempted to assess the relative importance of its individual and collective dimensions and have touched briefly on the extraordinarily difficult question of moral determinants. In discussion organisation, I have attempted to locate developments within China within traditional organisational theory of which both Chinese and Soviet leaders were acutely conscious. As I suggested in the Introduction, I have not discussed contemporary approaches to organisation, not because I do not consider them important, but because the nature of my research material precluded the kind of tests they required.

Throughout this work I have tried to specify the contradictions between a political system dedicated to the proposition that the workers were masters of society and elements of industrial organisation more conducive to bureaucratism and authoritarianism. In Chapter 7 in particular, I have examined those institutions within Chinese industrial enterprises that were designed to check such bureaucratism and authoritarianism and through which workers might participate effectively in decision making. As far as the period 1948–53 is concerned, my conclusions are somewhat pessimistic. In this final chapter therefore, in addition to summing up my observations for that period, I shall attempt to relate those observations to subsequent developments in the history of the Chinese Peoples Republic about which I feel more optimistic. As I suggested in the Introduction, my aim is the very limited one of documenting the reception of an alien model. At a time when many developing countries are adopting alien models of industrial organisation which derive from the capitalist West, it is salutory to reflect upon the fact that socialist countries or potentially socialist countries have also adopted the alien model of the Soviet Union with, I believe, equally unfortunate results. Other people are currently engaged in the far more significant task of examining the maturing indigenous Chinese alternative; they may only succeed if, like the Chinese themselves, they are conscious of past mistakes.

The contradiction between policy and resources

It is perhaps inevitable that any regime that wishes to do something more than just adapt itself to an existing situation will manifest a contradiction between policy and resources and the more radical the regime, the more acute is the contradiction likely to be. Such a contradiction was already apparent during the radical period after 1942 when Mao Tse-tung called for the introduction of *khozraschët* and progressive piecework systems[1] in a situation where the economy was only partially a monetary one.[2] In our period of study, it has been apparent that the Soviet model of planning could not be implemented fully when there were considerable supply problems and when there were wide cost disparities between sections of the same industry. The Soviet model of incentive could not be implemented so long as there were insufficient criteria for evaluating the qualities of line management and so long as piecework systems of remuneration could not be backed up by an educational programme that made the establishment of higher norms a desirable goal for the workers. The Soviet model of organisation could not be implemented in its entirety so long as there were not enough competent foremen to make staff-line systems of command a realistic possibility, so long as there were not enough competent personnel to attach to various points on the line and so long as the movement to root out gang-bosses was only partially implemented.

At the root of this contradiction between policy and resources was the problem of education. The functions of factory management committees could not be fulfilled effectively so long as the level of political education of management was so low that they held the workers in contempt and so long as the level of technical and political education of the workers was so low that they did not earn the confidence of management. Democratic reforms could not be successful so long as there remained a confusion between gang-bosses and skilled workers. The establishment of staff-line systems of command could not be undertaken effectively so long as it was necessary to maintain lines of functional supervision to compensate for the low level of education of junior line management. The establishment of complex technical norms and systems of piecework payment could not proceed if workers did not understand them adequately. The participation of workers in planning was frustrated by a lack of knowledge of the technical factors in that process, as was the incorporation of planned targets into collective and other contracts. The propaganda function of the Party and unions could only be as effective as was permitted by the literacy of lower level propagandists, and union cadres would remain 'fourth class' so long as the more educated and politically conscious of their number were creamed off into other organisations.

In this early period China was faced with a limited amount of skilled and politically conscious personnel, but this situation was gradually improved by a rapid training programme and by 1953 various movements could be launched to implement the prescribed policies more closely. The emphasis in this period seems in practice to have been on the *selection* of competent personnel, in marked contrast to the Great Leap Forward and Cultural Revolution where one may interpret the ideological approach to education as being concerned with the *creation* of personnel by first changing the environment in which education was carried on. The contradiction between a selective and creative approach was most marked in our period of study in the role of the factory management committees and the labour unions. The literature seems to imply that one of the prime functions of the management committees and of the labour unions was to *create* workers who were competent in managerial skills and yet in practice they were frequently used to *select* the most competent to *become managers*.

Herein lies a problem central to our discussion of education as a resource. Education was, of course, only one of the key resources that China lacked for a programme of rapid organisational change. In stating, however, that the problem of education lay at the core of the contradiction between policy and resources, I am implying that education is a resource qualitatively different from other resources in that it is able to *create* resources and may provide an understanding of how a resource lack in other fields might be compensated for. If education is regarded merely as another input into industry like coal, iron or capital and is measured primarily in terms of the number of graduates contributed to the system, then the speed of effective change is seen to depend directly upon the rate of growth of the formal education system which in turn depends upon the availability of other resources. On the other hand if education is seen not as a mere *input* but as a creative '*withinput*', set into motion it is true by external stimuli but depending largely on internal resources not usually considered as part of the formal education system, then a tremendous volume of resources may be mobilised from within industry independent of the external formal education system. This I believe was to be a fundamental theme of the Great Leap Forward. In the early 1950s however it was probably only dimly understood.

How clear was the Soviet model?

It was not, however, only the nature of resources that lacked clarity in the New Democratic period. The received Soviet model itself was unclear. Some of the institutions adopted during the period belonged not to the Soviet model of the late 1940s but to the Soviet Union of a much earlier period. However much the Chinese literature of the time condemned the 'parliamentary system' of management, the formal structure of management committees bore a striking resemblance to those forms of management organisation long discarded in the Soviet Union. The literature of the early 1950s went to great pains to point out that the 'responsibility system' did not contradict the 'democratisation of management' nor indeed need it have so long as responsibility was defined as specificity of function and the fulfilment of specific work tasks. Nevertheless as we have seen, right from the Movement to Create New Records of 1949, there was a tendency to regard the 'responsibility system' and 'one-man management' as one and the same thing and, in the provisions of 1953, I see no essential difference between the system of 'sole responsibility by the factory general manager' and 'one-man management'. In such a situation, the factory management committee could not but be relatively ineffective.

Not only was it not always clear which aspects of which Soviet model were to be implemented, it was also not clear which elements of the Soviet model of the late 1940s were inherently contradictory. I have mentioned some here such as a desire for innovation coupled with a stress on output targets but, since my main concern has not been with economic problems, much more attention has been devoted to those areas where the imported Soviet model clashed with tradition and the experiences of the Chinese Communist Party during its Yenan period. In attempting to portray this, it is hoped that something might be added to the 'logic of industrialism' debate.

To what extent was there a conflict between different leadership types and different approaches to conflict management?

We saw in Chapter 1 that the leadership in China's first attempt to industrialise was provided by what Kerr and others would call a 'dynastic élite'. Alongside those early industries and increasingly superimposed upon them was an important foreign sector that provided leadership more in tune with Kerr's 'colonial administration' type. In the 1930s a new type of leadership emerged in the form of conservative nationalists and these three types of leadership co-existed right down to the liberation of 1948–9. As a result of this three-fold leadership, the central strategy of China's industrialising élites was an odd mixture of preserving traditional society whilst strengthening defence and servicing the foreign imperialist countries mized with an occasional and ineffective protestation of national independence depending upon which imperialist power was the major target. There co-existed traditional paternalism, alien systems under alien control and a considerable state sector under the control of a comprador class which vacillated between subserviance to imperialism and ineffective nationalism. The mixed élites tended to regard industrial workers as dependent. They sought to suppress all conflict except in those instances where the Kuomintang tried out its own version of 'police socialism' and adopted tactics of control rather than suppression.

The Communist Party leadership which took over the task of industrialisation in the late 1940s came from a milieu very different from both the existing industrial managers and Soviet advisors. Obscuring the differences between the Soviet Union and China, the Kerr school argue that after 1949 'revolutionary intellectual' leadership in China was committed to a strategy of 'forced draft' industrialisation within a highly centralised state where the worker was converted into a 'dutiful producer'. In such a situation the attitude of the leadership towards conflict was one of suppression. I have attempted to show in this essay that there existed within the Communist Party a tradition of 'centralised leadership and divided operations', a genuine commitment to participatory democracy and an attitude towards conflict that was not merely 'suppressive'. During the period under review this tradition conflicted with the model of organisation borrowed from the Soviet Union and from whence Kerr and his school obviously derive their inspiration. There are, of course, many modes of conflict management – conflict suppression, conflict prevention, conflict avoidance, conflict resolution and conflict development and I have tried to demonstrate in this essay that there co-existed in Chinese industry at least two of the above types of conflict management. Considerable attention has been given to the loci of tension (and conflict) within industrial enterprises. We have seen that such tension (conflict) might exist between staff and line, between a factory general manager and a factory management committee, between 'feudal' and non-feudal line management, between union and management, union and Party, Party and management and even between model workers shorn of their prestige and ordinary workers. In all these situations, the Party organisation was ideally the conflict manager but the mode of conflict management differed from period to period. During the Democratic Reform Movement, it was seen that the only way to solve problems arising from a situation where enterprise leadership was instructed to unite with skilled workers and technicians and also eliminate the gang-bosses who were themselves considered by many to be skilled workers was creatively to stimulate conflict. It is the hallmark of Mao Tse-tung's approach to conflict management that unity is only effectively fostered through struggle. The many are united to struggle against the few and the product of that struggle is a new and higher stage of unity.[3] Such an approach is only possible when the 'enemy' at any given stage is clearly defined. In a situation where Soviet patterns of organisation were *superimposed* upon existing forms of organisation, the targets may have been obscured. Clarity could only be achieved not by conflict suppression but by conflict development.

The series of movements that began in May 1951 and ended in mid 1952 differed from those which preceded them and those which came immediately after them precisely in that they called for mass mobilisation and conflict development. They represented that tradition which began with land reform and extended through the Great Leap Forward and Cultural Revolution and which was subsequently associated with the name of Mao Tse-tung as opposed to the more suppressive movements which became associated with the name of Liu Shao-ch'i. One might, of course, argue that the various movements of 1951 were but the prelude to a new and more effective policy of conflict suppression. Objectively they were, but I doubt very much whether such was the intention of those who launched them. In initiating the movements of 1951, China's leadership brought about a reversal of the post-liberation process of centralisation but it is true that the strengthening of horizontal linkages and the growth in power of the Party organisation was but a temporary phenomenon. The removal of corrupt elements during those movements certainly facilitated the imposition of centralised Soviet forms of organisation after the movements. If, however, one adheres to the Kerr model of undifferentiated 'revolutionary intellectual' leadership, one has to explain why the Soviet centralised model was dismantled in the mid 1950s, why 'one-man management' was repudiated several times and why the concept of 'worker activism' (a far cry from the 'dutiful producer') was given particular prominence.

I would suggest that a more fruitful way of looking at China's leadership after 1949 is in terms of those ideal leadership types formulated by Franz Schurmann and described in the Introduction – the two types of bureaucratic leadership (traditional and modern), managerial leadership and Yenan-type 'cadre' leadership. Of these four types, the Soviet model tended to prescribe what has been called 'managerial leadership' (commitment to change within a network of technological solidarity) whereas the Yenan model tended to prescribe leadership according to the 'cadre' type (commitment to change within a network of human solidarity). It is thus possible to see all the various deviations that have been noted – persistent egalitarianism, the free supply mentality and adherence to *pao-kung* forms of organisation as stemming from this latter form of leadership. One must ask the question: how did various groups of what Kerr calls 'revolutionary intellectuals' (and I have very serious doubts about the utility of the term 'intellectuals') subjectively interpret their relationship with the new 'masters of society' and what in fact was their objective relationship. We saw in Chapter 7 that there were some who saw themselves as representatives of the working class by virtue of their relationship to the state as its employees whilst there were others who delighted Li Hsüeh-feng in violating Party instructions and adhering to the mass line tradition of the 1940s. To evaluate their objective relationship to the working class we must examine patterns of mobility between workers and management and the degree to which these two categories merged over time. We must examine also the way in which they merge. Both Marxists and the 'logic of industrialism' school foresee a process whereby the two categories merge – the former, however, foresee the development of the multi-faceted man enjoying an increasing degree of freedom in all his roles whereas the latter foresee some of the many roles that man will play demanding enslavement to technology and others allowing for 'Bohemian' creativity. The kind of study that is required calls for a scope far broader than this present essay and calls for something more than the crude inductive approach which the nature of my research material has forced me to follow.

To what extent were there different approaches to planning?

Having identified two distinct leadership types associated with the two models one can then proceed to ask questions concerning the attitude of these types to certain motivational and organisational problems. Let us first consider the question of planning. I have suggested that during the early 1950s, it was probably difficult to see to what extent elements of the Soviet model were inherently irrational (in terms of its own goals), to what extent they were irrational in terms of the ideals inherited by the Communist Party from Yenan days and to what extent problems were caused by the low level of technical resources that existed in China. One would expect that leadership of the 'cadre' type would give greater stress to the second source of irrationality and Soviet style 'managers' would give particular stress to China's lack of human and technical resources. During the New Democratic period most discussion in the literature focussed on this third category but with the generalisation of the Yenan heritage in the middle 1950s much more attention was given to the second. During the Great Leap Forward of 1957–9, less stress was laid on central planning and a greater degree of autonomy was located at levels higher than that of the factory general manager (province and municipality) (Schurmann's decentralisation II)[4] and lower than that of the factory general manager (shops and teams)[5] with whole process ideally linked by a Party organisation responsive to mass demands. Jack Gray has argued that such an approach stemmed from two contradictory policies. On the one hand, he sees Mao Tse-tung pressing for greater decentralisation of authority within productive units and, on the other, other elements within the Chinese leadership pressing for a type of decentralisation then being advocated in the Soviet Union by a leadership which saw the Stalinist system as irrational even in terms of its own goals. What ensued was an attempt to create a modern industrial complex in each provincial capital which led to the collapse of national planning and an over-stretching of the labour force.[6] The result was frequently excessive horizontal mobilisation and excessive 'commandism' which was the very opposite to that which was intended. Despite this development, however, the work of Steve Andors shows that in many cases meaningful decentralisation of authority within industrial enterprises was achieved and many of the reforms of this time persisted throughout the 1960s.[7]

We noted in Chapter 4 that the considerable stress on output targets during the First Five Year Plan period contributed to the isolation of management from workers. The Great Leap Forward did not, however, give less stress of output targets. On the contrary, output targets, were if anything, given greater weight. On the other hand, it would seem that a recognition of the alienating effect of such targets resulted in a parallel policy of giving unprecedented stress to technical innovations and on getting management down on to the shop floor. The Great Leap Forward was a period when the excessive form filling and red tape described earlier was attacked. It has been claimed that, at that time there was a 70% reduction in the number of forms used in planning[8], which is understandable in the light of the discussion in Chapter 4. Perhaps, however, this development contributed to the breakdown of the planning machinery. For years a fierce debate has raged both within China and outside as to what extent the breakdown in the planning machinery was responsible for the economic crisis which followed and to what extent the crisis of the early 1960s was due to the three bad harvest years, the removal of Soviet experts and blueprints or internal opposition. It is beyond the scope of this work to go into the debate here save to note that any experimentation was bound to be modified in the light of the food shortages of the early 1960s and that the economic crisis saw the restoration to positions of power of those who advocated more conservative policies.

Following the Great Leap Forward a new strategy was adopted. The relatively low priority given to centralised planning remained but, this time, more autonomy was located at the level of the factory general manager who was now subject to a much greater degree to market influences.[9] Franz Schurmann has pointed to that period as being a Chinese equivalent of the Soviet New Economic Policy[10] and his contention has been given added force by the claims made in Cultural Revolution material that Liu Shao-ch'i advocated forms of economic management similar to those of the Soviet Union in the early 1920s. The 1960s saw the flourishing of horizontally-integrated trust-like organisations which were 'economic accounting' rather than budgetary organs.[11] It was not however for this kind of 'trust' that Liu Shao-ch'i was subsequently attacked but for his alleged proposal to turn over part of industry to organisations similar to British public corporations dedicated to profitability and not amenable to Party supervision.[12] Perhaps the *cause célèbre* in the polemic over trusts concerned Liu's alleged proposal to set up an agricultural machinery trust which would have deprived local regions of any control over integrated agricultural development.[13] I know of no parallel for this kind of proposal in the New Democratic period.

The attack on 'trusts' during the Cultural Revolution was part of a very wide debate concerning the relationship between agriculture and industry and the validity of Liberman-type proposals put forward by 'revisionists' such as Sun Yeh-fang for the restoration of some greater degree of market relationships. This debate inevitably had an effect on the kind of issues discussed in Chapter 4 such as whether the economic accounting system should represent the operational side of the planning network within the enterprise or merely be synonomous with cost accounting. These debates will not be entered into here. It is perhaps premature to assess the post-Cultural-Revolution situation. At the time of writing (1974) it is not at all clear exactly what the status of the up and down process of plan formulation is and it appears that, in recent months, attempts have been made to strengthen vertical communication between enterprises and the centre. The process of up and down communication and amendment described in Chapter 4 was simplified in the 1950s and further simplified in the 1960s. Barry Richman has described a process (just before the Cultural Revolution) whereby managers would attend material exchange conferences, (*wu-tzu chiao-liu-hui*) at various levels and thus maintain a continuing informal dialogue with higher level organs.[14] I do not know whether this process continues. Currently the centre sets quantitative targets mainly for the provinces but not below them though as far as intra-enterprise plan discussion is concerned, it would appear that a two down one up procedure has been restored[15] (with the recent strengthening of vertical communication).

To what extent were there different approaches to incentive?

The middle 1950s saw considerable changes in incentive policy and in evaluating personnel. We discussed in Chapter 5 some of the difficulties in grading cadres according to the *ts'ai, te* and *tzu* categories whilst still adhering to a policy that sought not to take into account political attitude. It was possible in the early 1950s to interpret all three concepts in terms of technical values. A criterion such as 'loyalty to the cause of the people' might be measured in terms of adherance to the mass line but more frequently it was measured in terms of how hard one works. 'Experience in struggle' as a criterion depends on how one defines 'struggle'; struggle in a Chinese context has a whole span of definition from class struggle to work itself.[16]

In 1958 Mao Tse-tung echoed An Tzu-wen in criticising those who sought to counterpose *ts'ai* and *te* (now known respectively as *chuan* (expert) and *hung* (red).[17] The difference between the formulation of the early 1950s and that of the Great Leap Forward, however, was that the former defined the *te* (*hung*) concept increasingly in terms of technological values whilst the latter defined the *ts'ai* (*chuan*) concept increasingly in terms of political values. Both views condemned any tendency for there to appear groups of people clearly defined as 'reds' and 'experts' in the enterprise; appointments to all leading posts were made in terms of both qualities only, in the Great Leap Forward, this was done quite consciously and explicitly without any pretence at adhering to a policy that discounted political factors in grading.

The Great Leap Forward tendency to put the *te* (*hung*) concept first was founded on the belief that proper *te* (*hung*) in itself led to a desire to gain expertise. The adherents to the Soviet model also put the *te* (*hung*) concept first in the belief that proper *te* (*hung*) in itself included a high degree of expertise.

In Chapter 5 we noted some of the criticisms levelled against piecework in the middle 1950s. They were included in that chapter because the policy which gave rise to those problems dated from the New Democratic Period and most of them were apparent in the period reviewed in the main body of this work. The criticisms of the mid 1950s culminated in 1958 in the abolition of what was considered to be an excessively individualist incentive policy which was said to be necessary only when the consciousness of workers was low. At that time the primacy of the *group* was asserted both in the field of material and non-material incentive. One might therefore create a matrix showing material and moral incentive in their individual and group dimensions (see Fig. 13). In the early 1950s the prescribed direction was from group to individual dimensions with material incentive occupying a dominant position. In 1958 the prescribed direction was from individual to group dimensions with moral incentive occupying a higher place than before. Nevertheless, just as non-material incentive occupied a significant place in the early 1950s, so material incentive continued to occupy an important place throughout the whole history of the Chinese Peoples Republic.

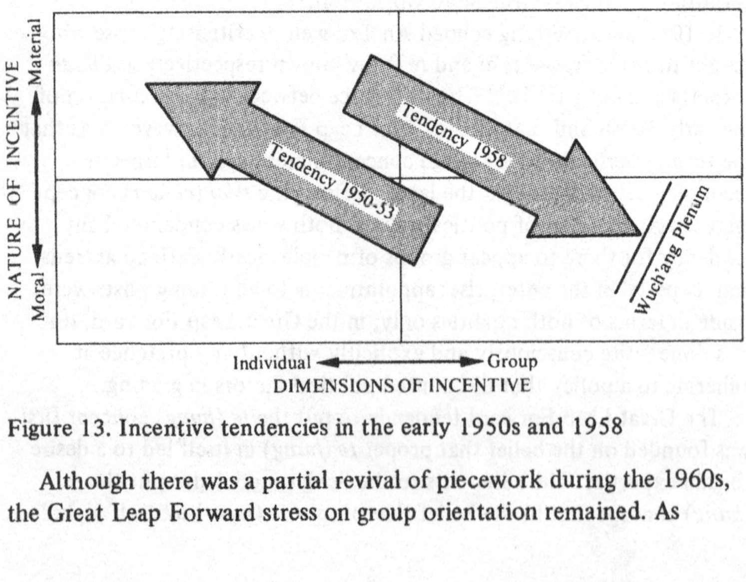

Figure 13. Incentive tendencies in the early 1950s and 1958

Although there was a partial revival of piecework during the 1960s, the Great Leap Forward stress on group orientation remained. As

Christopher Howe has noted, emulation campaigns actually increased in scale during the 1960s though this time with a stress on technical innovations and political performance rather than merely plan fulfilment as in the early 1950s.[18] From 1957–71, wages remained static indicating the stabilisation of real and money wages and the preference for direct controls over labour mobility rather than financial inducements which could exacerbate the gap in standard of living between rural and urban areas. Although extremely impressive, the stable wage policy created several problems. Firstly the system was perhaps somewhat too rigid which resulted in a preference for the flexibility of hiring relatively cheap temporary workers (often from the rural areas) thus leading to intra-urban differentials. Secondly, Howe argues, excessive rigidity prevented the adoption of different incentives schemes required by different technology. Thirdly the freeze on average wages led to a revival of bonus and welfare payments abolished in the mid 1950s as a possible loophole in wage control. Fourthly the stable wage policy led to some degree of dissatisfaction among labour unions who in 1966 were said to be once again guilty of 'economism'.[19]

The Cultural Revolution attacked the system of contract labour as exploitative and denounced a tendency (attributed to Liu Shao-ch'i) for the advocacy of a free labour market and thus the use of wages rather than direct controls over labour mobility. In harmony with their general condemnation of hierarchy the radicals attacked the formal system of grading and attempted once again to re-establish the spirit of Yenan. One of the immediate consequences of the explosion of local initiative in the Cultural Revolution however was that labour control tended to weaken and it would appear that the hiring of temporary contract labour continued, although with some left opposition.[20] Some progress has been made however in abolishing what remained of individual bonuses, surviving piecework systems and the system of assigning wage grades to particular occupations. Although the 10% wage rise of 1971 was 'egalitarian' in the sense that it raised the wages of the lower paid workers, the current stress on formalisation has led to a revival of a grading system for cadres, though simpler than that which prevailed in the 1950s. Once again less stress is paid to political criteria in grading than was paid in the heyday of the Cultural Revolution.[21]

The above developments might suggest that many of the achievements of the Cultural Revolution have been negated and that the 'Black Gang' discredited in that revolution is back in power. This seems even more so now Liu Shao-ch'i formerly considered to be a believer in excessive hierarchy and mechanical determinism is now condemned also for 'egalitarianism'[22] and for the belief that 'spirit can substitute for matter'.[23] The 'logic of industrialism' school might take comfort in that what they consider to be an inexorable drive toward professionalism seems to be continuing. They will see that the proportion of total compensation paid in kind has declined and the wage rate differentials between types of skill has narrowed. They will see also that performance criteria has once again been given more weight than political criteria. On the other hand, they will note that the wage-rate structure of job classifications and occupations within enterprises are less explicit than hitherto and that workers are encouraged to perform multiple roles rather than becoming more specialised. They will see also what looks like the beginnings of a revival of the left within the central leadership.[24] At the recent Tenth Congress of the Chinese Communist Party (1973) Mao Tse-tung's concept of 'continuous revolution' had given renewed stress.[25] I interpret this concept as one which recognises the inherent tendency for organisations to become more bureaucratised and that there is a need for constant revolutionary upheavals to offset this tendency;[26] a corollary of this notion of continuous revolution, therefore, is that the longer the interval between such revolutionary upheavals, the more severe the crisis when it comes. The current incentive policy has indeed failed to meet the expectations of the radicals during the Cultural Revolution but it is not the same as it was in the pre-Cultural Revolution situation. How it develops, depends upon the next revolutionary upheaval.

Most of the writing on incentive in China focusses on material rather than moral incentive. If we are to be in any position to evaluate the gains of the Cultural Revolution, then we must examine that kind of attitudinal change which of late has led to a new flowering of technical innovations. Such an attempt would require a full length study in itself. All I can do here is point out what I believe to be some of the more important elements in attitudinal change.

Surveying the history of the Chinese Peoples Republic, one may discern two views on work motivation and incentive. The first praises the hard-working individual and criticises the lazy. Such a stick-and-carrot policy pays according to piecework and is founded on the belief that status and material benefit are the prime determinants of work motivation.[27] The second view praises the individual not so much for his hard work but for his 'activism'. Such 'activism' is infectious,[28] hard work *per se* is not. Activism may be defined not just as enthusiasm for work but as infectious enthusiasm for work and the collectivity. This second view does not rule out status and material benefit as important factors in work motivation but attempts to reduce them to collective dimensions. As was suggested in Chapter 1, an additional ingredient is added – guilt. Under such a system the lazy individual is not only apprehensive of criticism but feels also a sense of guilt at having let down the collectivity.

There is a considerable amount of literature upon guilt as a determinant of work motivation in Western (particularly Protestant) society. It has been said that capitalism developed alongside a system of stable expectations which derived from the inner-worldly asceticism of the Puritans who, by depersonalising family and neighbours, achieved inter-personal reliability at the expense of emotional involvement.[29] The individual, truly alienated in a Marxian sense, misplaced his emotional involvement on to a symbol which in the period of the Protestant Reformation was God though later such a symbol was replaced by a more secularised version of ideal-self projection (duty, etc.). Guilt stemmed from the inadequacy of the residual self when confronted by the symbolised projection of the ideal self and one's state of grace came to be measured in terms of wealth or individual production.

It might be argued that the Soviet model evoked a similar confrontation except that God was replaced by the community. Mao also sees the community as a god-symbol as his essay 'The Foolish Old Man Who Moved the Mountains' makes clear[30] though there is a significant difference from the above pattern. If, as I have argued Mao is committed to an anti-individualist position, then the activist-guilt pattern of motivation that derived from the Yenan days and emerged again during the Great Leap Forward, whilst measuring activism and guilt in individual terms, would measure the functional equivalent of a state of grace in terms of the group.

It is true that the individual hero had been a feature of the Yenan Production Movement of the 1940s[31] and was again a feature of the Great Leap Forward but at no time was the individual model worker given so much kudos as during the period when the Soviet model was implemented. Both the Yenan-orientated radicals and the conservatives opposed the new stress on the individual. In 1951, Li Li-san called for the 'promotion of collective heroism' rather than individual merit. He saw the primary function of group labour agreements as shifting the focus away from the individual.[32] In view of Li's current economist line, he was probably speaking as a conservative trade unionist distrustful of the individual shock worker. An affirmation of *Gemeinschaft* may, however, be radical as well as conservative and it was a radical view of *Gemeinschaft* that informed the protesters against individualism during the Great Leap Forward and the Cultural Revolution. It is my belief that the most serious error made by the logic of industrialism school is the unquestioned belief that modern industrial society must inevitably be characterised by *Gesselschaft* – by technological solidarity. It is this belief that leads them to dismiss both Marx and Mayo, to regard the Japanese experience merely as an interesting synthesis of the traditional and the modern and not to look at the non-Soviet model Chinese experience at all.

To what extent were there different approaches to organisation?

The problem of *Gemeinschaft* versus *Gesselschaft*, of human solidarity versus technological solidarity leads us to pose the question, was there any difference between the Soviet and Yenan views of the relationship between formal and informal organisational structure?

From Frederick Taylor through to Stalin there have been organisational theorists who chose either to neglect informal organisational networks or to attempt to force them into prescribed formal patterns. Under such systems, personnel management is concerned with creating 'organisation men' (however 'Bohemian' Kerr and others would have them be in their spare time). An alternative approach seeks to focus loyalty not only upon the formal organisation but upon levels both higher and lower than the organisation. At the lower level, it seeks not to force people into subdivisions of the formal organisation, but to infuse existing levels of group solidarity with commitment to the same values as the formal organisation. At the higher levels, it seeks not to extend the focus of loyalty through a hierarchy of formal organisation, but to focus it upon a particular symbol cluster which is the source of legitimacy not only of different levels of formal organisation but also of informal groupings.

The above model, reminiscent of Protestant churches, is, I think relevant to a study of Chinese organisation. At the risk of grossly oversimplifying the situation, I would characterise the difference between the view of organisation inherited by the Communist Party from its Yenan experience and the Soviet view as follows. The former saw the individual's primary loyalty to the small group *and* to a cluster of symbols at the national level, whereas the latter saw the individual's primary loyalty to a level higher than the small group – to the organisation and an extension of that loyalty *through* a complex hierarchy, at the apex of which stood the same symbol cluster. In the Soviet view commitment to any group smaller than the organisation or its subdivisions was seen as potentially disruptive and this resulted in atomisation.[33] In the Chinese Yenan view, the key to unity lay not in smashing informal structures, but in politicising them, and the key actor in that process was the Party organisation.[34]

In this work, we have seen the curious phenomenon of traditional work-gangs continuing after liberation, after changing their names to 'teams', and a process of Democratic Reform which sought to create new forms of 'rational' organisation but, which, in fact, concentrated simply on rooting out gang-bosses leaving the individual gangs intact. We have seen a situation where groups were allowed to form 'spontaneously' (under labour-union leadership) to effect emergency repairs. The use of the word 'spontaneous' could well be a meaningless propaganda device, but it might also mean that there were some pre-existing patterns upon which groups could be formed, and initially all that really concerned Party and management was how such groups might be led. Such a view was very different from the Soviet prescription of the production territorial system, where the nature of production determined the structure of organisation and the network of command. In my opinion, it was not absolutely clear until 1953 whether existing structures should be politicised as a prelude for organisational change or whether organisational changes should be pushed through to provide a focus for new commitments. As long as the former was considered a realistic alternative, the independent role of the Party organisation was extremely important. After 1953, however, when the production territorial system and 'one-man management' were stressed most vigorously, the prescribed role of the Party could be no more than an adjunct to a process which sought to bring as much of the informal organisation as possible under the control of the formal organisation, rather than the former process which sought primarily to correct individual behaviour and focus loyalty on the new national symbol cluster. It was Mao's view (in 1962) that adherence to the Soviet model (until 1958) was unpleasant but necessary.[35] In a situation where the gang-boss system persisted and where traditional practices such as the employment of relatives were continued, perhaps some drastic policy was necessary. Nevertheless, in this field also, a reaction, was to develop in the middle 1950s culminating in the Great Leap Forward and again during the Cultural Revolution when the Yenan model was reaffirmed.

Following the abolition of one-man management in 1956, the formula of 'unified leadership under the enterprise Party committee' was adopted and the workers and staff congresses were brought back to life. Attempts were made to breathe life once again into the labour unions with exactly the same result as 1951. Demands for independence took the form of 'economism' which resulted in the unions once again being brought under Party control. Support for such union demands was later to be attributed to Liu Shao-ch'i who is said to have advocated the transfer of control over industry to the labour unions in much the same way as the Soviet Workers Opposition in 1920.[36] I find this charge impossible, however, to reconcile with the other charge that Liu demanded that people and organisations should be 'docile tools' of the Party.

All the above reforms, I have suggested, were part of a process whereby the Party acted as the major instrument to mobilise the latent energy of the workers through the politicisation of informal as well as formal structure. To achieve this aim, vertical control within enterprises was loosened and the Yenan policy of 'centralised leadership and divided operations' was reiterated thus strengthening the power of functional agents. The liaison function of the Party was considerably important but, as we saw in Chapter 7, where liaison is impossible, a body entrusted with this task either becomes utterly powerless or takes over leadership from both the bodies with which it is maintaining liaison and treats liaison as direction. There developed a tendency, therefore, similar to that in the period immediately following liberation for the Party organisation to take everything on to its own shoulders.[37] There also developed a tendency however, which has been described by Steve Andors for more and more workers to be involved in basic level decision making.[38] The degree of which these two tendencies constituted a paradox and the degree to which constituted what Mao would see as a contradiction seeking dialectical synthesis varied from situation to situation.

The stress on worker participation under the leadership of a Party committee that sought to politicise informal structure rather than force workers into the new structures dictated by the Soviet model saw a revival of *pao-kung* forms of organisation.[39] Considerable research needs to be done however before we can determine to what extent the reappearance of such forms was due to loose control over labour at a time of rapidly changing construction tasks and to what extent it was due to a belief in the intrinsically democratic nature of such organisations. From an economic point of view, commentators on *pao-kung* type agreements in the early 1950s noted that they led to hurried planning, material supply problems and a lack of liaison between staff departments and teams.[40] These were precisely the problems encountered in 1958.

I have suggested that in the early 1960s the situation was very mixed. Many of the reforms in the direction of participatory democracy introduced during the Great Leap Forward were retained and yet this was also a period when very stringent efforts were made to institute responsibility systems which might just be a synonym for 'one-man management'. The renewed stress on vertical control was partially offset by the continued functioning of worker and staff congresses which performed much the same functions as their counterparts in the early 1950s[41] but, like them, were increasingly concerned with questions of production.

Unlike the early 1950s, however, the authority of the enterprise Party committees usually remained fairly strong. To avoid a very mechanistic interpretation of the relationship of Party to management we have to ask ourselves to what extent did Party committees in the early 1960s perform the very important function of acting as a check against the bureaucratic tendency in management. It is my impression, on visiting Chinese factories during the period before the Cultural Revolution, that a high degree of congruence existed between senior management and Party committees except in the case where a significant number of senior managers were retained personnel. I neglected to document this observation and in fact only decided to undertake this study when I was no longer in a position to make that documentation. It is extremely difficult to find any contemporary written evidence to support my observation although it is supported in part by Cultural Revolution material attacking the conservative and bureaucratic policies adopted by Party secretaries. It is also supported indirectly by the decision taken in 1964–5 to transfer military personnel to undertake leading roles in the factories which normally would have been those of civilian Party secretaries.

It was probably the existence of these recently transferred personnel that led the observer Barry Richman to identify different groups of 'reds' and 'experts' in the factories he visited.[42] Although Liu Shao-ch'i is accused of advocating the policy that 'experts should run factories'[43] at no time did he or his opponents counterpose the concepts of 'red' and 'expert', despite the impression given by Western commentators. What I fear Richman might be doing is to assume that those who manifestly lacked expertise (*chuan/ts'ai*) were *ipso facto* red (*hung*). According to Kao Kang, personnel transferred from outside the industrial sphere in the early 1950s rapidly became imbued with expertise (*ts'ai*). Similarly political cadres transferred from the military in 1964–5 either rapidly achieved *ts'ai* or failed utterly to understand how production worked and were not much use from a *hung* point of view. Indeed the Cultural Revolution in the factories was essentially a battle not between two groups of people identifying themselves separately as *chuan* and *hung* but between two or more groups of people all identifying themselves as *hung*.

Accepting the idea of congruence between Party committee and senior management is perhaps the only way one can explain the charge that one-man management systems were reintroduced at a time when leadership was formally vested in the enterprise Party committee. According to Cultural Revolution material, 'one-man management' was described as 'revisionist' and the consequence of policies adopted by Liu Shao-ch'i and his henchmen who had embarked upon the capitalist road.[44] I mentioned above how it was difficult to reconcile Liu's alleged belief in union autonomy and his advocacy of 'docile tools of the Party'; I cannot imagine how one would further reconcile these two beliefs with the advocacy of a policy that demanded the subordination of both Party *and* unions to vertical managerial control; but then one should not be too much of a literalist.

According to Cultural Revolution material, 'one-man management' systems were usually introduced around 1956[45] or in the early 1960s[46] and dismantled during the Great Leap Forward[47] or Cultural Revolution.[48] 1956 is a most unlikely year for their introduction, since that was the year in which the culmination of attacks on one-man management resulted in its formal abandonment by the Eighth Party Congress. The choice of this date is probably linked to the fact that 1956 was the date that marked the formal commencement of the Sino-Soviet split (Khruschev's speech to the Twentieth Congress of the Communist Party of the Soviet Union) and the formal demotion of Mao Tse-tung thought in the Party constitution,[49] rather than the date that the introduction actually occurred. Furthermore, anyone who remembered the early 1950s would be quite sure that one-man management was primarily a Stalinist system. The attack on one-man management as 'revisionist' is an example of a process common in the Cultural Revolution where the substance of Stalinism was attacked although the label of Stalin was retained as a weapon with which to attack 'revisionism'.

Cultural Revolution material gives greatest stress on the revival of one-man management in some instances during the 1960s[50] and it is from this period that some of the most lurid descriptions of its abuse derive.[51] The heyday of the system was, however, the period from 1952–4, and it is possible to find in the literature of that time similar evidence of the exercise of dictatorial powers by factory general managers, even to the point of forbidding workers to have any dealing with the enterprise Party secretary.[52] My overwhelming impression is, however, that prescribed systems although of a stratified line type, were not excessively rigid and showed a marked degree of functional overlay.

The Cultural Revolution material was equally vitriolic in its condemnation of 'bureaucratism'. This may be defined as simply a fondness for red tape, rules and regulations or, as we noted earlier, as alienation from the masses consequent upon the adoption of a rigid staff-line system of command. With regard to the first definition, radicals during the Cultural Revolution gave particular weight to a new model collective contract (now called a 'constitution'). This was the Constitution of the Anshan Iron and Steel Corporation which was written by Mao in 1960 and was said to embody his theory of industrial organisation.[53] Apparently the earlier 'productivity deal' type contract had disappeared. The stress was on simplicity not only in administration but in the terms of the contract. It would seem that brevity that collective contracts gained by the removal of those clauses which were covered by regional or national regulations was more than compensated for by the growth in the number of factory regulations that were appended to them. These were by no means inconsiderable in 1949;[54] by the time of the Cultural Revolution, cases were on record of factory regulations which consisted of booklets of over 200,000 characters and which included strict regulations on everything down to the placing of teacups.[55] Again this development was attributed to Liu Shao-ch'i who apparently opposed the Anshan Constitution and put forward a counter document – the so-called Magnitogorsk Constitution which derived from the city of that name in the Soviet Union.[56] Liu was in general held to be responsible for what was called 'the ten thousand rules of bureaucracy'.

With regard to the second definition of bureaucratism, we noted in Chapter 6 the development of a 'bureaucratic cycle' from 1953–7 during which large numbers of white collar workers tended to concentrate at middle levels of enterprise organisation. By the end of the cycle in 1957, when administrative authority for a considerable part of industry was decentralised down to provincial or municipal level, a process of full scale retrenchment began. A similar cycle was to begin in the early 1960s which was to culminate in the organisational reforms begun in 1964 and which were a prelude to the Cultural Revolution. These reforms were almost the complete reverse of the process described earlier and provide a very neat contrast.

At the end of 1964 the Tsitsihar Vehicle Factory was put forward as a model of factory organisation and descriptions of this model achieved prominence in the 1965 *Peoples Handbook* (*Jen-min Shou-t'se*).[57] In this factory staff functions were transferred back to factory level and staff members instructed to lead production directly (i.e. to exercise functional leadership). Such steps were deemed the best possible method to counter the problem of overstaffing and over-bureaucratisation. The downward transfer of staff functions had evidently not been able to bring technical personnel closer to the shop floor and the Tsitsihar model attempted to achieve this by strengthening functional leadership and attempting to achieve ideological integration through a strengthened Party apparatus. The problem of alienation between staff members and workers was to be overcome by insisting that such personnel spend some time on the shop floor. This is very near to our ideologically integrated functional model.

We are now in a position to schematise the various approaches to organisation as exhibited during the early 1950s (described in Chapter 6) and during the period after 1964. One might create a matrix showing a tendency towards staff-line or functional systems integrated technologically or ideologically (see Fig. 14).

To what extent was there a parallel between the New Democratic Period and the Cultural Revolution?

The Tsitsihar model was put forward at a time when initial moves had been considered for reform in other spheres of enterprise management – as is illustrated by the transfer of military cadres into the factories. The process of reform was to extend into the Cultural Revolution. It would be useful at this stage to examine the main contours of that

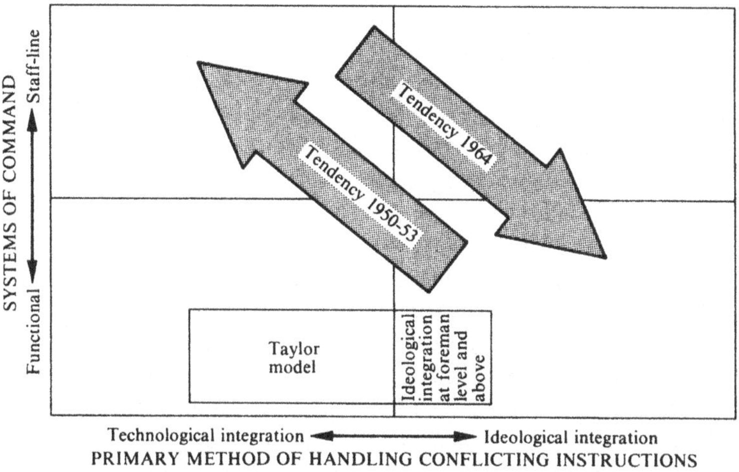

Figure 14. Organisational tendencies in the early 1950s and middle 1960s

reform and compare it with a similar process in the New Democratic Period. We have seen that the policy switch of May 1951 which inaugurated a series of mass movements led to 'democracy' being defined in a different sense from hitherto. During the earlier period 'democracy' within Chinese industrial enterprises was defined according to the criterion of controlled representation. After May 1951, the meaning of the word 'democratic' in the term 'democratic reform' was seen in a participatory sense. Workers themselves were to participate in the overthrow of gang-bosses and other undesirable elements rather than rely upon their representatives to do it for them. This is not to say that after 1951 the representative definition of democracy was given up, for the 1954 constitution was based upon such a definition and a similar definition was propounded in the 1950s. The period after 1964 saw a similar change. First a few attempts were made in 1964 to elect management committees but elections were vetted by Party and management and such committees had little power.[58] Then, attempts were made to reform management, to reduce the number of levels of administration and correct the bureaucratic behaviour of management, though not as part of a mass movement.[59] This process was seen to be not particularly successful and it would seem that managers sometimes still clung to that view of democracy (*min-chu*) that saw themselves as the *chu* (rulers) as opposed to the *min* (people) that we noted in

Chapter 7. As a consequence, a mass movement was launched which took as its first target the removal of 'irrational' management systems. At this stage the movement was led by enterprise Party committees who acted through the labour unions. Once again the labour unions soon came under attack from top to bottom for 'economism'.[60] Leading the movement, the Party often formed its own body of activists (for example the Shanghai *Ch'ih-wei-tui*)[61] and occasionally worker picket organisations (using the old designation *kung-jen chiu-ch'a-tui*) were formed to protect 'power holders' (*tang-ch'üan-pai*) and neutralise Red Rebel criticism.[62] Finally Party committees themselves came under attack from revolutionary groups with support from above[63] and with very strong horizontal links with local revolutionary organisations. The new leading group within industrial enterprises was to be the factory revolutionary committee organised according to a 'three in one' formula. One third of the leaders was to be provided by revolutionary rebel groups (the latter-day equivalent of the worker component in the factory management committee). One third was to be provided by personnel retained from the existing organisation (the latter-day equivalent of the retained management of the New Democratic period) and one third was to be provided by a military or some other functionally analogous organisation[64] such as the People's Militia (the latter-day equivalent of New Democratic military representation). As one might have expected from the experiences of 1950–1, the military component in the new organisation was gradually phased out as a new Party structure was built consisting of 'reformed' old Party personnel and activists who had emerged from the Cultural Revolution.[65] These activists 'emerged' in much the same way as an earlier generation of activists emerged from the Three and Five Anti Movements of 1951–2.

The parallel between the New Democratic period and the Cultural Revolution is a striking one but one cannot take it too far. The various mass movements of 1951–2 paved the way for the introduction of a highly centralised form of administration and one-man management forms of organisation. Although there has been a stress on discipline in the past few years and an attack on a previous tendency towards industrial anarchy,[66] the prescribed leadership formula is that of the mid 1950s and policy divisions are taken by revolutionary committees under Party leadership.[67] The early 1960s have shown that such a situation can lead to a *de facto* form of one-man management though, unlike some observers, I see no signs of that at present.[68] Indeed it would be highly unlikely that the newly formed Party committees have become instantaneously congruent with management though the events of the early 1960s have shown that we should not be blind to that possibility. There is indeed a similarity between the language used in the movement to establish responsibility movements of 1953 and the current movement to strengthen enterprise management. Just as some people criticised 'the working style of the warlords' at that time, so in 1972:

> Some comrades regard strengthening enterprise management as being opposed to giving full play to the people's revolutionary enthusiasm believing that all management systems can only tie the hands of the workers and dampen their enthusiasm.[69]

As in 1953, such attitudes are roundly criticised as indeed is the tendency to downgrade technical personnel. Too much spontaneity is again seen as a danger:

> Specialised management personnel are a backbone force in enterprise management. Particularly in large enterprises it is imperative to guard against the tendency to stress unduly management by the masses while ignoring management by specialised personnel.[70]

What seems to me to be a more immediate danger, however, is that a new bureaucratic cycle appears to have begun.[71] The Cultural Revolution went to great lengths to remove what were felt to be unnecessary staff personnel. It is highly likely that too many of such personnel were removed and some had to be restored. The impression one gets, however, is that a fairly large number have been restored which might warrant some further cut-back if and when a new stage in the continuous revolution gets under way. Much depends, of course, on the extent to which functional systems of administration such as the Tsitsihar model have been introduced for such systems require fewer specialist staff. Short of engaging in first-hand research I cannot determine the extent to which the ideologically integrated functional model described above has been realised. Even with such a system, however, there is a danger that, if a large number of specialist staff are located at enterprise level, they might offset the effectiveness of factory revolutionary committees which were in fact designed amongst other things to eliminate wasteful functional departments.[72]

A further set of problems emerge when one considers the relationship between the newly revamped Party committee, the factory revolutionary committees and the factory union organisations which for the most part have been established (at least under that name) in the past year.[73] One must examine how meaningful a separation is made between policy and operations. It would appear that, in a manner similar to the mid 1950s, the Party committee is concerned primarily with policy matters (planning and major production decisions).[74] To a more specific degree the revolutionary committee is also so engaged whereas leading groups at sub-enterprise level seem to be concerned mainly with operational decisions.[75] Ideally, I suppose, the Party committee should be concerned with what Andors would refer to as politics (the overall goals of society), whereas the revolutionary committee would be concerned more with policy (the specific implementation of these goals within the enterprise) but I cannot be sure how the distinction may be drawn. It would appear that the various factory organisations that fulfilled the function of labour unions before unions were formally reconstituted in 1972 performed also the function of providing the worker component on the revolutionary committee and of training cadres to serve as managers.[76] We saw in our study of the New Democratic Period that such a situation can emasculate the worker component on any senior management body as successful workers become managers and the unions are reduced to the home of 'fourth class cadres'. One might surmise that a memory of this fact together with the memory of the recurrent tendency of unions to degenerate into 'economism' might have accounted for the considerable delay in rebuilding the labour union structure. It may well be, however, that the lessons of the past have been well learnt and the new unions are substantially different from the old. Perhaps the increase in political consciousness engendered by the Cultural Revolution will be sufficient to ensure in the short run that the new union cadres do not harbour thoughts of 'fourth class' status. This is again something that only first-hand research can substantiate.

In the meantime one can merely note that certain institutional reforms have been introduced that must minimise the distance between workers and management. During the Great Leap Forward a system was introduced known as the 'two participations' and 'triple combination'.[77] The 'two participations' consisted of cadre participation in manual labour and worker participation in management and the 'triple combination' consisted of the formation of teams of management cadres, technicians and workers to facilitate making technical decisions and to short-circuit bureaucracy. These systems have been retained in the post Cultural Revolution structure. Combined teams still operate[78] in much the same way as 1958 and concentrate on specific tasks. In short-circuiting line management and reducing the dependence on specialised staff attached to line positions, they perform an important functional overlay which, if continued, will make the growth of rigid hierarchical systems extremely difficult.

When all is said and done, the future direction of factory management and worker participation will depend less on the structure of command and the pattern of control than on the consciousness of the work force, for without a sufficient level of consciousness any form of ideological integration is impossible. Here I see two very important reasons for hope. Firstly it was *worker* propaganda teams that solved some of the really serious problems created during the Cultural Revolution at a time when the Peoples Liberation Army was found to be too prone to wield the big stick. Workers began to participate *as workers* in all spheres of life outside the factory[79] and the tremendous kudos given to their role may have perhaps begun to create a climate where activist workers will not want to be anything else but workers. This I feel is not the same kind of pluralist role separation foreseen by the 'logic of industrialism' school where a worker alternates between a creative life outside the work place and slavery within it.

At the same time as there is greater participation by workers in life outside the factory, renewed efforts have been made to construct industrial communities. Early attempts were made in 1958–60 to create urban communes which united industrial, agricultural, trade, education and militia work.[80] More recently the Tach'ing Oil Field has been put forward as a model integrated industrial community. Mao Tse-tung has advocated an extension of the Tach'ing principle, whereby industrial workers engage also in agricultural work, to large iron and steel complexes such as Wuhan[81] and quite clearly any discussion of enterprise organisation and commitment that deals with the 1970s must consider the Tach'ing model. The wider aspects of industrial community have, however been beyond the scope of this essay which deals with the early 1950s.

My second reason for hope centres on one of the most notable gains of the Cultural Revolution. This is an affirmation of what I referred to earlier as the *creative* as opposed to the *selective* approach to education. The radicals during the Cultural Revolution condemned most severely the situation which we noted in Chapter 6 where graduates moved into high prestige staff-jobs leaving little scope for the promotion of workers. At one point 'ultra-left' criticism reached the point of calling for the abolition of universities.[82] In the aftermath of that revolution, the principle whereby a considerable stress is given to the creation of environmental conditions outside the formal education system which are conducive to the training of skilled personnel has remained of paramount importance. The manifest object of such a process is to abolish what Mao would call 'the three major differences' – between town and country, worker and peasant and between mental and manual labour. It is to avoid the creation of an élite, for Chinese leaders do not accept the natural law which the logic of industrialism school takes as axiomatic – the external division between semi-managers and semi-managed.

Finally one note of caution. In this work, I have not talked much about technological determinants mainly because of the limitations of my source material. I deliberately gave great stress to the iron and steel industry and the construction industry because they constituted apparently polar types but, beyond that, I did not raise some of the crucial questions which any student of Chinese management in 1973 must raise. In much of the Third World, societies are frequently distorted by the importation of complete plants designed overseas for a completely different economy and social system. By the end of the New Democratic period in China a large number of complete Soviet plants had begun to be imported and these were to be the élite showpieces of the First Five Year Plan. Recently China has taken the decision to import complete plants employing highly sophisticated technology from Japan and Western capitalist countries. There is a danger that an automated highly élitist sector of industry will grow up run by super-professionals who violate the principle of substitutability of roles that has been stressed by Chinese radicals. There is a danger that different incentive systems will apply to different sectors of industry (as indeed they did during the New Democratic period). In the modern sector an incentive system might be developed that encourages predictability whereas in other sectors an incentive system might develop that encourages creativity and relies to a greater degree on moral incentive.[83] It would, in my opinion, be a disaster for transition to socialism if that sector which stressed moral incentive and creativity is the poor cousin. Perhaps I am taking too technologically determinist a line here and perhaps China has no choice but to import sophisticated technology. I cannot but feel, however, that the principle of combining 'red' and 'expert' demands that technology should be shaped above all by social priorities. Once it is the other way round, the doctrine of letting 'experts run factories' comes into its own.

Appendix I

Some examples of wage point formulation

	North East Adm. Cttee. Wage pt. September 7 1948 (*fen*)	Hsin Chuang Coal Mine (N China) December 1948 (*hsi*)	Peking Municipal Wage pt. 9 Oct. 1951 (*fen*)
Rice }	1.63 *chin*	2 *chin*	0.48 *shih chin*
Wheat }		1 *chin*	0.32 *shih chin*
Coal	5.5 *chin*	1½ *chin*	2 *shih chin*
Oil	0.035 *chin*	5 *ch'ien*	0.05 *shih chin*
Salt	0.045 *chin*	5 *ch'ien*	0.02 *shih chin*
Cotton cloth	0.20 sq. ft	1 sq. metre	0.2 ft
Ranges			
Highest	Factory general manager	300 points	105 points
	White collar workers	180 points	
	Skilled workers	145 points	
	Ordinary workers in light work	120 points	
	Sundry workers	90 points	
Lowest	Apprentices	35 points	30 points
	Ordinary workers	60 points	
	Trainee technicians	50 points	
	Technicians	75 points	
	Management	100 points	

Note on weights and measures

The term *chin* referred to here is probably what is now referred to as an old chin (*chiu-chin*) = 0.597 kg.

1 *ch'ien* was the tenth part of 1 *liang* (ounce). According to the old

standard 1 *chin* = 16 *liang*, though later this was changed to 1 *shih chin* = 10 *liang*.

1 *shih chin* = 0.5 kg.

It is not clear what linear measurement the term foot refers to. According to the old standard 1 foot (*ch'ih*) = 0.32 metres whereas the new standard stipulated that 1 *shih ch'ih* = 0.333 metres.

Because of the uncertainty as to which standards are referred to, I have not converted the weights and measures.

Sources:

1. *Tung Pei Chan-shih Kung-ying Ch'i-yeh Kung-hsin Piao-chun* (Wartime Wage and Salary Standards for Publically-run Enterprises in the North East), 7 September 1948 in *Cheng-wu-yüan Ts'ai-cheng Ching-chi Wei-yüan-hui*, compendium, No. 1, pt. 2, pp. 710–13.
2. *Jen-min Jih-pao*, 25 December 1948, p. 2.
3. *Jen-min Jih-pao*, 11 October 1951, p. 2.

Appendix II

Collective contract of the glass factory under the Lushun–Talien Far East Electronics Bureau (Lu Ta Yüan-tung Tien-yeh Po-li Kung-ch'ang Chi-t'i Ho-t'ung) summary

The Contract was concluded between management (*kung-ch'ang tang-chü*) and labour union (*chih-kung-hui*) and signed by the factory general manager and labour union chairman in July 1949. It was ratified by special meeting of white and blue collar workers to be in force from 1 July 1949 until 31 December 1950; texts were in both Chinese and Russian.

I. *Aims and Objects*

To guarantee plan fulfilment, to raise the level of technical knowledge, to improve the organisation of production, to consolidate labour discipline, to implement a system for practising economy.

II. *Management undertakes*:–

1. to adopt all measures necessary for the fulfilment and over-fulfilment of stipulated production norms, to organise technical direction, to adopt measures for the supply of fuel and materials, and to ensure the timely installation and repair of technical equipment.
2. to transmit production plans to the shops, teams and individual workers at the latest 5 days before the commencement of each monthly or quarterly period and to assign workers to fixed work positions.
3. to provide favourable conditions and material help to those who put forward rationalisation proposals or suggest inventions, to propagate such proposals that are adopted and to award bonuses according to the regulations of the Electronics Bureau.
4. to guarantee the material conditions for the cultural and educational work of all employees and to designate a building as a temporary club before the end of this (Chinese) year.

III. *The Labour Union undertakes*:–

1. to employ every effort to improve the effectiveness of the emulation movement, to check up on adherance to technical standards and to propagate achievements.

2. to carry out daily education work with the aim of consolidating production and labour discipline and to inspire the workers to fulfil their daily production tasks and raise the labour productivity rate.

3. to organise voluntary labour to help decorate the club once designated.

Management and union undertake:–
in launching a 'creativity movement', to give all help to white and blue collar workers, to publish work achievements, sum up the emulation movement quarterly and to honour model workers by setting up a roll of honour, awarding badges, publishing photographs, biographies etc. (In addition to such moral incentive the general manager's office will make appropriate bonus payments from the bonus fund.)

IV. *Wages, production bonuses and allowances*

1. Basic wages will be paid according to the attached chart. Although the factory was classified as Grade 1, Grade 2 rates are shown since the contract was published as a model to be emulated by factories classified as both grade 1 (heavy industry) and grade 2 (light industry). The basic piece rate is calculated at the time rate + 10% (see Chapter 5). The hazard rate was paid to people working in high temperatures and where health might be damaged (a list of the various jobs covered by this rate is included in the contract). Apprentices were to be paid (according to Soviet practice) according to Grades 1 and 2 of the 7 Grade scale rate.

2. The scale for white collar workers was exactly the same as the fifteen grade scale prescribed for Lushun and Talien (see Chapter 5, Fig. 4) although, inexplicably, Grade 3 of a Grade 2 enterprise appears to be ¥300 lower than the official scale (probably a misprint). Contrary to the practice noted in Chapter 5, both technicians and line management were to be paid according to the fifteen grade scale.

3. Management and union undertook to draw up a concrete plan for the implementation of piecework systems; by the end of 1949, 70% of all workers were to be in receipt of payment by piecework or according to the progressive bonus system for over-fulfilling norms. A bonus system for white collar workers was also introduced. After 6 months norms and piecework standards were to be revised.

4. If a worker failed to fulfil his work norms due to accumulated completed but his pay was to be not less than two thirds of the basic wage. completed but his pay was not less than two thirds of the basic wage.

5. In the case of norm revision due to rationalisation proposals, the norm of the worker who put forward the proposals was not to be altered prematurely.

6. Overtime pay was not to be less than time-and-a-half and overtime was only to be practised when there was mutual agreement between management and union. Workers under 18 and pregnant women were forbidden to participate in overtime. Workers under the age of 18 were required to work only a seven hour day but the wages due to them were to be those of an eight hour day. If there were a work stoppage which was not due to a worker's mistakes and if management were unable to transfer a worker to another job, he would receive payment at half the time rate. If he were transferred to another job, he was to receive the full time rate.

If, due to a worker's errors, his production was completely sub-standard and constituted waste, he was to receive no payment; if his product were only partially sub-standard, payment would be reduced proportionally and if sub-standard products appeared which were not due to his errors, he would be paid according to the time rate rather than the piece rate. Management guaranteed to obtain grain at a low price and make monthly allocations to workers and their dependents. Management guaranteed further to provide the necessary industrial (rationed) goods and daily necessities.

When workers were absent from work due to electoral and other duties, management was to continue to pay their average wage. When on outside duty in connection with their work, workers would be paid according to their basic wage plus outside duty pay and travel allowances; (daily outside duty pay was equal to 3% of the monthly basic wage and hotel expenses were not to exceed 40% of the daily outside pay).

Losses incurred in the performance of work duties were to be recovered by management except in the case of carelessness. Management might deduct up to 30% of a worker's wage for losses due to carelessness except in the case of a court order when it was limited to 50%.

In the case of redundancy, management was required to pay severance pay equivalent to 12 days basic wage plus grants for rest days owing. In the case of temporary incapacity, workers would retain their original status and wage. In the case of sickness, this period was limited to three months and in the case of childbirth, 2½ months.

If a worker left the factory without good reason before an agreed time, he was to compensate the factory by repaying at current market prices the value of special work clothes given to him, grain allocation made during the month he left and industrial (rationed) goods allocated to him during the current quarter. In such case, management was empowered to give the said worker two weeks notice to move out of his dormitory. When a new worker was taken on, management was required to stipulate twelve to fourteen days as a trial period during which time his grade and duties would be determined.

In the case of white and blue collar workers whose place of residence was over 5 km. from the factory, management would provide expenses to help them move nearer. Management undertook to install a dormitory

Grade	Piecework coeffic-ients		Time rate basic	Piece rate basic (+10%)	Hazard rate	Time rate basic	Piece rate basic (+10%)	Hazard rate
		Hourly		12.9	13.5		10.8	11.3
1	1.0	Daily	94.1	103.5	108.2	73.4	86.3	90.2
		Monthly	2,400	2,640	2,760	2,000	2,200	2,300
		Hourly		15.5*	16.2		12.9	13.5
2	1.2	Daily	113.0	124.2	129.0	94.1	103.5	108.2
		Monthly	2,880	3,168	3,312	2,400	2,640	2,760
		Hourly		13.8*	19.6		15.6	16.3
3	1.45	Daily	136.5	150.1	156.9	113.7	125.1	130.8
		Monthly	3,480	3,828	4,002	2,900	3,190	3,335
		Hourly		22.6	23.7		18.9	19.7
4	1.75	Daily	164.7	181.1	189.4	137.3	151.0	157.8
		Monthly	4,200	4,620	4,830	3,500	3,850	4,025
		Hourly		27.8	29.2		23.2	24.2
5	2.15	Daily	202.4	222.6	235.0	168.6	185.5	193.9
		Monthly	5,160	5,675	5,934	4,300	4,730	4,945
		Hourly		33.6	35.2		28.0	29.3
6	2.6	Daily	244.7	268.6	261.4	203.9	224.3	234.5
		Monthly	6,240	6,364	7,176	5,200	5,720	5,980
		Hourly		41.4	43.5		34.5	36.1
7	3.2	Daily	301.2	331.5	346.4	251.0	276.1	288.6
		Monthly	7,680	8,448	8,833	6,400	7,040	7,360

*Possible error. Grade 3 is lower than Grade 2. On the basis of daily rate, hourly rate should be about 19.0 for Grade 3.

to hold 200–300 people before November 1949 (the text says 1940 – clearly a misprint). Technical personnel and skilled workers were given priority in accommodation. (Such a building was found on 30 July.)

V. *Working hours*

Normally these would not exceed eight hours daily (seven hours in the case of workers between the age of 14 and 17 and those working underground). Night shift workers were paid for nine hours on an eight hour shift, each hour being calculated at one and one seventh the day rate. Foremen and shift supervisors only received payment for eight hours and piecework norms would be calculated on an 8 hour basis.

Rest and lunch breaks were not included in working hours.

VI. *Rest periods*

Normally there was one rest day per week lasting 39 hours (from 5 p.m. on the previous day until 8 a.m. on the succeeding day). One day holiday was awarded at New Year, 2 days at Spring Festival, 2 days at the beginning of May and one day to celebrate victory over Japan (3 September). If such holidays could not be awarded, workers would be paid at time and a half. Those who had worked for an uninterrupted period of eleven months received 12 days holiday per year with pay according to the time rate. Workers in hazardous occupations could be awarded 18 days with pay according to the hazard rate. Those who had worked for an uninterrupted period of 2 years in the same enterprise were granted three days extra holiday per year though the number of accumulated holiday days was not to exceed 24 days in any one year. Management had the right to award from 6 to 12 days supplementary holiday for white and blue collar workers whose holidays were not fixed (a list of such people was to be determined by agreement by management and union). Workers under 17 years received 24 days per year.

VII. *Labour protection*

Management was to provide certain equipment to protect the workers health (a list of such equipment was given), conduct regular inspections, improve the clinic, etc. In addition, management was to provide an adequately heated and ventilated place for shift workers to spend the night which had to be completed by September 1949.

VIII. *Conciliation and arbitration*

A conciliation committee (*t'iao-chieh wei-yüan-hui*) was set up consisting of an equal number of delegates from the factory general office and the labour union with a system of rotating chairmen with a casting vote if necessary. The conciliation committee was required to discuss all labour disputes and its decisions were equally binding on management and labour union. In matters of great gravity, however, matters might be submitted to a higher body (the Electronics Bureau), which could convene an arbitration conference (*chung-ts'ai hui-i*) attended by representatives from the Bureau and the Lushun–Talien General Labour Union and representatives of each of the relevant departments of the factory. Such conferences could revise decisions taken by the conciliation committee.

IX. *Social insurance*

Management required to set up a social insurance fund which might not be used for any purpose other than social insurance. The fund would be calculated at 4% of that part of the total wages bill expressed in monetary terms. Management was expressly forbidden to make any deductions from wages in return for money received from this fund.

The social insurance fund was to be used as help towards medical expenses, as grants to those temporarily incapacitated or caring for sick relatives and as supplementary grants for wet-nurses, funerals, etc.

There followed concrete details of what constituted the period of pregnancy and what awards should be made in the case of death on duty. Payments for incapacitated workers varied according to length of service (*kung-ling*) ranging from 25% of basic wage (for less than six months' service) to 100% for over two years' service.

X. *Culture and education*

Management was required to set up a culture and education fund and money from this fund was paid monthly to the labour union for the provision of education. The fund was calculated at 1% of that part of the monthly wage bill which was expressed in monetary terms and deductions from workers wages in respect of educational expenses was forbidden. The fund was to be used for education in literacy and politics, for conducting propaganda and cultural activities, the purchase of books and expenses incurred in commemoration meetings.

Source

Chung-hua Ch'üan-kuo Tsung-kung-hui, Pien-chi Chu-pan-shih, August 1950, pp. 193–217.

Appendix III

Patriotic compact of the Wang Ch'ün-lao Team at the Wuch'ang Chen Huan spinning mill (Wu-ch'ang Chen Huan Sha-ch'ang Wang Ch'ün-lao Hsiao-tsu Ai-kuo Kung-yüeh) May 1951

1. Respond to the calls of the Party, management, labour union and Youth League. Actively participate in all factory activities.
2. Mobilise the masses to append their names to the resolution of the executive council (of the China Peace Committee) and carry out propaganda among the workers and their relatives concerning the United States rearming Japan.
3. Resolutely support the government's suppression of counter revolutionaries. Trace the origins of any (false) rumours that one may have heard.
4. Set up a newspaper-reading group to read newspapers for twenty minutes daily.
5. Appoint a worker picket before 1 June.
6. Appoint a Party propagandist before 1 June.
7. Undertake to attend classes run by the Party and Youth League.
8. Undertake that the entire team shall attend night school, will not come late or leave early and will maintain study discipline.
9. Guarantee the completion of the production plan, regularly inspect its completion and raise the level of the targets.
10. Every Saturday inspect the progress in implementing the compact.

Patriotic compact of the Chu Tsao-ti team of the Wuhan first spinning mill (Wu-han Ti-i Sha-ch'ang Chu Tsao-ti Hsiao-tsu Ai-kuo Kung-yüeh) April 1951

1. Study current affairs. Read newspapers from five to ten minutes daily. Raise the level of one's own understanding and publicise the news

amongst others.

2. Support and help the government in its suppression of counter revolutionaries. Protect the mill and search out secret agents.

3. Do not believe rumours one may hear. Explain (the true facts) to others and seek out the source of such rumours.

4. By means of effective action, improve production and fulfil work tasks in order to give thanks to Chairman Mao, the Communist Party and the Peoples government for their correct leadership. Support the Chinese Peoples Volunteer Army and oppose the American arming of Japan.

5. Improve unity and mutual help. Don't complain, and achieve ideological unity within the whole team. Establish relations with other groups.

6. Study technology, do research into technology together with other workers and management cadres who understand technology; study how to make minor repairs in machines. Raise the level of production.

7. Study 'culture' (i.e. improve literacy), undertake not to miss classes at night school so that one may become a person who understands, writes and is able to use (machinery). Help those who cannot attend night school.

8. Every two weeks investigate the implementation of the patriotic compact.

Source:

Chung Nan Jen-min Ch'u-pan-she, September 1951, pp. 50–1.

Brief biographical data of some of the more important names appearing in this book

I have listed here only the more important posts held during the New Democratic Period or the period in which their articles were written.

An Tzu-wen	Deputy Director CCP.CC Organisation Bureau. Minister of Personnel.
Chang Hsi	Ranking Party Secretary in Honan Party Committee. Chairman Honan Finance and Economics Committee. Member of State Planning Commission (1952–).
Chang Li-k'o	Chairman Shenyang General Labour Union.
Chang P'ing-hua	Member CSMAC (1950) and its Finance and Economics Committee. Chairman Wuhan Peoples Government (Sept. 1950–) demoted early 1952 and later reinstated.
Ch'en Po-ta	Deputy Director Party Propaganda Bureau.
Chi Ming-ta	Director Anshan Iron and Steel Company; Smelting Works Construction Corporation.
Chou Shu K'ang	Head of Wages Department NE General Labour Union.
Chu Hsüeh-fan	Adm. Cttee. member of Chinese Labour Assn. (1945). Delegate of Assn. to 6th Labour Conference. Held a number of posts 1949–65 including Minister of Posts and Telecommunications. Vice-Chairman ACFTU.
Hsü Ti-hsin	Vice-Chairman E. China Military Region Finance and Economics Cttee. (and later ECMAC Feb. 1950) June 1952. Vice-Chairman of All China Federation of Industry and Commerce.
Hsüeh Mu-ch'iao	Secretary General GAC Finance and Economics Cttee. (1949–52). Head of State Statistical Bureau. Member of State Planning Commission.
Jao Shu-shih	Chairman ECMAC (later E. China Adm. Cttee.). 1st Secretary CCP.CC E. China Bureau (1952–). Head of CCP Organisation Bureau. Disappeared Feb. 1954. Censured March 1955.
Kao Fang-ch'i	FGM Shenyang Wu San Factory.
Kao Kang	Chairman NEPG, Secy. CCP. CC NE Bureau (1952–). Chairman State Planning Commission. Disappeared Feb. 1954. Suicide 1954. Censured March 1955.
Ku Cho-hsin	Head of Finance Dept. NEPG (1952). Vice-Chairman NEPG Planning Cttee (1954–). Vice-

	Chairman State Planning Commission.
Lai Jo-yü	(Dec. 1951–) Member Central Austerity Examination Cttee. ACFL Secretary General and from 1953 ACFTU Chairman.
Li Fu-ch'un	(1949–) Vice-Chairman NEPG. (Oct. 1949) Member Central Finance and Economics Cttee. and later Vice-Chairman. Minister of Heavy Industry (1950–2). Vice-Chairman Central Austerity Committee (1951). Member and later Chairman of State Planning Commission (after dismissal of Kao Kang).
Li Hsiu-jen	Deputy Director of ACFTU General Office (1957).
Li Hsüeh-feng	Held a number of important posts in CSMAC (1950–4). Later Head CCP Industrial and Communications Work Dept.
Li Li-san	Better known for his career in the late 1920s. (1948) 1st Vice-Chairman ACFL (de facto Head) until union crisis of 1951–2. His errors exposed in 1953. Replaced by Lai Jo-yü at 7th Labour Conference.
Liu Ch'ang-sheng	Executive Cttee. member Shanghai Party Cttee. (1949–52) and 3rd Secretary (1952–3). Member of Central Govt. Finance and Economics Cttee. (1951–4). Head of ECMAC Labour Dept. and Director Shanghai Office of ACFL.
Liu Shao-ch'i	By 1945 second only to Mao Tse-tung in the Party. For full list of posts see Klein and Clark, 1971.
Liu Tzu-chiu	Director of a number of bodies directly under ACFL Centre and member of the ACFTU Executive Cttee., Praesidium and Secretariat.
Lü Tung	Deputy Director NEPG Industrial Dept. (1952–). Vice Minister of Heavy Industry.
Ma Heng-chang	Team leader in the 5th Machinery works in Shenyang. The most famous of all the model team leaders in the period.
Peng Chen	Best known as Mayor of Peking (1951–66).
Sun Yeh-fang	Economic theorist. (1949) Member ECMAC Finance and Economics Cttee. (1954–7) Deputy Director State Statistical Bureau. (1961) Director Institute of Economics. Attacked as a 'Chinese Liberman' in 1966.
T'ao Chu	(in 1960s) 1st Secretary of Central South Bureau CCP.CC and Vice-Premier.
Teng T'o	(1950) Deputy Managing Director *JMJP*. (1952) Editor in Chief *JMJP*. (1951) Head of Propaganda Cttee. of Peking Party Cttee. Later to become notorious in Cultural Revolution.
Teng Tzu-hui	Member Central South Finance and Economics

	Cttee. and (after 1952) Vice-Chairman, Ranking Vice-Chairman of CSMAC.
Wang Ho-shou	Director NEPG Industrial Dept. and member of NE Finance and Economics Cttee. Succeeded Li Fu-ch'un as Minister of Heavy Industry.

Notes to the text

Introduction

1 Kerr *et al.* 1962.
2 G.D.H. Cole defines a 'bourgeoisie' as 'a body of citizens asserting their collective as well as their individual independence of a social system dominated by feudal power based on land holding and on the services attached to it, whereas the words "middle class" call up a quite different image of a body of persons who are placed between two other bodies – or perhaps more than two – in some sort of stratified social order'. Cole, 1961, pp. 90–1.
3 For a discussion of 'bureaucratic capitalism' see Hsü Ti-hsin, 1949.
4 Bendix, 1956, p. 2.
5 *Ibid.* pp. 46–60.
6 Yoshino, 1968, Chapter 3.
7 See the debate between Abegglen, 1959 and Taira, 1970. This debate will be discussed in Chapter 1.
8 The idea of a bourgeois democratic revolution under proletarian hegemony was put forward by Trotsky in 1905. Later in that year, Lenin began to echo this idea interpreting 'revolutionary democratic dictatorship of workers and peasants' in terms of proletarian hegemony. See d'Encausse and Schram, 1969, pp. 19–20.
9 Many of these firms had never really recovered from the war and were squeezed our fairly easily by various forms of pressure. One last woollen mill remained under British management until 1959. See Donnithorne, 1967, p. 145.

On the take over of industries temporarily brought under the control of the Kuomintang government National Resources Commission in North East China (formerly Manchukuo) see *SCMP*, No. 50, 18 January 1951 and No. 52, 20 January 1951.

10 The Chinese define 'large' industrial enterprise in terms of two criteria – the number of employees and the extent to which mechanical power is used. Any establishment is classified as 'large' if there is a work force of 16 or more and if the establishment uses mechanical power. If, on the other hand, there is no mechanical power, then the establishment is classified as 'large' if there is a work force of 31 or more. In the case of independent electric power plants, the plant is classified as 'large' if the capacity is over 15 kilowatts regardless of the size of the work force employed. (Chen Nai-ruenn, 1967, p. 29.) According to these criteria there were some 9000 large scale industrial enterprises administered by central or local government by the end of our period of study (1953). (Chen

Nai-ruenn, 1967, p. 182.)

We shall be concerned here with a much more restricted definition of 'large'. In the main, I shall be concerned with industrial enterprises taken over by the state which employed over 100 persons and which by the end of 1949 amounted only to some 1000 units as is shown by the following table.

Size of employment	*Number of industrial concerns*	*Number of production workers*
Total	2,677	753,000
Below 100 persons	1,687	57,000
100–500 persons	686	151,000
500–1000 persons	145	104,000
1000–5000 persons	130	252,000
Over 5000 persons	14	189,000
Unknown	15	n.a.

Chen Nai-ruenn, 1967, p. 181.

I have used the word 'concern' here rather than enterprise for reasons suggested later in the Introduction.

I shall give particular attention to the iron and steel industry (some 100 enterprises with over 100 people employed by 1954 Chen Nai-ruenn, 1967, p. 184), because it was given planning priority as the Soviet model of administration was adopted and might be expected to exhibit what were considered to be 'advanced' features and the construction industry which might be expected to use more traditional features of organisation and commitment because of the necessity of relying initially on contract labour.

11 See, for example, *Chin-tai Ko-ming Li-shih-so, Hung-wei-ping Chan-tou Kung-ying chan*, 1967.

12 In the ideal form of Soviet organisation described by Cheng Hung-su, 1950, the enterprise consisted of more than one factory presided over by a director (Chinese translation *ching-li*) whereas each constituent factory was presided over by a factory general manager (*ch'ang-chang*). In fact, in China, most enterprises were single factories and were presided over by a factory general manager.

The New Democratic period was one in which enterprises were being formed and, in using this term, one should constantly be aware of the dichotomy between natural and prescribed organisational forms. One might suggest that the dichotomy between the natural village and the administrative village had its industrial counterpart, though this parallel should not be taken too far since in terms of personnel, the enterprise was usually coterminous with the natural factory except in the case of huge vertically integrated corporations (*kung-ssu*). Like the term 'commune' (*kung-she*), the term enterprise was used very loosely. It could mean an ideal form of organisation, a prescribed organisational form which temporarily fell short of that ideal or the actual existing industrial unit.

One should note also that the term *kung-ssu* was used both for a commercially defined 'company' and an administratively defined 'corporation'. Both types of *kung-ssu* were presided over by a director (*ching-li*).

13 Berliner 1957 (1968). A similar exercise is currently being undertaken for the Chinese textile industry by Kevin Bucknall of the Australian National University.

14 The best exposition of the 'mass line' may be found in Mao Tse-tung 1 June 1943 and has been commented on very ably by Selden in Barnett, 1969, and Selden, 1971. For a definition see p. 311.

15 For example the work of Christopher Howe, *Wage Patterns and Wage Policy in Modern China 1919–1972*, 1973.

16 Schurmann, 1966, pp. 165–7 and 236.

17 This decision-making pattern was seen most clearly in the various decisions taken by the Tao Kuang emperor in the period preceding and during the First Opium War and is similar to that which applied to twentieth-century Japanese industrial organisations as described by Yoshino, 1968, pp. 254–62.

18 Taylor, 1913.

19 Taylor (1911) in Taylor, 1947, p. 104.

20 *Ibid.* p. 123.

21 For example, a study of 100 firms made in South Essex in the 1950s showed 35 firms of predominantly line type organisation, 59 staff-line organisation, 4 unclassifiable and only 2 of functional organisation, Woodward, 1965, p. 18.

22 Pfiffner and Sherwood 1960, Chapter 2, 'Complexity of Organisation: The Concept of Overlays', pp. 16–32.

23 Reeves and Woodward in Woodward, 1970, pp. 37–56.

24 *Ibid.* p. 38.

25 *Ibid.* p. 45.

26 Schurmann, 1966, p. 192.

27 The distinction made by Schurmann is between *chien-ch'a* (监察) and *chien-tu* (监督). The term *chien-ch'a* (监察) is the term used in control commission (*chien-ch'a wei-yüan-hui*) and Procuratorate (*chien-ch'a-yüan*), which ideally judge legal cases after the event. In the industrial sphere, however, control organs (*chien-ch'a chi-kuan*) frequently became involved in checking up on actions whilst they were in progress. In addition to the above terms, two others are frequently used both pronounced *chien*^{3}-*ch'a*^{2}. The first of these (检察) is primarily a legal term indicating examination and prosecution and the second (检查) is an extremely common term indicating the process of checking up on actions during and after the event, both in the legal sphere and outside. The question is made even more complicated by the use of other terms, such as *tu-ch'a* (督察) (on-going inspection), *k'ao-ch'a* (考察) (exploratory research), *tiao-ch'a* (调查) (specific investigation), etc., all of which have some bearing on the English word 'control'. To avoid the discussion become too abstruse, when I am not using control in

the general sense of *k'ung-chih* (控制), I shall accept Schurmann's somewhat oversimplified distinction between *chien-tu* and *chien-ch'a* which I shall translate as 'supervision' and 'control'.

28 Mao Tse-tung, 1957.
29 Mao Tse-tung (January 1962) in *Mao Chu-hsi Wen-hsüan*, p. 74.
30 Schurmann unpublished manuscript, I. 16.
31 Andors [1969 (1971)] defines politics as the overall goals of society, policy as the specific formulation of these goals for a particular enterprise and operations as a process whereby policy is carried out.
32 Harper, 1969.

Chapter 1: The Chinese pattern of industrialisation in comparative perspective

1 The account of early Russian industrialisation is taken from Mavor, 1965, Chapter 3 and Dobb, 1966, Chapter 1.
2 Bendix, 1956, data from A.G. Rashin.
3 Mavor, 1965, Vol. I, p. 441. The figures are 99,000 to 241,000 and 43,000 to 71,000.
4 Bendix, 1956, p. 184.
5 This word is taken from Crane Brinton: *Anatomy of Revolution* and signifies a set of conditions which together make up a pre-revolutionary situation.
6 Bendix, 1956, p. 180.
7 i.e. the older view that increasing conservatism of workers produces revolution.
8 *Ibid.* p. 179.
9 Mavor, 1965, Vol. 2, p. 427.
10 Mavor, 1965, Vol. 2, p. 367.
11 Ungern-Sternberg cited in Bendix, 1956, p. 188.
12 Bendix, 1956, pp. 181–2.
13 Mavor, 1965, Vol. 2, pp. 378–9.
14 Posvolsky and Moulton cited in Dobb, 1966, p. 38.
15 Lenin *Selected Works* Vol. IX, p. 284, cited in Dobb, 1966, p. 83.
16 Dobb, 1966, p. 85.
17 Compare Dobb, 1966, and Wiles, 1964, pp. 33–4.
18 Dobb, 1966, p. 122.
19 The discussion of War Communism is taken from Dobb, 1966, Chapters 5 and 6.
20 *Ibid.* p. 369.
21 Cited in Cheng Hung-su, 1950: 'Su-lien ti Ch'i-yeh . . . '
22 Dobb, 1966, p. 370.
23 Arakelian, 1947 (1950), p. 92.
24 All such labour-union-organised conferences were of a mass nature and had no executive function. Chang Li-k'o, 1951.
25 Cheng Hung-su, 1950, Part II, p. 10.
26 Feuerwerker, 1958, pp. 43–4.

27 This general outline of Japanese industrialisation is taken from Yoshino, 1968, especially Chapter 3.
28 The discussion here of simulated-kinship structure is taken from Bennett and Ishino, 1963.
29 Bendix, 1956, pp. 53–8.
30 Yoshino, 1968, Chapter 3.
31 Abegglen, 1959, especially p. 13.
32 Taira, 1970, Chapter 5, pp. 97–127.
33 Suggested by *Ibid*. p. 99.
34 Yoshino, 1968, Chapter 3.
35 Taira, 1970, p. 144. The movement was inaugurated in 1938.
36 *Ibid*. p. 148.
37 *Ibid*. p. 149.
38 *Ibid*. pp. 160–3.
39 Yoshino, 1968, p. 126.
40 *Ibid*. p. 122.
41 *Ibid*. p. 27.
42 *Ibid*. pp. 28, 119.
43 *Ibid*. pp. 28–9.
44 *Ibid*. p. 119.
45 *Ibid*. p. 130.
46 The discussion here of *kuan-tu shang-pan* and the activities of Sheng Hsüan-huai is taken from Feuerwerker, 1958.
47 *Ibid*. Chapter 3. With the outbreak of the revolution of 1911, Sheng fled for his life. He subsequently returned to China and retained control of the Chinese Merchants Company and his textile mills. He died in 1916. Feuerwerker, 1958, p. 82.
48 See in particular the complaints of H.B. Morse in Feuerwerker, 1958, pp. 137–44.
49 Feuerwerker, 1958, pp. 101–3.
50 Wang Ching-yü cited in Feuerwerker, 1964, p. 84.
51 Cheng, Y.K., 1956, p. 27.
52 Remer (1933) says that foreign investment in modern factories was some $U.S.111 million in 1914: cited in Chen and Galenson, 1969, p. 16.
53 Feuerwerker, 1958, p. 16.
54 This account is taken from Feuerwerker, 1964.
55 Chesneaux, 1968; for a discussion of the size and distribution of the working class, see Chapter 2.
56 *Ibid*. Chapter 4.
57 *Ibid*. p. 76.
58 *Ibid*. p. 87.
59 *Ibid*. pp. 62–4.
60 Fong, H.D., 1937, p. 40.
61 Chesneaux, 1964, p. 115.
62 Selden, 1971, p. 243.
63 Fong, H.D., 1937, p. 38 (p. 956).
64 *Ibid*.

65 Chesneaux, 1968, p. 117.
66 Torgaschoff (1930) cited in Fong, 1937, p. 40 (p. 258).
67 Lamson (1934) cited in Fong, 1937, pp. 40–1 (pp. 958–9).
68 Lieberthal, 1973.
69 South Manchurian Railway Company, 1938, pp. 40–1.
70 *Ibid.*
71 Chesneaux, 1964, p. 115.
72 South Manchurian Railway Company, 1938, pp. 40–1.
73 Chesneaux, 1968, pp. 123, 127.
74 *Ibid.* p. 127.
75 *Ibid.* Chapters 8–9.
76 *Ibid.* Chapter 9.
77 *Ibid.* pp. 243–50.
78 *Ibid.* pp. 253–58.
79 *Ibid.* p. 288.
80 *Ibid.* Chapter 12.
81 *Ibid.* Chapter 13.
82 *Ibid.* Chapter 14.
83 Chu Hsüeh-fan, 1948.
84 Barnett, 1963, pp. 76–8.
85 Chu Hsüeh-fan, 1948.
86 Barnett, 1963, p. 76.
87 *Ibid.* p. 78.
88 Hubbard, 1935, p. 204.
89 *Ibid.* Hubbard makes the point that 'the labour laws set a standard very materially beyond what is immediately attainable in China and if applied literally would completely dislocate the industries concerned'.
90 Barnett, 1963, p. 79.
91 *Ibid.*
92 *Ibid.* p. 77.
93 *Ibid.* p. 78.
94 Eastman, 1972.
95 The four families were the Chiang, Ch'en, Sung and K'ung.
96 King, 1968, p. 113.
97 Chiang Kai-shek, 1947.
98 Myrdal, 1970, Chapter 7.
99 Ministry of Economic Affairs, Republic of China 1943, cited in Chen and Galenson, 1969, p. 17.
100 Chen and Galenson, 1969, p. 19.
101 Cheng, Y.K., 1956, p. 266.
102 Hsüeh Mu-ch'iao, 1964, p. 16.
103 Donnithorne, 1967, p. 145.
104 Winfield, 1948, pp. 329–30. The proposed transfer was put forward in February 1947 as part of an anti-inflationary programme. It excluded heavy industry.
105 Cheng, Y.K., 1956, p. 158 and Pauley (1946) cited in Chen and Galenson, 1969, p. 19.

106 Pauley's statistics cited in Cheng, Y.K., 1956, p. 266.
107 Statistics collected by Japanese technicians cited in Cheng, Y.K., 1956, p. 266.
108 Cheng Tsu-yüan, 1955, p. 20.
109 *Ibid.*
110 Cheng, Y.K., 1956, p. 158.
111 Chao I-wen (1957), cited in Chen and Galenson, 1969, p. 20.
112 State Statistical Bureau, Dept. of Ind. Stats., 1958, cited in Chen and Galenson, 1969, p. 20.
113 Winfield, 1948, pp. 96–7. Winfield describes how 200,000 tons of machinery was transferred to the interior in 1939 (pp. 216–18).
114 *T'ung-chi Kung-tso T'ung-hsüng Tzu-liao-shih*, 1957, p. 70.
115 Tseng Wen-chin (1958) cited in Chen and Galenson, 1969, p. 21.
116 State Statistical Bureau Department of Industrial Statistics, 1958, cited in Chen and Galenson, 1969, p. 21.
117 Chao I-wen (1957) cited in Chen and Galenson, 1969, p. 22.
118 The following discussion of the Shen Kan Ning area is taken from Selden, 1971, pp. 254–67.
119 de Tocqueville, 1956, pp. 62–72.
120 Mao Tse-tung, December 1942.
121 Tawney, 1932, p. 135.
122 This idea was suggested to me by Franz Schurmann.
123 Tawney, 1932, pp. 130–1.
124 Yoshino, 1968, Chapter 9.
125 See note 48 above.
126 V.I. Lenin, April 1918, *SW*, 1967, Vol. II, p. 664.
127 For example, Cheng Hung-su, 1950. 'Su-lien ti Ch'i-yeh . . .'
128 Lenin, April 1918, pp. 672–3.
129 Abegglen, 1959, p. 13.
130 Crankshaw, 1959, p. 69. Schapiro (1960, p. 564) does not record any fundamental changes in Party composition in the first five years after Stalin's death but does note its completely changed relationship to government and sees the Khruschev–Malenkov dispute in this light (p. 576). Except perhaps for the Kao Kang issue,the supremacy of the Party in China seems to have been unchallenged at the highest levels although, at lower levels, the Party organisation was frequently eclipsed.
131 Yoshino, 1968, pp. 218–19.
132 This discussion of incentives in Japanese industry is taken largely from R.E. Cole, 1971, Chapter 3.
133 Taira, 1970, pp. 183–4.
134 Chesneaux, 1968, p. 88.
135 For an account of payment systems, *Ibid.* pp. 88–97.
136 *Ibid.* pp.90–1.
137 This resolution was reprinted in *Kan-pu Hsüeh-hsi Tzu-liao*, No. 5, May 1950, as being particularly relevant to the present time.
138 Lindsay, 1970, p. 3.
139 Mao Tse-tung, December 1942, p. 274.

140 Ch'en Tzu-hsün, 1950.

Chapter 2: The moderate phase

1 *Chung-kuo Kung-ch'an-tang Chung-yang Wei-yüan-hui Tung Pei chü*, 10 June 1948.
2 Mao Tse-tung, 25 December 1947.
3 e.g. *Chung-kuo Kung-ch'an-tang Chung-yang Wei-yüan-hui Tung Pei chü*, 10 June 1948. *Hsin-min-chu Ch'u-pan-she*, 1949, pp. 56–61. Mao Tse-tung, 27 February 1948. Mao Tse-tung *et al.*, 1949, pp. 163–72.
4 *Chung-kuo Ti-liu-chieh Ch'üan-kuo Lao-tung Ta-hui*, 8 August 1948.
5 *Chin-tai Ko-ming Li-shih-so* and Lieberthal, 1971.
6 e.g. Lieberthal, 1971.
7 *Hsin-hua-she* (*Tung Pei*), 23 August 1948.
8 *Chung-kuo Kung-ch'an-tang Chung-yang Wei-yüan-hui Tung Pei chü*, 10 June 1948. In the earlier period material had been stolen on the grounds that it belonged to the Chiang regime.
9 Cheng Tsu-yüan, 1955, p. 22.
10 *Ibid.* p. 25.
11 *Ibid.* p. 26.
12 *Chung-kuo Kung-ch'an-tang Chung-yang Wei-yüan hui Tung Pei chü*, 1 August 1948.
13 Winfield, 1948, p. 165.
14 *Chung-kuo Kung-ch'an-tang Chung-yang Wei-yüan-hui Tung Pei chü*, 1 August 1948.
15 Shenyang (no author) in *Hsin-hua Shu-tien*, 1949.
16 Shanghai (no publisher stated), *Chieh-fang hou* . . .
17 *Chung-kuo Kung-ch'an-tang Chung-yang Wei-yüan-hui Tung Pei chü*, 1 August 1948.
18 Liu Shao-ch'i, May 1949, 'Tsai Hua Pei . . . '.
19 *Jen-min Jih-pao*, 12 September 1948, p. 1.
20 *Jen-min Jih-pao*, 17 September 1948.
21 Compare Shenyang (no author) and Liu Shao-ch'i, May 1949, 'Tsai Hua Pei . . . '.
22 Liu Shao-ch'i, May 1949, 'Tsai Hua Pei . . . '.
23 e.g. *Kung-jen Ch'u-pan-she*, 1953, p. 55 and Liu Shao-ch'i, May 1949, 'Tsai Hua Pei . . . '.
24 Ch'en Po-ta in *Hsin-hua Shu-tien*, 1949.
25 Liu Shao-ch'i, May 1949, 'Tsai Hua Pei . . . '.
26 *Chung-kuo Kung-ch'an-tang Chung-yang Wei-yüan-hui Tung Pei chü*, 18 April 1950.
27 Lieberthal, 1971, p. 511.
28 Li Hsüeh-feng, 1956.
29 Ling Hua-ch'un, 1951.
30 Li Hsüeh-feng, 1956.
31 An Tzu-wen, August 1951.
32 Shanghai (no publisher stated), *Chieh-fang-hou* . . . , pp. 1, 4, 12

et passim.
33 Chang Li-chih, 1950 and Chu Hsüeh-fan, 1948.
34 Shanghai (no publisher stated), *Chieh-fang hou* . . . , p. 1.
35 *Ibid.*
36 *Ibid.* pp. 3–4.
37 *Kung-jen Jih-pao*, 30 August 1951 and Shanghai *Ta Kung Pao*, 17 July 1951 (*SCMP*, 140, 22–3 July 1951, p. 29).
38 Shanghai (no publisher stated), *Chieh-fang hou* . . . , p. 1.
39 *Ibid.* p. 12.
40 *Ibid.* p. 2.
41 Jao Shu-shih, 1949.
42 Liu Shao-ch'i, May 1949, 'Tsai Hua Pei . . . '.
43 Barnett, 1963, p. 340.
44 *Ibid.*
45 Shanghai (no publisher stated), *Chieh-fang hou* . . . , p. 17.
46 *Jen-min Jih-pao*, 3 June 1949, p. 1.
47 The description of stock-taking is taken from Shanghai (no publisher stated), *Chieh-fang hou* . . . , pp. 17–21.
48 Barnett, 1963, p. 340.
49 Teng Tzu-hui, 1950, p. 23.
50 Ch'en Po-ta, in *Hsin-hua Shu-tien*, 1949.
51 Teng Tzu-hui, 1950.
52 Schurmann unpublished manuscript I – 4–5 cites Li Li-san *How to Manage A Factory*, Hong Kong, 1949, pp. 23–5. I have been unable to check the original.
53 Barnett, 1963, pp. 339–40.
54 *Chung-kuo Ti-liu-chieh Ch'üan-kuo Lao-tung Ta-hui*, 8 August 1948. *Hua Pei Ti-i-chieh Chih-kung Tai-piao hui-i*, 28 February 1950.
55 *Chung-hua Ch'üan-kuo Tsung-kung-hui*, August 1950.
56 Liu Shao-ch'i, May 1949, 'Tsai Hua Pei . . . '.
57 Chinese Communist Party Central Committee, March 1955.
58 Kuan Shui-hsin, 1950.
59 Kao Kang, 2 June 1951.
60 Selden, 1971, pp. 216–24.
61 Harper, 1969, p. 90.
62 The total nature of labour union membership and the abolition of craft unions is succinctly stated in the following quotation: 'Any membership restrictions based on political trend, the degree of political consciousness, sectarianism and exclusionism for the benefit of individual trades must be abolished'. *Chung-hua Ch'üan-kuo Tsung-kung-hui*, 1 May 1950.
63 e.g. see Appendix II.
64 Liu Ch'ang-sheng, June 1950.
65 *Kung-jen Jih-pao she*, 1950, Question 21, pp. 18–19.
66 On the formation of these national unions, see *Chung-kuo Kung-jen*, 1950, where the establishment of each national union is discussed. See also Harper, 1969, p. 91.
67 Liu Ch'ang-sheng, June 1950.

68 *Chung-hua Ch'üan-kuo Tsung-kung-hui, Wu-i Wai-pin Chao-tai Wei-yüan-hui*, 1952, p. 4.
69 *Chung-hua Ch'üan-kuo Tsung-kung-hui*, 9 August 1949.
70 *Kung-jen Jih-pao she*, pp. 25–31. Even the factory general manager in public enterprises could join the labour union.
71 *Ibid.* p. 2, Question 3, also section 4, p. 25.
72 Chao Ch'ao-kou, 1946, p. 202.
73 Liu Ch'ang-sheng (ed.), 1951, and Shanghai (no author stated), *Chieh-fang hou . . .*
74 Kao Kang, 13 March 1950.
75 Lieberthal, 1971, p. 511.
76 Harper, 1969, p. 92.
77 Chu Hsüeh-fan, 1948, and most of the essays in Liu Ch'ang-sheng (ed.), 1951, discuss these strikes.
78 Explicit reference is made to the authoritative nature of Liu's Tientsin Talks in *Chung-hua Tsung-kung-hui*, 1 May 1950.
79 Of the four articles cited by Harper as evidence of disruption, two refer to disruption in the *private sector* (*Kung-jen Jih-pao* editorial, 1 January 1951, and *SCMP*, 136, 1951, pp. 11–12). The other two discuss economism at length but make no mention of strikes (*Kung-jen Jih-pao*, 11 February 1953, and Lai Jo-yü's report to the 7th Labour Conference, 3 May 1953).
80 At this time cases such as that of Yang Ch'üan, which is described later in this chapter, were uncovered.
81 Han Yi and Wu Tung-min, 1950.
82 Kao Kang, 1 October 1952.
83 *Chung-kuo Kung-ch'an-tang Chung-yang Wei-yüan-hui Tung Pei chü*, May 1951.
84 Shanghai, *Ta Kung Pao* (November 1950–February 1951), collected and translated in *CB*, 108, 20 August 1951, p. 40.
85 *Chung-hua Ch'üan-kuo Tsung-kung-hui, Wu-i Wai-pin Chao-tai Wei-yüan-hui*, 1952, pp. 5–6.
86 *Kung-jen Jih-pao*, 11 January 1952. The first three classes were 1. Party cadres, 2 Government cadres, 3. Engineers (Liu Shao-ch'i, May 1949 'Tsai Hua Pei . . . '). In the model Wu San factory in Shenyang, union cadres considered themselves only third class; I am not sure which species of cadre was omitted. (*Kung-jen Ch'u-pan-she*, 1953, pp. 119–21.)
87 Li Li-san, 29 June 1950.
88 *Jen-min Jih-pao*, 3 March, 24 March and 20 April 1950.
89 *Chung-hua Ch'üan-kuo Tsung-kung-hui, Wu-i Wai-pin Chao-tai Wei-yüan-hui*, 1952, p. 4.
90 *Hsin-hua-she*, 10 February 1953. In a speech Hsü Chih-chen (29 January 1953) announced that over 90% of all industrial workers had joined unions.
91 *Ch'ang-chiang Jih-pao*, 13 June 1951 and Liu Tzu-chiu, 1951.
92 *Chung-yang Jen-min Cheng-fu Wei-yüan-hui*, 28 June 1950.
93 Li Li-san, 29 June 1950.

94 *Ibid.*
95 *Ibid.*
96 *Pei-p'ing Chieh-fang-pao*, 25 March 1949, p. 1.
97 Schapiro, 1960, pp. 310–13. Note also Trotsky's comment, Trotsky, 1945, pp. 97–8.
98 *Jen-min Jih-pao*, April 1950, 'An-tung-shih-wei . . . '.
99 *Tung Pei Jih-pao*, April 1950, 'An-tung Tsao-chih-ch'ang . . . '.
100 Hsiao Feng, 1951.
101 Kao Kang, 2 June 1951.
102 An Tzu-wen, August 1951.
103 *Ibid.*
104 Kao Kang, 8 September 1949.
105 *Ibid.*
106 Kao Kang, 31 August 1951.
107 Strictly speaking the Party Central Committee had no official theoretical journal until 1958 when *Hung Ch'i* (Red Flag) began publication. In practice however *Hsüeh-hsi* (Study) served this function.
108 Li Lung, 1951.
109 *Kung-jen Ch'u-pan-she*, 1953, p. 80.
110 Chinese Communist Party, Central Committee, March 1955. The only conclusion we can come to at this stage is that there remained a number of leadership groups within the Party which at some stage in the past forty years were identified in a particular context, e.g. the December 9th Group which came under attack in the Cultural Revolution (see Klein, 1968, pp. 89–91) and the various field army groups (see Whitson, 1969). To what extent this kind of grouping reflected a potential two party situation is difficult to say. It is also impossible to determine how Kao defined the rural-military and white area orientation for there was considerable movement between the liberated and white areas during the war. It could be that Kao was only reflecting a continuation of the tension that had existed between local and transferred cadres which had existed from Yenan days. Selden (1971, pp. 145–8) describes a situation where different types of cadre occupied different levels of administration.
111 Ai Wu, 1961.
112 *Kung-jen Ch'u-pan-she*, 1953, p. 102.
113 *Ibid.* p. 55.
114 *Chung-kuo Kung-ch'an-tang Chung-yang Wei-yüan-hui Tung Pei chü*, 1 August 1948.
115 Kao Kang, 2 June 1951.
116 *Ibid.*
117 In a situation where the main link with local government was via the Party organisation, and where management was more concerned with vertical than horizontal channels of communication, the relations between the Party organisation and the local labour bureaux would seem to be very important. Howe (1971, pp. 78–80) gives the impression however, that the labour bureaux were

ineffective in maintaining good relationships with enterprises due to the fact that they were grossly inefficient and made a 'hiring charge' for their services. This led to the appearance of an illegal labour market which grew in size until labour regulations were partially lifted in 1956. Since it was the function of local Party committees to correct the illegal behaviour of enterprise cadres, the growth of this market does not attest to their success except in a situation where mass mobilisation techniques were employed (The Three Anti Movement) when the labour bureaux appeared to be most ineffective (Howe, 1971, p. 96).

118 *NCNA*, 30 July 1951, p. 1; *SCMP*, 31 July 1951, pp. 7–8.
119 *Lao-tung pu*, 15 May 1951.
120 See Howe, 1971, Chapter 5.
121 Selden, 1971, pp. 216–24.
122 *Kung-jen Ch'u-pan-she*, 1953, p. 36.
123 *Kung-jen Jih-pao*, April 1950, 'K'uang-shan Kuan-li . . . '.
124 *Kung-jen Jih-pao*, 25 August 1951.
125 H.D. Fong, 1937.
126 Lin Li, April 1950.
127 *Ibid.* and *Jen-min Jih-pao*, April 1950, 'Hua Pei Mei-k'uang . . . '.
128 See for example the order abolishing the gang-boss system in the transportation industry, *Chung-kuo Kung-jen*, No. 3, 15 April 1950, p. 15.
129 Liu Tzu-chiu, 1951.
130 *Hsin-hua-she*, 25 June 1949.
131 *Hua Pei Ti-i-chieh Chih-kung Tai-piao-hui-i*, 28 February 1950.
132 *Jen-min Jih-pao*, April 1950, 'Ching Chin . . . '.
133 *NCNA* Peking, 4 August 1951 (*SCMP*, 150, 9 August 1951, pp. 7–10).
134 The following account is taken from *Tung Pei Jih-pao*, 3 April 1950, 'Pen-hsi Mei-t'ieh . . . ' and 'Fan-tui Ch'i-yeh Kuan-li chung . . . ', Ch'ang T'ai-tz'u, 3 April 1950 and Lai Han-ying, 7 April 1950.
135 Mao Tse-tung, 6 June 1950.
136 See Teng T'o, 1950 and Chang P'ing-hua, 1950. Chang describes commandism as 'virulent bureaucratism'.

Chapter 3: From radicalism to stability (1951–3)

1 Teng Tzu-hui, 30 July 1950.
2 *Chung-kuo Kung-jen*, No. 15, April 1951, p. 36.
3 *Ibid.*
4 *Chung-kuo Kung-jen*, No. 16, 24 May 1951, Index.
5 Harper, 1969, p. 91.
6 *Ibid.* pp. 95–6.
7 This will be discussed in Chapter 5 below.
8 *Tung Pei Jih-pao* July 1951, 'Tung Pei Kung-hui . . . '.
9 *Ibid.*

10 Harper, 1969, p. 96.
11 See also Harper, 1969, p. 96.
12 *Tung Pei Jih-pao*, July 1951, 'Tung Pei Kung-hui . . .'.
13 Shanghai, *Chieh-fang Jih-pao*, 24 September 1951 (*SCMP*, 185, 30 September 1951, p. 15). The figure for the preceding month was 307 (*Chieh-fang Jih-pao*, 2 September 1951, *SCMP*, 169, September 7–8 1951, p. 32).

This followed a directive of the Shanghai General Labour Union. Labour union teams were reorganised according to production criteria. The process was linked with democratic reform since some of the old labour union officers were found to be counter revolutionary elements.

T'ao Chih-ch'üan 1951. For further details on re-elections in Shanghai see *Lao-tung Ch'u-pan-she*, October 1951.
14 *Kung-jen Jih-pao*, 11 February 1953.
15 *Ibid.*
16 See Carr, 1966, Vol. 1, pp. 202–19.
17 See the collection of articles in *Kan-pu Hsüeh-hsi Tzu-liao*, No. 37, September 1951.
18 Liu Tzu-chiu, 1951, Tai Chi-ying, 1951 and also the various articles on the subject in *Kung-jen Jih-pao* throughout August–September 1951.
19 *Ch'ang-chiang Jih-pao*, 13 June 1951.
20 Liu Tzu-chiu, 1951.
21 On links with secret agents see *Chung-kuo Kung-ch'an-tang Chung-yang Wei-yüan-hui Chung Nan chü*, 1 August 1951.
22 Liu Tzu-chiu, 1951.
23 *Ibid.*
24 *Ch'ang-chiang Jih-pao*, 13 June 1951.
25 For an account of the various activities of secret agents in factories see *Hua Tung Jen-min Ch'u-pan-she*, May 1951.
26 Liu Tzu-chiu, 1951.
27 *Chung-kuo Kung-ch'an-tang Chung yang Wei-yüan-hui Chung Nan chü*, 1 August 1951.
28 *Ch'ang-chaing Jih-pao*, 13 June 1951.
29 *Ibid.*
30 *Ibid.*
31 *Ibid.*
32 Liu Tzu-chiu, 1951.
33 *Chung-kuo Kung-ch'an-tang Chung-yang Wei-yüan-hui Hua Nan Fen-chü*, 5 August 1951.
34 e.g. *Ch'ang-chiang Jih-pao*, 5 July 1951 in *CB*, 115, 10 September 1951, p. 13.
35 *Ibid.* This formula was laid down by Yeh Chien-ying, at that time Chairman of the Chinese Communist Party Central Committee South China Sub-bureau.
36 *Ibid.*
37 Liu Tzu-chiu, 1951.

38 *SCMP*, 170, 9–10 September 1951, pp. 11–12.
39 *Chung-kuo Kung-ch'an-tang Chung-yang Wei-yüan-hui Hua Nan Fen-chü*, 5 August 1951.
40 *Chung-kuo Kung-ch'an-tang Chung-yang Wei-yüan-hui Chung Nan chü*, 1 August 1951, expounded on at greater length in Liu Tzu-chiu, 1951.
41 Chang Hsi, 1951, p. 76.
42 *Chung-kuo Kung-ch'an-tang Chung-yang Wei-yüan hui Chung Nan chü*, 1 August 1951, Chang P'ing-hua, July 1951.
43 *Kung-jen Jih-pao*, 30 August 1951, p. 1.
44 Liu Tzu-chiu, 1951.
45 *Ch'ang-chiang Jih-pao*, 19 August 1951 in *CB*, 115, 10 September 1951, pp. 16–19.
46 *Ch'ang-chiang Jih-pao*, 20 July 1951.
47 Liu Tzu-chiu, 1951.
48 *Chung-kuo Kung-ch'an-tang, Chung-yang Wei-yüan-hui Chung Nan chü*, 1 August 1951. See also *Nan-fang Jih-pao*, 20 August 1951 in *CB*, 115, 10 September 1951, p. 12.
49 Liu Tzu-chiu, 1951.
50 *Chung-kuo Kung-ch'an-tang Chung-yang Wei-yüan-hui Chung Nan chü*, 1 August 1951.
51 *Ch'ang-chiang Jih-pao*, 13 June 1951.
52 Liu Tzu-chiu, 1951.
53 Chang Hsi, 1951.
54 This formula was laid down by Mao (1 June 1943). He talks about mass response to a movement consisting of three groups – the small number of active elements, the large intermediate group and the group of relatively backward elements.
55 *Chung-kuo Kung-ch'an-tang Chung-yang Wei-yüan-hui Chung Nan chü*, 1 August 1951.
56 Liu Tzu-chiu, 1951.
57 *Ibid.*
58 *Ibid.*
59 Bennett and Ishino, 1963, pp. 119–22.
60 *Ibid.* p. 116.
61 Kao Kang, 31 August 1951.
62 *Jen-min Jih-pao*, 16 June 1951, p. 1.
63 e.g. *Ch'ün-chung Jih-pao* (Sian), 8 October 1951.
64 The following quote from Kao Kang illustrates this process: 'By uncovering the bureaucratism existing in the leadership, many cadres have come to realise that they have consciously fallen into the pit of corruption just because of their lack of self examination. In the course of self criticism the leadership has found that they have lost no prestige before the workers but, instead have been able to see ways of improving their leadership.' Kao Kang, 31 August 1951.
65 This process was first articulated by Mao (June 1943). Mao describes the changes in the composition of a movement's 'leading

group' as new activists come forward and reveal the old leadership as degenerate (*SW*, English, III, pp. 117–22). In the original version, these activists who emerge to replace former members of the leading group are referred to as 'heroes' though this word is omitted from the Selected Works version.

66 Jao Shu-shih, 17 December 1951.
67 The composition of the Shanghai Municipal committee is described in Gardner, 1969.
68 Kao Kang, 26 October 1951.
69 Kao Kang, 2 June 1951.
70 Jao Shu-shih, 17 December 1951.
71 Provision for these was made in *Chung Nan Chün-cheng Wei-yüan-hui*, 21 November 1951.
72 Kao Kang, 26 October 1951.
73 *Tung Pei Jih-pao*, 6 December 1951.
74 This crime became one of the 'antis' in the Five Anti Campaign and received considerable publicity at the beginning of 1952. See *Jen-min Jih-pao*, 21 February 1952. According to the head of the North East Peoples Government Industrial Department, Wang Ho-shou, many cadres in the North East were selling documents to 'bad merchants'. Wang Ho-shou, 9 February 1952.
75 Jao Shu-shih, 17 December 1951.
76 Ho Kan-chih, *Chung-kuo Hsien-tai Ko-ming shih* (*The Contemporary Revolutionary History of China*), Hong Kong, 1958, pp. 366–7, cited in Schurmann, 1966, p. 318.
77 Kao Kang, 10 January 1952.
78 *Kung-jen Jih-pao*, 9 January 1952, 'Chin-i-pu . . . '.
79 *Kung-jen Jih-pao*, 9 January 1952, 'Wa-chüeh . . . '.
80 *Ibid.*
81 *Kung-jen Jih-pao*, 11 January 1952.
82 Liu Shao-ch'i, May 1949, 'Tsai Hua Pei . . . '.
83 *Chung-kuo Kung-ch'an-tang Chung-yang Wei-yüan-hui Tung Pei chü*, 20 February 1951.
84 *Ibid.*
85 *Ibid.*
86 The five antis were graft, tax evasion, theft of state property, cheating on government contracts and stealing state economic information.
87 *Chung-kuo Kung-ch'an-tang Chung-yang Wei-yüan-hui Tung Pei chü*, 20 February 1951.
88 See *CB*, 201, 12 August 1952. Here a number of articles are translated dealing with the conclusion of the Three Anti and Five Anti Movements in various regions and the renewed stress on increasing production and practising economy. According to Howe (1971, p. 96), the unemployment consequences of the Five Anti Movement was one of the major factors in bringing it to a halt in May 1952.
89 Ku Cho-hsin, 1959.
90 Klein and Clark, 1971, pp. 211 and 433–4.

91 The basic decisions regarding Kao Kang were taken at a politburo meeting in December 1953 and, in February 1954, the Party's Central Committee (4th plenum) attacked the idea of an independent kingdom attributed to Kao Kang (speech by Liu Shao-ch'i). The government reorganisation took place in September 1954 and Kao Kang was publically disgraced at the 5th plenum in March 1955. The exact date of his suicide in 1954 is uncertain. See Klein and Clark, 1971, p. 434.

92 This process began with the publication of financial and economic control (*chien-ch'a*) regulations (27 December 1952) which demanded that a control group be set up in each enterprise. This group was to concern itself with both political and economic matters. At this stage control personnel were selected from the personnel roster of the enterprise itself. Schurmann notes that one of the first accounts of the operation of an enterprise control organ was that of the Shih-ching-shan Iron and Steel Works in July 1953 where workers were enjoined to voice their complaints to this group rather than higher level organs or the newspapers. At this stage enterprise control work was more concerned with political than economic questions and control officers were probably under the tight control of the factory general manager. By the end of 1953 control work became more concerned with economic matters. In 1954 the Harbin System of external economic control was put forward and a Ministry of State Control set up. See Schurmann 1966, Chapter 5 and in particular pp. 322–39.

93 An Tzu-wen, 7 January 1953.

94 *Ibid.*

95 *Jen-min Jih-pao*, 6 June 1954. At that time judicial committees (*shen-p'an-hui*) linked to local People's Courts were set up within enterprises.

96 *Ibid.*

97 *Ibid.*

98 *Chung-kung-yeh T'ung-hsün*, No. 7, 1 March 1953.

99 *Ibid.*

100 *Ibid.*

101 *Ibid.*

Chapter 4: Planning and accounting

1 Simon, 1950, pp. 75–7.

2 Schurmann, 1966, pp. 231–5.

3 Bendix, 1960, p. 245.

4 For some light on this see the debate between Bendix and Eckstein in Grossman, 1960.

5 In particular Talcott Parsons.

6 e.g. Almond and Coleman, *The Politics of the Developing Areas*, introduction and conclusion.

7 Chu P'u, 1950, p. 5; his words exactly.

8 Li Fu-ch'un, excerpts of speech to Mobilisation Meeting of North East Industrial Department in *Jen-min Jih-pao*, 1 November 1949, p. 2.
9 Chu P'u, 1950.
10 *Tung Pei Jen-min Cheng-fu, Kung-yeh-pu*, 6 October 1949: 'Kuan-yü K'ai-chan . . . '; *Chung-kuo Kung-ch'an-tang Chung-yang Wei-yüan-hui, Tung Pei chü*, 6 October 1949.
11 *Tung Pei Jen-min Cheng-fu, Kung-yeh-pu*, 6 October 1949: 'Kuan-yü Chi-hsü . . . '
12 Chu P'u, 1950, p. 4.
13 *NCNA*, 16 March 1950, recounted in Chu P'u, 1950.
14 Chu P'u, 1950, pp. 12–13.
15 *Ibid.* pp. 8–9.
16 Li Fu-ch'un summary of speech to 3rd Financial and Economic Conference of the North East Liberated Areas in *Jen-min Jih-pao*, 16 December 1947, p. 1. See also *Jen-min Jih-pao*, 20 November 1947, p. 1 and Ku Cho-hsin, 1959.
17 Chu P'u, 1950, p. 13.
18 *Ibid.*
19 *Tung Pei Jen-min Cheng-fu, Kung-yeh-pu*, 28 February 1950.
20 *Tung Pei Jih-pao*, 4 March 1950.
21 *Tung Pei Jen-min Cheng-fu, Kung-yeh-pu*, 28 February 1950 and *Tung Pei Jih-pao*, 4 March 1950.
22 *Ibid.*
23 *Jen-min Jih-pao*, 6 December 1948, p. 1.
24 Donnithorne, 1967, p. 403.
25 *Cheng-wu-yüan*, April 1950.
26 Donnithorne, 1967, p. 406.
27 *Ibid.* and Perkins, 1968, p. 620.
28 Donnithorne, 1967, p. 421.
29 *Ibid.* p. 411.
30 Perkins, 1968, p. 601 from *T'ung-chi Kung-tso*, 14 July 1957, (*ECMM*, 97, pp. 21–7).
31 Perkins, 1968, p. 605 from *Yu-se Chin-shu*, 18 February 1959 (in *JPRS*, 1090D, 21 December 1959, pp. 1–9).
32 Perkins, 1968, pp. 610–13.
33 Schurmann, unpublished manuscript II, 14–15 and 28.
34 Granick, 1960, pp. 267–70.
35 Yao P'u, 1952.
36 e.g. *Ibid.*
37 *Tung Pei Jen-min Cheng-fu*, 18 September 1950. See also Chou Shu-k'ang, 1950 on union supervision.
38 Wang Ch'i-fan and Li Tsu-yin, 1951.
39 Ho Jen, 1951.
40 Schurmann, unpublished manuscript II, 14–15 and 28.
41 Kao Fang-ch'i, 1953.
42 *Chung-kuo Kung-ch'an-tang Chung-yang Wei-yüan-hui Tung Pei chü*, May 1951, and *Kung-jen Ch'u-pan-she*, 1953, pp. 80–1.

43 *Chung-kung-yeh T'ung-hsün*, No. 30, 21 October 1953, pp. 30–1.
44 The best definition of the Mass Line may be found in Mao Tse-tung, 1 June 1943: 'In all our Party's actual work, correct leadership must come from the masses and go to the masses. This means taking the views of the masses (unintegrated, unrelated views) and subjecting them to concentration (they are transformed through research into concentrated systematized views), then going to the masses with propaganda and explanation in order to transform the views of the masses, and seeing that these [views] are maintained by the masses and carried over into their activities. It also means an examination of mass activities to ascertain the correctness of these views. Then again there is concentration from the masses and maintenance among the masses. Thus the process is repeated indefinitely, each time more correctly vitally and fruitfully. This is the epistomology and methodology of Marxism Leninism.' Compton, 1966, p. 179. Another translation may be found in *Selected Works*, II, p. 119.
45 *Kung-jen Jih-pao she*, 1950, pp. 46–7, Question 74.
46 See Chapter 3.
47 Kao Kang, 10 January 1952.
48 Berliner, 1957 (1968).
49 *Kung-jen Ch'u-pan-she*, 1953, p. 80.
50 Shanghai (no publisher stated), *Chieh-fang hou . . .*, p. 28.
51 *Tung Pei Kung-yeh*, No. 94, 11 May 1952, p. 7.
52 Perkins, 1968, pp. 600 and 606–7.
53 Schurmann, unpublished manuscript, III, C-15. See also Sun Yeh-fang, 1957.
54 e.g. Wang Chih-fang, 1953.
55 Liu Hsien-shu, 1953.
56 *Chung-kung-yeh T'ung-hsün*, No. 19, 1 July 1953.
57 Perkins, 1968, p. 618.
58 Kao Kang, 13 March 1950.
59 Perkins, 1968, p. 619.
60 Kao Kang, 10 January 1952 and Wang Ho-shou, 9 February 1952.
61 *Chung-kuo Kung-ch'an-tang Chung-yang Wei-yüan-hui Tung Pei chü*, 20 February 1952.
62 Perkins, 1968, p. 626.
63 Granick, 1960, p. 159.
64 Perkins, 1968, p. 626.
65 *Ibid.* and *Chung-kuo Jen-min Yin-hang*, 30 March 1955.
66 Berliner, 1957 (1968), Chapter XII, pp. 207–30.
67 Donnithorne, 1967, pp. 290–1 from *Chieh-fang Jih-pao*, 7 May 1958 (*SCMP*, 1794), 'Ch'ing-lien-ko Tea-house in Shanghai Enters a New Era' and *Kuo-wu-yüan Fa-chih chü* compendium, Vol. VI, pp. 375–6.
68 Arakelian, 1950, p. 64.
69 Cheng Hung-su, February 1950, 'Ching-chi Ho-suan-chih . . .'.
70 *Ibid.* and Arakelian, 1950, p. 92.

71 Schurmann, unpublished manuscript, III.
72 *Tung Pei Jih-pao*, 7 April 1950.
73 *Tung Pei-Jen-min Cheng-fu, Kung-yeh-pu*, directive, 29 July 1949 cited in Chu P'u, 1950.
74 Cheng Hung-su, February 1950, 'Ching-chi Ho-suan-chih . . . '.
75 Kao Kang, 31 August 1951.
76 *Tung Pei Jih-pao*, 7 April 1950.
77 Schurmann, unpublished manuscript, III, 20.
78 Yü Wen-ch'ing, 1950.
79 e.g. Cheng Hung-su, February 1950, 'Ching-chi Ho-suan-chih . . . '.
80 Shao Li-sheng, 1950.
81 It is doubtful whether a statistical network was operational on a national level until 1953. See Li Choh-ming, 1962, p. 8.
82 *Chung-kung-yeh-pu, Chien-she Kung-ch'eng Kung-ssu*, July 1953.
83 This will be discussed further in Chapter 6.
84 Tso Ch'un-t'ai, 'Wo-kuo Ching-chi Ho-suan ti Chien-li ho Fa-chan', 'The Establishment and Development of Economic Accounting in Our Country', *Ta Kung Pao*, 3 June 1962 cited in Schurmann, unpublished manuscript, III, 31.
85 For a description of the confused state currency at the time of liberation see Hsieh Chia, 1950.
86 Yü Wen-ch'ing, 1950.

Chapter 5: Incentives and labour agreements

1 *Tung Pei Kung-yeh*, No. 20, 16 April 1950, pp. 50–3.
2 Liu Pao, 1952.
3 Chu P'u, 1950, p. 10.
4 *Ibid.*
5 Lai Jo-yü, 20 September 1952.
6 For the national (May 1954) regulations see *NCNA*, 1723, 30, August 1954, Peking Foreign Languages Press, 1956, pp. 54–64; also Hoffman, 1964.
7 Chu P'u, 1950, pp. 10–13.
8 *Chung-kuo Ti-liu-chieh Ch'üan-kuo Lao-tung Ta-hui*, August 1948, 'Yu-kuan Kung-tzu . . . '.
9 Schran, 1961, p. 250.
10 The description of methods of payment in Lushun and Talien is taken from Chu P'u, 1950.
11 *Ibid.*
12 *Ts'ai-ching Yen-chiu*, No. 18, 15 November 1958, pp. 34–7 (in *JPRS*, 1337-N, 12 March 1959, p. 2).
13 *Ibid.*
14 Schran, 1961, p. 290.
15 In North China, the wage point was usually known as a '*hsi*' and in North East China as a '*fen*'. *Chung-kuo Ti-liu-chieh Ch'üan-kuo Lao-tung Ta-hui*, August 1948. 'Yu-kuan Kung-tzu . . . '. Later the term '*fen*' was also used in North China. *Jen-min Jih-pao*, 11 October

1951, p. 2.
16 Some examples of wage point composition are given in Appendix I.
17 Schran, 1961, p. 250.
18 State Council Decision on Wage Reform, 16 June 1956, in *Kung-jen Jih-pao*, 5 July 1956, pp. 1–2, translated in *JPRS*, Report No. 515, *Wages in Communist China*, July–December 1956, p. 1.
19 e.g. *Jen-min Jih-pao*, 25 December 1948, p. 2. During this time various standards were published, e.g. *Tung Pei Hsing-cheng Wei-yüan-hui*, 7 September 1948.
20 Schran, 1961, p. 257.
21 *Tung Pei Hsing-cheng Wei-yüan-hui*, 7 September 1948.
22 Kao Kang, 8 September 1949.
23 Schran, 1961, p. 285.
24 *Jen-min Jih-pao*, 27 November 1948, p. 1.
25 *Chung-kuo Ti-liu-chieh Ch'üan-kuo Lao-tung Ta-hui*, 8 August 1948, 'Kuan-yü Chung-kuo Chih-kung Yün-tung . . .'.
26 Chou Shu-k'ang, 1950.
27 Wang Tzu-mien, 1951.
28 Schran, 1961, p. 284, Chou Shu-k'ang, 1950, p. 6. An example of such a range is in *Tung Pei Jen-min Cheng-fu*, 19 June 1950 and 7 July 1950.
29 *Tung Pei Jen-min Cheng-fu*, 19 June 1950 and 7 July 1950.
30 *Tung Pei Jen-min Cheng-fu*, 7 July 1950.
31 Wang Tzu-mien, 1951.
32 e.g. Chang Li-chih, 1950.
33 e.g. *Jen-min Jih-pao*, 25 December 1948, p. 2.
34 Chou Shu-k'ang, 1950.
35 e.g. *Lao-tung*, No. 11, 6 November 1956, pp. 8–9, translated in *JPRS*, Report No. 515.
36 Kao Kang, 8 September 1949.
37 e.g. *Jen-min Jih-pao*, 9 April 1952, p. 1.
38 An Tzu-wen, 7 January 1953.
39 *Lao-tung*, No. 4, 18 February 1957, pp. 13–14 and *Lao-tung*, No. 8, 18 April 1957, p. 14, in *JPRS*, Report No. 754, *Wages in Communist China*, January–June 1957, pp. 34–5.
40 *Lao-tung*, No. 11, 3 June 1957, pp. 19–21 in *JPRS*, Report No. 754, p. 36.
41 *Ibid.*
42 See Vogel, 1967, pp. 49–51.
43 *Lao-tung*, No. 11, 3 June 1957, pp. 19–21, in *JPRS*, Report No. 754, p. 36.
44 Schran, 1961, pp. 293–4.
45 The Wage Reform of 1956 was particularly weighted in favour of technicians. It introduced special technical bonuses and allowed for 'individual' wage standards for those technicians who were already on wage scales higher than line management.
46 *Chung-kuo Ch'ing-nien*, No. 5, 1 March 1955, pp. 5–7, cited in Vogel, 1967, p. 48.
47 *Lao-tung*, No. 8, 18 April 1957, p. 14, in *JPRS*, Report No. 754, p. 35.

48 Ho Fu-pen, 1958.
49 A good example of the deleterious effects of an 'egalitarian' wage system upon technical education is provided by the Shantung Aluminium Works where the workers felt that 'studying technology was not as good as going home and growing vegetables', *Lao-tung-pu, Kung-tzu-ssu, Shan-tung Kung-tso tsu*, 1951.
50 Schran, 1961, p. 302.
51 See the various articles collected and translated in *JPRS*, Report 1337-N.
52 At that time there was much discussion of introducing payment according to need (the 'Communist' principle) to supplement payment according to work (the 'socialist' principle) (see *JPRS*, Report 1337-N). There is no evidence to my knowledge, however, that any element of 'payment according to need' was actually introduced into factories. At the Wuch'ang Plenum of December 1958 the idea of 'payment according to need' was given up.
53 Schran, 1961, p. 309.
54 Chou Shu-k'ang, 1950.
55 *Ts'ai-ching Yen-chiu*, No. 7, 15 October 1958, pp. 22–4, in *JPRS* Report 1337-N, p. 4.
56 *Lao-tung-pu, Kung-tzu-ssu, Shan-tung Kung-tso-tsu*, 1951.
57 Chou Shu-k'ang, 1950.
58 *Ts'ai-ching Yen-chiu*, No. 8, 15 November 1958, pp. 34–7, in *JPRS* Report 1337-N, p. 1.
59 Ch'en Wei-shuo, 1951 (*Tung Pei Kung-yeh*, No. 50, p. 41).
60 Chou Shu-k'ang, 1950.
61 *Ibid.*
62 Chang Chien, 1954.
63 P'an-Heng-yü, 1954, p. 27.
64 *Lao-tung*, No. 11, 3 June 1957, p. 18, in *JPRS*, Report No. 754, p. 42.
65 *Lao-tung*, No. 3, 3 February 1957, pp. 13–14, in *JPRS*, Report No. 754, p. 32.
66 *Ts'ai-ching Yen-chiu*, 1958, No. 6, pp. 49–52, in *JPRS*, Report 1337-N, pp. 2–3.
67 *Lao-tung*, No. 3, 3 February 1957, p. 12, in *JPRS*, Report No. 754, p. 29.
68 *Tung Pei Jen-min Cheng-fu Kung-yeh-pu, Tien-yeh Kuan-li Tsung-chü*, February 1950; *Tung Pei Jen-min Cheng-fu Kung-yeh-pu Chü-chang Ching-li Lien-hsi Hui-i*, 7 December 1949.
69 *Ha-erh-pin Tsung-kung-hui Pan-kung-shih*, 'Kai-chan . . . '. December 1950.
70 e.g. Chou Ch'i-yu, 1951.
71 e.g. *NCNA* (Talien), 20 July 1951.
72 e.g. *Ha-erh-pin Tsung-kung-hui*, December 1950, 'Kuan-yü Tang-ch'ien . . . '. and *Ha-erh-pin Tsung-kung-hui Pan-kung-shih*, December 1950, 'Kai-chan . . .'.
73 *Ibid.*
74 *Ibid.*
75 *Tung Pei Jen-min Cheng-fu Kung-yeh-pu Chü-chang Ching-li Lien-*

hsi Hui-i, 7 December 1949.

76 Shao Li-sheng, 1950.

77 For example *Tung Pei Jih-pao* carried a regular column entitled '*Hung-pang*' (Red Roll) (e.g. *Tung Pei Jih-pao*, 8 May 1950, p. 4).

78 Ai Wu, 1961.

79 *Tung Pei Jen-min Cheng-fu, Kung-yeh-pu*, 6 October 1949, 'Kuan-yü K'ai-chan . . . '.

80 *Tung Pei Jih-pao*, 6 October 1949.

81 *CB*, 99, 15 July 1951, p. 1 from Hong Kong *Ta Kung Pao*, 22 March 1951.

82 A whole hierarchy of such congresses was set up. In addition to model workers selected at enterprise level, municipal model workers were to be selected twice a year (before May Day and National Day) and those model workers who were to represent a national labour union were to be selected annually or biennially. Li Li-san, 17 November 1950.

83 *CB*, 99, p. 1.

84 Chang Li-k'o, April 1951, 'T'ui-kuang . . . '.

85 *Jen-min Jih-pao*, 20 January 1951, p. 2.

86 *Chung-kuo Kung-jen*, No. 15, April 1951, p. 7.

87 *NCNA*, Shanghai, 24 March 1951 (*SCMP*, 87, 22–4 March 1951, p. 21).

88 *NCNA*, Peking, 27 March 1951 (*SCMP*, 89, 28–31 March 1951, p. 33).

89 *NCNA*, K'aifeng Chengchow, 28 March 1951 (*SCMP*, 89, p. 33).

90 Li Li-san, 1 July 1951.

91 1 May 1951 (*Chung-kuo Kung-jen*, No. 16, 1951, p. 31); late June 1951, (*SCMP*, 126, 29–30 June 1951, p. 12), 29 September 1951 (*SCMP*, 185).

92 *NCNA*, Shenyang, 28 April 1951 (*SCMP*, 100, 28–30 April 1951, p. 8

93 Ma Heng-chang, June 1951.

94 *Chieh-fang Jih-pao*, 15 July 1951.

95 Li Li-san, 1 July 1951.

96 Lai Jo-yü, 20 September 1952, p. 152.

97 See Appendix II taken from *Chung-hua Ch'üan-kuo Tsung-kung-hui, Pien-chi Ch'u-pan-shih*, August 1950, pp. 193–209.

98 *Ibid.* A decision on collective contracts was taken by the Lushun–Talien General Labour Union on 1 March, an order issued by local government on 1 June and the glass factory contract drawn up one month later.

99 Perhaps the clearest example of Mao Tse-tung's views on the role of the Party branches in industry was when he castigated Party cadres for not dealing with the problem of bureaucratism by educative means before the strikes of 1956. The implication was that the Party should stop disputes coming to a head. Mao Tse-tung, 27 February 1957.

100 On the role of the labour bureaux, see Howe, 1971, Chapter 5.

101 It is unlikely that the process of conciliation and arbitration made much headway until after the labour union crisis and the Three and

Five Anti Movements were over. The Three Anti Movement was one in which direct action by the Party organisation was brought to bear on intra-factory problems (see Chapter 3) and this led to a large number of sackings. (Howe, 1971, p. 96). This did not indicate much success in conciliation and arbitration. By 1953, Howe notes that the mediating role of the labour bureaux was not given so much stress (p. 100). The formal regulations for settling labour disputes may be found in Peking Foreign Languages Press, 1951, *The Trade Union Law of the Peoples Republic of China*, pp. 27–32.

102 *Chung-hua Ch'üan-kuo Tsung-kung-hui, Pien-chi Ch'u-pan-shih*, 1950, pp. 249–63.

103 *Ibid.* pp. 265–73.

104 *Ibid.* p. 187.

105 *Kung-jen Ch'u-pan-she*, 1953, p. 46.

106 *Ibid.* p. 127.

107 *Chung-hua Ch'üan-kuo Tsung-kung-hui, Pien-chi Ch'u-pan-shih*, 1950, pp. 188–9.

108 *NCNA*, Peking, 18 May 1951; *SCMP*, No. 106, 21–3 May 1951, pp. 30–1.

109 On the difference between internal and external *pao-kung* systems see *An-shan Kang-t'ieh Kung-ssu Chi-pen Chien-she-ch'u*, 1951.

110 *Chung-hua Ch'üan-kuo Tsung-kung-hui Pien-chi Ch'u-pan-shih*, 1950, p. 188.

111 *Tung Pei Kung-yeh*, No. 87, 1 March 1952, pp. 12–14.

112 *Chung-hua Ch'üan-kuo Tsung-kung-hui, Pien-chi Ch'u-pan-shih*, 1950, p. 188.

113 *Ibid.*

114 Huang Yu-feng and Lin Ming-chang, 1951.

115 *Chung-hua Ch'üan-kuo Tsung-kung-hui, Pien-chi Ch'u-pan-shih*, 1950, p. 188.

116 Huang Yu-feng and Lin Ming-chang, 1951.

117 *Chung-hua Ch'üan-kuo Tsung-kung-hui, Pien-chi Ch'u-pan-shih*, 1950, pp. 189–90.

118 *Ibid.*

119 *Chung-hua Ch'üan-kuo Tsung-kung-hui, Sheng-ch'an-pu*, May 1950, pp. 231–2.

120 *Chung-hua Ch'üan-kuo Tsung-kung-hui, Pien-chi Ch'u-pan-shih*, 1950, p. 189.

121 *Chung-hua Ch'üan-kuo Tsung-kung-hui, Sheng-ch'an-pu*, May 1950, pp. 231–2. The joint contract was described as a method of securing co-ordination in a situation where there was imbalance between the degree of mass mobilisation and the development of the Movement to Create New Records. It was a way of bringing backward shops up to the level of advanced shops.

122 *NCNA*, 7 June 1951; *SCMP*, No. 112, 8–9 June 1951, p. 2.

123 e.g. *SCMP*, 122, 22–3 June 1951, p. 9.

124 *Jen-min Jih-pao*, 2 June 1951.

125 *NCNA*, 13 June 1951; *SCMP*, No. 116, 14 June 1951, p. 5.

126 *Jen-min Jih-pao*, 2 June 1951.
127 *Ibid.* For a warning against this tendency.
128 Chang Ch'ing-chi, 1951.
129 The first compact was drawn up on 7 November 1950. *Jen-min Jih-pao*, 29 July 1951, p. 1.
130 See Appendix III.
131 Hu P'ing, 1951.
132 Ting Tan and Chou Su-chen, 1951.
133 e.g. *Chung Nan Jen-min Ch'u-pan-she*, September 1951.
134 Chin Feng, 1951.
135 See Appendix III.
136 *Tung Pei Jih-pao*, July 1951, 'Chien-ch'a Ai-kuo . . . '.
137 *NCNA*, 8 August 1951; *SCMP*, No. 150, 9 August 1951, pp. 10–11.
138 Hu P'ing, 1951.
139 Chin Feng, 1951.
140 *Chung-kuo Min-chu T'ung-meng Tsung-pu Hsüan-ch'uan Wei-yüan-hui*, 1951, pp. 122–3.
141 *Ibid.* p. 126.
142 *Ibid.* pp. 127 and 116.
143 *Ibid.* pp. 127 and 111.
144 *Kung-jen Ch'u-pan-she*, 1953, pp. 127–8.

Chapter 6: A discrete command structure

1 Issue No. 1 of *Chung-kuo Kung-yeh* was published on 16 April 1949. Shanghai was completely liberated by the 28 May 1949 and issue No. 2 appeared on 19 June 1949.
2 Yin Ku, 1949.
3 *Chung-kuo Kung-yeh*, Vol. I, No. 2, editorial.
4 Yin Ku attributes this preferred system to a certain I-tun. This is obviously a transliteration but I have not been able to identify him.
5 Yin Ku, 1949.
6 Chu P'u, 1950.
7 *Tung Pei Jen-min Cheng-fu Kung-yeh-pu*, 23 November 1949.
8 For a catalogue of waste and accidents during the movement see *Tung Pei Jen-min Cheng-fu Kung-yeh-pu, Tien-yeh Kuan-li Tsung-chü*, February 1950.
9 *Tung Pei Jen-min Cheng-fu Kung-yeh-pu Chü-chang Ching-li Lien-hsi, Hui-i*, 7 December 1949.
10 Chu P'u, 1950.
11 See for example the section in *Chung-kuo Kung-jen*, No. 5, 15 June 1950, pp. 8–21 entitled 'Kuan-ch'e Sheng-ch'an Tse-jen-chih' ('Implement the Production Responsibility System') which includes a *Tung Pei Jih-pao* editorial 'Hsin Chi-lu Yün-tung ti Hsin Fang-hsiang' ('The New Direction of the New Record Movement'), pp. 8–9.
12 Li Li-san, 1 July 1951.
13 Lai Jo-yü, 3 May 1953.

14 *Tung Pei Jen-min Cheng-fu Kung-yeh-pu*, 28 February 1950 and *Tung Pei Jih-pao*, 4 March 1950.
15 *Tung Pei Jen-min Cheng-fu Kung-yeh-pu*, 18 March 1950.
16 Chu P'u, 1950, p. 14.
17 Cheng Hung-su, June 1950, 'Su-lien ti Ch'i-yeh . . .'.
18 The standard translation was *i-chang-chih* (as used in the translation of the Lokshin article, 1950).
19 In the Lokshin article, 'functional management' (as abolished in 1934) is translated as *tse-jen fen-san ti ling-tao* (literally: 'system of divided responsibility in leadership'). Current Taiwan works on industrial management translate the functional approach as *kuan-li kung-neng fang-fa*. See Kung P'ing-pang, 1970, p. 20.
20 e.g. Lokshin, 1950.
21 As in *Chung-kung-yeh-pu*, 28 May. 1953.
22 See Chapter 3.
23 See in particular *Chung-kung-yeh-pu*, 28 May 1953.
24 Schurmann, 1966, p. 264.
25 Li Hsüeh-feng, 24 September 1956.
26 See Chapter 2 and in particular the Yang Ch'üan case.
27 Alley, 1952, pp. 21–2 and Lieberthal, 1973.
28 Fong, 1937.
29 See Chapter 2, the Yang Ch'üan case.
30 This term is mine and was not to my knowledge used in contemporary literature.
31 Ho Fu-pen, 1953.
32 *Chung-kung-yeh T'ung-hsün*, No. 33, 21 November 1953, pp. 16–17.
33 Fong, 1937, p. 53.
34 Ho Fu-pen, 1953.
35 *Chung-kung-yeh T'ung-hsün*, No. 33, pp. 16–17.
36 *Ibid.*
37 *Ibid.*
38 *Tung Pei Jen-min Cheng-fu, Kung-yeh-pu*, 18 June 1951. See also Lü Tung, 1952.
39 Yao P'u, 1952.
40 *Chung-kung-yeh T'ung-hsün*, No. 19, 1 July 1953, p. 28.
41 Lo Han, 1953, p. 26.
42 Chi Ming-ta, 1953.
43 The corollary of this was that each particular job of work should only be carried on in one place. See *Chung-kung-yeh T'ung-hsün*, No. 33, 21 November 1953, pp. 2–4.
44 Ho Fu-pen, 1953.
45 *Ibid.*
46 Wang Yung-kang, 1953.
47 Lo Han, 1953.
48 Kao Kang, 13 March 1950.
49 *Ibid.*, for a most vehement attack.
50 Schurmann, 1966, p. 235.

51 *Chung-kung-yeh-pu*, 28 May 1953.
52 *Ibid.* There was frequently a level lower than *kung-tuan*, the *hsiao-tsu* ('team', sometimes translated as 'brigade').
53 During the movement to establish responsibility systems, the Chinese People's University edited and disseminated material on 'one-man management' and labour discipline. See Huang K'un-i, 1953.
54 *Chung-kung-yeh-pu*, 28 May 1953.
55 Schurmann, 1966, pp. 252–3.
56 *Chung-kung-yeh T'ung-hsün*, No. 16, 1 June 1953, p. 8.
57 *Tung Pei Jen-min Cheng-fu, Kung-yeh-pu*, 1 April 1951.
58 *Ibid.*
59 *Tung Pei Jih-pao*, April 1951, 'Kung-ch'eng Chi-shu . . . '.
60 *Chung-kung-yeh-pu, Hua-hsüeh Kung-yeh Kuan-li-chü*, November 1954.
61 *Ibid.*
62 This body would seem to be a successor to the territorially organised 'Increase Production and Practise Economy Committees' which appeared during the Three Anti Movement. See Chapter 2.
63 Ch'i Kuo-chien and Chang Yi-chün, 1953.
64 *Chung-kung-yeh-pu, Huà-hsüeh Kung-yeh Kuan-li-chü*, November 1954.
65 *Ibid.*
66 Huang K'un-i, 1953.
67 Wang Yung-kang, 1953.
68 *Ibid.*
69 Liu Pao, 1952.
70 *Anshan Kang-t'ieh Kung-ssu*, September 1953.
71 Huang K'un-i, 1953.
72 Granick, 1960, pp. 64 and 39.
73 Huang K'un-i, 1953.
74 Schurmann unpublished manuscript, IV, 10 and 27.
75 *Tung Pei Jen-min Cheng-fu Kung-yeh-pu, Pan-kung-shih, Yen-chiu-k'o*, 1951.
76 *Ibid.*
77 Plans at shop level included production plan, material supply plan, power equipment and transport plan, inspection and repair plan, plan for improving labour organisation, cost plan, plan for technical and organisational measures. Li Ch'ang-yüan, 1952.
On team and individual plans, see for example *Ha-erh-pin Tsung-kung-hui, Pan-kung-shih*, 20 December 1950.
78 *Chung-kung-yeh T'ung-hsün*, No. 33, 21 November 1953, pp. 2–4.
79 Yen Yü-hsü and Shen Kuo-jung, 1953.
80 *Chung-kung-yeh T'ung-hsün*, No. 33, 21 November 1953, pp. 2–4. The majority of factories within the network of the Ministry of Heavy Industry operated a three shift system in 1953.
81 Yen Yü-hsü and Shen Kuo-jung, 1953.
82 Ai Wu, 1961.

83 Berliner, 1957 (1968), p. 15.
84 Li Mao-ch'i, 1953, p. 15.
Note: in the very early period the term *kung-chang* was sometimes used for shop supervisor. For example Cheng Hung-su uses the term *chih-ch'ang kung-chang* for shop supervisor. Afterwards the term *che-chien chu-jen* came into standard usage for shop supervisor. See Cheng Hung-su, June 1950, 'Su-lien ti Ch'i-yeh . . . '.
85 *Chung-kung-yeh T'ung-hsün*, No. 33, 21 November 1953, pp. 2–4.
86 Wu Mo-hua, 1953.
87 Chang Te-sheng, 1953.
88 *Ibid.*
89 Wu Mo-hua, 1953.
90 *Chung-kung-yeh T'ung-hsün*, No. 33, 21 November 1953, pp. 2–4.
91 *Chung-kung-yeh T'ung-hsün*, No. 33, 21 November 1953, pp. 16–17.
92 Chang Te-sheng, 1953.
93 See Chapter 3.
94 Lin Chiang-yün, 1955.
95 Schurmann (1966, p. 264) discusses this intensifying critique.

Chapter 7: Checks on managerial bureaucratism and authoritarianism

1 *Chung-kuo Ti-liu-chieh Ch'üan-kuo Lao-tung Ta-hui*, 8 August 1948. 'Kuan-yü Chung-kuo Chih-kung Yün-tung . . . '.
2 *Hua Pei Ti-i-chieh Chih-kung Tai-piao-hui-i*, 28 February 1950.
3 *Kung-jen Jih-pao she*, December 1949, pp. 48–9.
4 *Ibid.*
5 *Hua Pei Ti-i-chieh Chih-kung Tai-piao-hui-i*, 28 February 1950.
6 *Kung-jen Jih-pao she*, December 1949, pp. 47–8 (Question 75).
7 Schurmann (1966, Chapter IV) uses the dichotomy of 'organisation' and 'institution' expounded by Selznick, 1957, pp. 5–21.
8 This is best expounded in Mao Tse-tung, 27 February 1957.
9 *Kung-jen Jih-pao she*, pp. 46–7 (Question 74).
10 Carr, 1966, Vol. I, p. 219.
11 *Hua Pei Ti-i-chieh Chih-kung Tai-piao-hui-i*, 28 February 1950.
12 *Kung-jen Jih-pao she*, pp. 45–6 (Question 72).
13 *Ibid.* p. 45 (Question 70).
14 *Ibid.* pp. 46–7 (Question 73).
15 By 1952, 90% of those eligible for membership had joined. *Chung-hua Ch'üan-kuo Tsung-kung-hui, Wu-i Wai-pin Chao-tai Wei-yüan-hui*, 1952, p. 4.
16 The account of the Third Mill is taken from Chang Li-chih, 1950.
17 5 May 1949.
18 'Directive on Work in Tientsin', *Chin-tai Ko-ming Li-shih-so, Hung-wei-ping, Chan-tou Kung-yung-chan*, 1967.
19 Chang Li-chih, 1950.
20 *Hua Pei Ti-i-chieh Chih-kung Tai-piao-hui-i*, 28 February 1950.
21 On the bombing of North Chinese cities see Bodde, 1967, p. 178.

22 See *Hua Pei Ti-i-chieh Chih-kung Tai-piao-hui-i*, 28 February 1950.
23 e.g. *Jen-min Jih-pao*, 7 February 1950. This editorial became required reading for all enterprise personnel and was reprinted many times.
24 *Ibid.*
25 Chang Li-chih, 1950. The Third Textile Mill committee was required to carry out propaganda amongst white collar workers on how to rely on the masses and to approve documents for study.
26 *Jen-min Jih-pao*, 7 February 1950.
27 *Ibid.*
28 *Pei-ching-shih Tsung-kung-hui Wu-chin Kung-tso Wei-yüan-hui*, 1951.
29 Chang Li-k'o, 1951, 'Ju-ho K'o-fu . . . '.
30 *Pei-ching-shih Tsung-kung-hui Wu-chin Kung-tso Wei-yüan-hui*, 1951.
31 Chang Li-k'o, 1951, 'Ju-ho K'o-fu . . . '.
32 *Pei-ching-shih Tsung-kung-hui Wu-chin Kung-tso Wei-yüan-hui*, 1951.
33 Chang Li-k'o, 1951, 'Ju-ho K'o-fu . . . '.
34 *Ibid.*
35 *Pei-ching-shih Tsung-kung-hui Wu-chin Kung-tso Wei-yüan-hui*, 1951.
36 e.g. the Shih-ching-shan Forging Department, *Ibid.*
37 Chang Li-k'o, 1951, 'Ju-ho K'o-fu . . . '.
38 *Ibid.*
39 Ling Hua-ch'un, 1951.
40 *Chung-hua Ch'üan-kuo Tsung-kung-hui*, 1 May 1950.
41 *Pei-ching-shih Tsung-kung-hui Wu-chin Kung-tso Wei-yüan-hui*, 1951.
42 e.g. Kao Kang (13 March 1950) talks about the Party committees usurpation of managerial authority as a violation of 'co-ordinated leadership'.
43 *Ibid.*
44 Chang Li-k'o, 1951, 'Ju-ho K'o-fu . . . '.
45 *Ibid.*
46 *Tung Pei Jih-pao*, April 1950, 'An-tung Tsao-chih-ch'ang . . . '.
47 Ling Hua-ch'un, 1951.
48 Kao Kang, 13 March 1950.
49 The phrase 'political work is the lifeblood of all economic work' (*cheng-chih kung-tso shih i-ch'ieh ching-chi kung-tso ti sheng-ming-hsien*) was first put forward by Mao in 1955 in his introductory note to 'Yen-chung ti Chiao-hsün' ('A Serious Lesson') in *Chung-kuo Kung-ch'an-tang, Chung-yang Wei-yüan-hui, Pan-kung-t'ing*, 1956, p. 255. This was at a time when the reaction against an excessive concentration on economic work was beginning. The reaction was to culminate in 1958 when the slogan *cheng-chih kua-shuai* 'politics in command' was given prominence. The particular relationship between politics and economics had, however, long

been a tenet of Leninism. See V.I. Lenin, January 1921 (*SW*, 3 vol. ed., Vol. 3, p. 527) in which Lenin says '. . . politics is a concentrated expression of economics . . . Politics must take precedence over economics. To argue otherwise is to forget the ABC of Marxism.'

50 *Kung-jen Ch'u-pan-she*, 1953, pp. 58 and 81.
51 Such was the implication of Li Hsüeh-feng's attack on one-man management. Li Hsüeh-feng, 24 September 1956.
52 Pfiffner and Sherwood, 1960, p. 336.
53 This process is discussed with reference to Stalin in Schapiro and Lewis, 1970, p. 125.
54 Schurmann, 1966, p. 192.
55 Dubin cited in Pfiffner and Sherwood, 1960, p. 337.
56 Pfiffner and Sherwood, 1960, p. 297.
57 Vogel, 1971, pp. 313–19.
58 An Tzu-wen, 7 January 1953.
59 *Chung-kuo Kung-ch'an-tang Chung-yang Wei-yüan-hui Tung Pei chü*, May 1951.
60 *Tung Pei Jih-pao*, 3 and 8 April 1950, reprinted in Shanghai *Hsin-hua Shu-tien*, September 1950, pp. 95–106.
61 *Ibid.*
62 Shanghai, *Hsin-hua Shu-tien*, September 1950, pp. 3–9.
63 *Chung-kuo Kung-ch'an-tang Chung-yang Wei-yüan-hui Tung Pei chü*, May 1951.
64 Kao Kang, 31 August 1951.
65 *Kung-jen Ch'u-pan-she*, 1953, p. 80.
66 Li Hsüeh-feng, 24 September 1956.
67 Li Cho-jen, 26 May 1950.
68 *Ibid.*
69 Liu Chih-ming, 1950.
70 *Ibid.*
71 *Shanghai Tsung-kung-hui, Wen-chiao-pu*, 1950, preface, pp. 1–3.
72 *Chung-kuo Kung-ch'an-tang Chung-yang Wei-yüan-hui*, 1 January 1951.
73 *Ibid.*
74 *NCNA*, Shenyang, 19 January 1951 (*CB*, 54, 23 January 1951, p. 9).
75 *NCNA*, 7 June 1951 (*SCMP*, 112, 8–9 June 1951, p. 23).
76 *NCNA*, Shenyang, 19 January 1951 (*CB*, 54, 23 January 1951, p. 9).
77 *Kung-jen Ch'u-pan-she*, 1953, pp. 35 and 68. Here two different reports give the figures for propagandists in the factory as 316 (+ 157 propaganda activists) (p. 35) and 248 (+ 157) (p. 68). These two undated articles were probably written at different times. Party membership was 9.2% in mid 1952 although the rapid employment of new personnel after the Three-Five Anti Movement reduced this ratio (p. 74).
78 Gardner, 1969, p. 501.

79 *Kung-jen Ch'u-pan-she*, 1953, p. 68.
80 This figure is deduced from a statement by the labour union chairman that 2,400 people had participated in cultural classes. Since this figure probably included all blue collar workers, most white collar workers and also probably some workers who had left the factory (which might cancel out those workers who were not attending classes) a figure of 2–3,000 is perhaps a reasonable estimate. *Kung-jen Ch'u-pan-she*, 1953, p. 50. It is also stated that there were 10 workshops each containing some 200 men (pp. 64–5).
81 Shanghai, *Wan-yeh Shu-tien*, 1952.
82 Kao Kang, 13 March 1950.
83 *Kung-jen Ch'u-pan-she*, 1953, p. 73. The term used is *wen-hua hsüeh-hsi* which at least means literacy and at most means education.
84 *Shang-hai Jen-min Kuang-po Tien-t'ai*, 1950.
85 Schurmann (1966, p. 295) explains the atmosphere at that time as strict adherence to policy but with considerable operational leeway.
86 e.g. *NCNA* report on the Shanghai No. 17 cotton mill (*SWB*, 4 June 1969). See also Chapter 8.
87 See Gardner, 1969.
88 *Kung-jen Ch'u-pan-she*, 1953, p. 1.
89 *Ibid.* pp. 43–5.
90 *Ibid.* pp. 47–8.
91 *Ibid.* pp. 48–9.
92 *Ibid.* p. 50.
93 *Ibid.* pp. 50 and 86–93.
94 *Ibid.* p. 93.
95 *Chung-kuo Kung-ch'an-tang Chung-yang Wei-yüan-hui Hua Nan Fen-chü*, 5 August 1951.
96 Cheng Hung-su, June 1950, 'Su-lien ti Ch'i-yeh'.

Chapter 8 : Conclusion

1 Mao Tse-tung, December 1942, pp. 273–4.
2 Lindsay, 1970.
3 Mao Tse-tung, 27 February 1957.
4 Schurmann, 1966, p. 207.
5 Andors, 1969, p. 404.
6 Gray, 1973, pp. 130–5.
7 Andors, 1969.
8 Donnithorne, 1967, p. 467 (from *Chi-hua Ching-chi*, No. 9, September 1958, pp. 14–15).
9 Schurmann, 1966, p. 303; Wheelwright and McFarlane, 1970, pp. 68–76; Schurmann, 1964, pp. 65–91.
10 Schurmann, 1964.
11 Richman, 1969, pp. 688–704.
12 '57 United Detachment of the Revolutionary Rebels of the 8th Ministry of Machine Building', 1967.

13 Gray, 1973, pp. 145–8.
14 Richman, 1969, pp. 710–20.
15 Bastid, 1973, p. 169.
16 The slogan 'Work is struggle' has always been one of the most widely used of Mao Tse-tung's quotations. See Mao Chu-hsi Yü-lu, 1965, p. 171 'Kuan-yü Ch'ung-ch'ing T'an-p'an, 17 October 1945, *Hsüan-chi*, Vol. 4, p. 1160.
17 Mao Tse-tung, 31 January 1958.
18 Howe, 1973, pp. 238–9.
19 *Ibid.* pp. 239–41.
20 MacDougall, 1968.
21 Howe, 1973, pp. 251–2. For a discussion of grading see Meisner, 1972.
22 *SWB* FE/4090/B II/1, 12 September 1972.
23 *SWB* FE/4080/B II/13, 31 August 1972.
24 See Domes, 1973.
25 Wang Hung-wen, 1973.
26 The theory is of course much more complicated than suggested here. Although Mao has never spelt it out, the logic of the Cultural Revolution and the criticism of the Soviet Union would indicate that Mao see bureaucratism leading to the growth of new class formations which tend to identify with the remnants of former ruling classes.
27 For a stimulating discussion of the two views on work motivation and incentive see Wheelwright and McFarlane, 1970, especially Chapter 8.
28 The infectious nature of activism is amply illustrated by Hinton in the following quote which describes the land reform process: 'The mobilisation of the population could spread only slowly and in concentric circles like the waves on the surface of a pond when a stone is thrown in. The stone in this case was a small group of *chi chi fen tse* [*sic*] or 'activists' as the cadres of the new administration and the core of its militia were called.' Hinton, 1966, p. 115.
29 Bendix, 1960.
30 Mao Tse-tung, 11 June 1945.
31 Sheridan, 1968.
32 Li Li-san, 1 July 1951. See p. 166.
33 e.g. Moore, 1958 (1965), p. 26.
34 This is discussed in Schurmann, 1966, p. 424.
35 Mao Tse-tung, January 1962.
36 'All China Federation of Trade Unions Revolutionaries', 1968.
37 Schurmann, 1966, pp. 293–6.
38 Andors, 1969.
39 Schurmann, 1966, p. 294.
40 Huang Yu-feng and Lin Ming-chang, 1951.
41 *Jen-min Jih-pao*, 11 October 1961. 'Give Full Play to the Role of the Workers Representative Conferences' in *SCMP*, 2604, 24

October 1961, pp. 15–16.

42 Richman, 1969, pp. 52, 145, 211, 229, 288, 435–6.

43 Liu seems to have said many contradictory things. The contradiction between 'letting experts run factories' and 'neglecting economic accounting' is noted in *SWB* FE/4067/B II/1, 15 August 1972.

44 *Shang-hai Kung-jen Ko-ming Tsao-fan Tsung-ssu-ling-pu*, 1968.

45 *Ibid.*

46 *Kung-ko-hui* in *SCMP*, 4369, 5 March 1969, pp. 7–10.

47 *Shang-hai Kung-jen Ko-ming Tsao-fan Tsung-ssu-ling-pu*, 1968.

48 *Kung-ko-hui*, 1969.

49 Mao in fact traced the origin of this split to a much earlier date. See Mao Tse-tung, 24 September 1962.

50 *Kung-ko-hui*, 1969.

51 Yeh Hsiu-ch'ing for example was able to get rid of two Party secretaries with whom he disagreed and was said to have been supported by T'ao Chu, First Secretary of the recreated Central South Bureau of the Party. *Kung-ko-hui*, 1969.

52 *Tung Pei Kung-yeh*, No. 84, 1 February 1952, p. 15.

53 See *Peking Review*, 1970, No. 16, p. 3 and 1970, No. 14, p. 11. See also the other translated articles in *SCMP*, 4627, 1 April 1970, pp. 78–110.

The Anshan constitution was formulated on 22 March 1960, but was not implemented until 22 March 1968 when the Anshan Municipal Revolutionary Committee was set up and Liu Shao-ch'i discredited. In the Anshan Constitution, 5 principles were laid down for running socialist enterprises:

1. 'keep politics firmly in command'
2. 'strengthen Party leadership'
3. 'launch vigorous mass movements'
4. 'institute the system of cadre participation in productive labour and worker participation in management, of the reform of irrational and outdated rules and regulations and of close co-operation among workers cadres and technicians'
5. 'go full steam ahead with technical innovations and the technical revolution'

This order of priorities was quite different from the earlier collective contracts.

54 *Chung-hua Ch'üan-kuo Tsung-kung-hui, Pien-chi Ch'u-pan-shih*, 1950, pp. 231–4.

55 See for example the *NCNA* report on the Shanghai, No. 17 cotton mill (*SWB*, 4 June 1969). See also the various articles on the Anshan Iron and Steel Company in Peking Review and *SCMP* (e.g. *Peking Review*, 1970, No. 14, p. 11).

56 *Peking Review*, 1970, No. 16, p. 3.

57 Chang Ta-k'ai and Sung Chin-sheng.

58 Richman, 1969, pp. 255–6. 40% of the enterprises surveyed by Richman were implementing this system. The mechanics for

election were the same as for delegates to people's congresses.
59 *Jen-min Jih-pao*, 24 December 1965, p. 1.
60 Harper, 1969.
61 Hunter, 1969, pp. 167–72.
62 Ito and Shibata, 1968. See also *URS*, Vol. 56, No. 11, 5 August 1969.
63 Hunter, 1969, Chapters 10–11.
64 Wheelwright and McFarlane, 1970, p. 132.
65 Watson, 1973, pp. 314–15.
66 e.g. *Jen-min Jih-pao*, 24 September 1969 (in *SCMP* 4510). Significantly the previous trend towards anarchism is also laid at the feet of Liu Shao-ch'i (*SWB* FE/4079/B II/5, 30 August 1972).
67 Bastid, 1973, p. 187.
68 Domes, 1973, p. 6.
69 *SWB* FE/4080/B II/13, 31 August 1972.
70 *SWB* FE/4135/B II/4, 3 November 1972.
71 This is discussed in Howe, 1973, pp. 249–50.
72 Howe, 1973, p. 250.
73 The revival of the labour unions was officially announced in April 1973.
74 Bastid, 1973, p. 187.
75 Watson, 1973, p. 317.
76 *Ibid.* p. 316.
77 Andors, 1969.
78 *Jen-min Jih-pao*, 5 April 1972.
79 Watson, 1973, p. 317 on the new social esteem accorded to workers.
80 For a discussion of urban communes see Salaff, 1967.
81 *NCNA*, Tach'ing, 18 January, 1973 in *Hsin-hua Selected News*, No. 5, 29 January 1973. This is one of a series of 5 articles on Tach'ing, the remaining four can be found in *Ibid.* pp. 21–2 and *CB*, No. 979, 2 March 1973, pp. 4–15.
82 *Jen-min Jih-pao*, 29 March 1969. 'How Should Socialist Universities be Run' in *SCMM*, No. 881, 26 May 1969, p. 4.
83 Howe (1973, p. 240) would welcome such a situation and by no means consider it a danger.

Bibliography

For ease of reference, I have put together all books and articles whether in Chinese or English in one comprehensive list. For material in Chinese, I have used the Wade-Giles system of transliteration. For materials in English written by Chinese authors, I have used the same system of transliteration as the author.

Abegglen, J. *The Japanese Factory: Aspects of its Social Organisation*, Bombay, Asia Publishing House, 1959.

Ai Wu. *Steeled and Tempered*, Peking, Foreign Languages Press, 1961, 437 pp.

All China Federation of Trade Union Proletarian Revolutionaries. 'The Struggle Between the Two Lines in China's Trade Union Movement', *Peking Review*, No. 26, 28 June 1968, pp. 17–21.

Alley, Rewi. *Yo Banfa*, Shanghai, China Monthly Review, 1952, 193 pp.

An-shan Kang-t'ieh Kung-ssu. 'Kuan-yü tsai Ko Sheng-ch'an Tan-wei Chien-li Hsing-cheng Chuan-tse-chih ti Chih-shih' ('Directive on the Establishment of a Managerial Responsibility System in Each Unit of Production'), *Chung-kung-yeh T'ung-hsün*, No. 26, 11 September 1953, p. 8.

An-shan Kang-t'ieh Kung-ssu Chi-pen Chien-she-ch'u. 'Tsen-yang Chih-hsing Chi-pen Chien-she ti Nei-pao-kung Chih-tu' ('How to Implement the Internal *Pao-kung* System in Basic Construction'), *Tung Pei Kung-yeh*, No. 63, 1 July 1951, pp. 11–14.

An Tzu-wen. 'Tsen-yang I-k'ao Kung-jen Chieh-chi' (How to Rely Upon the Working Class), speech to meeting at labour union cadres school, basic level union cadres training class, *Kung-jen Jih-pao*, 31 August 1951, pp. 1 and 4.

An Tzu-wen, 7 January 1953. 'Wei Hsiao-ch'u Tang Tsu-chih nei ti Hsiao-chi ti ho Pu-chien-k'ang ti Hsien-hsiang erh Tou-cheng' ('Struggle to Get Rid of Passive and Unhealthy Phenomena in Party Organisations'), speech to staff meeting of cadres of directly subordinate organs of Party Central Committee, *Jen-min Jih-pao*, 12 February 1953, pp. 1 and 3.

Andors, S. 'Revolution and Modernisation: Man and Machine in Industrialising Society, the Chinese Case' in Friedman and Selden, 1969, pp. 393–444.

Arakelian, R. *Industrial Management in the U.S.S.R.* (translated by Ellsworth L. Raymond) Washington D.C., Public Affairs Press, 1950, 168 pp. originally published in Russian *Upravlenie Sotsialisticheskoi Promyshlennost'iu*, Moscow, Worker Press, 1947, and issued by the Economics Institute of the Academy of Sciences of the U.S.S.R.

Barnett, A. Doak. *China on the Eve of Communist Takeover*, New York, Praeger, 1963 (second printing 1966), 371 pp.

(ed.). *Chinese Communist Politics in Action*, Seattle and London, University of Washington Press, 1969, 620 pp.

Bastid, M. 'Levels of Economic Decision Making', in Schram, 1973, pp. 159–97.

Bendix, R. *Work and Authority in Industry: Ideologies of Management in the Course of Industrialization*, New York, John Wiley and Sons, 1956, 466 pp.

'The Cultural and Political Setting of Economic Rationality in Western and Eastern Europe' in Grossman (ed.), 1960.

Bennett, J. and Ishino Iwao. *Paternalism in the Japanese Economy*, Minneapolis, University of Minnesota Press, 1963, 307 pp.

Berliner, J. *Factory and Manager in the U.S.S.R.*, Cambridge Mass., Harvard University Press, 1957 (second printing 1968), 386 pp.

Bernstein, T. 'Problems of Village Leadership after Land Reform', *China Quarterly*, No. 36, October–December 1968, pp. 1–22.

Bodde, D. *Peking Diary*, New York, Fawcett World Library, 1967, first published Abelard Schuman, 1950, 288 pp.

Carr, E.H. *The Bolshevik Revolution*, Vol. I, Harmondsworth, Penguin Books (Pelican), 1966, 448 pp. first published, MacMillan, 1950.

Chai. *Essential Works of Chinese Communism*, New York, Pica Press, 1970, 464 pp.

Chang Chien. 'Kung-tzu Kung-tso chung ti Pu Ho-li Hsien-hsiang Shih Wo-man Lang-fei-le Kung-tzu Chi-chin' ('Irrational Phenomena in Wages Work has Caused us to Waste the Wage Fund'), *Chung-kung-yeh T'ung-hsün*, No. 69 (33) November 1954, p. 28.

Chang Ch'ing-chi. 'Pei-ching-shih ti Ai-kuo Kung-yüeh Yün-tung' ('The Patriotic Compact Movement in Peking Municipality'), *Jen-min Jih-pao*, 10 July 1951, reprinted in *Chung Nan Jen-min Ch'u-pan-she*, September 1951, pp. 34–7.

Chang Hsi. 'K'ai-chan Ch'i-yeh Min-chu Kai-ko Yün-tung' ('On Developing the Democratic Reform Movement in Enterprises'), *Kan-pu Hsüeh-hsi Tzu-liao*, No. 37, 1951.

Chang, J.K. 'Industrial Development of Mainland China 1912–49', *The Journal of Economic History*, Vol. 27, March 1967, pp. 56–81.

Chang Li-chih. 'T'ien-chin Chung Fang San Ch'ang Shih-hsing Kuan-li Min-chu-hua ti Ching-yen' ('The Experiences of the Third [Chinese Textile Construction Company's] Textile Mill in Tientsin in Implementing the Democratisation of Management'), in Li T'ao and Lin Keng, 1950, pp. 1–9.

Chang Li-k'o. 'Ju-ho K'o-fu Ch'i-yeh Kuan-li Min-chu-hua chung ti Hsing-shih-chu-i' ('How to Overcome Formalism in the Democratisation of Enterprise Management'), in *Lao-tung Ch'u-pan-she Pien-shen-pu*, 1951, pp. 33–42.

'T'ui-kuang Hsien-chin Ching-yen Shen-ju Kung-ku Ai-kuo-chu-i Ching-sai' ('Propagate Advance Experiences, Enter Deep and Consolidate Patriotic Competitions'), *Chung-kuo Kung-jen*, No.

15, 20 April 1951, p. 3.

Chang P'ing-hua. 'Kuan-yü Tsung-chieh Kung-tso Cheng-tun Ssu-hsiang Tso-feng ti Pao-kao' ('Report on Summing up Work and Rectifying Ideology and Working Style'), to a conference of Party cadres in Wuhan, in *Kan-pu Hsüeh-hsi Tzu-liao*, No. 16, September 1950, pp. 106–14.

'Tui-yü (Wei Kuan-ch'e Min-chu Kai-ko erh Tou-cheng) ti Pu-ch'ung Fa-yen' ('Supplementary speech on the Struggle to Implement Democratic Reform'), at first session of the 2nd Congress of People from All Circles in Wuhan. *Ch'ang-chiang Jih-pao*, 9 July 1951, reprinted in *Kan-pu Hsüeh-hsi Tzu-liao*, No. 37, pp. 65–73.

Chang Shih-lin. 'Chinese People Resolved to Make Every Undertaking a Great School of Mao Tse-tung's Thought', *Peking Review*, No. 36, 2 September 1966, p. 22.

Chang Ta-k'ai and Sung Chin-sheng. 'Ch'i-yeh Kuan-li-shang I-ko Ken-pen-hsing ti Pien-ko' ('A Fundamental Revolutionary Change in Enterprise Management'), *Jen-min Shou-ts'e*, 1965, pp. 564–6.

Chang Te-sheng. 'Chi-ts'eng Tsu-chih Sui i Kai-pien, Kung-ch'ang Jeng shih Yu-chih Wu-ch'üan' ('Although Basic Level Organisation has Been Changed, the Foreman Still has Responsibility but No Power'), *Chung-kung-yeh T'ung-hsün*, No. 33, 21 November 1953, p. 18.

Ch'ang-chiang Jih-pao, 13 June 1951. 'Lun Kung-ying Ch'i-yeh chung ti Min-chu Kai-ko' ('On Democratic Reform in State-run Enterprises') reprinted in *Kan-pu Hsüeh-hsi Tzu-liao*, No. 37, pp. 28–31.

20 July 1951. 'Lun Fa-tung Kung-jen Ch'ün-chung Chien-chüeh Kuan-ch'e Ch'i-yeh Min-chu Kai-ko' ('On Mobilising the Worker Masses to Persist in Implementing the Democratic Reform of Enterprises'), reprinted in *Kan-pu Hsüeh-hsi Tzu-liao*, No. 37, pp. 37–42.

Ch'ang T'ai-tz'u. 'Shen-su-hsin Yüan-wen' ('Letter of Complaint [to editor of *Tung Pei Jih-pao*] Original Text') 3 April 1950, reprinted in Shanghai *Hsin-hua Shu-tien*, 1950, pp. 40–7.

Chao Ch'ao-kou. *Yen-an I-yüeh* (*One Month in Yenan*), 2nd edition, Nanking, *Hsin Min Pao*, 1946, 252 pp.

Chen Nai-ruenn. *Chinese Economic Statistics: A Handbook for Mainland China*, Edinburgh, the University Press, 1967, 539 pp.

Chen Nai-ruenn and Galenson W. *The Chinese Economy Under Communism*, Edinburgh, the University Press, 1969, 250 pp.

Ch'en Po-ta. 'Pu-yao Ta-luan Yüan-lai Ch'i-yeh Chi-kou' ('Do Not Throw Into Confusion Existing Enterprise Structure'), in *Hsin-hua Shu-tien*, 1949 (presumed), pp. 17–29.

Ch'en Tzu-hsün. 'Yü Chih-kung Hsiung-ti-men T'an-t'an Kung tzu Wen-t'i' ('Chatting About Wage Problems With Our White and Blue Collar Worker Brothers'), *Chung-kuo Kung-yeh*, Vol. 2, No. 4, August 1950, pp. 20–30.

Ch'en Wei-shuo. 'Tsou Hsiang Ho-li Kung-tzu Chih-tu ti Tao-lu' ('Walk

Along the Road Towards a Rational Wages System'), *Tung Pei Kung-yeh*, No. 47 (1 January 1951), pp. 25–9, No. 48 (1 February 1951), pp. 32–4, No. 49 (11 February 1951), pp. 37–9, No. 50 (21 February 1951), pp. 40–2.

Cheng Hung-su. 'Su-lien ti Ch'i-yeh Kuan-li shih Tsen-yang T'iao-cheng ti' ('How Soviet Enterprise Management was Put in Order'), *Chung-kuo Kung-yeh*, Vol. 2, No. 2, June 1950, pp. 21–5 and Vol. 2, No. 3, July 1950, pp. 7–13.

'Ching-chi Ho-suan-chih ti Li-lun yu Shih-chien' ('The Theory and Practice of the Economic Accounting System'), *Chung-kuo Kung-yeh*, Vol. 1, No. 10, 15 February 1950, pp. 19–26.

Cheng Tsu-yüan. *Anshan Steel Factory in Communist China*, Hong Kong, Union Research Institute, 1955, 88 pp.

Cheng-wu-yüan, April 1950. 'Kuan-yü Shih-hsing Kuo-chia Chi-kuan ti Hsien-chin Kuan-li ti Chüeh-ting' ('Decision on Carrying out the Management of Ready Cash in State Organs'). Passed at 27th meeting. *Hsin-hua-she*, Peking, 7 April 1950, *Hsin-hua Yüeh-pao*, No. 7, May 1950, p. 128.

Cheng-wu-yüan, Ts'ai-cheng Ching-chi Wei-yüan-hui. *Chung-yang Ts'ai-ching Cheng-ts'e Fa-ling Hui-pien* (*Compendium of Financial and Economic Policies Laws and Decrees*), No. 1 (parts 1 and 2), August 1950, 824 pp.; No. 2 (parts 1–4), June 1951, 1,149 pp.; No. 3 (parts 1–3), March 1952, 1,096 pp.

28 February 1950. 'Kuan-yü Kuo-ying Kung-ying Kung-ch'ang Chien-li Kung-ch'ang Kuan-li Wei-yüan-hui ti Chih-shih' ('Directive on the Establishment of Factory Management Committees in State and Publically-run Factories'), in *Lao-tung Ch'u-pan-she, Pien-shen-pu*, 1951.

Cheng Yu-kwei. *Foreign Trade and Industrial Development of China*, Washington D.C. University Press, 1956, 278 pp.

Chesneaux, J. 'The Chinese Labour Force in the First Part of the Twentieth Century', in Cowan, 1964, pp. 111–27.

The Chinese Labour Movement 1919–1927, Stanford, Stanford University Press, 1968, 574 pp. Originally published as *Le Movement Ouvrier Chinois de 1919 à 1927*, Paris, Mouton, 1962, 652 pp.

Chi Ming-ta. 'Kung-tuan Tsu-chih chung ti Chi-ko Chung-yao Wen-t'i' ('Some Important Questions on Work Section Organisation'), *Chung-kung-yeh T'ung-hsün*, No. 30, 21 October 1953, pp. 10–12.

Ch'i Kuo-chien and Chang Yi-chün. 'Pao-t'ou T'ieh-ch'ang Ch'ang-chang Kuan-liao-chu-i Tso-feng Yen-chung' ('The Bureaucratic Working Style of the Factory General Manager of the Paotow Iron Works is Serious'), *Kung-jen Jih-pao*, 8 January 1953, p. 3.

Chiang Kai-shek. *China's Destiny and Chinese Economic Theory*, New York, Roy Publishers, 1947, 347 pp.

Chiao Yi-fu (ed.). *Hung-wei-ping Hsüan-chi* (*Selections from the Red Guards*), Hong Kong, *Ta-lu Ch'u-pan-she*, July 1967, 255 pp.

Chieh-fang Jih-pao. 15 July 1951. 'Too Many Meetings Affect Model

Worker Yüan Kai-li's [*sic*] Production Work and Health', in *SCMP*, 14 July 1951, pp. 14–15 (the surname should more properly be read Juan).

Chieh-fang-she. Chung-kuo Chih-kung Yün-tung ti Tang-ch'ien Jen-wu (*The Current Tasks of the Movement of Chinese White and Blue Collar Workers*), Shanghai, June 1949, 94 pp.

Chin Feng. 'Tsen-yang Chien-ch'a ho Hsiu-ting Ai-kuo Kung-yüeh' ('How to Check up on and Amend Patriotic Compacts'), *Jen-min Jih-pao*, 23 May 1951, in *Chung Nan Jen-min Ch'u-pan-she*, September 1951, pp. 30–3.

Chin-tai Ko-ming Li-shih-so, Hung-wei-ping Chan-tou Kung-ying-chan. 'Liu Shao-ch'i ti Tzu-ch'an-chieh-chi Chien-kuo Kang-ling' ('Liu Shao-ch'i's Bourgeois Programme for Setting Up the State'), originally in *Chin Chün Pao* (*Advance the Troops Newspaper*) and reprinted in Chiao Yi-fu (ed.), 1967, pp. 28–37.

Chinese Communist Party, Central Committee. 'Resolution on the Anti Party Block of Kao Kang and Jao Shu-shih', March 1955, extract in Chai, 1970, pp. 342–5.

Chou Ch'i-yü. 'Shou-tu Shih-ching-shan Fa-tien-ch'ang Shih-hsing Ch'e-chien Ai-kuo Ching-sai Kung-yüeh' ('The Capital's Shih-ching-shan Electrical Power Plant Implements Workshop Patriotic Competition Compacts'), *Kung-jen Jih-pao*, 24 July 1951, p. 1.

Chou Shu-k'ang, 26 December 1950. 'Kuo-ying Ch'i-yeh chung Kung-hui Ying-kai Tsen-yang Tso Kung-tzu Kung-tso' ('How Ought the Labour Unions Conduct Wage Work in State-run Enterprises'), report to meeting of basic level cadres at An Kang. *Chung-kuo Kung-jen*, No. 16, 24 May 1951, p. 6.

Chu Hsüeh-fan. 'Kuan-yü Kuo-min-tang T'ung-chih-ch'ü ti Chih-kung Yün-tung' ('On the Movement of White and Blue Collar Workers in Districts Under Kuomintang Rule'), speech to 6th All China Labour Conference 10–11 August 1948, excerpts in *Chieh-fang-she*, 1949, pp. 15–29.

Chu P'u. 'Wei-ta ti Ch'uang Hsin Chi-lu Yün-tung' ('The Great Movement to Create New Records'), *Chung-kuo Kung-yeh*, Vol. 1, No. 12, 24 April 1950.

Chu Tz'u-shou. 'Shih-lun Hsin Chung-kuo Kung-yeh Kuan-li ti Chi-pen Fang-ts'e' ('A Tentative Discussion on the Basic Policy for Industrial Management in New China'), *Chung-kuo Kung-yeh*, Vol. 3, No. 5, September 1951, pp. 3–10.

Ch'ün-chung Jih-pao (Sian). 'CCP Committees in Party and Mass Organs Map put Plans to Study Party Reform Work', translated in *CB*, 158, 15 February 1952, pp. 30–1.

Chung-hua Ch'üan-kuo Tsung-kung-hui, 9 August 1949. 'Kuan-yü Hui-yüan Wen-t'i ti Chüeh-ting *ts'ao-an*)' ('Draft Decision on the Question of Membership') in Shanghai (no author stated), *Chieh-fang-hou . . .*, pp. 175–7.

1 May 1950. 'I nien lai ti Kung-tso Pao-kao' ('Report on the Work of the Past Year'), *Chung-kuo Kung-jen*, No. 4, 15 May 1950.

pp. 18–21.

'Cheng-tun Kung-hui Tsu-chih yü Kung-hui Kan-pu ti Kung-tso Tso-feng' ('Rectify Labour Union Organisation and the Working Style of Labour Union Cadres'), *Kung-jen Jih-pao*, 30 August 1950, reprinted in *Chung-kuo Kung-jen*, No. 8, September 1950, p. 6.

Chung-hua Ch'üan-kuo Tsung-kung-hui, Pien-chi Ch'u-pan-shih. Chi-t'i Ho-t'ung Shou-ts'e (*Collective Contract Handbook*), Vol. 2, Peking, *Kung-jen Ch'u-pan-she*, August 1950, 303 pp. (2 vols.).

Chung-hua Ch'üan-kuo Tsung-kung-hui Sheng-ch'an-pu. Sheng-ch'an Kung-tso Shou-ts'e (*Production Work Handbook*), Vol. 1, Peking, *Kung-jen Ch'u-pan-she*, May 1950, 265 pp.

Chung-hua Ch'üan-kuo Tsung-kung-hui, Wu-i Wai-pin Chao-tai Wei-yüan-hui. Chieh-fang-le ti Chung-Kuo Kung-jen (*The Liberated Chinese Workers*), Peking, *Kung-jen Ch'u-pan-she*, August 1953, 3rd printing (1st printing April 1952), 24 pp.

Chung-kung-yeh-pu. 28 May 1953. 'Kuan-yü tsai Sheng-ch'an Ch'ang K'uang Chien-li Tse-jen-chih ti Chih-shih' ('Directive on the Establishment of a Responsibility System in Production Factories and Mines'), *Chung-kung-yeh T'ung-hsün*, No. 16, 1 June 1953, p. 105.

Chung-kung-yeh-pu, Chien-she Kung-ch'eng Kung-ssu. 'Chieh-shao "Hsiao-tsu Ching-chi Ho-suan Shou-ts'e" ' ('Introducing "the Team Economic Accounting Handbook" '), *Chung-kung-yeh T'ung-hsün*, No. 21, 21 July 1953, pp. 18–19.

Chung-kung-yeh-pu, Hua-hsüeh Kung-yeh Kuan-li-chü. 'Kai-chin ho T'i-kao Sheng-ch'an Fu-ch'ang-chang ti Ling-tao Fang-fa; Chia-ch'iang Sheng-ch'an Chi-shu Ling-tao' ('Improve and Raise the Level of the Methods of Leadership of the Deputy Factory General Manager in Charge of Production; Strengthen Leadership in Production Technology'), *Chung-Kung-yeh T'ung-hsün*, No. 68 (1954 No. 32), 11 November 1954, pp. 16–20.

Chung-kung-yeh T'ung-hsün, No. 7, 1 March 1953, pp. 25–8. 'Ha-erh-pin Kung-yeh Ta-hsüeh Kung-ti shih Ju-ho K'ai-chan Tse-jen-chih Yün-tung ti' ('How the Movement to Launch a Responsibility System was Developed at the Work Site of the Harbin Industrial University').

No. 16, 1 June 1953, p. 8. 'Tsai Chia-ch'iang Chi-hua Kuan-li ti Chi-ch'u shang Chan-k'ai Chien-li Tse-jen-chih Yün-tung; Ch'i-yeh Kuan-li chung ti Wu-jen Fu-tse Hsien-hsiang' ('On the Basis of Strengthening Planned Management, Develop the Establishment of Responsibility Systems; the Serious Phenomenon of No-one Being Responsible in Enterprise Management').

No. 19, 1 July 1953, pp. 1–2. 'Kuan-ch'e Tso-yeh-chi-hua Tsu-chih Chün-heng Sheng-ch'an' ('Implement the Work Plan and Organise Balanced Production').

No. 19, 1 July 1953, p. 28. 'T'ang-shan Kang-ch'ang K'ai-shih-le Chien-li Tse-jen-chih ti Chun-pei Kung-tso' ('Tangshan Steel Works Begins Preparatory Work for Establishing a Responsibility

System').

No. 30, 21 October 1953, pp. 30–1. 'Tsai Kai-shan Lao-tung Tsu-chih ti Chi-ch'u shang Ting-ch'u Hsien-chin ti Sheng-ch'an Lao-tung Chi-hua' ('On the Basis of Improving Labour Organisation, Draw Up an Advanced Production-Labour Plan').

No. 33, 21 November 1953, pp. 2–4. 'Shih-hsing Sheng-ch'an Ch'ü-yü Kuan-li-chih' ('Implement the Production Territorial Management System').

No. 33, 21 November 1953, pp. 16–17. 'T'ui-hsing Chi-ts'eng Hsing-cheng Tse-jen-chih Kai-pien-le To-t'ou-ling-tao ti Hun-luan Hsien-hsiang' ('Promote the Managerial Responsibility System at the Basic Level and Change the Confused Phenomenon of Multi-headed Leadership').

Chung Kung-Yen-chiu Tsa-chih she, (Taipei). *Liu Shao-ch'i Wen-t'i Tzu-liao Chuan-chi* (*A Special Collection of Materials on Liu Shao-ch'i*), December 1970, 774 pp.

Chung-kuo Ch'ing-nien-pao, 6 September 1961, p. 1. 'Study in Earnest for the Cause of Socialist Construction', translated in *URS*, Vol. 25, pp. 308–12.

Chung-kuo Jen-min Yin-hang, 30 March 1955. 'Kuan-yü Ch'ü-hsiao Kuo-ying Kung-yeh chien Yi-chi Kuo-ying Kung-yeh ho Ch'i-ta Kuo-ying Ch'i-yeh chien ti Shang-yeh Hsin-yung Tai i Yin-hang Chieh-suan ti Pao-kao' ('Report on Eliminating the Use of Commercial Credit Within State Industry and Between State Industry and Other State Enterprises as a Substitute for Bank Balances'), in *Kuo-wu-yüan, Fa-chih-chü*, 1956, Vol. I, pp. 270–3.

Chung-kuo Kung-ch'an-tang Chung-yang Wei-yüan-hui, 1 January 1951. 'Kuan-yü tsai Ch'üan Tang Chien-li tui Jen-min Ch'ün-chung ti Hsüan-ch'uan-kang ti Chüeh-ting' ('Decision on the Establishment Throughout the Party of a Propaganda Network for the Popular Masses'), *Jen-min Jih-pao*, 3 January 1951, p. 1.

Chung-kuo Kung-ch'an-tang Chung-yang Wei-yüan-hui Pan-kung-t'ing. Chung-kuo Nung-ts'un ti She-hui-chu-i Kao-ch'ao (*Socialist Upsurge in The Chinese Countryside*), selections, Peking, *Jen-min Ch'u-pan-she*, 1956, 438 pp.

Chung-kuo Kung-ch'an-tang Ti-pa-tz'u Ch'üan-kuo Tai-piao-ta-hui Wen-hsien (*Documents of the Chinese Communist Party Eighth Congress*), Peking, *Jen-min Ch'u-pan-she*, February 1957, 1,101 pp.

Chung-kuo Kung-ch'an-tang Chung-yang Wei-yüan-hui Chung Nan chü, August 1951. 'Kuan-yü Fa-tung Kung-jen Ch'ün-chung K'ai-chan Min-chu Kai-ko Yün-tung ti Chih-shih' ('Directive on Launching a Movement of the Worker Masses to Develop the Democratic Reform Movement'), *Ch'ang-chiang Jih-pao*, 8 August 1951, reprinted in *Kan-pu Hsüeh-hsi Tzu-liao*, No. 37, pp. 1–16.

Chung-kuo Kung-ch'an-tang Chung-yang Wei-yüan-hui Hua Nan Fen-chü, 5 August 1951. 'Kuan-yü tsai Ch'eng-shih Fa-tung Kung-jen Ch'ün-chung chung K'ai-chan Min-chu Kai-ko Yün-tung ti Chüeh-ting (Wei Kuan-ch'e Min-chu Kai-ko Yün-tung erh Tou-cheng)' ('Resolution Concerning Mobilisation of the Working Masses in Cities to Develop the Democratic Reform Movement [Struggle for the Implementation of the Democratic Reform Movement]'), *Nan-fang Jih-pao*, 31 August 1951, reprinted in *Kan-pu Hsüeh-hsi Tzu-liao*, No. 37, September 1951, p. 26.

Chung-kuo Kung-ch'an-tang Chung-yang Wei-yüan-hui Tung Pei chü, 10 June 1948. 'Kuan-yü Pao-hu Hsin Shou-fu Ch'eng-shih ti Chih-shih' ('Directive on Maintaining Newly Recovered Cities'), in Liu Shao-ch'i et al, 1949.

1 August 1948. 'Kuan-yü Kung-ying Ch'i-yeh chung Chih-yüan Wen-t'i ti Chüeh-ting' ('Resolution on the Question of White Collar Workers in Publically-run Enterprises'), *Jen-min Jih-pao*, 7 August 1948, p. 2.

6 October 1949. 'Kuan-yü Kuan-ch'a (Kung-yeh-pu Chi-hsü Kuan-ch'e Ching-chi Ho-suan-chih ti Chih-shih yü K'ai-chan Ch'ün-chung-hsing ti Ch'uang-tsao Sheng-ch'an Hsin Chi-lu ti Chüeh-ting) ti Chüeh-ting ('Decision on Implementing the Industrial Department's Directive on the Continued Implementation of the Economic Accounting System and its Decision on Developing the Movement of a Mass Nature to Create New Production Records') *Chung-kuo Kung-jen*, Vol. 1, No. 1, 15 February 1950, p. 28.

18 April 1950. 'Kuan-yü Chin-i-pu T'uan-chieh Kung-ying Ch'i-yeh chung Chi-shu Jen-yüan yü Chih-yüan ti Chih-shih' ('Directive on Furthering Unity between Technical Personnel and White Collar Workers in Publically-run Enterprises'), *Tung Pei Kung-yeh*, No. 21, 1 May 1950, pp. 2–4.

May 1951. 'Kuan-yü Tang tui Kuo-ying Ch'i-yeh Ling-tao ti Chüeh-i' ('Resolution on the Party Exercising Leadership over State Enterprises'), *Tung Pei Jih-pao*, 5 September 1951, pp. 1–2.

20 February 1952. 'Kuan-yü tsai (San Fan) Yün-tung chung Chia-ch'iang Kuo-ying Ch'ang K'uang Ch'i-yeh Sheng-ch'an Ling-tao ti T'ung-hsün' ('Communiqué Concerning Strengthening Production Leadership in State-run Industrial and Mining Enterprises During the Three Anti Movement'), *Hsin-hua Yüeh-pao*, 1952, No. 3, pp. 7–8.

Chung-kuo Kung-jen, No. 15, April 1951, p. 36. 'Kung-hui Ying-kai Chan tsai Tsen-yang ti Li-ch'ang shang' ('What Kind of Standpoint Should the Labour Unions Take?').

Chung-kuo Min-chu T'ung-meng Tsung-pu Hsüan-ch'uan Wei-yüan-hui. Ts'eng-ch'an Chieh-yüeh Fan T'an-wu; Fan Lang-fei: Fan Kuan-liao-ch-i (*Increase Production and Practise Economy; Oppose Graft Waste and Bureaucratism*), December 1951, 132 pp.

Chung-kuo Ti-liu-chieh Ch'üan-kuo Lao-tung Ta-hui, 8 August 1948. 'Kuan-yü Chung-kuo Chih-kung Yün-tung ti Tang-ch'ien Jen-wu ti Chüeh-i' ('Resolution on the Current Tasks of the Movement of the Chinese White and Blue Collar Workers') in *Lao-tung Ch'u-pan-she Pien-shen-pu*, July 1951, pp. 1–3 and *Jen-min Jih-pao*,

10 November 1948, p. 3.
August 1948. 'Yu-kuan Kung-tzu Wen-t'i ti Chüeh-i' ('Resolution on Wages') in *Cheng-wu-yüan Ts'ai-cheng Ching-chi Wei-yüan-hui*, 1950, Vol. I, part 2, pp. 720–1.

Chung Nan Chün-cheng Wei-yüan-hui, 21 November 1951 (4th session). 'Kuan-yü K'ai-chan Tseng-ch'an Chieh-yüeh Yün-tung Pan-pa ti Chüeh-i' ('Resolution on Measures for the Development of the Movement to Increase Production and Practise Economy'), *Kan-pu Hsüeh-hsi Tzu-liao*, No. 41, December 1951 (reprinted January 1952).

Chung Nan Jen-min Ch'u-pan-she. Hsüan-ch'uan-yüan Kung-tso Wen-chi (*Documents on the Work of Propagandists*), Hankow, April 1951, 170 pp.

Tsen-yang Ting-li ho Chih-hsing Ai-kuo Kung-yüeh (*How to Draw up and Implement Patriotic Compacts*), Hankow, September 1951, 67 pp.

Chung-yang Jen-min Cheng-fu Wei-yüan-hui. Chung-hua Jen-min Kung-ho-kuo Kung-hui-fa (*Labour Union Law of the Peoples Republic of China*), passed at 8th session. Promulgated 28 June 1950, *Chung-kuo Kung-jen*, Vol. 1, No. 6, 15 July 1950, pp. 1–5.

Cole, G.D.H. *Studies in Class Structure*, London, Routledge and Kegan Paul, 1955 (2nd impression 1961), 195 pp.

Cole, R.E. *Japanese Blue Collar: The Changing Tradition*, Berkeley and Los Angeles, University of California Press, 1971, 300 pp.

Compton, Boyd. *Mao's China: Party Reform Documents 1942–44*, Seattle and London, University of Washington Press, 1966, 278 pp. (first published 1952).

Cowan, C.D. (ed.). *The Economic Development of China and Japan*, London, George Allen and Unwin, 1964, 255 pp.

Crankshaw, E. *Khruschev's Russia*, Harmondsworth, Penguin, 1959 (reprinted 1963), 183 pp.

Dobb, M. *Soviet Economic Development since 1917*, London, Routledge and Kegan Paul, 1966, 515 pp. (first published 1948).

Domes, J. 'A Rift in the New Course', *Far Eastern Economic Review*, 1 October 1973, supplement pp. 3–8.

Donnithorne, A. *China's Economic System*, London, George Allen and Unwin, 1967, 592 pp.

Eastman, L. 'Fascism in Kuomintang China: The Blue Shirts', *China Quarterly*, No. 49, January–March 1972, pp. 1–31.

Eckstein, A., Galenson W. and Liu Ta-chung (eds.). *Economic Trends in Communist China*, Edinburgh, The University Press, 1968, 757 pp.

d'Encausse, H. and Schram, S. *Marxism and Asia*, London, Allen Lane the Penguin Press, 1969, 404 pp. First published in France as *Le Marxisme et l'Asie* by Armand Colin, 1965.

Feuerwerker, A. 'China's Nineteenth Century Industrialisation: The Case of the Hanyehping Coal and Iron Company Limited', in Cowan, 1964, pp. 79–110.

China's Early Industrialisation: Sheng Hsüan-huai (1844–1916) and

Mandarin Enterprise, Cambridge Mass, Harvard University Press, 1958, 311 pp.

'57' United Detachment of the Revolutionary Rebels of the Eight Ministry of Machine Building. 'Wipe out State Monopoly and Promote Mechanisation on the Basis of Self Reliance in a Big Way', *Nung-yeh Chi-chieh Chi-shu*, No. 6, September 1967, translated in *SCMM*, No. 610, 15 January 1968, pp. 26–8.

Fong, H.D. (Fang Hsien-ting). *Industrial Organisation in China*, Tientsin, Nankai University Institute of Economics, 1937, 88 pp., originally in *Nankai Social and Economic Quarterly*, Vol. IX, No. 4, January 1937, pp. 919–1006.

Friedman, E. and Selden, M. *America's Asia: Dissenting Essays on Asian American Relations*, New York, Random House, 1969, 458 pp.

Gardner, J. 'The Wu-fan Campaign in Shanghai: A study in the Consolidation of Urban Control' in Barnett, 1969, pp. 477–539.

Granick, D. *The Red Executive*, London, MacMillan, 1960, 334 pp.

Gray, J. 'The Two Roads: Alternative Strategies of Social Change and Economic Growth in China', in Schram (ed.), 1973, pp. 109–57.

Grossman, G. (ed.). *Value and Plan*, Berkeley and Los Angeles, University of California Press, 1960, 370 pp.

Ha-erh-pin Tsung-kung-hui. 'Kuan-yü Tang-ch'ien Ai-kuo-chu-i Ching-sai ti Chih-shih' ('Directive on the Current Patriotic Competitions'), *Chung-kuo Kung-yeh*, Vol. 2, No. 8, 20 December 1950, pp. 53–6.

Ha-erh-pin Tsung-kung-hui-Pen-kung-shih. 'K'ai-chan Ai-kuo-chu-i Sheng-ch'an Ching-sai chung Ju-ho Ting-hao Ko-jen ho Hsiao-tsu ti Sheng-ch'an Chi-hua' ('How to Draw up Individual and Team Production Plans During the Development of Patriotic Production Competitions'), *Chung-kuo Kung-yeh*, Vol. 2, No. 8, 20 December 1950, pp. 51–3.

Han Yi and Wu Tung-min. 'Chi-lin-sheng Tsung-kung-hui ti Tsu-chih Kung-tso' ('The Organisational Work of the Kirin General Labour Union'), *Chung-kuo Kung-jen*, No. 2, 15 March 1950, p. 38.

Harper, P. 'The Party and the Unions in Communist China' *China Quarterly*, No. 37, January–March 1969, pp. 84–119.

Hinton, W. *Fanshen: A Documentary of Revolution in a Chinese Village*, New York, Vintage Books 1966, 637 pp.

Ho Fu-pen. 'Chi-ts'eng Hsing-cheng Tse-jen-chih Shih-tien Ching-yen' ('Experience of a Trial Point for the Basic Level Managerial Responsibility System'), *Chung-kung-yeh T'ung-hsün*, No. 36, 21 December 1953, pp. 22–5.

Ho Jen. 'Hsing-cheng shang Ch'iang-p'o Kung-jen Chia-pan Chüan-hsien' ('Management Forces Workers to Work Extra Shifts as a Donation'), letter to the editor of *Kung-jen Jih-pao*, 25 July 1951, p. 2.

Hoffman, C. 'Work Incentive Policy in Communist China', *China Quarterly*, No. 17, 1964, pp. 92–100.

Howe, C. *Employment and Economic Growth in Urban China*, London, Cambridge University Press, 1971, 170 pp.

'Labour Organisation and Incentives in Industry, Before and After

the Cultural Revolution', in Schram (ed.), 1973, pp. 233–56.
Wage Patterns and Wage Policy in Modern China 1919–1972, London, Cambridge University Press, 1973, 171 pp.

Hsiao Feng. 'Tung Pei Yeh-lien-ch'ang shih Ts'en-yang Kuan-ch'e Kuan-li Min-chu-hua ti' ('How the North East Smelting Works Implemented the Democratisation of Management'), in *Lao-tung Ch'u-pan-she, Pien-shen-pu*, 1951, pp. 55–67.

Hsieh Chia. *Huo-pi Wen-t'i* (*The Problems of Currency*), Tientsin *Chih-shih Shu-tien*, July 1950, 113 pp.

Hsin-hua-she, 7 February 1948. 'Chien-ch'ih Chih-kung Yün-tung Cheng-ch'üeh Lu-hsien, Fan-tui (Tso)-ch'ing Mao-hsien-chu-i' ('Maintain the Correct Line in the Movement of White and Blue Collar Workers and Oppose Left Adventurism'), in *Hsin-min-chu Ch'u-pan-she*, 1949, pp. 56–61.

25 June 1949. 'Pao-hu Jen-min Tsu-kuo ti Ts'ai-ch'an' ('Protect the Property of the Peoples Motherland'), in Liu Shao-ch'i et al, 1949, pp. 29–31.

10 February 1953. 'Chung-hua Tsung-kung-hui Chao-k'ai Liu-chieh Erh-ts'u Chih-hsing Wei-yüan-hui K'uo-ta Hui-i' (All China Federation of Labour Convenes an Enlarged Second Session of the Sixth Executive Committee'), *Kung-jen Jih-pao*, 11 February 1953, p. 1.

Hsin-hua-she (*Tung Pei*), 23 August 1948. 'Tung Pei San-nien Kao-shu' ('An Outline Account of the North East in the Past Three Years'), in *Jen-min Jih-pao*, 26 August 1948, p. 2.

Hsin-hua Shu-tien. Chung-kuo Jen-min Chieh-fang-chün Ju-ch'eng Cheng-ts'e (*Policy for the Peoples Liberation Army on Entering Cities*), no date (presumably 1949), 109 pp.

Hsin-min-chu Ch'u-pan-she. I-chiu-ssu-ch'i-nien I-lai Chung-kuo Kung-ch'an-tang Chung-yao Wen-chien-chi (*Important Documents of the Chinese Communist Party Since 1947*), Hong Kong, February 1949, 149 pp.

Hsü Ti-hsin. *Kuan-liao Tzu-pen lun* (*On Bureaucratic Capital*), Shanghai, *Hai-yen Shu-tien*, 1949, 148 pp.

Hsüeh Mu-ch'iao. *Chung-kuo Kuo-min Ching-chi ti She-hui-chu-i Kai-tsao* (*Socialist Transformation of China's National Economy*), Peking, *Jen-min Ch'u-pan-she*, April 1964 (revised edition), 154 pp.

Hu P'ing. 'Tsen-yang tsai Kung-ch'ang Ch'i-yeh chung Ting-li Ai-kuo Kung-yüeh' ('How to Formulate Patriotic Compacts in Factories and Enterprises'), *Jen-min Jih-pao*, 22 May 1951, reprinted in *Chung Nan Jen-min Ch'u-pan-she*, September 1951, pp. 7–10.

Hua-Pei Ti-i-chieh Chih-kung Tai-piao-hui-i, 28 February 1950. 'Kuan-yü tsai Kuo-ying Kung-ying Kung-yeh Ch'i-yeh chung Chien-li Kung-ch'ang Kuan-li Wei-yüan-hui ti Shih-shih T'iao-li' ('Effective Regulations of the First North China Congress of White and Blue Collar Workers Concerning the Establishment of Factory Management Committees in State-run and Publically-run Industrial

Enterprises'), in *Lao-tung Ch'u-pan-she, Pien-shen-pu*, 1951, pp. 5–10.

Hua-Tung Jen-min Ch'u-pan-she. T'e-wu P'o-huai Kung-ch'ang ti Tsui-hsing (*The Crimes of the Special Agents who Sabotage Factories*), Shanghai, *Hua-Tung Jen-min Ch'u-pan-she*, May 1951, 55 pp.

Huang K'un-i. 'K'ai-chan Tse-jen-chih Yün-tung, Pi-hsü tsai Ssu-hsiang shang Tsu-chih shang Tso-hao Ch'ung-fen Chun-pei' ('In Order to Develop the Responsibility System, We Must Make Adequate Preparation Both Ideologically and Organisationally'), *Chung-kung-yeh T'ung-hsün*, No. 26, 11 September 1953, p. 10.

Huang Yu-feng and Lin Ming-chang. 'Wo-men Yung (Nei-pao-kung Chi-chien-chih) Chin-hsing Tung-chi Ta-chien-hsiu Kung-tso' ('We use the [Internal] *Pao-kung* Piecework System to Carry Out the Great Winter Inspection and Repairs'), *Tung Pei Kung-yeh*, No. 45, 1 January 1951, pp. 23–4.

Hubbard, G.E. *Eastern Industrialisation and its Effect on the West*, London, Oxford University Press, 1935, 395 pp.

Hunter, N. *Shanghai Journal*, New York, Praeger, 1969, 311 pp.

Ito Kikuzo and Shibata Minoru. 'The Dilemma of Mao Tse-tung', *China Quarterly*, No. 35, July–September 1968, pp. 58–77.

Jao Shu-shih, 8 August 1949. 'Tsai Shang-hai Ko-chieh Jen-min Tai-piao-hui-i shang ti Pao-kao' ('Report to Congress of Representatives from All Circles in Shanghai'), in Shanghai (no publisher stated), 1949, *Chieh-fang hou . . .*

17 December 1951. 'Wei K'ai-chan Tseng-ch'an Chieh-yüeh Fan-tui T'an-wu Fan-tui Lang-fei, Fan-tui Kuan-liao-chu-i erh Tou-cheng' ('Struggle to Develop [a Movement to] Increase Production and Practise Economy, Oppose Graft, Waste and Bureaucratism') (excerpts), mobilisation report to East China Higher Level Government Cadres Meeting, *Hsin-hui Yüeh-pao*, No. 1, 1952, pp. 19–20.

Jen-min Ch'u-pan-she. Chung-hua Jen-min Kung-ho-kuo San-nien-lai Wei-ta Ch'eng-chiu (*The Great Achievements of the Chinese People's Republic in the Past Three Years*), Peking, December 1952, (4th printing August 1953), 172 pp.

Jen-min Jih-pao, 20 November 1947, p. 1. 'Tung Pei I-chiu-ssu-pa-nien Chien-she Ta-kang' ('General Outline for Construction in the North East in 1948').

16 December 1947, p. 1. 'Tung Pei Ts'ai-ching Hui-i Pi-mu Chüeh-ting Ts'ai-ching Chien-she Ta-kang' ('At the Closing of the Financial and Economic Conference in the North East, The General Outline for Financial and Economic Construction is Determined').

12 September 1948, p. 1. 'Cheng-tun Ch'i-yeh, T'i-kao Sheng-ch'an' ('Rectify Enterprises and Raise the Level of Production').

17 September 1948. 'An-tung Chao-k'ai Ch'ang-chang Hui-i' ('Antung Convenes a Conference of Factory General Managers').

25 December 1948, p. 2. 'Hsin Chuang Mei-k'uang Hsi-mi K'ao-kung

Kung-tzu P'ing-ting Chiao-ch'ien Ho-li' ('The Hsin Chuang Coal Mine Conducts a Meticulous Examination of Workers; Wage Assessment is More Rational Than Hitherto').

3 June 1949, p. 1. 'Ta Shang-hai Chieh-kuan Shun-li' ('Take-over in Greater Shanghai has Proceeded Smoothly').

7 February 1950. 'Hsüeh-hsi Kuan-li Ch'i-yeh' ('Learn How to Manage an Enterprise').

3 March, 24 March and 20 April 1950. 'Hua Pei Shih-ching-shan Kang-t'ieh-ch'ang Ta Chien-ch'a Ch'ien-hou' ('The Circumstances of the Great Investigation of the North China Shih-ching-shan Iron and Steel Works'). Summarised in Shanghai, *Hsin-hua Shu-tien*, 1950, pp. 3–9.

'Hua Pei Mei-k'uang Kuan-li-tsung-chü Chih-ling Yang Ch'üan K'uang-wu-chü Chien-ch'a Yang Ch'üan Mei-k'uang Wen-t'i' ('North China General Mining Bureau Orders the Yang Ch'üan Mining Bureau to Investigate the Problem of the Yang Ch'üan Coal Mines'), *Chung-kuo Kung-jen*, No. 3, 15 April 1950, p. 15.

'Ching Chin teng Ta Kung-ying ch'ang Chan-k'ai Ch'ün-chung Ta Chien-ch'a' ('A Great Mass Inspection is launched in Large Publically-run Factories in the Peking Tientsin etc., Areas'), *Chung-kuo Kung-jen*, No. 3, 15 April 1950, p. 15.

'An-tung-shih-wei Ch'uang-tsao Ch'i-yeh chung Tang ti Kung-tso Hsin Fang-shih' ('The New Method Adopted by the Antung Municipal Party Committee in Establishing Party Work in Enterprises'), reprinted in *Chung-kuo Kung-jen*, No. 3, 15 April 1950, pp. 31–2.

2 June 1951. 'Kuang-fan Ting-li ping Jen-chen Chih-hsing Ai-kuo-kung-yüeh' ('Establish Far and Wide Patriotic Compacts and Conscientiously Implement Them'), reprinted in *Chung Nan Jen-min Ch'u-pan-she*, September 1951, pp. 1–6.

16 June 1951, p. 1. 'Mei-yu Kung-ch'eng She-chi chiu Pu K'o-neng Shih-kung' ('Without Engineering Design, One Cannot Undertake the Work').

29 July 1951, p. 1. 'Cheng-ch'ü An-shih Wan-ch'eng Tseng-ch'an Chüan-hsien Chi-hua' ('Strive to Complete on Time Plans for Increasing Production and Making Donations').

11 October 1951, p. 2. 'Pei-ching-shih Ts'ai-cheng Ching-chi Wei-yüan-hui Kung-pu (fen) Chi-suan Pan-fa' ('Peking Municipality Finance and Economics Committee Publishes Method of Calculating Wage Points').

21 February 1952. 'Fan-tui Tao-ch'ieh Kuo-chia Ching-chi Ch'ing-pao ti Tsui-hsing' ('Oppose the Crime of Stealing State Economic Information'), reprinted in *Hsin-hua Yüeh-pao*, No. 3, pp. 4–5.

9 April 1952, p. 1. 'Ta-tan Fang-shou T'i-pa Kan-pu' ('Boldly Set About Promoting Cadres').

6 June 1954. 'Chin-i-pu Kung-ku Lao-tung Chi-lü' ('Further Consolidate Labour Discipline'), in *Hsin-hua Yüeh-pao*, 1954, No. 7, p. 37.

24 September 1965, p. 1. 'Mien Hsiang Pan Tsu, Mien Hsiang Ch'ün-chung, Wei Sheng-ch'an Fu-wu' ('Face the Shifts, Face the Teams, Serve Production').

24 September 1969. 'Intensify Disciplinary Education and Raise Young Workers' Revolutionary Consciousness', in *SCMP*, No. 4510, 6 October 1969, pp. 6–8.

5 April 1972. 'Maintain Placing Proletarian Politics in Command, Strengthen Technical Management in An All-round Manner' in *SCMP*, No. 5116, 19 April 1972, pp. 111–14.

Joint Publications Research Service (Washington). *Wages in Communist China*, Report No. 754, January–June 1957.

Joint Publications Research Service. *Wages, Manpower and Standard of Living in Communist China*, Report No. 1337-N, 12 March 1959, 45 pp.

Kallgren, J. 'Social Welfare and China's Industrial Workers', in Barnett, 1969, pp. 540–73.

Kao Fang-ch'i. 'Wo-men shih Tsen-yang I-K'ao Kung-jen Chieh-chi Kuan-li Kung-ch'ang ti' ('How We Relied Upon the Working Class to Manage the Factory'), in *Kung-jen Ch'u-pan-she*, 1953, pp. 86–101.

Kao Kang, 8 September 1949. 'Jung-yü shih Shu-yü Shei-ti' ('To Whom Belongs the Glory?'), speech to meeting of cadres in the North East, *Kan-pu Hsüeh-hsi Tzu-liao*, No. 2, April 1950, pp. 23–32.

13 March 1950. 'Chan tsai Tung Pei Ching-chi Chien-she ti Tsui Ch'ien-mien' ('Stand at the Forefront of Economic Construction in the North East'), report to 1st conference of Chinese Communist Party members in the North East, *Tung Pei Jih-pao*, 6 June 1950, p. 1.

2 June 1951. 'Tsai Tung Pei Chü Ch'eng-shih Kung-tso Hui-i ti Tsung-chieh' ('Summing up Speech at North East Bureau Urban Work Conference') 18 May–2nd June 1951, *Tung Pei Jih-pao*, 25 June 1951, reprinted in *Hsin-hua Yueh-pao*, Vol. 4, No. 4, 25 August 1951, pp. 839–41.

31 August 1951. 'Fan-tui Tan-wu T'ui-hua, Fan-tui Kuan-liao-chu-i' ('Oppose Graft and Degeneration, Oppose Bureaucratism'), speech to top-level Party members and cadres conference in the North East, *Tung Pei Jih-pao*, 1 December 1951, reprinted in *Chung-kuo Min-chu T'ung-meng Tsung-pu Hsüan-ch'uan Wei-yüan-hui*, 1951, pp. 14–25.

26 October 1951. 'Ch'üan-mien K'ai-chan Tseng-ch'an Chieh-yüeh Yün-tung; Chin-i-pu Shen-ju Fan T'an-wu Fan Lang-fei, Fan Kuan-liao-chu-i ti Tou-cheng' ('Carry Further the Struggle Against Graft Waste and Bureaucratism in the Overall Campaign for Increasing Production and Practising Economy'), speech to top level cadres in the North East, *Tung Pei Jih-pao*, 1 December 1951, reprinted in *Kung-jen Jih-pao*, 1 December 1951, p. 1.

10 January 1952. 'K'o-fu Tzu-ch'an-chieh-chi Ssu-hsiang tui Tang ti Ch'in-shih; Fan-tui Tang-nei ti Yu-ch'ing Ssu-hsiang' ('Overcome

the Corrosion of Bourgeois Ideology; Oppose the Rightist Trend in the Party'), report given at higher level cadres meeting of the Communist Party Central Committee, North East Bureau, *Jen-min Jih-pao*, 24 January 1952 reprinted in *Kan-pu Hsüeh-hsi Tzu-liao*, No. 44, February 1952.

October 1962. 'Ying-chieh Ching chi Chien-she ti Hsin Shih-ch'i' ('Usher in the New Period of Economic Construction'), *Jen-min Jih-pao*, 1 October 1952, reprinted in *Hsin-hua Yüeh-pao*, No. 36, October 1952, pp. 7–10.

Kerr, C., Dunlop, J.T., Harbison, F.H. and Myers, C.A. *Industrialism and Industrial Man*, London, Heinemann, 1962, 317 pp.

King, F. *A Concise Economic History of Modern China (1840–1961)*, New York, Praeger, 1968, 243 pp.

Klein, D. 'The State Council and the Cultural Revolution', *China Quarterly*, No. 35, July–September, 1968.

Klein, D. and Clark, A. *Biographic Dictionary of Chinese Communism 1921–1965*, Cambridge Mass., Harvard University Press, 1971.

Ku Cho-hsin. 'The Development of Planning in Industrial Construction in the Past Decade', *Chi-hua yü T'ung-chi*, No. 13, 1959, translated in *ECMM*, No. 204, 14 March 1960.

Kuan Shui-hsin. 'San nien lai Tung Pei ti Ching-chi Chien-she' ('Economic Construction in the North East in the Past Three Years'), *Chung-kuo Kung-yeh*, Vol. 1, No. 11, 17 March 1950, pp. 18–22.

Kung-jen Ch'u-pan-she. Wu San Kung-ch'ang Kung-hui Kung-tso Ching-yen (The Experiences of Labour Union Work in the Wu San Factory), Peking, March 1953, 188 pp. (1st ed. January 1953).

Kung-jen Jih-pao. 'Ho K'uang-shan Kuan-li shang ti Kuan-liao-chu-i yü Feng-chien Chien-yü Tso Tou-cheng' ('Struggle Against Bureaucratism and Feudal Remnants in Mine Management'), *Chung-kuo Kung-jen*, No. 3, 15 April 1950, p. 9.

Kung-jen Jih-pao. 'K'uang-shan Kuan-li Kuan liao-chu-i yü Feng-chien Chien-yü ti Hou-kuo' ('The Results of Bureaucratism and the [Continued Existence of] Feudal Remnants in Mine Management'), *Chung-kuo Kung-jen*, No. 3, 15 April 1950, p. 11.

25 August 1951, p. 1. 'Chia-ch'ang Ch'üan-kuo Chien-chu Kung-hui Kung-tso' ('Strengthen Labour Union Work in the Building Industry Throughout the Country').

30 August 1951. 'Pei-ching Kung-ying Yung Mao Chien-chu Kung-ch'eng Kung-ssu Kung-hui Ling-tao Kung-jen Ta-tao Feng-chien Pa-t'ou' ('The Labour Union of the Publically-run Yung Mao Building Corporation in Peking Leads the Workers to Overthrow the Feudal Gang-Bosses').

9 January 1952. 'Chin-i-pu Chan-k'ai ho Fei-kung-jen-chieh-chi Ssu-hsiang ti Chan-tou' ('Develop Further the Struggle Against Non-working-class Thought').

9 January 1952. 'Wa-chüeh Fei-kung-jen-chieh-chi ti Ssu-hsiang; Ta-chia lai Hsi-tsao' ('Root Out Non-working-class Thought; Everyone

Take a Bath').
11 January 1952. 'Kung-hui Kan-pu shih Ssu-teng Kan-pu ma' ('Are Labour Union Cadres Fourth Class?').
11 February 1953, p. 1. 'Kuan-ch'e Ch'üan-kuo Tsung-kung-hui Liu-chieh Erh-tz'u Chih-wei K'uo-ta Hui-i ti Chüeh-i; Chi-chi Ying-chieh Ti Ch'i-tz'u Ch'üan-kuo Lao-tung Ta-hui' ('Implement the Resolution of the Enlarged Second Session of the All China Federation of Labour 6th Executive Committee; Actively Greet the Seventh All China Labour Conference').

Kung-jen Jih-pao she. Kung-yün Wen-t'i i-pai-ko, Vol. 1, (*One Hundred Questions on the Labour Movement*), *Kung-jen Jih-pao she*, 1950, (1st ed. December 1949), 72 pp.

Kung ko-hui (Canton Heavy-duty Machine Works Committee). 'Down with Counter-revolutionary Revisionist Yeh Hsiu-ch'ing', in Canton, *Chih-tao Chung Nan*, 21 July 1968, translated in *SCMP*, 4369, 5 March 1969, pp. 7–10.

Kung P'ing-pang. *Hsien-tai Ch'i-yeh Kuan-li* (*Modern Enterprise Management*), T'ai-chung, *San-min Shu-chü*, July 1970.

Kuo-wu-yüan, Fa-chih-chü. Chung-hua Jen-min Kung-ho-kuo Fa-kuei Hui-pien (*Compendium of Laws and Regulations of the People's Republic of China*) Vol. I (September 1954–June 1955), published 1956, 556 pp.

Lai Han-ying. 'Kuan-yü Ch'u-li Ch'ang T'ai-tz'u Wen-t'i ti Tzu-wo Chien-t'ao' ('Self Confession on Dealing with the Question of Ch'ang T'ai-tz'u'), *Tung Pei Jih-pao*, 7 April 1950, reprinted in Shanghai: *Hsin-hua Shu-tien*, pp. 53–4.

Lai Jo-yü, 20 September 1952. 'Ta Kuei-mo Ching-chi Chien-she Ch'ien-yeh ti Chung-kuo Kung-jen-chieh-chi' ('The Chinese Working Class on the Eve of Large Scale Economic Construction'), in *Jen-min Ch'u-pan-she*, December 1952, pp. 151–6.
3 May 1953. 'Wei Wan-ch'eng Kuo-chia Kung-yeh Chien-she ti Jen-wu erh Fen-tou' ('Struggle for the Completion of the Nation's Task of Industrial Construction'), report to the 7th Labour Conference, *Jen-min Jih-pao*, 11 May 1953, pp. 1–2.

Lao-tung Ch'u-pan-she. Shang-hai Kung-hui Chi-ts'eng Tsu-chih Kai-hsüan Kung-tso Tien-ti Ching-yen (*Focal Point Experiences of Re-election of Basic Level Labour Union Organisations in Shanghai*), Shanghai, October 1951, 88 pp.

Lao-tung Ch'u-pan-she, Pien-shen-pu. Ch'i-yeh Kuan-li Min-chu-hua (*The Democratisation of Enterprise Management*), Shanghai, July 1951, 94 pp.

Lao-tung-pu, 15 May 1951. 'Kuan-yü Ko-ti Chao-p'in Chih-kung ti Chan-hsing Kuei-ting' ('Temporary Regulations on Each Area Offering Employment to White and Blue Collar Workers'), in *Cheng-wu-yüan. Ts'ai-cheng Ching-chi Wei-yüan-hui*, Compendium, 1952, Vol. 3, Part 3, p. 1066.

Lao-tung-pu, Kung-tzu-ssu, Shan-tung Kung-tso-tsu. 'Shan-tung Lü-ch'ang T'iao-cheng Kung-tzu ti Ching-yen' ('Experiences of the

Shantung Aluminium Factory in Adjusting Wage Systems'), *Kung-jen Jih-pao*, 6 October 1951, p. 1.

Lenin, V.I. *Selected Works*, Moscow: Progress Publishers, 1967, 3 Vols. 894 + 814 + 912 pp.

'What is to be Done', 1902, *Selected Works*, 1967, Vol. I, pp. 97–256.

'The Immediate Tasks of the Soviet Government', 1918, *Selected Works*, 1967, Vol. II, pp. 643–80.

'Once Again on the Trade Unions, the Current Situation and the Mistakes of Trotsky and Bukharin', 1921, *Selected Works*, 1967, Vol. III, pp. 561–97.

Li Ch'ang-yüan. 'Tsai Hsien-yu ti Chi-ch'u shang T'i-kao I-pu' ('Advance Further Upon the Present Basis'), *Tung Pei Kung-yeh*, No. 81, 1 January 1952, pp. 28–9.

Li Cho-jen, 26 May 1950. 'Tsai Tung Pei Kung K'uang Ch'i-yeh Hsüan-ch'uan Ku-tung Kung-tso Hui-i shang ti Chiang-hua' ('Speech at the Work Conference on Agitprop Work in Industrial and Mining Enterprises in the North East'), *Tung Pei Jih-pao*, 3 June 1950, reprinted in *Shang-hai Tsung-kung-hui, Wen-chiao-pu*, 1950, pp. 7–13.

Li Choh-ming. *The Statistical System of Communist China*, Berkeley and Los Angeles, University of California Press, 1962, 149 pp.

Li Hsiu-jen. ' "8,000 li Hurried Tour of Inspection" report on Inspection of Ten Cities along the Peking-Canton Railway', *Kung-jen Jih-pao*, 9 May 1957 in *JPRS*, 665 (summary), pp. 33–6.

Li Hsüeh-feng, 24 September 1956. Speech to Eighth Party Congress, in *Chung-kuo Kung-ch'an-tang Chung-yang Wei-yüan-hui Pan-kung-t'ing*, 1957, pp. 457–64.

Li Li-san, 25 August 1948. 'Kuan-yü Chung-hua Ch'üan-kuo Tsung-kung-hui Chang-ch'eng' ('On the Charter of the All China Federation of Labour') report of this speech in *Chieh-fang-she*, 1949, pp. 33–4.

29 June 1950. 'Kuan-yü Chung-hua Jen-min Kung-ho-kuo Kung-hui-fa Ts'ao-an ti Chi-tien Shuo-ming' ('Explanation of Some Points in the Draft Labour Union Law of the People's Republic of China'), in *Cheng-wu-yüan, Ts'ai-cheng Ching-chi Wei-yüan-hui*, Compendium, 1960, Vol. I, Part 2, pp. 655–64.

17 November 1950. 'Report to 59th Meeting of Government Affairs Council on the National Congress of Model Workers' (held in Peking from 25 September to 2 October 1950 together with the National Conference of Combat Heroes), *CB*, No. 54, 12 January 1951, pp. 1–4.

'K'ai-chan Lao-tung Ching-sai Ch'ing-chu Tang ti San-shih chou-nien Chi-nien' ('Develop Labour Competitions to Celebrate the Thirtieth Anniversary of the Party'), *Kung-jen Jih-pao*, 1 July 1951, p. 5.

Li Lung. 'Wei-shen-mo Pi-hsü K'o-fu (Kung-ch'en) Ssu-hsiang' ('Why Must We Overcome the Ideology of the Meritorious'), letter to the editor of *Hsüeh-hsi*, Vol. 3, No. 7, 1 January 1951, p. 8.

Li Mao-ch'i. 'Mo-fan Lu-chang Li Shao-k'uei Tsen-yang Ling-tao Sheng-ch'an' ('How The Model Furnace Chief Li Shao-k'uei Led Production'), *Chung-kung-yeh T'ung-hsün*, No. 35, 11 December 1953, p. 15.

Li T'ao and Lin Keng. *Hsüeh-hui Kuan-li Ch'i-yeh chung ti Chi-ko Wen-t'i* (*Some Questions on Learning How to Manage an Enterprise*), Tientsin, *Tu-che Shu-tien*, April 1950, 78 pp.

Lieberthal, K. 'Mao Versus Liu? Policy Towards Industry and Commerce 1946–9', *China Quarterly*, No. 47, July–September 1971, pp. 494–520.

'The Suppression of Secret Societies in Post Liberation Tientsin', *China Quarterly*, No. 54, April–June 1973, pp. 242–66.

Lin Chiang-yün. 'Certain Problems in the Control of Labour Power', *Lao-tung*, No. 11, November 1955, translated in *ECMM*, No. 27, 12 March 1956, pp. 22–6.

Lin Li. 'Yang Ch'üan Kuo-ying Mei-k'uang Tsun-tsai ti Yen-chung Wen-t'i' ('The Serious Problems that Exist at the Yang Ch'üan State Coal Mines'), *Chung-kuo Kung-jen*, No. 3, 15 April 1950, pp. 12–13 (originally in *Jen-min Jih-pao*).

'Yang Ch'üan Kuo-ying Mei-k'uang Wei-shen-mo Pao-hu Pa-t'ou-chih' ('Why the Gang-Boss System was Maintained in the Yang Ch'üan State Coal Mines'), *Chung-kuo Kung-jen*, No. 3, 15 April 1950, pp. 14 and 13.

Lindsay, M. 'The Taxation System of the Shensi–Chahar–Hopei Border Region 1938–45', *China Quarterly*, No. 42, April–June 1970, pp. 1–15.

Ling Hua-ch'un. [an account of] '(Kung-yeh-pu) Kuan-yü Kung-ch'ang Kuan-li Wei-yüan-hui Yen-chiu Pao-kao' ('Research Report of the [North East People's Government], Industrial Department on Factory Management Committees'), *Tung Pei Kung-yeh*, No. 56, 21 April 1951, pp. 19–21. Note in issue No. 57, 1 May 1951, a corrigendum appeared (p. 27) removing the characters *Kung-yeh-pu* (North East People's Government Industrial Department) from the title.

Liu Ch'ang-sheng. 'Kuan-yü Kung-hui Kung-tso' ('On Labour Union Work'), in *Shang-hai Tsung-kung-hui, Wen-chiao-pu*, June 1950, pp. 21–31.

Liu Ch'ang-sheng (ed.). *Chung-kuo Kung-ch'an-tang yü Shang-hai Kung-jen* (*The Chinese Communist Party and the Shanghai Workers*, Shanghai: *Lao-tung Ch'u-pan-she*, August 1951, 88 pp.

Liu Ch'en-jui, Hung Sui-chih, Yang Chen, Kang Tso-wu and Ko Ling-p'ing. ('Contradiction in the Piece-wage System Enforced in Industrial Enterprises'), *Chiao-hsüeh yü Yen-chiu*, No. 9, 1958, in *ECMM*, No. 153, 12 January 1956, p. 17.

Liu Chih-ming. 'Ch'i-yeh Hsüan-ch'uan Ku-tung Kung-tso chung ti Chi-ko Wen-t'i' ('Several Questions on Agitprop Work in Enterprises'), in *Shang-hai Tsung-kung-hui, Wen-chiao-pu*, 1950, pp. 14–24.

Liu Hsien-shu. 'Yao Cheng-chüeh Tui-tai Kuo-chia Chi-hua, Sheng-ch'an Kuo-chia Hsü-yao ti Ch'an-p'in' ('Treat the State Plan Correctly and Turn Out Products Which the State Needs'), letter to the editor of *Chung-kung-yeh T'ung-hsün*, No. 20, 11 July 1953, pp. 41–2.

Liu Pao. 'Pi-hsü Ta-tao Chi-shu Jen-yüan Ssu-hsiang shang ti Ti-jen' ('We Must Overthrow the Enemy in the Thinking of Technical Personnel'), *Tung Pei Kung-yeh*, No. 91, 11 April 1952, p. 40.

Liu Shao-ch'i. 'Tsai Hua Pei Chih-kung Tai-piao-hui-i shang Kuan-yü Kung-hui Kung-tso Wen-t'i ti Pao-kao' ('Report On Labour Union Work to North China Congress of White and Blue Collar Workers'), May 1949, originally published in Red Guard publication *Liu Shao-ch'i Wu-ko Ts'ai-liao* (1967), and reprinted in Taipei, *Chung-kung Yen-chiu Tsa-chih she*, 1970, pp. 200–7.

'Tsai Kan-pu Hui-shang ti Chiang-hua' ('Speech to Cadre Conference'), May 1949, originally in *Liu Shao-ch'i Wu-ko Ts'ai-liao* (1967) and reprinted in Taipei, *Chung-kung Yen-chiu Tsa-chih she*, 1970, pp. 207–20.

Liu Shao-ch'i et al. *Hsin-min-chu-chu-i Ch'eng-shih Cheng-ts'e* (*New Democratic Urban Policy*), Hong Kong, *Hsin-min-chu Ch'u-pan-she*, August 1949, 198 pp.

Liu Ta-chung and Yeh Kung-chia. *The Economy of the Chinese Mainland: National Income and Economic Development 1933–1959*, Princeton NJ: Princeton University Press, 1965, 771 pp.

Liu Tzu-chiu. 'Lun Ch'ang k'uang Ch'i-yeh chung Min-chu Kai-ko ti Pu-k'o Wen-t'i' ('On the Question of the Supplementary Lesson of Democratic Reform in Factory and Mining Enterprises'), *Kung-jen Jih-pao*, 12 September 1951.

Lo Han. 'Pi-hsü an Shang-ch'an Ch'ü-yü Kuan-li-chih ti Yüan-tse lai Tsu-chih Tiao-tu Kung-tso' ('Production Order Work Must Be Organised According to the Principles of the Production Territorial Management System') (a summary of experiences discussed at the An-kang forum on Production order work), *Chung-kung-yeh T'ung-hsün*, No. 34, 1 December 1953, p. 26.

Lokshin, E. (Chinese Translation of Russian original) 'Ch'i-yeh nei ti I-chang-chih' ('The One-Man Management System in the Enterprise'), in *Ta-chung Shu-tien*, 1950, pp. 31–55.

Lü Tung. 'Chia-ch'iang Tse-jen-chih, T'i-kao Kung-ch'eng Chih-liang Wei Wan-ch'eng I-chiu-wu-erh-nien ti Kung-ch'eng Chi-hua erh Fen-tou' ('Strengthen the Responsibility System, Improve the Quality of Construction Work and Struggle for the Completion of the Construction Plan for 1952'), *Tung Pei Kung-yeh*, No. 99, 1 July 1952, pp. 1–6.

Ma Heng-chang. 'Letter to Chairman Mao to Commemorate 30th Anniversary of the Founding of the Chinese Communist Party', *NCNA*, Peking, 30 June 1951, in *SCMP*, 127, 1–3 July 1951, p. 15.

MacDougall, C. 'Second Class Workers', *Far Eastern Economic Review*,

LX, No. 19, 9 May 1968, pp. 306–8.

Mao Tse-tung. *Hsüan-chi* (*Selected Works*), Peking, *Jen-min Ch'u-pan-she*, 4 Vols., 1951, 1952, 1953 and 1960.

Mao Tse-tung Chu-tso Hsüan-tu Chia-chung-pen (*Selected Readings from Mao Tse-tung's Works* (*first selection*), Peking, *Jen-min Ch'u-pan-she*, 1965, 526 pp.

Mao Chu-hsi Yü-lu (*Quotations from Chairman Mao*), Peking, *Chung-kuo Jen-min Chieh-fang-chün Tsung-cheng-chih-pu* (People's Liberation Army General Political Department), August 1965.

Untitled Collection, no publication details, Red Guard source, 38 pp.

Mao Tse-tung Ssu-hsiang Wan-sui (*Long Live Mao Tse-tung Thought*), no publication details, Red Guard source, April 1967, 46 pp.

Mao Chu-hsi Wen-hsüan (*Selections from Chairman Mao*), no publication details, Red Guard source, 120 pp.

Mao Tse-tung Chi (*Collected Writings of Mao Tse-tung*), Vol. 8, Tokyo: Hokubosha, 1971, 354 pp.

December 1942. 'Ching-chi Wen-t'i yü Ts'ai-cheng Wen-t'i' ('Economic and Financial Problems') report to higher levels cadres meeting of the Shen Kan Ning Border Region. *Mao Tse-tung Hsüan-chi*, 1944 edition, Vol. 4, 1947 edition, Vol. 5, reprinted in *Mao Tse-tung Chi*, 1971, pp. 259–75.

1 June 1943. 'Kuan-yü Ling-tao Fang-fa ti Jo-kan Wen-t'i' ('Some Questions Concerning Methods of Leadership'), *Hsüan-chi*, Vol. III, pp. 899–904. *Selected Works* (English), Vol. III, pp. 117–22.

11 June 1945. 'Yü Kung Yi Shan' ('The Foolish Old Man Who Removed the Mountains'), *Hsüan-chi*, Vol. III, pp. 1101–1104. *Selected Works* (English), Vol. III, pp. 321–4.

25 December 1947. 'Mu-ch'ien Hsing-shih ho Wo-men ti Jen-wu' ('The Present Situation and Our Tasks') in collection of articles of same title, 1949, pp. 20–41.

27 February 1948. 'Kuan-yü Kung-shang-yeh Cheng-ts'e' ('On the Policy Concerning Industry and Commerce') *Hsüan-chi*, Vol. IV, pp. 1283–1284, *Selected Works* (English), Vol. IV, pp. 203–5.

Mao Tse-tung et al. *Mu-ch'ien Hsing-shih ho Wo-men ti Jen-wu* (*The Present Situation and Our Tasks*), *Chieh-fang-she*, November 1949, 188 pp.

Mao Tse-tung, 6 June 1950. 'Wei Cheng-ch'ü Kuo-chia Ts'ai-cheng Ching-chi Chuang-k'uang ti Chi-pan Hao-chuan erh Tou-cheng' ('Struggle for the Attainment of a Basic Turn for the Better in the National Financial and Economic Situation'), speech to 3rd Plenum of the 7th Central Committee, *Jen-min Jih-pao*, 13 June 1950.

27 February 1957. 'Kuan-yü Cheng-ch'üeh Ch'u-li Jen-min Nei-pu Mao-tun Wen-t'i' ('On the Correct Handling of Contradictions Among the People'), in *Mao Tse-tung Chu-tso Hsüan-tu Chia-chung-pen*, pp. 448–99.

31 January 1958. 'Kung-tso Fang-fa Liu-shih t'iao (ts'ao-an)' ('Sixty Work Methods [draft]') in untitled collection of writings of Mao,

pp. 29–38.

31 January 1958. 'Kuan-yü Hung Chuan Wen-t'i ti Chih-shih' ('Directive on the Question of Red and Expert'), in *Mao Tse-tung Ssu-hsiang Wan-sui*, 1967, p. 17.

28 June 1958. 'Speech at the Group Leaders Forum of the Enlarged Conference of the Military Affairs Commission' from a Red Guard pamphlet *Mao Chu-hsi Tui P'eng, Huang, Chang, Chou Fan-Tang Chi-t'uan ti P'i-p'an* (*Chairman Mao's Denunciation of the P'eng, Huang, Chang, Chou Anti Party Clique*), translated in *Chinese Law and Government*, Vol. I, No. 4, Winter 1968–9, p. 19.

January 1962. 'Min-chu Chi-chung-chih' ('Democratic Centralism') speech to 7,000 Cadre Conference in *Mao Chu-hsi Wen-hsüan*, pp. 64–78.

24 September 1962. 'Speech at the Tenth Plenary Session of the Eighth Central Committee' in *Chinese Law and Government*, Vol. I, No. 4, Winter 1968–9. pp. 88–9.

Mavor, J. *An Economic History of Russia*, 2 vols, New York, Russell and Russell, 1965 (first published 1914).

Meisner, Mitch. 'The Shenyang Transformer Factory – a Profile', *China Quarterly*, No. 52, October–December 1972, pp. 717–37.

Moore, Barrington Jr. *Political Power and Social Theory*, New York, Harper Torchbooks, 1958 (1965), 243 pp.

Myrdal, G. *The Challenge of World Poverty: A World Anti-Poverty Programme in Outline*, Harmondsworth, Penguin Books (Pelican), 1971, 464 pp. first published 1970.

NCNA (Talien). 20 July 1951. 'Women Crew of March 8th Locomotive Take up Challenge of Soviet Sisters', in *SCMP*, 199, 20–1 July 1951, p. 11.

P'an Heng-yü. 'Shen-yang Ye-lien-ch'ang Kung-tzu Kung-tso chung Tsun-tsai-che Ching-chi-chu-i P'ing-chün-chu-i Hsien-hsiang' ('There Exists the Phenomena of Economism and Egalitarianism in Wage Work at the Shenyang Smelting Works'), *Chung-kung-yeh T'ung-hsün*' No. 69 (33), 21 November 1954, p. 27.

Pei-ching Shih-fan Ta-hsüeh Li-shih-hsi. Men-t'ou-kou Mei-K'uang Shih-kao (*Draft History of the Men-t'ou-kou Coal Mine*), Peking, *Jen-min ch'u-pan-she*, September 1958, 128 pp.

Pei-ching-shih, Tsung-kung-hui Wu-chin Kung-tso Wei-yüan-hui. 'Kuan-ch'e Kung-ch'ang Kuan-li Min-chu-hua' ('Implement the Democratisation of Factory Management), in *Lao-tung Ch'u-pan-she, Pien-shen-pu*, 1951, pp. 22–7.

Pei-p'ing Chieh-fang-pao, 25 March 1949. 'Chung Kung Ch'i-chieh Erh-chung Ch'üan-hui Wan-man Pi-mu' ('The Second Plenum of the 7th Central Committee Closes').

Peking Foreign Languages Press. The Trade Union Law of the People's Republic of China, Peking, 1951, 38 pp.

Labour Laws and Regulations of the Chinese People's Republic, Peking, 1956.

The Great Socialist Cultural Revolution in China, No. 3, Peking, 1966, 21 pp.

Peking Review. 1970, No. 14, p. 11. 'Long Live the Victory of the Constitution of Anshan Iron and Steel Company'.

1970, No. 16, p. 3. 'Constitution of Anshan Iron and Steel Company Spurs Revolution and Production'.

Perkins, D. 'Industrial Planning and Management' in Eckstein, Galenson and Liu (eds.), 1968.

Pfiffner, J.M. and Sherwood, F.P. *Administrative Organisation*, Englewood Cliffs N.J., Prentice Hall, 1960, 481 pp.

Richman, B. *Industrial Society in Communist China*, New York, Random House, 1969, 968 pp.

Salaff, J. 'The Urban Communes and Anti-City Experiment in Communist China', *China Quarterly*, No. 29, January–March 1967, pp. 82–110.

Schapiro, L. *The Communist Party of the Soviet Union*, New York, Random House, 1960, 631 pp.

Schapiro, L. and Lewis, J. 'The Role of the Monolithic Party under the Totalitarian Leader' in Lewis *Party Leadership and Revolutionary Power in China*, London, Cambridge University Press, 1970, pp. 114–45.

Schram, S. *The Political Thought of Mao Tse-tung* (enlarged and revised edition), Harmondsworth, Penguin Books (Pelican), 1969, 479 pp.

Schram, S. (ed.). *Authority, Participation and Cultural Change in China*, London, Cambridge University Press, 1973, 350 pp.

Schran, P. *The Structure of Income in Communist China*, Unpublished PhD. dissertation in Economics, University of California, Berkeley, 1961, 374 pp.

Schurmann, H.F. 'China's "New Economic Policy" – Transition or Beginning', *China Quarterly*, 1964, No. 17, pp. 65–91.

Ideology and Organisation in Communist China, Berkeley and Los Angeles: University of California Press, 1966, 540 pp.

Unpublished manuscript on industrial management in China.

Selden, M. *The Yenan Way in Revolutionary China*, Cambridge Mass., Harvard University Press, 1971, 311 pp.

Selznick, P. *Leadership in Administration: A Sociological Interpretation*, Evanston Ill., Row, Peterson, 1957, 162 pp.

Shanghai (no publisher stated). *Chieh-fang-hou Shang-hai Kung-yün Tzu-liao* (*Materials on the Shanghai Workers Movement after Liberation*) (May–December 1949), Hong Kong, reprint, no date, 254 pp.

Shanghai *Hsin-hua Shu-tien. Fan-tui Kuan-liao-chu-i* (*Oppose Bureaucratism*), September 1950.

Shang-hai Jen-min Kuang-po Tien-t'ai. 'Kuang-po shih Hsüan-ch'uan Kutung ti Yu-li Wu-ch'i' ('Broadcasting is a Powerful Weapon in Agitprop') in *Shang-hai Tsung-kung-hui, Wen-chiao-pu*, 1950, pp. 91–4.

Shang-hai Kung-jen Ko-ming Tsao-fan Tsung-ssu-ling-pu. 'Kung-ch'ang

Ch'i-yeh Kuan-li shang Liang-t'iao Lu-hsien ti Tou-cheng' ('The Struggle Between the Two Lines in the Management of Factory Enterprises'), *Kung-jen Tsao-fan pao* (*Workers' Rebel Newspaper*), No. 187, 28 November 1968.

Shang-hai-shih Jen-min-cheng-fu Lao-tung-chü. Lao-tung Shou-ts'e (*Labour Handbook*), Shanghai, *Hua Tung Jen-min Ch'u-pan-she*, 1951, 230 pp.

Shang-hai Tsung-kung-hui, Wen-chiao-pu. Ch'üan-kuo Kung-hui Kung-tso Hui-i (*T'e-chi*) (*All China Conference on Labour Union Work* [*Special Edition*]), Shanghai, *Lao-tung Ch'u-pan-she*, June 1950, 100 pp.

Kung-ch'ang chung ti Hsüan-ch'uan Ku-tung Kung-tso (*Agitprop Work in Factories*) Shanghai, *Lao-tung Ch'u-pan-she*, October 1950, 196 pp.

'Chia-ch'iang Kung-ch'ang Hsüan-ch'uan Ku-tung Kung-tso' ('Strengthen Agitprop Work in Factories'), preface to *Shang-hai Tsung-kung-hui, Wen-chiao-pu*, October 1950, pp. 1–3.

Shang-hai Wan-yeh Shu-tien. Hui-ch'ang Pu-chih-fa (*The Layout of a Meeting Hall*), 20 May 1952 (1st edn.), 26 July 1952.

Shao Li-sheng. 'Ko-jen Ching-chi Ho-suan-chih' ('The Individual Economic Accounting System'), *Chung-kuo Kung-yeh*, Vol. 2, No. 11, 24 March 1950, pp. 21–8.

Shenyang (no author). 'Shen-yang ti Chieh-shou ho Hui-fu Kung-tso ti Ch'eng-kung Ching-yen' ('The Successful Experiences in Take-over and Rehabilitation Work in Shenyang'), in *Hsin-hua Shu-tien*, 1949 (?), pp. 104–5.

Sheridan, M. 'The Emulation of Heroes', *China Quarterly*, No. 47, January–March 1968, pp. 47–72.

Simon, H. *Administrative Behaviour: A Study of Decision Making Processes in Administrative Organisation*, New York, MacMillan, 1950.

South Manchurian Railway Company. 'Labour Management at the Fushun Coal Mines', *Contemporary Manchuria*, Vol. II, No. 5, September 1938.

State Statistical Bureau. *Ten Great Years, Statistics of the Economic and Cultural Achievements of the People's Republic of China*, Peking Foreign Languages Press, 1960.

Sun Yeh-fang. 'Ts'ung "Tsung-ch'an-chih" T'an-ch'i' ('Speaking of "Gross Value" of Output'), *T'ung-chi Kung-tso*, No. 13, 14 July 1957, pp. 8–14.

Ta-chung Shu-tien (Peking). *Kuan-yü Ch'i-yeh Kuan-li Wen-t'i* (*On Problems of Enterprise Management*), a collection of articles translated from Russian, May 1950.

Tai Chi-ying. 'Kuan-ch'e She-hui-chu-i Kai-ko, Kung-ku ho K'uo-ta Fan Feng-chien Chan-hsien' ('Consolidate and Enlarge the Anti Feudal United Front'), *Ho-nan Jih-pao*, 22 July 1951, reprinted in *Kan-pu Hsüeh-hsi Tzu-liao*, No. 37.

Taira Koji. *Economic Development and the Labor Market in Japan*,

New York and London, Columbia University Press, 1970, 280 pp.

T'ao Chih-ch'üan. 'Shang-hai Ko Kung-hui Chi-ts'eng Tsu-chih Ch'ung-fen Fa-yang Min-chu, P'u-pien Chin-hsing Kai-hsüan' ('Each Basic Level Labour Union Organisation in Shanghai Promotes Democracy and Carries out Universal Re-election'), *Kung-jen Jih-pao*, 3 November 1951.

Tawney, R.H. *Land and Labour in China*, London, George Allen and Unwin, 1932, 207 pp.

Taylor, F.W. *The Principles of Scientific Management*, New York, Harper, 1913, 144 pp.

'Shop Management' (1911) in F. Taylor *Scientific Management*, New York, Harper and Row, 1947 (10th ptg), pp. 1–207.

Teng T'o. 'Cheng-feng Yün-tung tsai Kuo-chia Chien-she Kung-tso chung ti Chung-yao-hsing' ('The Importance of the Rectification Movement in National Construction Work'). *Hsüeh-hsi*, Vol. 2, No. 11, 16 August 1950, pp. 3–5.

Teng Tzu-hui. 'Chung Nan Kung-ying Kung-k'uang-yeh Chin-hou San Ta Jen-wu yü Ch'i-yeh Kuan-li Min-chu-hua' ('The Three Major Tasks Facing Publically-run Industry and Mining in the Central South and the Democratisation of Enterprise Management'), *Kan-pu Hsüeh-hsi Tzu-liao*, No. 9, May 1950.

Teng Tzu-hui, 30 July 1950. 'Kuan-yü Kung-hui Kung-tso chung ti San-ko Chi-pen Wen-t'i' ('On the Three Basic Questions in Labour Union Work'), report to an enlarged meeting of the preparatory committee for labour unions in the Central South Region, *Chung-kuo Kung-jen*, No. 8, September 1950, pp. 1–5.

Ting Tan and Chou Su-chen. 'Wu-ch'ang Chen-huan Sha-ch'ang T'ui-hsing Ai-kuo Kung-yüeh ti Ching-kuo' ('The Experiences of the Chen Huan [World Shaking] Spinning Mill in Wuch'ang in Promoting Patriotic Compacts'), *Ta Kung Pao*, 5 July 1951, reprinted in *Chung Nan Jen-min Ch'u-pan-she*, September 1951, pp. 42–7.

de Tocqueville, A. *Democracy In America* (abridged by R.D. Heffner), Mentor Books, 1956.

Trotsky, L. *The Revolution Betrayed*, New York. Pioneer Publishers, 1945, 308 pp.

Tung Pei Hsing-cheng Wei-yüan-hui, 7 September 1948. 'Tung Pei Chan-shih Kung-ying Ch'i-yeh Kung-hsin Piao-chun' ('Wartime Wage and Salary Standards for Publically-run Enterprises in the North East'), in *Cheng-wu-yüan, Ts'ai-cheng Ching-chi Wei-yüan-hui*, Compendium, 1950, Vol. I, Part 2, pp. 710–13.

Tung Pei Jen-min Cheng-fu, 19 June 1950. 'Kuan-yü T'iao-cheng Kung-ying Ch'an-yeh Kung-jen, Chi-shu Jen-yüan Kung-hsin chi Kai-hsing Pa-chi Kung-tzu-chih ti Chih-shih' ('Directive on Adjusting Wages for Industrial Workers and Technical Personnel in Public Enterprises and Altering Grading to the Eight Grade System'), *Chung-kuo Kung-jen*, No. 7, August 1950, p. 50.

7 July 1950. 'Wei Chih-hsing T'iao-cheng Kung-ying Ch'i-yeh

Kung-jen Chi-shu Jen-yüan chi Kai-hsing Pa-chi King-tzu-chih chung Jo-kan Wen-t'i ti Chih-shih' ('Directive on Certain Questions in Carrying out the Adjustment of the Wages of Workers and Technical Personnel in Publically-run Enterprises and Altering Grading to the Eight Grade System'), *Chung-kuo Kung-jen*, No. 7, August 1950, p. 51,

18 September 1950. 'Kuan-yü Kung-ying Ch'i-yeh Chien-ting Chi-t'i Ho-t'ung ti Chih-shih' ('Directive on Concluding Collective Contracts in Publically-run Enterprises'), *Lao-tung Kung-pao*, No. 6, January 1951, pp. 27–8.

Tung Pei Jen-min Cheng-fu, Kung-yeh-pu, 6 October 1949, 'Kuan-yü Chi-hsü Kuan-ch'e Ching-chi Ho-suan-chih ti Chih-shih' ('Directive on the Continued Implementation of the Economic Accounting System'), *Tung Pei Jih-pao*, 6 October 1949, reprinted in *Jen-min Jih-pao*, 14 October 1949, p. 2, and *Chung-kuo Kung-jen*, Vol. 1, No. 1, 15 February 1950, pp. 25–7.

6 October 1949. 'Kuan-yü K'ai-chan Ch'ün-chung-hsing Ch'uang-tsao Sheng-ch'an Hsin Chi-lu ti Chüeh-ting' ('Decision on Developing the Movement of a Movement of a mass Nature to Establish New Production Records'), *Jen-min Jih-pao*, 15 October 1949, p. 2, and *Chung-kuo Kung-jen*, Vol. 1, No. 1, 15 February 1950.

23 November 1949. 'Kuan-yü tsai Ch'uang Hsin Chi-lu Yün-tung chung Fang-chih P'ien-hsiang ti T'ung-pao' ('Communication of Preventing [Certain] Tendencies in the Movement to Create New Records'), *Chung-kuo Kung-jen*, Vol. 1, No. 1, 15 February 1950, p. 32.

28 February 1950. 'Kuan-yü Sheng-ch'an Tse-jen-chih ti Chüeh-ting' ('Decision on the Production Responsibility System'), in *Chung-hua Ch'üan-kuo Tsung-kung-hui, Sheng-ch'an-pu*, May 1950, pp. 207–12.

18 March 1950. 'Kuan-yü Chia-ch'iang An-ch'üan Tse-jen-chih Chin-hsing Pao-an Ta Chien-ch'a Chih-shih' ('Directive on Strengthening the System of Responsibility for Safety and Carrying out a Large Scale Inspection of Safety Measures'), *Lao-tung Kung-pao*, No. 2, May 1950, p. 21.

'Kung-ch'eng Chi-shu Jen-yüan Chih-tse Chan-hsing T'iao-li' ('Temporary Regulations concerning the Responsibilities of Engineering and Technical Personnel'), *Tung Pei Kung-yeh*, No. 54, 1 April 1951, pp. 7–8.

18 June 1952. 'Kuan-yü Mu-ch'ien Chi-pen Chien-she Kung-tso ti Chih-shih' ('Directive on Current Basic Construction Work'), *Tung Pei Kung-yeh*, No. 98, 21 June 1952, pp. 1–4.

Tung Pei Jen-min Cheng-fu Kung-yeh-pu Chü-chang Ching-li Lien-hsi Hui-i, 7 December 1949. 'Tao-lun Hsin Chi-lu Yün-tung ti Chieh-lun' ('Conclusions of Discussion of the Movement to Create New Records'), *Chung-kuo Kung-jen*, Vol. 1, No. 1, 15 February 1950, p. 36.

Tung Pei Jen-min Cheng-fu Kung-yeh-pu, Pan-kung-shih, Yen-chiu-k'o.

'Ko Tan-wei tsai Chia-ch'iang Ch'e-chien Kuan-li Fang-mien Tso-le Na-hsieh Kung-tso' ('What Work Has Been Done by Each Unit with Regard to Strengthening Shop Management?'), *Tung Pei Kung-yeh*, No. 58, 11 May 1951, pp. 37–8.

Tung Pei Jen-min Cheng-fu Kung-yeh-pu, Tien-yeh Kuan-li Tsung-chü. 'Hsin Chi-lu Yün-tung ti Ch'u-pu Tsung-chieh' ('Initial Summary of the Movement to Create New Records'), *Chung-kuo Kung-jen*, Vol. 1, No. 1, 15 February 1950, pp. 38–40.

Tung Pei Jih-pao, 6 October 1949. 'Chan-k'ai Ch'uang Chi-lu Yün-tung' ('Develop The Movement to Create Records'), reprinted in *Chung-kuo Kung-jen*, Vol. 1, No. 1, 15 February 1950, p. 31.

4 March 1950. 'Kuan-ch'e Sheng-ch'an Tse-jen-chih shih Mu-ch'ien Kai-chin Kung-yeh Kuan-li ti Kuan-lien' ('Implementing the Production Responsibility System is the key to Advancing Industrial Management at the Present Time'), in *Chung-hua Ch'üan-kuo Tsung-kung-hui Sheng-ch'an-pu*, May 1950, pp. 212–15.

3 April 1950. 'Fan-tui Ch'i-yeh Kuan-li chung ti Pu Min-chu yü Kuan-liao-chu-i Tsò-feng' ('Oppose an Undemocratic Bureaucratic Working-style in Enterprise Management'), reprinted in Shanghai, *Hsin-hua Shu-tien*, 1950, pp. 50–2.

3 April 1950. 'Pen-hsi Mei-t'ieh Kung-ssu Mei-k'uang-pu Kung-jen Ch'ang T'ai-tz'u Chieh-fa Ling-tao Pu Min-chu ti Ching-kuo ho Tiao-ch'a Chieh-lun' ('The Circumstances of the Disclosure of a Lack of Democracy on the Party of the Leadership by Ch'ang T'ai-tz'u a Worker in the Coal Mining Department of the Penki Coal and Iron Corporation and the Conclusions of an Investigation') (amended slightly to give background information and reprinted in Shanghai, *Hsin-hua Shu-tien*, 1950, pp. 37–9.

7 April 1950. 'Ju-ho Kuan-ch'e Ching-chi Ho-suan-chih' ('How to Implement the Economic Accounting System'), *Chung-kuo Kung-yeh*, Vol. 1, No. 12, 14 April 1950, pp. 37–8.

'An-tung Tsao-chih-ch'ang Yüan-liao-k'o Chih-pu Sheng-li ti T'ui-chin-le Ch'uang Chi-lu Yün-tung' ('The Party Branch of the Raw Materials Department of the Antung Paper Works Promotes Successfully the Movement to Create Records') reprinted in *Chung-kuo Kung-jen*, Vol. 1, No. 3, 15 April 1950, pp. 32–3.

'Kung-ch'eng Chi-shu Jen-yüan Chih-tse T'iao-li – I-ko Chi wei Chung-yao ti Cheng-ts'e Wen-t'i' ('Regulations Concerning the Responsibilities of Engineering and Technical Personnel – An Extremely Important Policy Question'), reprinted in *Tung Pei Kung-yeh*, No. 54, 1 April 1951, pp. 5–6.

'Tung Pei Kung-hui Kung-tso Hsü Chin-i-pu Chia-ch'iang' ('Labour Union Work in the North East Should be Further Strengthened'), reprinted in *Jen-min Jih-pao*, 9 July 1951, p. 2.

'Chien-ch'a Ai-kuo Kung-yüeh Chiu-cheng Hu-shih Cheng-chih Ch'ing-hsiang' ('Investigate Patriotic Compacts and Rectify the Tendency to Overlook Politics'), reprinted in *Jen-min Jih-pao*,

14 July 1951, p. 1.

6 December 1951. 'Kao Kang T'ung-chih Chih-shih Chia-ch'iang Kung-ch'ang Ch'e-chien Kung-ts'o' ('Comrade Kao Kang Issues Directive on Strengthening Work in the Shops'), reprinted in *Hsin-hua Yüeh-pao*, 1952, No. 1, p. 149.

Tung Pei Kung-yeh, No. 84, 1 February 1952, p. 15. 'Pu-chun Ya-chih Min-chu' ('It is Forbidden to Suppress Democracy').

No. 87, 1 March 1952, pp. 12–14. 'Chi-pen Chien-she Pu-men ti T'an-wu Fen-tzu Tsen-yang Chin-hsing T'an-wu' ('How Corrupt Elements Practise their Corruption in Basic Construction Departments').

T'ung-chi Kung-tso T'ung-hsün Tzu-liao-shih. 'Kuan-yü Wo-kuo She-hui-chu-i Kung-yeh-hua ti Chi-ko Wen-t'i' ('Some Questions in our Country's Socialist Industrialisation'), *Hsin-hua Pan-yueh-k'en*, No. 99, 1957, pp. 67–71.

Vogel, E. 'From Revolutionary to Semi Bureaucrat: The Regularisation of Cadres', *China Quarterly*, No. 29, January–March 1967, pp. 36–60.

Canton Under Communism: Programmes and Politics in a Provincial Capital 1949–1968, New York, Harper Torchbooks, 1971, 448 pp. Originally published Harvard University Press, 1969.

Wang Ch'i-fan and Li Tsu-yin. 'Tsen-yang Fang-chih T'ieh-lu Kung-jen Chia-pan Chia-tien' ('How to Stop Extra Shifts and Overtime for Railway Workers'), *Kung-jen Jih-pao*, 29 August, 1951, p. 4.

Wang Chih-fang. 'Wan-ch'eng Sheng-ch'an Tsung-chih Pu Teng-yü Ch'üan-mien Wan-ch'eng Kuo-chia Chi-hua' ('Fulfilling the Gross Value of Production Target Does Not Equal the Complete Fulfilment of the State Plan'), *Chung-kung-yeh T'ung-hsün*, No. 8, 11 March 1953, pp. 20–1.

Wang Ho-shou, 9 February 1952. 'K'o-fu Fan T'an-wu Fan Lang-fei Fan Kuan-liao-chu-i Yün-tung chung ti Yu-ch'ing Ssu-hsiang' ('Overcome Rightist Thinking in the Movement to Oppose Graft, Waste and Bureaucratism'), report to meeting of cadres of North East People's Government Industrial Department, *Tung Pei Kung-yeh*, No. 85, 11 February 1952, pp. 1–4.

Wang Hung-wen, 24 August 1973. 'Report on the Revision of the Party Constitution' delivered at 10th National Congress of the Chinese Communist Party. Adopted 28 August 1973, *Peking Review*, Nos. 35–6, 7 September 1973, pp. 29–33.

Wang Tzu-mien. 'Shih-ching-shan Fa-tien-ch'ang Shih-hsing Pa-chi Kung-tzu-chih ti Ching-yen' ('The Experiences of the Shih-ching-shan Electrical Power Plant in Implementing the Eight Grade System'), *Kung-jen Jih-pao*, 12 October 1951, p. 4.

Wang Yung-kang. 'Chien-li Tiao-tu Tse-jen-chih Ch'ung-fen Fa-hui Tiao-tu Kung-tso ti Tso-yung' ('Establish a Responsibility System for Production Order and Fulfil completely the Functions of Production Order'), *Chung-kung-yeh T'ung-hsün*, No. 26, 11 September 1953, pp. 16–18.

Watson, A. 'A Revolution to Touch Men's Souls: The Family, Interpersonal Relations and Daily Life', in Schram (ed.), 1973, pp. 291–330.

Wheelwright, E.L. and McFarlane, B. *The Chinese Road to Socialism*, New York and London, Monthly Review Press, 1970, 256 pp.

Whitson, W. 'The Field Army In Chinese Communist Military Politics', *China Quarterly*, No. 37, January–March 1969, pp. 1–30.

Wiles, P.J.D. *The Political Economy of Communism*, Oxford, Basil Blackwell, 1964, 404 pp.

Winfield, G.F. *China: The Land and the People*, New York, William Sloane Associates, 1948, 437 pp.

Woodward, J. *Industrial Organisation: Theory and Practice*, London, Oxford University Press, 1965, 281 pp.

Woodward, J. (ed.). *Industrial Organisation: Behaviour and Control*, London, Oxford University Press, 1970, 262 pp.

Wu Mo-hua. 'Cheng-tun Chi-ts'eng Tsu-chih, Ming-chüeh Chi-ts'eng Kan-pu ti Tse-jen' ('Sort Out Basic Level Organisation; Define Clearly the Responsibilities of Basic Level Cadres'), *Chung-kung-yeh T'ung-hsün*, No. 33, 21 November 1953, pp. 10–12.

Yao P'u. 'Tsung I-ko Kung-ch'ang Kung-tso Chiao-tu T'i-hui-tao ti Chi-chien Kung-tso chung ti i-hsieh Wen-t'i' ('Some Questions Concerning Basic Construction as seen from the Angle of Work in One Factory'), *Tung Pei Kung-yeh*, No. 101, 21 July 1952, pp. 14–17.

Yen Yü-hsü and Shen Kuo-jung. 'Chieh-shao Fu-shun Chih-kang-ch'ang ti Tse-jen-chih' ('Introducing the Responsibility System at the Fushun Steel Making Works'), *Chung-kung-yeh T'ung-hsün*, No. 16, 1 June 1953, pp. 9–13.

Yin Ku. 'Kung-ch'ang Kuan-li' ('Factory Management'), *Chung-kuo Kung-yeh*, Vol. 1, No. 1, 1949, pp. 17–22 and No. 2, pp. 28–36.

Yoshino, M.Y. *Japan's Managerial System: Tradition and Innovation*, Cambridge Mass., The MIT Press, 1968, 292 pp.

Yü Wen-ch'ing. 'T'ung Pei Kung K'uang Ch'i-yeh ti Ch'eng-pen Chi-suan [Chieh-shao Tung Pei Jen-min Cheng-fu Kung-yeh-pu Chan-hsing Ch'eng-pen Chi-suan Kuei-ch'eng]' ('Cost Accounting in Industrial and Mining Enterprises in the North East [Introducing the North East People's Government Industrial Department's Temporary Regulations for Cost Accounting]'), *Chung-kuo Kung-yeh*, Vol. 2, No. 4, 23 August 1950, pp. 5–9.

Index

Made in the USA
Monee, IL
14 September 2026

63198322R00225